MEGARA

The Political History of a
Greek City-State to 336 B.C.

Miniature bronze Herakles with Megarian lettering on the left leg. Executed circa 500. Reproduced by courtesy of the Benaki Museum, Athens.

MEGARA

The Political History of a
Greek City-State to 336 B.C.

RONALD P. LEGON

Cornell University Press

ITHACA AND LONDON

First published 1981 by Cornell University Press.
Published in the United Kingdom by Cornell University Press Ltd.,
Ely House, 37 Dover Street, London W1X 4HQ.

International Standard Book Number 0-8014-1370-2
Library of Congress Catalog Card Number 80-25668
Printed in the United States of America
*Librarians: Library of Congress cataloging information appears
on the last page of the book.*

IN MEMORY OF MY FATHER,
SAMUEL LEGON

The lands of Pelasgian Argos surpass all others;
so do the horses of Thessaly, the women of Lacedaemon,
and the men who drink from the lovely Arethusa.
But even better than these are those who live between
Tirynthos and Arcadia, rich in flocks,—the Argives,
with their linen breastplates, the goads of war.
But you, O Megarians, stand neither third, nor fourth, nor twelfth;
you are not fit to be considered or ranked at all.

—*The Greek Anthology* 14.73

Contents

Plates and Maps

8

Preface

THIS BOOK attempts to test the limits to which we can recapture the political life and milieu of ancient Megara in its own terms. In the following pages, I have endeavored to trace the political history of Megara in a more single-minded fashion than is often attempted in books devoted to the lesser city-states (*poleis*) of ancient Greece. This is not to say that other aspects of Megarian affairs are completely ignored. I consider any evidence, literary, mythological, artistic, that can throw light on an aspect of the state's political development, or on the socioeconomic and cultural basis of that development.

The history of such states as Megara adds an important dimension to our understanding of the Greek world. That world was composed of hundreds of poleis as well as communities organized on a more primitive tribal basis; all of them were small by modern standards, and most were indeed minuscule. It is impossible to grasp the variety of their experience by concentrating exclusively on the larger and more prominent among them. For a true appreciation, one must understand the inner workings of a wide range of states. Nor can the interrelationships of the many independent communities in this complex system be adequately approached from the perspective of the dominant states alone. I am also convinced that to concentrate on relatively well-known but isolated incidents of local history is insufficient to correct the balance; such episodes can be badly misinterpreted and their significance misunderstood unless they are examined in the context of local development. Nor will generalized contexts serve; they mislead us further by assuming what needs to be proved and obscuring the uniqueness of local experience.

The picture of Megara presented here is not necessarily typical of her sister poleis (though in many respects she was more like most of them than were Athens, Sparta, and Argos). Although her population and land area were small, she possessed important assets. Her key location on the Isthmus of Corinth gave her unique opportunities and subjected her to extraordinary pressures from the major states. Archaic Megara emerged as a pioneer in political, economic, colonial, technological, and artistic matters. She produced one of the great poets of the age, Theognis; settled what was to become the most important of the eastern colonies, Byzantium; and gave birth to possibly the earliest democratic movement in Greece—to name only some of her more notable accomplishments. And though she later sank to a dependent position, she enjoyed a remarkable renaissance in the fourth century.

I have tried to avoid the temptation to clarify obscure episodes of Megarian history either by making frequent references to analogous circumstances in other Greek poleis or by leaning too heavily on our understanding of general trends and phenomena. Even so, the reader may note a few direct analogies, including some, I suspect, of which I am unconscious. My concern, however, is to avoid the trap of assuming that Megara followed a pattern of development that is demonstrable elsewhere. That assumption might seriously diminish the value of any lessons to be learned from the Megarian experience.

Do we have enough information to attempt a political history of Megara? I believe we do, but the question raises an issue that affects the study of all the smaller and even many of the larger poleis of ancient Greece. If one demands ample documentation in the form of contemporary inscriptions and reasonably full and reliable ancient narrative history, few Greek states are fitting subjects for political history, and I would concede that what follows is not an entirely satisfactory narrative of Megarian history; yet I hope it is a significant improvement over what has been available. Even if many issues must be left unresolved and the solutions to others are tentative, I believe I have at least provided a full matrix for the history of archaic and classical Megara and a sound basis for further discussion of both specific problems and general political development.

10

I do not wish to make light of the problem of evidence for Megarian history. This book would have been substantially shorter if we had had more information, for many points must be argued at length on the basis of extremely fragmentary evidence—sometimes the merest inference of Megarian involvement in larger events. Few local inscriptions have come to light from periods earlier than the third century B.C., and archaeological investigation has barely scratched the surface of the Megarid. Although Megara produced a small number of historians (the *Megareis*) in the fourth and third centuries, their attention was concentrated almost exclusively on her legendary early history, rather than on the political currents of the archaic and classical periods, to judge from the fragments of their works—none of which comes down to us intact. Only the poems of Theognis, the *Theognidaea,* furnish us with a compact body of evidence reflecting on one period of Megarian history (the sixth century), but even here the evidence must be used with extreme caution, since both the integrity and the provenance of the collection are matters of dispute. The historian of Megara is therefore thrown back on references to Megarian affairs that are scattered throughout the corpus of ancient literature. In such notices Megara was seldom the writer's principal concern. There is, in addition, a widespread anti-Megarian attitude in the surviving sources. It is most pronounced in Athenian literature, which frequently abuses the Megarians and projects the stereotype of an ignorant, brutish, and vulgar folk. But bias against Megara was not confined to Athens, and, in fact, the ancient tradition is largely unfriendly.

The epigraph to this volume is a good illustration of the problems facing the investigator of Megarian history. Here we have what appears to be the Delphic Oracle's response to an early inquiry from Megara regarding her standing among the Greek states. The rebuff could scarcely have been more blunt or severe. Closer examination, however, shows that it is not quite what it seems to be. The three opening lines constitute a self-contained statement, listing the outstanding qualities of a number of leading states— Argos in Thessaly has the best land, Thrace the finest horses, Sparta the prettiest women, and Chalcis in Euboea the bravest men. Whether or not the Delphic Oracle was responsible for these lines, most likely they originally stood alone. It is reasonably clear that they belong to the first half of the seventh century at the latest, given the characterizations of Chalcis and Sparta. The following three lines were apparently added at a later date, in order to top the initial statement, proclaiming the superiority of Peloponnesian Argos. The description seems most appropriate to the seventh or early sixth century, before Argos was decisively eclipsed by Sparta. The final two lines are an insult tagged on at a still later date, though how much later is impossible to determine. The earliest quotations of the saying come from the late fifth and fourth centuries B.C. Another disquieting fact for an interpreter is that in several versions, including the oldest surviving one in Ion of Chios, Aegium, a small town on the coast of Achaea in the Peloponnese, rather than Megara, is the butt of the joke. Historians do not agree on which version is the original, if such a designation has meaning for such an obviously composite statement, and the case seems hopeless. On the one hand, Aegium could more fittingly be described as a nonentity; on the other hand, the insult has more sting if directed against a middling state with some pretensions, such as Megara. Thus what appears at first glance to be a piece of evidence nearly vanishes on closer examination. This seemingly archaic Delphic rebuke to Megara cannot be treated as anything more than a classical taunt applied to Megara, Aegium, and who knows how many other states. The problem serves as an example of how the investigator must make his way through a great quantity of material that is centuries removed from the events with which he deals, material that is variable in quality and riddled with prejudice.

There is no substitute for discussing the merits of the evidence on a case-by-case basis, but scholars have such widely varying approaches to the use of evidence that some general statement of my attitude on this subject seems in order. I have relied primarily on contemporary or near-contemporary sources where they exist, but have not rejected later information when it has not been in conflict with the earlier and is not inherently illogical, implausible, or so biased that its significance cannot be penetrated. Obviously, this is a subjective procedure, but I believe that it is the best available for a subject on which evidence is in short supply. Also it has the advantage of allowing the reader to see and judge a greater proportion of the evidence that has survived. I must admit to my frequent use of what Keith Hopkins has aptly named the "wigwam argument": "There are several pieces of evidence, each insufficient or untrustworthy in itself, which seem collectively to confirm [a conclusion]. Each pole would fall down by itself, but together the poles stand up, by leaning on each other; they point roughly in the same direction, and circumscribe 'truth'" (*Conquerors and Slaves*, Cambridge, 1978, pp. 19-20).

A half century has passed since the last general studies of ancient Megara were published. When E. L. Highbarger's *History and Civilization of Ancient Megara* appeared in 1927, it was judged woefully inadequate on most counts, and time has not improved it. The political history it presents is haphazard, inconsistent, and wedded to theories that were out of date even when it was written. Highbarger's grasp of general political developments in Greece was also uninformed. In the following pages, I have cited Highbarger where his insights are valuable, but I have not belabored his deficiencies. In 1931, Ernst Meyer's article on Megara appeared in the Pauly-Wissowa *Realenzyklopädie der klassischen Altertumswissenschaft*, Vol. 15, providing generally excellent coverage within a limited compass. I have found this the most helpful older work. K. Hanell's *Megarische Studien*, which appeared in 1934, supplanted Highbarger as effectively on matters relating to Megara's cults and colonies as Meyer had on questions of topography and history; but half a century has produced major changes in Greek studies and given rise to new views that illuminate all periods of Megarian history. Archaeology, though still meager, has also made substantial contributions since the early thirties to our understanding of ancient Megara: excavations in the agora by Threpsiades and Travlos from 1934 to 1940; study of the fountainhouse by Gruben in the 1950's; and work on the ancient walls and the town plan by members of the Greek Archaeological Service since the mid-1960's. One has only to compare the map of Pausanias' itinerary prepared by Highbarger in 1927 with recent ones by Alexandris and Travlos to realize how much progress has been made. In addition, a number of important articles and monographs on specific problems of Megarian political, social, topographical, and art-historical development have appeared in recent decades by such scholars as

Bol, Beattie, French, Jeffery, N. G. L. Hammond, Oost, Salmon, Payne, Vallet, Villard, and Wiseman. Almost every major issue is affected by this recent work, and the time seems appropriate for a reconsideration of the overall development of ancient Megara.

There are many to thank for their help, support, and advice with this project. Visits to the Megarid were generously funded by the American Council of Learned Societies in 1976 and the American Philosophical Society in 1978. Much of the writing was accomplished during a sabbatical leave in 1977-78 granted by the University of Illinois at Chicago Circle. I owe a debt of gratitude to David Stockton and the other Fellows of Brasenose College, Oxford, who extended warm hospitality during my sabbatical year and facilitated my work. I am especially indebted to the staff of the Ashmolean Museum Library at Oxford—the most congenial environment known to me for the study of ancient history. In Greece the staff of the Greek Archaeological Service gave generously of their time to answer my questions and to guide me through Megarian antiquities. I particularly wish to thank Olga Alexandris, ephor of the Attic Region; one of her assistants, Helen Xylas; and Mando Economides, director of the Athens Numismatic Collection. The staff of the American School of Classical Studies in Athens was also very helpful. Colin Edmonson, associate director of the school, shared his extensive knowledge of the terrain and archaeological remains of the Megarid and guided me on a day-long walk through the Megarian Vathikhoria—an unforgettable experience.

I am indebted to more scholars than I can thank here, but two deserve special mention: Donald Kagan, of Yale University, my mentor, whose intellectual stimulation and moral support and, most of all, tremendous enthusiasm for Greek history have inspired me in this as in all my projects; and Chester G. Starr, of the University of Michigan, who encouraged me and offered sage advice about the book as it developed. Earlier drafts of several sections benefited as well from the advice and criticism of members of the University of Illinois at Chicago Circle Classics Department: Jack Davis, Matthew Dickie, Elizabeth Gebhard, and other participants in our Archaeological Studies Seminar, as well as some of those present at the 1979 meeting of the American Association of Ancient Historians, especially Hunter Rawlings III. I also thank the anonymous readers of my manuscript, who saved me from many blunders.

Services provided by the University of Illinois at Chicago Circle Cartographic Laboratory, Ray Brod cartographer, were used in the preparation of the maps, and are gratefully acknowledged. John Travlos kindly gave permission to have Maps 1 and 2 based on those that appeared in his article, "Megara," *Encyclopedia Dome*, 274/5 (1978). I am grateful to the Benaki Museum in Athens and the Greek Ministry of Culture and Science for their generous permission to reproduce photographs. Except for several brief passages noted in the text, the translations are my own.

My family have lived with this book fully as much as I have, and it could never have been completed without their patience and constant support. Carol will understand that I owe her more than words can express. Finally, I must acknowledge an immeasurable debt to my father, who heard the earlier, but not the later, chapters. He was my greatest booster, sharpest critic, and most influential teacher.

RONALD P. LEGON

Oak Park, Illinois

15

Abbreviations and Short Titles

Ancient authors are cited in the standard abbreviations to be found in the *Oxford Classical Dictionary*. Short titles and abbreviations are used for the following journals, widely known reference works, and frequently cited books and articles.

AA	*Archäologischer Anzeiger.*
AAA	*Athens Annals of Archaeology.*
AD	*Archaiologikon Deltion.*
AE	*Archaiologikē Ephemeris.*
AJP	*American Journal of Philology.*
AM	*Mitteilungen des deutschen archäologischen Instituts: Athenische Abteilung.*
BCH	*Bulletin de correspondance hellénique.*
BSA	*Annual of the British School at Athens.*
Burn, *Lyric Age*	A. R. Burn, *The Lyric Age of Greece*, London, 1960.
CP	*Classical Philology.*
CQ	*Classical Quarterly.*
CRAI	*Comptes rendus de l'Académie des Inscriptions et Belles-lettres.*
CW	*Classical World.*
Dunbabin, "Early Corinth"	T. J. Dunbabin, "The Early History of Corinth," *JHS*, 68 (1948), 59-69.
FGrH	Felix Jacoby, *Die Fragmente der griechischen Historiker*, Berlin and Leiden, 1923———.
G&R	*Greece and Rome.*
GHI	Russell Meiggs and D. M. Lewis, *A Selection of Greek Historical Inscriptions to the End of the Fifth Century B.C.*, Oxford, 1969.
Gomme, *HCT*	A. W. Gomme, *A Historical Commentary on Thucydides*, Vols. 1-3, Oxford, 1945-56.

Hammond, *HG*	N. G. L. Hammond, *A History of Greece to 322 B.C.*, 2d ed., Oxford, 1967.
Hammond, "Heraeum"	———,"The Heraeum at Perachora, and Corinthian Encroachment," *BSA*, 49 (1954), 93-102.
Hammond, "Main Road"	———,"The Main Road from Boeotia to the Peloponnese through the Northern Megarid," *BSA*, 49 (1954), 103-122.
Hanell, *Studien*	Krister Hanell, *Megarische Studien*, Lund, 1934.
Highbarger, *Megara*	E. L. Highbarger, *The History and Civilization of Ancient Megara*, Baltimore, 1927.
HSCP	*Harvard Studies in Classical Philology.*
IG	*Inscriptiones Graecae*, 1873——.
JHS	*Journal of Hellenic Studies.*
Kagan, *Outbreak*	Donald Kagan, *The Outbreak of the Peloponnesian War*, Ithaca, 1969.
MAE	M. Sakellariou and N. Faraklas, *Megaris, Aegosthena, Ereneia*, Vol. 14 of Ancient Greek Cities, Athens, 1972.
Meyer, "Megara"	Ernst Meyer, "Megara," *RE*, Vol. 15, pt. 1 (Stuttgart, 1931), cols. 152-205.
NC	*Numismatic Chronicle.*
Oost, "Theagenes and Theognis"	Stewart I. Oost, "The Megara of Theagenes and Theognis," *CP*, 68 (1973), 186-196.
PAAH	*Praktika tēs en Athenais Archaiologikēs Hetaireias.*
RE	A. Pauly, G. Wissowa, and W. Kroll, *Realenzyklopädie der klassischen Altertumswissenschaft*, Stuttgart, 1893——.
REG	*Revue des études grecques.*
Salmon, "Heraeum"	John Salmon, "The Heraeum at Perachora and the Early History of Corinth and Megara," *BSA*, 67 (1972), 159-204.
de Ste Croix, *OPW*	G. E. M. de Ste Croix, *The Origins of the Peloponnesian War*, Ithaca, 1972.
TAPA	*Transactions of the American Philological Association.*
Travlos, "Megara"	John Travlos, "Megara," *Encyclopedia Domē*, 274/5 (1978), 202-208.
VDI	*Vestnik drevnei istorii.*
Will, *Korinthiaka*	Edouard Will, *Korinthiaka*, Paris, 1955.
YCS	*Yale Classical Studies.*

MEGARA

The Political History of a
Greek City-State to 336 B.C.

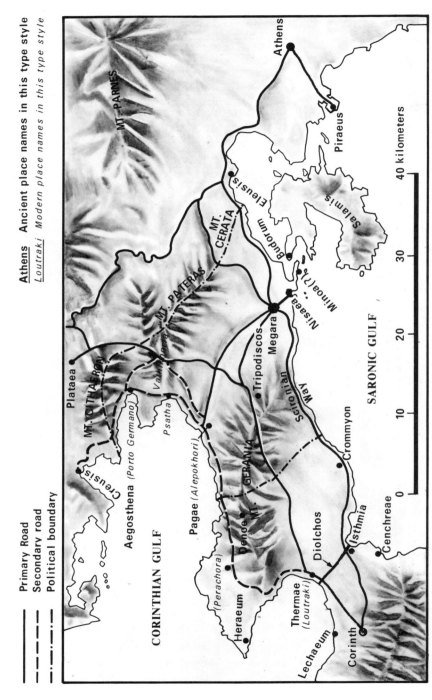

Primary Road
Secondary road
Political boundary

Athens Ancient place names in this type style
Loutraki Modern place names in this type style

Map 1. The Megarid. Based on John Travlos, "Megara," p. 203.

CHAPTER 1

The Geography of
the Megarid

Megara is a miserable town. . . . The soil is generally sterile, and the
climate insalubrious.

—Dodwell (1819)

We no sooner drew nigh to MEGARA, than the prospect of a beauti-
ful and extensive plan opened before us. . . . From a view of this
important field, it must be evident that the town of Megara owed
its celebrity more to its fertile domain, than to its position with
respect to the sea.

—Clarke (1814)

The redeeming attribute of the Megaric territory was its excellent
position for the pursuit of commerce both by land and sea; and it
was undoubtedly to this advantage that Megara owed an opu-
lence and splendour, which were quite disproportionate to its
natural resources.

—Leake (1835)

THE TERRITORY of ancient Megara lay entirely within the Isthmus
that links the Peloponnese with the rest of mainland Greece. This
narrow strip of land, known as the Isthmus of Corinth, though
serving as a bridge between the northern and southern portions of
Greece, runs more nearly east to west. Its northern coast is washed
by the Gulf of Corinth and its southern coast by the Saronic Gulf.
The Isthmus itself is predominantly mountainous. In the east,
where it joins central Greece, a continuous chain of mountains
extends from the Cerata range near the southeast coast, through
the Pateras range, to the Cithaeron range in the northeast. This
barrier defined the political boundaries between the Megarid and
both the Eleusinian plain of Attica and the towns of southern
Boeotia throughout the period that concerns us. The western half

of the Isthmus is almost entirely covered by the sprawling Gerania range, which, however, terminates in a narrow elevated plain where the Isthmus joins the Peloponnese. For most of the period we will consider, the heights of Gerania constituted the effective boundary between Corinthia and the Megarid, but at an early date Megarian territory included the Perachora peninsula—the north-western extremity of Gerania—and may have extended as far west as the neck of the Isthmus.

In the eighth century[1] Megarian territory may have approached 700 square kilometers, but during the classical period it comprised only about 470 square kilometers, making Megara one of the small-est of mainland states. Probably no more than one fifth of this area, under 100 square kilometers, was of much use to the Megar-ians. The rest was too rugged for systematic economic develop-ment or permanent settlement, though the mountains are not especially lofty when compared, for example, with the more dis-tant peaks of Cithaeron, Helicon, and Parnassus, all clearly visible from higher ground in the Megarid. The Megarian summits sel-dom exceed 1,000 meters, and the highest point in Gerania is roughly 1,350 meters. Nonetheless, these mountains constituted formidable obstacles to agriculture and transportation in antiquity. Apart from the mountains themselves, most of the Megarid was inhospitable highland—stony, with only a thin soil cover, if any, and blanketed with scrub and pine trees.

The only significant plain, some 70 square kilometers in extent, is wedged between Gerania and the eastern mountains. It stretches approximately 10 kilometers along the coast of the Saronic Gulf, narrowing as it penetrates the interior of the Isthmus and merges into the foothills of Gerania and Pateras. Most of this nearly triangular plain is well above sea level. The soil, which consists of sandy marls and friable limestone, was aptly described by Theophrastus as *psaphos*, "crumbling."[2] When mixed with the clay alluvium that washes down into the plain from the eastern slopes of Gerania, the soil takes on a pale whitish appearance. This accounts for ancient references to the Megarian plain as the White Plain, *Leukon Pedion*.[3] An abundant supply of subsoil water, origi-

[1]All ancient dates are B.C. unless A.D. is specified.
[2]*Hist. Pl.* 8.2.11.
[3]*Etym. Magn.* 561.43; Hsch. 741.

nating in the surrounding mountains, supplemented the limited rainfall that penetrated the Gerania watershed, but no rivers flowed through the plain.[4] Ancient writers judged the fertility of this valley meager or worse. Theophrastus described the soil as poor; Strabo, likening it to that of Attica, pronounced it "very sterile"; and, in a hyperbolic passage, Isocrates said the Megarians farmed rocks.[5] As the epigraphs to this chapter indicate, modern verdicts have not been so unanimous. Judgments on such questions depend to a certain extent on one's frame of reference, but there is no doubt that, like Attica, the Megarid could be made agriculturally productive, and was so in antiquity. The major limitation on the region's productivity was the small quantity of arable land, rather than its quality or the nature of the local climate.

Our incomplete understanding of ancient agriculture and diet enables us to make only a rough estimate of the size of the population that could be sustained by local agriculture in the Megarid.[6] There were roughly 90 square kilometers of good farmland, and most of this, say 80 square kilometers, could have been devoted to the production of diet staples—for example, barley and wheat. Since half the land would have lain fallow each year, only 40 square kilometers would have been available for annual use. If we use barley, the higher yield crop, as a basis, the Megarid could have harvested as much as 1,800 hectoliters per square kilometer, or a total of 72,000 hectoliters (254,160 cubic feet) of barley. Since an average of 2.6 hectoliters were required per person, this crop could have fed about 27,700 people. Under more realistic conditions, such as a mixed crop of wheat and barley, 25,000 is probably a sound estimate of the maximum population that a totally self-reliant Megarid could sustain. No census statistics survive to be compared with this figure, but evidence of Megara's military strength in various periods permits us to estimate the actual number of inhabitants. Discussion of this evidence is reserved for later chapters, where it can be evaluated in its historical context, but some of the conclusions may be briefly summarized. The total population

[4]MAE, p. 7, gives the average rainfall since 1946 as 58 centimeters.
[5]Theophr. Hist. Pl. 2.8.1; Strab. 9.1.9; Isoc. 8.117.
[6]I have adapted the method of calculation employed by C. Roebuck in "The Economic Development of Ionia," CP, 48 (1953), 12-13.

seems never to have exceeded 40,000, nor the citizen population 25,000. This level was reached by the early fifth century, and very likely a century or more before that (though we have no direct evidence for the earlier period), and was sustained, with temporary periods of decline, to the late fourth century. During these same centuries, and particularly in the fourth, there was an increase in the proportion of slaves and probably of resident aliens as well. From the end of the fourth century there was a sharp decline in Megarian population and prosperity. The 40,000 estimate makes it apparent that Megara was overshadowed by all three of her immediate neighbors, Athens, Boeotia, and Corinth, in population, total area, and arable land.[7] It also suggests that Megara came to rely in some measure on grain imports, though she was always capable of producing the greater part of her food supply.

In addition to barley and wheat, Megara's modest domain was suitable for growing a variety of fruits and vegetables, and for the olive culture which is much in evidence today. In the historical period her export crops included onions and garlic, giving rise to many jokes at her expense, but cucumbers, pomegranates, and apples, though provoking less comment, may have been equally important.[8] In the field of animal husbandry Megara achieved great success in sheep-rearing and developed an export trade in wool and woolen garments.[9] The highlands could at least serve a useful purpose as grazing land. The Megarians may also have raised pigs for export, if we seek a factual basis for Aristophanes' jest in the *Acharnians*.[10]

[7] K. J. Beloch, *Gr. Gesch.* 3.1[2], pp. 273-86, gives estimates of the land area and late fifth-century populations of the four regions in question:

State	Square Km.	Population
Megara	470	40,000
Corinthia	900	100,000
Attica	2,350	200,000
Boeotia	2,600	150,000

It should further be noted that Beloch's figure for the Athenian population is among the lowest proposed by any scholar. For example, A. W. Gomme, in *The Population of Athens* (Oxford, 1933), pp. 24-28, gives 315,000 as a minimum for this period.

[8] For references to bulbs of the onion and garlic family, see Ar. *Ach.* 521 and 761. *Pax* 500 ff., 1,000-03, and the scholia to 246 and 249; Pliny *HN* 19.93 and 20.105; Cato *Agr.* 8.2; Ath. 64d. For additional references to these and other Megarian crops, see Meyer, "Megara," cols. 172-73. Pliny (*HN* 20.105) says that Megarian garlic was a powerful aphrodisiac!

[9] See, e.g., Xen. *Mem.* 2.7.6. This subject is treated more fully in Chapter 4, below.

[10] *Ach.* 736 ff. This scene is analyzed in Chapter 10, below.

We often assume that mountainous regions possess mineral wealth to compensate for their agricultural poverty. Such was not the case in ancient Megara. She had no significant deposits of metals. Nor did her quarries produce anything beyond mediocre limestone. Her only marketable natural resource was salt, which was collected from salt flats along the south coast.[11] This salt was famed for its strong and distinctive flavor. Clay suitable for a local pottery industry was to be found in Gerania, but the existence of a clay industry has not yet been clearly established by archaeologists and is therefore still a subject for conjecture.[12]

The town of Megara stands today, as it has since antiquity, near the southwestern corner of the central plain, less than 2 kilometers from the coast. It occupies the slopes and the area around the base of a distinctive twin-peaked hill, whose summits rise nearly 300 meters. The eastern acropolis was known in antiquity as Caria, the western and slightly higher one as Alcathoa. From either summit one has an excellent view of the Megarian plain and the mountains that define it, of the Saronic Gulf coastline from Cerata to Gerania, and of Salamis and Aegina (in clear weather) in the Gulf itself. The logic of controlling the Megarian plain from this point and no other is compelling, and must account for its continuous occupation since prehistoric times. Megara's 3.5-meter thick circuit walls have been the subject of archaeological investigation in recent years; portions of the southern flank have been unearthed, and the approximate line of the entire circuit has been established.[13] This wall stood in the fourth century, and it undoubtedly shows the city at its greatest extent. It encloses an area of approximately 1.4 square kilometers (350 acres). Both Caria and Alcathoa lie within its perimeter. The modern town, which is only slightly more extensive than the area enclosed by the fourth-century wall, sits precise-

---

[11]*Ach.* 520 and 760-61. The scholiast to this latter passage locates the salt-pans in the vicinity of Nisaea. Cf. Pliny *HN* 31.87 and 36.18 on the distinctive, strong flavor of Megarian salt.

[12]Pliny (*HN* 17.42) refers to the white clay of Megara—*leukargillon*—which he says was spread over the soil to protect seedlings from the cold. A lone reference to Megarian "jars"—*pithaknia*—occurs in a fragment of the fourth-century comic poet Eubulus, quoted in Ath. 28c. See below, Chapter 3, for a discussion of the possibility of a Megarian pottery industry.

[13]See O. Alexandri, "The Ancient Wall of Megara," *AAA*, 3 (1970), 21-29 (in Greek).

ly over the classical settlement. Even the street plan seems unchanged in its essentials. This circumstance, together with the
town's relatively modest reputation in ancient times, has discour-
aged extensive archaeological projects.

Only one ancient building, the so-called fountainhouse of
Theagenes, has remained continuously visible since antiquity,
though in a ruined state. The fountainhouse was first excavated in
the 1890's and again, more extensively, in the 1950's. Even here,
archaeologists have been hampered by the presence of modern
buildings, which crowd the site on two sides, making it impossible
to trace the entrance to the ancient structure and to resolve questions concerning periods of construction earlier than the circa 500
date assigned to the surviving monument.[14] Excavations in the
central square of the modern town, the Platea Metaxa, in the 1930's
uncovered the foundations of a fourth-century stoa and a late Ro-
man-Byzantine public bath. They also established the southern
limits of the ancient agora and the roads that converged there.[15]
These traces are now once more obscured. Some work was done
on the acropolis of Alcathoa in the same period, where both temple
foundations and part of the acropolis wall were found.[16] Otherwise, archaeological investigation has been confined to the perimeter of the inhabited area and to the countryside, and to rescue
excavations where modern buildings have been demolished with a
view of their replacement. These studies have brought to light a
number of grave sites and private houses, mostly of the Roman
and Christian eras, but have shed relatively little light on the
archaic and classical town.[17]

Much we would like to know about the ancient city remains,
therefore, a mystery. But scholars have been able to establish the
general town plan with some confidence by setting the limited

[14]For the conclusions of the most recent excavations, see G. Gruben, "Das Quellhaus von Megara," AD, 19A (1964), 37-41. These findings supersede those of R.
Delbrück and K. G. Vollmöller, "Das Brunnenhaus des Theagenes," AM, 25 (1900),
23-33.
[15]See J. Threpsiades, "Excavations in Megara," PAAH (1936), 43-56, and J. Travlos, pp. 206-08, in the same volume (both in Greek).
[16]See J. Threpsiades and J. Travlos, "Archaeological Investigations in Megara,"
PAAH (1934), 39-57, and Travlos, p. 206, in the same volume (in Greek).
[17]Reports of these excavations occasionally appear in AD and AAA, but much
remains unpublished.

archaeological record against our one detailed description of ancient Megara, that of Pausanias. (The most recent conclusions concerning the locations of the monuments, streets, and defenses of ancient Megara are summarized on Map 2, where the monuments are keyed to Pausanias' itinerary.)[18] It is probable that no more than 250 to 275 of the 350 enclosed acres were residential, if we allow for the extensive public areas of the town and the uninhabited steeper slopes of the two hills. Accepting as a rule of thumb a maximum of 50 persons per acre, we arrive at a total urban population of no more than 14,000.[19] This figure compares with the current population of over 17,000.[20]

Megara's principle port, Nisaea, stood on the Saronic Gulf coast near the city. Its precise locale and the dimensions of the town are matters of conjecture, though the site of the harbor itself is reasonably certain. Thucydides puts Nisaea eight stades (approximately 1.4 kilometers) from Megara itself, although Strabo makes it eighteen stades (3.2 kilometers).[21] These figures are impossible to reconcile with a single site, and one or the other (or possibly both) must be in error.[22] From the early 450's until the winter of 424/3 and again from the late 340's until at least the end of the first century A.D., long-walls connected Nisaea to the metropolis. If we knew the precise line of these walls, we could resolve some of the doubts about Nisaea's location, but although some earlier investigators claim to have seen traces of walls and paving running toward the coast, no positive identification of the long-walls has been made. All the same, the attention of scholars has focused on a stretch of

[18]For additional detail, see the plans in Travlos, "Megara," p. 205, and in *MAE*, fig. 27 (based on the work of O. Alexandri).
[19]This density per acre is proposed by R. A. Tomlinson, *Argos and the Argolid* (London, 1972), p. 18.
[20]Greek census of 1971, as cited in Travlos, "Megara," p. 202. *MAE*, table 1, compiles earlier census data:

1889	6,249
1920	9,531
1951	13,863
1961	15,450

[21]Thuc. 4.66.3; Strab. 9.1.4.
[22]The closest possible location of the harbor of Nisaea—i.e., in front of Paleokastro—would have been approximately ten stades from the nearest point in Megara's circuit walls.

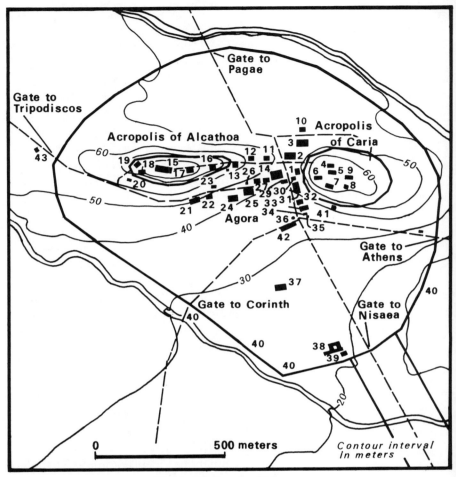

Map 2. The town of Megara.

The numbers refer to the monuments noted in Pausanias' itinerary (1.39-44): 1. Theagenes' fountainhouse. 2. Sanctuary of Artemis. 3. Olympieum. 4. Temple of Nocturnal Dionysus. 5. Sanctuary of Epistrophian Aphrodite. 6. Shrine of the Oracle of the Night. 7. Temple of Dusty Zeus. 8. Statues of Aesculapius and Health. 9. Megaron of Demeter. 10. Tomb of Alcmena. 11. Tomb of Megaraeus. 12. Hearth of the Prodomeis. 13. Apollo's stone. 14. Council House (Aesymnaton). 15. Temple of Athena. 16. Sanctuary of Athena Nike. 17. Sanctuary of Ajacian Athena. 18. Temple of Apollo. 19. Sanctuary of Lawgiver Demeter. 20. Tomb of Callipolis. 21. Shrine of Ino. 22. Shrine of Iphigenia. 23. Tomb of Adrastus. 24. Sanctuary of Artemis. 25. Prytaneum. 26. Anaclethra. 27. Tomb of the Persian War Dead. 28. = 14. 29. Tomb of Pyrgo. 30. Tomb of Iphinoe. 31. Shrine of Alcathous. 32. Sanctuary of Dionysus. 33. Temple of Aphrodite. 34. Sanctuary of Fortune. 35. Tomb of Coroebus. 36. Tomb of Orsippus. 37. Sanctuary of Tutelary Apollo. 38. Gymnasium. 39. Sanctuary of Ilithyias. 40. Discovered portions of the city wall. 41. Cave. 42. Southern Stoa of the Agora. 43. Ancient fountain. Based on John Travlos, "Megara," p. 205.

coast from a small hill on which ancient and medieval fortifications are visible (Paleokastro), to the loftier and steeper Hill of St. George about half a kilometer to the east, which also exhibits traces of ancient defensive works (Map 3). Between the two hills but near the base of St. George, a small headland known today as Skala juts out at right angles to the coast. To the west of Skala and somewhat protected by it is a broad, curved beach, which most scholars identify as the main harbor of ancient Nisaea. East of Skala, directly below St. George, is a modern wharf and a small deep-water harbor, which may also have been used by the ancient Megarians. The main source of disagreement among those who have considered the question is whether Paleokastro or St. George was the site of the acropolis and fortified area of the ancient port.[23]

This issue is compounded by the even greater difficulty of identifying the offshore island of Minoa in relation to Nisaea. Thucydides gives a detailed but confusing picture of Minoa's situation in connection with Nicias' seizure of the island in 427, when Athens was attempting to blockade Nisaea:

> The Athenians, led by Nicias . . . made an expedition against the island of Minoa, which lies in front of Megara. The Megarians, having built a tower there, used it as a guard-post. But Nicias wanted to establish the Athenian blockade at this nearer point, rather than at Budorum and Salamis, in order to prevent the Peloponnesians from sending out triremes or privateers undetected, as they had done previously, and, at the same time, to prevent any ships from reaching Megara. First, with the aid of siege engines mounted on his ships, he captured two towers which faced Nisaea. Having cleared the channel between the island and the coast, he walled the island off from the mainland where the distance was not great and relief might be brought to the island by

[23]The earliest solution, proposed by Spratt in "Remarks on the Supposed Situation of Minoa and Nisaea," *Journal of the Royal Geographic Society*, 8 (1838), 205 ff., was that Paleokastro was Minoa and St. George was Nisaea. This view has subsequently been defended by H. G. Lolling, "Nisaea and Minoa," *AM*, 5 (1880), 1-19; S. Casson, "The Topography of Megara," *BSA*, 19 (1912/13), 70-81; and Highbarger, *Megara*, pp. 20-23. F. Bölte and G. Weicker argued in "Nisaia und Minoa," *AM*, 29 (1904), 79-100, that these identifications should be reversed. Among those who have supported their view are Meyer, "Megara," col. 162, and A. W. Gomme, *HCT*, 2, pp. 334-36. A. J. Beattie, in "Nisaea and Minoa," *RM*, 103 (1960), 20-43, rejects both Paleokastro and St. George as possible sites for Minoa, returning to Spratt's view that St. George should be identified as Nisaea.

means of a bridge across a marsh. This was completed in a few days, and afterwards Nicias built a fort on the island, left a garrison there, and evacuated the rest of his forces.[24]

This passage conveys the picture of an island separated from the mainland by a narrow channel, a portion of which was marshy and could easily be bridged and which had several towers guarding the entrance nearest Nisaea. No such island exists in modern times. Five islets lie between the Megarian coast and Salamis, but all are too far from the shore to be reached in the manner Thucydides describes. The problem is further complicated by a conflicting description of Minoa by Strabo, who calls it a promontory (*akra prokeitai*) forming the harbor of Nisaea, rather than an island.[25] Until recently, investigators have rejected this conflicting evidence and concentrated on attempting to determine whether either Paleokastro or St. George could have been an island in antiquity. This would seem to have been possible only if the entire coast from Paleokastro to Teicho had been detached from the mainland, which cannot have been the case, since it would have meant that all likely sites for Nisaea as well would have been on this rather large island.

A new solution to the puzzle, proposed by A. J. Beattie, attempts to reconcile Strabo's description with that of Thucydides by identifying *two* Minoas: the promontory of Teicho, stretching southeast from the ridge that begins at St. George, and the islet of Tripika, which lies off the southeastern tip of Teicho.[26] I am persuaded by many of Beattie's agruments, especially those he musters to reject the possibility that either Paleokastro or St. George was Minoa and those which stress the suitability of Teicho for some of the military movements along the coast of the Megarid from 427 to 421, as described by Thucydides. I might add that Athenian possession of Teicho after 427 would explain how the Athenians could prevent

[24]3.51. Cf. 4.67.1, where Athenian troops sail to Minoa at night and then move to a position on the mainland, just outside the Megarian long-walls, apparently having crossed over from Minoa under cover of darkness. Though Thucydides neglects to say so, they may well have made use of just such a temporary bridge as 3.51 suggests; it could easily have been thrown across the marsh separating Minoa from the mainland.
[25]9.1.4.
[26]Beattie, pp. 20-43. His view has been largely adopted in *MAE*, pp. 56-63.

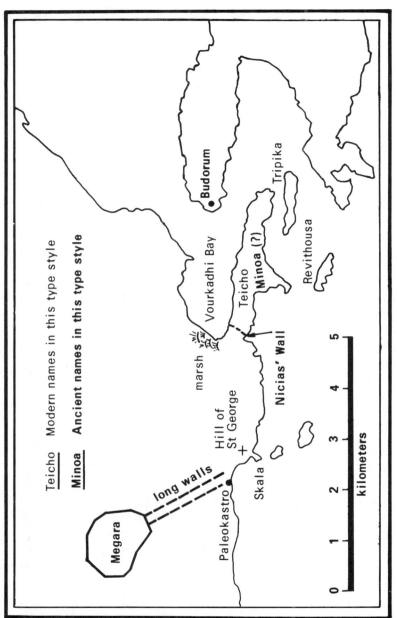

Teicho   Modern names in this type style

Minoa   **Ancient names in this type style**

Megara

long walls

Paleokastro

Skala

Hill of
St George

Nicias' Wall

marsh

Vourkadhi Bay

Teicho

Minoa (?)

Tripika

Revithousa

Budorum

0   1   2   3   4   5

kilometers

Map 3. Megara, Nisaea, and Minoa.

the Megarians from collecting salt from the pans along the shore, as Aristophanes seems to say they did.[27] Salt pans existed on the shore of Vourkadhi Bay, just opposite Teicho to the north. But I am not convinced by Beattie that Thucydides' account of the seizure of Minoa in 427 can be read as involving *both* an island *and* a promontory. I do not believe that a definitive identification can be made without further archaeological and geological study, but Beattie's approach has led me to consider that Teicho itself may be the *island* of Minoa, subsequently joined to the mainland by the silting up of the channel or by artificial works. The base of this promontory is only 300 meters wide, and the northern coast of this stretch is still marshy. Nor did I note any rock formations that would preclude the earlier existence of a channel separating Teicho from the mainland. Definitive solution of this problem will, I believe, require the study of the terrain by geologists.

The tentative identification of Teicho as the island of Minoa does not, however, resolve the problem of locating Nisaea, by far the more important of the two sites. In fact, this solution of the identity of Minoa leaves both Paleokastro and St. George eligible. Again, a definitive answer is not possible at the present time. The shallow harbor between the two hills could have been associated with either, and the fortified area may well have included both. I am inclined at present to favor the identification of Paleokastro as the Nisaean acropolis. It lies closer to the beach and to Megara itself, and it would have been considerably easier to inhabit on a regular basis. This is a question which further excavation, particularly the tracing of fortifications, ought to answer conclusively.

No similar uncertainty surrounds the identification of Megara's Corinthian Gulf ports. Ancient references, local inscriptions, archaeological remains, and even coins confirm the locations of Pagae (modern Alepochori) and Aegosthena (modern Porto Germano). Pagae was the more important during archaic and classical times, because of its greater accessibility from Megara. Aegosthena, though possessing an excellent protected habor, was isolated between Pateras and Cithaeron at the northeastern extremity of the Megarid, and was at least as difficult to reach from Megara as from

[27]*Ach.* 760-61.

southern Boeotia. It became significant only when it was granted independence during the Hellenistic period, and it must have remained a very small community even then.[28] The fine bay and gentle beach at modern Psatha, which lies midway between Pagae and Aegosthena, was too inaccessible by land ever to have either commercial or strategic value, and so it remains today. Ancient fortifications can be seen above ground at both Pagae and Aegosthena. A long section of the latter port's Hellenistic defensive works, including seven nearly intact towers, is one of the best preserved examples of ancient fortification in the whole of Greece.[29]

The site of the town of Tripodiscos has been tentatively identified in the central depression of Gerania, near the western edge of the Megarian plain. Grave sites have been excavated along the route that led from Megara to Tripodiscos, but no systematic investigation of the site itself has yet been undertaken.[30] The town's existence was justified by its situation along a major trans-Isthmian route and its easy accessibility from Megara. The names of other towns—such as Aegeiros, Eirenea, and Cynosura—are known, but their locations remain problematic. (Proposed sites for some of these are indicated on Map 1.) None of them was very large, and it is safe to say that the urban population of the Megarid was overwhelmingly concentrated in Megara itself.

Since it was impossible to travel by land from northern and central Greece into the Peloponnese without traversing the Megarid, its commercial and strategic importance was considerable. Megara was necessarily involved in all peaceful contacts and hostilities between the Peloponnesian states and the rest of mainland Greece, including a great many situations in which her role has been entirely ignored by historians. The issue constantly before the Megarians was whether to encourage, aid, obstruct, or ignore this

[28]Ephebe lists from third-century Aegosthena (*IG* 7.209-18 and 220-22) yield an average of seven youths reaching military age each year. This suggests a hoplite population of under 200 and a total hoplite citizen class of roughly 800. There is no basis for calculating the size of the other elements of the population at this period. See the epilogue for further discussion of the ephebe evidence.
[29]See E. F. Benson, "Aegosthena," *JHS*, 15 (1895), 314-24.
[30]See Y. Nicopoulou, "Report from the Megarid," *AAA*, 2 (1969), 339-43, and *AD*, 25B (1970), 99-120 (both in Greek).

33

traffic, weighing such factors as friendship, profit, and security. Conversely, states that had a particular interest in securing safe passage through the Isthmus had also to consider how best to influence the Megarians' behavior, whether through friendship, reward, intimidation, or outright coercion.

Let us consider the roads that traversed Megarian territory in ancient times.[31] The northern and southern coasts of the Megarid were joined by a single road, which ran northwest from Megara toward Pagae. After crossing the Megarian plain, this route climbed the gentle slope of the Gerania foothills to the watershed near the northern coast of the Isthmus, whence it descended more steeply to the harbor at Pagae. It was an easy trip for traffic of all kinds over its entire length of roughly 20 kilometers and served as the main link between the city and its two major ports.

The routes which crossed the Megarid from east to west present a more complex picture. The road most familiar to modern visitors to Greece followed the southern coast along the same line taken by the two modern highways and the railway from Athens to Corinth. Leaving the plain of Eleusis in western Attica, one skirted Mt. Cerata along the coast and entered the Megarian plain. The road continued across the plain to Megara and thence began the ascent over the southern cliffs of Gerania, the infamous Scironian Way. Unlike the modern roads, which are cut into the mountainside at higher elevations, the ancient path narrowed here to a treacherous ledge. As Strabo describes it, "The road approaches so near the rocks that in many places it runs along the edge of precipices, for the overhanging mountain is of great height, and impassable."[32] One false step meant a drop of more than 200 meters into the Saronic Gulf. Here the legendary robber Sciron was supposed to have thrown his victims to the waiting jaws of a monster turtle in the sea below, until Theseus gave him a taste of his own medicine. This precipice was easily blocked in time of war, and was probably impassable by vehicles under the best of circumstances until the

[31]On the road system in general, see N. G. L. Hammond's indispensable article, "Main Road," pp. 103-22. Cf. James Wiseman, *The Land of the Ancient Corinthians*, Studies in Mediterranean Archaeology, Vol. 50 (Göteborg, 1978) chapter 2, for a more detailed description of the roads linking Megara and Corinth.

[32]Strab. 9.1.4. Strabo is cited here and elsewhere in the translation of H. C. Hamilton and W. Falconer, *The Geography of Strabo*, 3 vols., London, 1892.

ledge was widened by order of the Emperor Hadrian.[33] Once past this dangerous stretch, however, the route on to the neck of the Isthmus presented no problems.

It has often been assumed that this road was the main highway between the Peloponnese and the rest of Greece, but as just pointed out, that was not likely until later antiquity. For the first thousand years of Megara's existence, an alternate road was probably of greater commercial and strategic significance. One might avoid the Scironian Way by following the first route west only as far as the town of Megara and then turning inland toward Tripodiscos. Taking a path through the central depression of the Gerania range, one emerged at the neck of the Isthmus near Thermae (modern Loutraki). It was also possible to avoid the southern coast altogether. To do so, one took the route which Hammond has labeled "the Road of the Towers" from southern Boeotia or western Attica into the Megarian plain and then cut across the plain to join the central Gerania road near Tripodiscos. This was the shortest and fastest route through the Isthmus, but it was not entirely without difficulties. One first crossed the eastern slopes of Cithaeron from the vicinity of Plataea and then, in the most arduous part of the journey, ascended the flank of Mt. Karydi in the Pateras range and descended into the valley of the Megalo and Mikro Vathikhori. The climb over Karydi, approximately 900 meters high, is fairly steep, but has remarkably few and gentle turns for a mountain road. It is buttressed in a number of places and is wide enough to have accommodated wagons. At the summit of Karydi the terrain is so rugged that it is impossible to tell the precise path followed by the ancient road. Once in the Vathikhoria, however, the Road of the Towers presented no further difficulties. It skirted the eastern edge of the smaller depression, the Mikro Vathikhori, and descended gradually into the Megarian plain along the southern slopes of Pateras. From this point, one could either continue west across the plain to Tripodiscos and the Peloponnese or veer south toward Megara.

In the Vathikhoria a number of lesser tracks from Pagae and Aegosthena converged on the main road, and a rugged footpath

---

[33]Paus. 1.44.6. On the robber Sciron, see Plut. *Thes.* 10. The Corinthians blocked the Scironian Way against the Persians in 480, according to Hdt. 8.71.

suitable only for men and pack animals ran eastward over Pateras into the Koundoura Valley of Attica. One or more Megarian settlements must have stood in the Vathikhoria, but no systematic search for these communities has yet been undertaken.[34] What has been found are the ruins of at least seven ancient stone towers on the western flank of Karydi.[35] Judging from the different techniques employed by the stone masons, these towers seem to have been built at various times in the fourth and third centuries. Some stand alongside the road, while others are several hundred meters from it. All are well below the summit of Karydi, nor do any of the towers occupy particularly elevated ground in relation to the road. Though at least some of the towers command a view of the Megarian plain and beyond to Gerania, none has an unobstructed view of Megara itself, or of the road on the far side of Karydi. Such considerations have created some doubt about the function of these apparently military towers. By themselves, they could not have provided Megara with early warning of an invasion via Attica or Boeotia, and although there are traces of fortification walls linking some of the towers, it seems doubtful that they could have held back an army advancing along the Road of the Towers toward the Megarian plain. One possibility is that they were intended merely to provide temporary refuge for the local populace in time of war. Another is that they were not built by the Megarians at all, but were constructed by powers north of the Isthmus—for example, Thebes or Athens—who required early warning of the advance of Peloponnesian forces along the central Gerania road, and who planned to hold the pass over Mt. Karydi. In either case, the towers were built in periods when Megara's control of the Vathikhoria and her military strength in general were negligible, and, as we shall see, there is ample evidence to suggest that this was indeed the state of affairs in much of the fourth and third centuries.

There was yet a third route through the Isthmus in addition to

[34]Some scholars have placed Ereinea in this region. See, e.g., Meyer, "Megara," col. 163, and *MAE*, app. 2, pp. 5-6. Hammond, "Main Road," pp. 118-20, proposes the Megalo Vathikhori as the site of ancient Aegeiros.

[35]See H. J. W. Tillyard, "Two Watch-Towers in the Megarid," *BSA*, 12 (1905/6), 101-08 and Hammond, "Main Road," pp. 108-11. I am indebted to Professor Colin Edmonson for guiding me through this region and pointing out features of the towers and other ancient remains. I, of course, accept full responsibility for the inferences drawn here.

the southern road and the Road of the Towers. It followed the northern coast, starting from the Bay of Creusis in Boeotia. One first scrambled over the Cithaeron cliffs to reach Aegosthena, climbed Mt. Mytikas (400 meters) and descended to the coastal plain of Psatha, and climbed once again, this time over the sheer cliff which divides Psatha from Pagae. With only slightly less difficulty, one could continue along the coast to and across the base of the Perachora peninsula, reaching the neck of the Isthmus of Thermae. Many parts of this route were hazardous for men and pack animals and impossible for wheeled vehicles. In recounting the Spartan's retreat from Boeotia in 379, Xenophon vividly describes some of the extraordinary hazards that one might encounter on the portion of this route which ran between Creusis and Aegosthena:

> Cleombrotus led the troops under his command home via Creusis. . . . En route they encountered an extraordinary wind. . . . In addition to many other consequences of the wind's violence, when he had left Creusis with his army and was crossing the mountain ridge that slopes down to the sea, numbers of pack-asses with their loads were hurled down the precipice, and a great many shields, torn from the soldiers' grasp, plunged into the sea. Finally, many who were unable to make headway with their heavy arms left their shields lying flat here and there on the ridge, filled with stones. And that day they dined at Aegosthena in the Megarid as best they could. But the next day they went back to recover their arms.[36]

The wind was not often so severe, but climbing these exposed cliffs was always difficult and the footing dangerous. It is clear that this route had no commercial value, and its military use was restricted to situations in which the Road of the Towers was being held by a hostile force, or when the advantage of surprise outweighed the risks and rigors of the journey. It was possible to abandon the route along the northern coast and join the Road of the Towers by means of many tracks which led into the Vathikhoria or by traversing the depression between Cithaeron and Karydi. The reader can work out the permutations. Few would have chosen to remain on the coastal road any longer than necessary.

[36]*Hell.* 5.4.16-18.

Megara's position was of some importance in naval affairs as well. The Saronic Gulf was the focal point of shipping on the western shores of the Aegean from time immemorial, and from the late eighth century the Gulf of Corinth served the Greek world as the safest and most direct route to the Ionian and Adriatic Seas and to the western Mediterranean. The exchange of goods among the far-flung states of the Greek world therefore converged on the shores of the Isthmus. Here, both states and individuals could grow rich on the proceeds of commerce. Tolls, duties on the exchange of goods, portage fees, the rental of market and storage facilities, the provision of lodging, food, and other amenities (including female companionship) for the merchants and travelers, not to mention the ready opportunities for direct participation in commercial ventures themselves—all played a part.

Megara did not, however, control the entire Isthmus during most of her history, although she may have had control at an early date. Corinth, too, had a share, and, in fact, possessed much the narrowest portion, where the two gulfs are only 7 kilometers apart, as compared to the more than 20 kilometers separating Nisaea from Pagae. The Corinthians built a paved road, known as the *diolchos*, across the neck of the Isthmus as early as the sixth century.[37] This ancient tramway, which followed almost precisely the same line as the modern Corinth Canal, was used to hoist heavy-laden wagons over the Isthmus. Wheel ruts are visible on the surviving segments of the diolchos. While some historians have maintained that this path was used to transfer merchant ships themselves from one gulf to the other, making it possible to continue a long sea voyage in the same vessel without undertaking the dangerous and time-consuming circumvallation of the Peloponnese, others believe that its use was restricted to the transportation of merchandise and, occasionally, triremes and lighter craft.[38] The

[37]See N. M. Verdelis, "Der Diolkos am Isthmus von Korinth," *AM*, 71 (1956), 51-59.

[38]Verdelis argues for the use of the diolchos by transport ships. Among recent authorities who dispute this conclusion are H. Michell, *The Economics of Ancient Greece*, 2d ed. (Cambridge, 1957), p. 237; L. Casson, *Ships and Seamanship in the Ancient World* (Princeton, 1971), p. 255; Wiseman, pp. 45-46; and de Ste Croix, *OPW*, p. 216. My own view was expressed earlier in "The Megarian Decree and the Balance of Greek Naval Power," *CP*, 68 (1973), 166-67. See Thuc. 3.15 for evidence that the diolchos was used to transship the lighter triremes.

unlikely possibility of hauling a bulky cargo ship, 7.6 to 10 meters wide[39] on a carriage whose track was a mere 1.5 meters wide, from sea level over a ridge more than 200 meters high and down to sea level again, persuades me that the latter view is the more probable. I believe that goods normally changed hands at the Isthmus, and that merchandise and passengers heading for more remote destinations changed ships at this juncture. Yet even if we regard the diolchos as employed primarily for the transshipment of cargo, the efficiency of means and the shorter distance to be traversed must have given Corinth a decisive advantage over Megara in the competition to attract commercial shipping.[40] Any captain heading for the Isthmus with passengers or merchandise whose final destination was anywhere other than Megara itself was sure to make for one of the Corinthian ports unless, of course, either he or a vessel from his home port or, perhaps, his cargo was unwelcome there. In that uncommon circumstance, Megara was always available as a feasible alternative transit point.[41]

The advantages of the Corinthian over the Megarian section of the Isthmus may be summed up by observing that if an isthmus has strategic and commercial value, that value is greatest where the isthmus is narrowest. Throughout the historical period Corinth possessed this considerable advantage over her neighbor. That was probably inevitable in light of geographic factors which favored Corinth in any protracted contest for control of the neck of the Isthmus. When one considers the location of the main valleys and population centers of the two states relative to this valuable border territory, it is clear that the Corinthians were much better placed to keep it under constant surveillance and to reach it in strength rapidly. The Acrocorinth commands a view of the area, and there is but a short distance and no natural obstacles between the diolchos and the city of Corinth. Megara, on the other hand, is

[39]For these dimensions, see Casson, p. 173.

[40]A similar view is adopted by de Ste Croix, *OPW*, p. 187. Even without the diolchos, the Corinthians would have had an easier time hauling merchandise across the Isthmus, since their ports were less than half the distance apart that separated Pagae from Nisaea.

[41]From the standpoint of the land passage into the Peloponnese, the neck of the Isthmus, controlled by Corinth, had the greatest strategic potential. It was here, for example, that the Greek allies undertook to build a wall in 480 to block Xerxes' advance. See Hdt. 8.71 ff. and 9.6 ff.

cut off by Gerania. The neck of the Isthmus is concealed from direct observation, and a time-consuming trek across the mountain passes would have been necessary before the Megarians could bring their main forces to bear on any sudden crisis in the area. Under these conditions, Corinth would probably have won control of the region in the long run, even if she had lacked other material advantages over Megara.

The overriding conclusion of this survey is that while Megara possessed the assets to achieve moderate prosperity and to sustain her viability as an independent city-state, her territory was not large enough or richly enough endowed to place her in the first rank of Greek poleis. As we shall see, she prospered during the archaic period as a result of her rapid maturation, and flourished during extended periods of peace thereafter. On occasion she even played a pivotal role in the power struggles of the Greek world. But on the whole she was destined to play a lesser and usually subordinate role compared with her immediate neighbors and the more distant Spartans. Through most of her history, Megara was incapable even of preserving her territorial integrity unaided, and she had ultimately to reconcile herself to the modest, though worthwhile, goals of achieving political stability and economic prosperity under the shadow of other powers.

CHAPTER 2

The Formative Centuries

In olden times the Megarians lived in villages (*komas*), with the citizens divided into five units. These were called Heraeis, Piraeis, Megareis, Cynosouries, and Tripodiscioi.
—Plutarch, *Greek Questions* 17

PRIOR to the middle of the seventh century, even the barest outline of Megarian history is problematic. Archaeology has not yet succeeded in providing us with a framework for developments in the Megarid during the post-Mycenaean era. Artifacts dated to these centuries are rare, and no tradition of local pottery has yet been identified. (An attractive hypothesis concerning the existence of distinctive Megarian pottery during the late Geometric and Pro-to-Corinthian periods, circa 750-700, is discussed in the following chapter, but even if it is borne out by further study, it falls far short of establishing continuous tradition we have for Attica, Corinth, or Argos.) Without a substantial material record to guide us, it is impossible to gauge the degree of continuity or discontinuity in the culture of the Megarid during these centuries, or, indeed, to verify Megarian occupation of a given site. As a consequence, our picture of the origins of Megara depends to a much greater extent than in the case of surrounding states on a literary tradition that is late, incomplete, contradictory, and embedded in a fabric of aetiological and self-serving myth. Only occasionally does the better estab-lished material record of neighboring communities enable us to correct this picture. Given this state of affairs, it is not surprising that historians have drawn widely different conclusions on issues fundamental to the development of Megara. It is perhaps more remarkable that in recent decades the areas of dispute among schol-ars have narrowed considerably, and consensus has emerged on a number of issues, though it is a consensus based on lamentably little hard evidence.

Our story properly begins with the founding of the Megarian state, but some comments about the preceding period may help to set the stage. Sufficient remains of pottery and fortifications have been noted at Megara, Paleokastro, and the Hill of St. George to establish that the Megarid was occupied during the Mycenaean era.[1] This is hardly surprising in light of the many Mycenaean settlements that have been found north and south of the Isthmus. There has been too little investigation in the Megarid, however, to determine the chronology, distribution, and importance of Bronze Age settlements in the region, nor have their cultural links with other Mycenaean areas been traced. If we turn to the legends, we find two conflicting traditions regarding the ethnic and political associations of the pre-Dorian inhabitants of the Megarid. One series of anecdotes connects them with Attica and another with Boeotia.[2] Both may be late inventions meant to serve Athenian or Boeotian ambitions on the Isthmus, and the dynastic links that each tradition asserts are not the kind to inspire much confidence. One is hard put to choose between such figures as Pandion II of Attica and Megareus of Onchestus in Boeotia as authentic kings of Megara. The Boeotian connection draws dubious support from the Homeric catalogue of ships, where, although Megara is not mentioned, a certain Nisa is noted in the Boeotian contingent.[3] Since no such place name survives in Boeotia, it has been proposed that Megara or Megarian Nisaea is meant. The Athenian tradition, on

[1] See R. Hope Simpson and O. T. P. K. Dickinson, *A Gazetteer of Aegean Civilization in the Bronze Age*, Vol. 1: *The Mainland and Islands*, Studies in Mediterranean Archaeology, 52 (Göteborg, 1979), 73-74, for a summary of Mycenaean finds in the Megarid and bibliography on the subject. Objects from the early, middle, and late Helladic periods have been identified.

[2] The Attic tradition rests on the legend that Pandion II of Athens also ruled the Megarid, and that his son Nisus was given this domain as his inheritance. Nisus is alleged to have ruled over the region called Nisa or Nisaea, before it became known as Megara. See Strab. 9.1.6; Paus. 1.5.3, 39.4, and 2.34.7; Steph. Byz., *s.v. Nisaea*; Apollod. 3.15.5, 8; Pind. *Pyth.* 9.91, *Nem.* 5.46; Eur. *Heracl.* 954. Another Attic tradition, not specifically linked to the first, records Theseus' conquest of the Megarid. See Plut. *Thes.* 25.

The Boeotian connection is established by the story that Nisus married Megara of Onchestus in Boeotia, and that her brother Megareus came to Nisus' aid when the latter's kingdom was under attack by the Cretans. Megareus succeeded to the throne, and the name of his realm was altered in due course to Megara. See Paus. 1.39.5; Plut. *Quaest. Graec.* 16; Steph. Byz., *s.v. Nisaea*; Apollod. 3.15.8; Hom. *Od.* 11.269.

[3] *Il.* 2.508. Onchestus appears two lines earlier.

the other hand, makes marginally greater geographic sense, and could provide a plausible basis for the conflicting claims of Athens and Megara to possession of Salamis in later times. Given the length of the Mycenaean era and the uncertainties of the Sub-Mycenaean period, it is even possible that there is some truth in both accounts. Modern scholars, at any rate, are about evenly divided on the question.[4] At this stage, no more can be confidently said than that the Megarid was occupied by a Mycenaean population whose culture was submerged or swept away by Dorian invaders in the period after 1150.

The course of this Dorian take-over is equally a matter of dispute, and at the present time our expanding physical record for the Dark Ages seems to be complicating the problems, rather than resolving them. The old controversy over whether the Dorians marched steadily southward through Greece, conquering as they went and moving into the Peloponnese after taking the Isthmus, or, on the other hand, somehow established themselves in the eastern Peloponnese and extended their power in all directions from that base, has been resolved in favor of the second view. But subtler debates over the sequence of Dorian conquests (and even over the existence of an ethnic group that can meaningfully be labeled Dorian at this early period) are very much alive. These issues are directly relevant to an attempt to estimate the date at which the Megarid was occupied by the Dorians and the relationship between that development and the settlement of Corinth and other neighboring districts by the Dorians. One current view holds that the conquerors systematically extended their control from an entrenched position at Argos, moving first into the northern Argolid, next into Corinthia and Sicyon, and finally attacking the Megarid and Attica.[5] Since the occupation of Corinth is believed on archaeological grounds to have taken place circa 900,[6] this

---

[4]For the pro-Attic position, see, e.g., Ed. Meyer, *Gesch. des Alt.*, Vol. 2, pp. 286 ff.; Beloch, *Gr. Gesch.* 1.1², p. 142; Highbarger, *Megara*, pp. 84-85; and Meyer, "Megara," cols. 180-81. The Boeotian claims are supported by U. von Wilamowitz, *Homer. Unters.*, p. 252, and G. Busolt, *Gr. Gesch.*, Vol. 1, pp. 220-21, but argued most fully and persuasively by Hanell, *Studien*, pp. 18-68.

[5]This view is explicitly stated by Dunbabin, "Early Corinth," pp. 95-96, and is implicit in H. Payne, *Perachora*, Vol. 1 (Oxford, 1940), 20-23, and Hammond, "Heraeum," *passim*.

[6]See Dunbabin, "Early Corinth," p. 62.

pattern of expansion would put the Dorians in the Megarian plain at roughly the same date or a little later. The other view would push the conquest of the Megarid back more than a hundred years, into the late eleventh century, only a generation or two after the Dorian occupation of Argos and at about the same time as the Ionian migration from Attica.[7] In this scenario, the Dorians swept through intervening districts in their push toward Attica, established Megara as their northern outpost when they were repulsed, and then gradually reduced the entire northeastern Peloponnese.

The literary sources do not provide unequivocal support for either picture. Herodotus, our earliest source, says only that the city of Megara was built by the Dorians the first time they invaded Attica.[8] Pausanias provides a more detailed account:

> When Codrus was king (of Athens), the Peloponnesians attacked Attica; and having achieved no great success there, they afterwards took Megara from the Athenians for those among their Corinthian and other allies who desired to settle there. The Megarians thus changed their customs and dialect and became Dorians.[9]

Strabo purports to have an even more detailed understanding of this remote event:

> When Attica became populous by the accession of fugitives [driven there by the previous conquests of the Heraclidae and their Dorian followers in the Peloponnese], the Heraclidae were alarmed and invaded Attica, chiefly at the instigation of the Corinthians and Messenians; the former of whom were influenced by the proximity of the situation, the latter by the circumstance that Codrus, the son of Melanthus [who had been king of Messenia before being driven out by the Dorians], was at that time king of Attica. They were, however, defeated in battle and relinquished the whole of the country, except for the territory of Megara, of which they kept possession, and founded the city of Megara, where they introduced as inhabitants Dorians in place of Ionians. They also destroyed the pillar which was the boundary of the country of the Ionians and the Peloponnesians.[10]

[7]See Salmon, "Heraeum," pp. 192-204.
[8]5.76.
[9]1.39.4-5.
[10]9.1.7. Cf. Ps.-Scymn. 503-05, which credits the Corinthians and Messenians with settling the Megarid.

Strabo had earlier stated that this pillar had been erected at the Peloponnesian end of the Isthmus by "the Ionians who took possession of Attica and the Megarid when they were driven out of the Peloponnese."[11] Later, he connected the conquest of the Megarid with further Dorian expansion:

> Some of the Dorians who founded Megara after the death of Codrus remained there; others associated themselves with the colony which went to Crete under the conduct of Althemenes the Argive; the rest were distributed at Rhodes, and among [Halicarnassus, Cnidus, and Cos].[12]

These accounts could be made to fit either theory of Dorian expansion outlined above.

We cannot, however, allow ourselves to be taken in by the apparent concreteness of these sources. Their dynastic associations are questionable, as is the involvement of Corinth or Messenia *per se* at any date between the mid-eleventh and early ninth century, although the participation of Dorians from Messenia and Corinthia in a northern campaign is credible. (The even more extreme fifth-century assertion that Megara was a Corinthian colony [*apoikia*] is universally rejected.)[13] Several hints in the invasion stories have stimulated speculation as to whether Megara was founded directly by Argos.[14] Although there is scant evidence for the close political ties between Megara and Argos which might be expected to exist if Argos had established the settlement at Megara, their dialects and cults reveal sufficient similarities to lend plausibility to such a relationship. It is argued, for example, that the worship of Apollo Archegetes (Apollo the Founder) at Megara suggests that Apollo Pythaeus at Argos was regarded as the divine patron of the new settlement.[15] The homogeneity of Dorian culture in the northeastern Peloponnese was such, however, that a similar case could be

[11]3.5.5.
[12]14.2.6.
[13]Schol. Pind. *Nem.* 7.155 and Schol. Pl. *Euthd.* 292. A. J. Graham, in *Colony and Mother City* (Manchester, 1964), pp. 233-34, and some others appear to credit this assertion, but a close reading of their interpretations indicates that all they really accept is the primary role of settlers from Corinth—not a literal *apoikia*.
[14]The most convincing case is made by Hanell, *Studien*, pp. 69-91.
[15]Hanell, *Studien*, pp. 82 ff.

made for a special relationship between almost any pair of communities. All the same, it must be acknowledged that Argos may have reached political maturity early enough to have consciously sponsored other settlements, and, indeed, she is credited in legend with the founding of both Epidaurus and Sicyon.[16] It is even more pertinent that Coroebus, the legendary founder of Tripodiscos in the Megarid, was an Argive.[17] Finally, a good case can be made that Hera worship was introduced to the Isthmus at Perachora by the Argives.[18] In light of all these factors, it is plausible that the Argives played a significant role in the Dorian campaign against Attica which resulted in the conquest of the Megarid. But this expedition is more likely to have involved warriors from a wide area of the Peloponnese in a more general and spontaneous movement than to have been a systematic campaign of conquest under the close control of the Argive state. Our only hope of resolving the question of the date of the Dorian occupation of the Megarid is future excavation of sites in the Megarid. Of one thing, however, we can be relatively certain: The Dorian settlement of the Isthmus was a gradual process, rather than a single event. Thus while further investigation may prove that the Dorians were present at Megara earlier than at Corinth, it is highly improbable that the Dorians had settled everywhere in the Megarid before establishing themselves anywhere in Corinthia.

Although the above discussion makes clear that we cannot at present resolve the problem of dating the arrival of the Dorians in the Megarid, I am inclined toward a date in the late eleventh or early tenth century, largely on the grounds that a substantial period of time seems necessary to account for the early evolution of political institutions in the region prior to the first recorded events in the ninth century. With the Dorian occupation, the border with Attica became the new frontier between Ionian and Dorian Greece,[19] though no one could have anticipated at the time that this

[16]Paus. 2.26.1-2 (on Epidaurus) and 2.6.7 (on Sicyon).
[17]Paus.1.43.8.
[18]See below, Chapter 3.
[19]The Athenians were supposed to have erected a pillar on the border with Megara, which said, "This is no longer Peloponnesus, but Ionia," on the side facing

boundary was to endure for more than a thousand years. By historical times, the pre-invasion population of the Isthmus had disappeared without a trace. Perhaps this phenomenon was part of the general depopulation of the Mycenaean world during its declining days.[20] But some refugees must have fled into neighboring Attica, and these may well have taken part in the Ionian migration, particularly if a relatively early (pre-1000) date for the Dorian invasion of the Megarid is correct. Still others must have remained under Dorian domination, but there is no evidence from the existence of a permanent underclass, such as we find in some other Dorian communities. Nor was the tribal structure of ancient Megara altered to accommodate a non-Doric element, as often occurred elsewhere. The three Dorian tribes, the Hylleis, Pamphyleis, and Dymaneis, remained intact and exclusive down to the second century of the Christian era.[21]

The quotation at the beginning of this chapter indicates that the Megarid was once settled in five village communities or *komai*: Heraea, Piraea, Megara, Cynosura, and Tripodiscos. Halliday's view that Aristotle's lost *Constitution of the Megarians* was Plutarch's source for this and other statements about early Megarian history has gained wide acceptance, but his opinion that the division of the Megarid into five komai reflects pre-Dorian conditions has not.[22] The komai were prominent fixtures of the Dorian state. Throughout the history of the *polis* a five part structure was characteristic of Megarian magistracies, probouleutic bodies, and commissions. Inscriptions also demonstrate that Megarians continued to be identi-

---

Megara, and "This is Peloponnesus, not Ionia," on the opposite face. See Strab. 3.5.5 and Plut. *Thes.* 25.

[20]See, e.g., the comments of V. R. d'A. Desborough, *The Greek Dark Ages* (London, 1972), pp. 19 ff.

[21]See, e.g., IG 4².41 and 7.70, 72. A fourth tribe was created in honor of the Emperor Hadrian in the second century of the Christian era, the Hadrianidae. See IG 7.72, 74, 101. We cannot confidently reconstruct the relationship in Megarian military, administrative, and demographic structure between the tripartite tribal-based system and the five-part village-based one, given the limited evidence available. One possibility is that each tribe was subdivided into five units, one for each komē, and that at some period these subdivisions might have been referred to as centuries.

[22]W. R. Halliday, *The Greek Questions of Plutarch with a New Translation and Commentary* (Oxford, 1928), pp. 92, 95-97.

fied by their komai, much as Athenians were by their *demes*, and that the komai long retained political significance in the state.[23] That the Megarians did indeed equate their komai with the Athenian demes is confirmed by the local tradition of the Megarian invention of comedy reported by Aristotle:

> They treat the name itself as a proof. For they say that they call their outlying districts *komai*, while the Athenians call theirs *demes*, and they believe that comedians were so designated not from *komazein* (to revel), but from going *kata komas* (among the *komai*), since they were judged unworthy to enter the *asty* (town of Megara).[24]

Aristotle offers no opinion on the plausibility of this etymology of "comedy." We may remain skeptical on that point without discarding his acknowledgment of the komai in archaic Megara, although this passage does not confirm their names or number.

If, as seems evident, the komai were embedded in the fabric of Dorian Megara, it is difficult to believe that they were holdovers from the pre-Dorian period.[25] In fact, the pattern of Dorian settlement in komai is hardly confined to the Megarid. Aristotle goes so

[23]As a rule, Megara seems to have appointed five generals (*strategoi*). See *IG* 7.8-14 and R. M. Heath, "Proxeny Decrees from Megara," *BSA*, 19 (1912/13), 82-88, nos. 1 and 2. But there was one period in the last decade of the fourth century when the five annually rotated generals gave way to a board of six strategoi who remained in office for at least four years. See *IG* 7.1-7 and Heath, no. 3. There were also five demiourgoi (*IG* 7.41) and, for a period in the third century, five polemarchs (*IG* 7.27-28). Demosthenes (19.295) mentions a high court of 300—possibly identical with the ruling council of fourth-century Megara. Cf. below, Chapter 11.

The Epidaurus inscriptions (*IG* 4².71) record Megarian commissions of thirty-one and 151. In the latter case, two tribes are represented by fifty men each, and the third by fifty-one. A certain Dionysus is referred to in a third-century inscription (*IG* 4².42) as a member of the *hekatostyes* (century) of Cynosura, suggesting not only the survival of that komē, but its continuing role in the military organization of the Megarid. See Hanell's comments, *Studien*, pp. 140 ff. Cf. *IG* 7.17 for evidence of the special status of the komai in the Hellenistic period.

[24]*Poet.* 1448a.

[25]We gain some idea of the Megarians' own picture of the pre-Dorian divisions of the Megarid from the lines which, according to Strabo (9.1.10), they used to quote in order to contradict Athens' use of Homer in support of the latter's claim to Salamis. The Megarians cited the following suspect lines: "Ajax conducted ships from Salamis, Polichna, Aegirussa, Nisaea, and Tripodes." Only Tripodes can be immediately identified as one of the five komai. The absence of the name Megara from this interpolation in the Catalogue of Ships, points to the likelihood that it was intended to portray pre-Dorian circumstances, when the settlement on the twin hills was known as Nisaea.

far as to describe such village communities as the general rule before the emergence of poleis.[26] The five villages of early Sparta are well known, and a similar organization has been argued for Corinthia as well.[27] Such communities were initially self-governing, and it is both unnecessary and unreasonable to assume that they were all established simultaneously in an entire region like the Megarid. Apart from the reference to Coroebus' founding of Tripodiscos, our literary tradition is confined to the Dorian settlement of Megara itself and has virtually nothing to say about the other four komai. We cannot determine whether the lesser villages were secondary offshoots of the initial Dorian community at Megara or the result of fresh invasions from the Peloponnese. (In the former case, the basis for eventual *synoikism* [unification] would have been marginally stronger.) Though it may never be possible to date the founding of each *komē*, or to trace their roots, we must be conscious of the fallacy in debating the relative dates of Megara, Corinth, and other Dorian states as if a single date could be fixed for each region.

The location of some of the Megarian komai is a matter of conjecture. Megara and Tripodiscos were undoubtedly in the districts occupied by the identically named classical towns, but the other three present serious difficulties, since they do not correspond to sites either known or attested in the historical period. The problems of Heraea and Piraea have been more tractable than that of Cynosura.[28] Heraea, in fact, has long been identified to the general satisfaction of scholars. The name Heraeis for one element of the Megarian populace suggests that they had some special connection with the worship of Hera. The importance of Hera worship in the early period is also attested in the presence of her cult in Megara's eighth- and seventh-century colonies. Yet there was no shrine or temple of Hera in the later Megarid—that is, east of the heights of Gerania. This seeming paradox is resolved if we widen our search for an *early* Megarian shrine to include the Perachora peninsula,

---

[26]*Pol.* 1252b.

[27]For Sparta, see, e.g., Thuc. 1.10 and Paus. 3.16.9-10. Will, *Korinthiaka,* p. 358, bases his picture of Dorian komai in Corinth partly on what he regards as the better-founded case of Megara.

[28]Important recent discussions appear in Payne, pp. 16 ff.; Hammond, "Heraeum," pp. 95-97; and Salmon, "Heraeum," pp. 193-96.

where the worship of Hera Acraea has been traced back to the later ninth century and may have been present centuries earlier.[29] This shrine was in the hands of Corinth in later times, but there is a lively dispute over when the Corinthians gained custody. One view dates Corinthian control from the building of the first temple of Hera Acraea. The other dates it from circa 725, when a new temple was dedicated to Hera Limnea and the earlier one appears to have become derelict. We shall return to this controversy in the next chapter, for it has a bearing on the problem of early relations between Megara and Corinth, but here it is sufficient to note that advocates of both positions concede the probability that the worship of Hera Acraea at Perachora was introduced under Argive influence, and that the likeliest early custodians of the shrine were the inhabitants of Megarian Heraea. Agreement breaks down over the question of the extensiveness of the early komē. The shrine of Hera Acraea is located around a tiny cove at the furthest extremity of the Perachora peninsula (Plate 1). It can be argued that the komē was confined to the district immediately surrounding the shrine or extended to include all of Perachora. This question cannot be separated from the problem of locating Piraea.

While no Piraea is to be found in or near classical Megara, the name Peraea was used for the entire Perachora peninsula and the area at its base, possibly including Thermae (modern Loutraki). It is tempting to accept the striking similarity in name to locate Piraea at Perachora, and a majority of historians have taken this view. Though several objections have been raised against this hypothesis, none is fatal.[30] It is asserted that the resources of Perachora were too meager to support two communities, and that if Perachora held only one komē, Heraea has the stronger claim. But this argument assumes we know something about the size of these village communities, and we do not. There is no reason to believe they were either large or at all comparable in size to one another.

[29]A date of c. 850 for the first temple of Hera Acraea was proposed by Dunbabin, "Early Corinth," p. 64, and more recent discussions have accepted a date in the second half of the ninth century. But the issue is complicated by the possibility that the cult may have existed for generations or even centuries before any permanent, stone temple was built. See below, Chapter 3.

[30]See Salmon, "Heraeum," pp. 194-96, for the case against identifying Perachora as Piraea.

1. The remains of the temple of Hera Acraea at Perachora.

Furthermore, the economic potential of Perachora should not be lightly dismissed. In the fourth century, during the Corinthian War, the Corinthians, when the rest of their territory lay exposed to Spartan attack, maintained all their livestock and a considerable portion of their population on the Perachora peninsula. This would suggest that two modest-sized settlements would have been feasible in an earlier time. If there were two komai in the region of Perachora, it is likely from the nature of the terrain that the raising of livestock played a relatively important role in their economy. It has also been objected that the designation Peraea or Piraea, "land opposite," is an appropriate description of Perachora as seen from Corinth or Lechaeum, but not as seen from Megara or anywhere on the eastern half of the Isthmus. This is not strictly true, since Perachora can, in fact, be described as "land opposite" from the vantage point of Mt. Karydi and other heights in the northeastern Megarid, although the designation from the south is more natural. The corollary that the Megarians must have referred to some district other than Piraea, however, is far from inevitable. There is no reason to assume that place names in and around the Isthmus were parceled out by the inhabitants of Megara in the centuries before the Dorian settlement there became the urban center of a unified polis.[31] It is possible that Perachora was given the name Piraea from the perspective of Greeks in the Peloponnese sometime during the Bronze or early Iron Age, and that the initially autonomous Dorian community on the peninsula, which eventually came to be regarded as one of the Megarian komai, simply adopted the already familiar designation. My preference, therefore, is to locate Heraea on the further, more westerly extremity of Perachora, and Piraea at the base of the peninsula, perhaps extending down the western slopes of Gerania some distance toward the neck of the Isthmus. At the present time, the identification of more precise boundaries is hopeless.

[31]Salmon proposes the Saronic Gulf coast of the Peloponnese as an appropriate region to warrant the designation "Piraea" from the Megarian point of view. But this region seems too remote, and it is largely obscured from view from Megara itself by the Scironides. There are other objections as well: Control of this region by Megara presupposes Megarian domination of the intervening territory, including the plain of Isthmia and the western slopes of Gerania—the very land which the more conservative hypothesis associates with Piraea. Cf. the critique of Salmon's hypothesis in Wiseman, pp. 41-42, f.n. 109.

Several sites in the eastern Megarid have been proposed for Cynosura, but ancient evidence is entirely lacking. Historians and geographers are probably more influenced by a desire to balance the settlement pattern than by any positive considerations. With Tripodiscos and Megara in the central part of the region and Heraea and Piraea in the west—in fact, spilling over its boundaries—a vacuum in the eastern sector would appear to exist. How better to fill it than by placing the unknown Cynosura there? Thus it is commonly located in the northeast, embracing the region of Pagae and Aegosthena, or in the southeast, along the route to Eleusis.[32] The first view is the more attractive, and the ridge of Mt. Mytikas, extending into the Corinthian Gulf between Pagae and Aegosthena, might, as Hammond suggests, appropriately bear the epithet "Dog's Tail." Cynosura, however, remains the most elusive of the Megarian komai.

Although the existence of komai is widely attested, very little is known about their internal organization, in the Megarid or elsewhere. Monarchy was still a vital institution among the Dorians at this early date, yet we cannot say whether each komē would have had its own king, or have recognized the authority of a more remote figure in one of the relatively few larger communities, such as Argos, or perhaps Megara, in the case of the smaller komai on the Isthmus. One suspects that despite the existence of kings, the local warrior class would have dominated affairs in the komai, appropriating the best land for its personal estates, shaping policy through its advisory role or in its capacity as the kings' representatives, and extending its patronage to the less privileged. The *oikoi*, relatively self-contained aristocratic household units, may have been more significant in economic and social relations than the komai in which they existed. The Dorian tribes under royal or aristocratic leadership, rather than the komai or the oikoi, were probably the dominant forces in military and religious affairs. We must not exaggerate the activity or sophistication of the early komai.

The next stage of Megarian development was the merger of the

---

[32]Hammond, "Main Road," p. 117, and Meyer, "Megara," col. 182, e.g., defend the northeastern locale, while *MAE*, pp. 22-23, prefers the southeast. Cf. E. Kirsten and A. Philippson, *Die Griesch. Lands.*, Vol. 1, Part 3 (Frankfort, 1952), p. 946.

komai to form the polis of Megara. Here again, there is a near total absence of solid evidence to guide us. A number of developments discussed in detail in the following chapter fix the *terminus ante quem* of Megarian synoikism by inference in the middle years of the eighth century. These phenomena included Megara's protracted conflict with Corinth, which resulted in the loss of Heraea and Piraea no later than the last quarter of the eighth century, and her colonial expansion, which began with the founding of Megara Hyblaea in Sicily around 730 or possibly a few decades earlier. Synoikism might have occurred substantially earlier than the mid-eighth century, but I am inclined to place it close to that time, partly because it was a period of similar developments in many parts of the Greek mainland and, more importantly, because recent synoikism would help to explain the basis of conflict with Corinth and the genesis of Megarian colonialism.[33]

Something of the character of the synoikism and the relations between the Megarian komai in this period may be preserved in the body of Plutarch's essay whose opening sentence identifies the five villages. Here he is explaining the origin of the term *dorixenos*, "spear-friend":

> The Corinthians fomented war among them [the *komai*], for they continually connived to gain control of the Megarid. All the same, because of their moderation the Megarians fought in a mild and kinsmanly way. No one harmed those working in the fields, and those who were captured were freed on payment of a set ransom. The captor only received his ransom after he had set his captive free, not before, but he took the captive to his house, and, having shared salt and food with him, sent him home. The man, therefore, who paid his ransom was applauded and was ever after the friend of his captor; and he who had been captured by the spear was henceforth called a "spear-friend."[34]

If this passage has historical value, it appears to record a struggle in the period leading up to synoikism, or one intended to undo the results of unification. For, this is the issue likeliest to have brought the five komai to blows. Corinth's role as agent provocateur

[33]The same conclusion is reached by M. Moggi, *I sinecismi Interstati Greci*, Vol. 1 (Pisa, 1976), pp. 29-34.
[34]*Quaest. Graec.* 17.

accords well with the evidence for her subsequent relations with Megara and her acquisition of Megara's western komai. (We shall explore this element of the tale further in Chapter 3.) The restraint exercised in this conflict may be taken as a sign of the affinity that worked to cement these communities together after a long period of mutual contact on the Isthmus, but the fact of the conflict itself indicates that elements in some or most of the komai either resisted synoikism or soon became disenchanted with it. Megara, undoubtedly the largest and most powerful, must have been the prime mover behind the synoikism and gave her name to the new state.

Apart from Plutarch's reference to a war that must have involved the issue of synoikism, we can form no picture of the process. We will have substantially better luck in describing some of the institutions of the early polis. That is not to say that we possess detailed sources dealing with the organization of Megara during this period, but political inscriptions from the Hellenistic period can be used to illuminate it. The relevance of this information is established by the fact that the seventh-century Megarian colonies reveal many of the same political features. These must have been well rooted in the metropolis before being transplanted.

Kingship probably survived the synoikism, but it did not last much longer. In later centuries the *basileus* was the annual eponymous official of Megara.[35] This was rare prominence for the defunct kingship in a Greek polis. It is paralleled in most of the seventh-century and later Megarian colonies and virtually nowhere else[36]— strong indication that the basileus was eliminated as the effective ruler after the formation of the polis, but no later than the beginning of the seventh century. A date even closer to the political unification of the Megarid could be inferred from the absence of all reference to royal involvement in the conflict with Corinth which began no later than the last quarter of the eighth century.

[35]See, e.g., *IG* 7.1-14. At some point during the third-century association of Megara and the Boeotian League, an eponymous archon replaced the basileus, and the same office is attested for contemporary Aegosthena (*IG* 7.207-09).

[36]See Hanell, *Studien*, pp. 149-60, for the widely scattered evidence for an eponymous basileus at Chalcedon, Chersonesos, Herakleia Pontica, and Kallatis. Hanell rejects the view of Pick that the basileus was eponymous at Byzantium too, although a king archon existed there.

Another fixture of the early polis was a council known as the *aesymnatae*, whose title apparently derives from the verb *aesymnaō* (to regulate, judge, or preside).[37] This body is well attested in late Megarian inscriptions, and is a fixture in all the Megarian colonies whose internal structure is known to us.[38] Its likely presence in Megara Hyblaea, founded in the eighth century, pushes its existence at Megara back to the earliest days of the polis and perhaps, like the monarchy, even earlier. Because of constitutional changes at Megara and in the colonies over the centuries, details of the council's early composition cannot be safely inferred from our later sources. Doubtless it was an aristocratic body at the outset, but its size and the length of its members' tenure cannot be determined.

Pausanias records a tradition that purports to describe the overthrow of the monarchy and links it to the creation of the *aesymnaton*:

> When Hyperion, the son of Agamemnon—who was the last of the Megarian kings—was killed by Sandion because of his greed and arrogance, they (the Megarians) decided not to be ruled by a king any longer, but to choose magistrates (archons) and obey one another by lot. Then Aesymnus, whose prestige was second to none among the Megarians, went to the god at Delphi and asked what the Megarians should do to gain prosperity. Among other things, the god answered that the Megarians would succeed if they deliberated among the majority. Believing that this oracle referred to the dead, they built their council house so that the tomb of the heroes would be within the chamber.[39]

The anachronistic democratic motivation, improbable Delphic intervention, and implied etymology for the aesymnatae call into question the historical value of this unattributed passage. But though it would be futile to attempt to verify the details, or to inquire about the historicity of the named principals, we may see here a distorted recollection of the violent overthrow of the monarchy and its replacement by the direct rule of the aristocratic council.

[37]First proposed by F. T. Welker, *Theognidis Reliquae* (Frankfort, 1826), p. xviii.

[38]For Megara, see *IG* 7.15 and Paus. 1.43.3. Hanell, *Studien*, pp. 149-60, assembles the evidence for aesymnatae at Chalcedon, Selymbria, Chersonesos, Kallatis, and possibly at Megara Hyblaea.

[39]1.43.3.

It seems reasonable to conclude that effective monarchy in Megara did not long survive territorial and political synoikism.[40] In a more politically decentralized society, such as had characterized the Megarid in the centuries preceding synoikism, the aristocrats may have tolerated the nominal authority of a royal figure, and obliged his occasional demands for support and service; the king could not seriously threaten the aristocracy's influence over affairs in their own districts. But the creation of the polis increased the king's managerial role, simultaneously diminishing the prerogatives of the local nobility. This threat to their independence may very well account for aristocratic opposition to synoikism itself, but, ironically, the centralization of polis affairs handed to the aristocracy the means to destroy monarchy itself in the long run. It was only a matter of time before the right combination of circumstances gave the corporate aristocracy the opportunity to overthrow the king or relegate him to a diminished and, ultimately, ceremonial role. He disappears, to be replaced by an annual official, the eponymous basileus—drawn, no doubt, from the ranks of the aristocracy itself.

The early Megarian polis must have had a tribal assembly of citizens, but its functions were probably limited to ratification of declarations of war and peace, and no explicit record of its activity earlier than the third century survives. Various magistracies must also have come into existence to assist the aesymnatae in the business of governing Megara. The eponymous basileus was obviously one. His functions in later times were, not surprisingly, religious and ceremonial, but he may have held wider responsibility in the period immediately after the coup. The names of other Megarian magistracies are known, but there is no way to determine how early they were established. We have evidence for a board of five *strategoi* (generals), five *demiourgoi* (officials, public servants), and a *grammateus* (secretary of the council and assembly of the people), but though the Hellenistic functions of these officials are clear, we can scarcely claim to know anything about their existence or activity in the eighth century.[41]

---

[40]See, e.g., the comments of C. G. Starr, *The Origins of Greek Civilization, 1100–650 B.C.* (New York, 1961), pp. 329–45.

[41]See note 23 above for references to the strategoi and demiourgoi. The *gram-*

To sum up our modest picture of the formative centuries in Megara, by the later part of the eighth century she had become a city-state out of a collection of village communities, and had gone through a political revolution from kingship to aristocracy. A sense of identity was already evident among the constituent elements of the newly formed state, but the komai may not have been entirely reconciled to their absorption into the Megarian polis. The new state was to face a major challenge from its equally young and ambitious neighbor, Corinth, before it had sufficient time to consolidate its position. The outcome of that contest so soon after her creation was to have a permanent impact on the role of Megara in the Hellenic world, relegating her to the second rank among Greek states. To this conflict we must now turn.

---

mateus boulas kai demou is named in many Hellenistic Megarian inscriptions, e.g., *IG* 7.1-14 and 3473. He is probably identical with the *grammateos tou damou* in *IG* 7.29 and the *grammateos ton synhedron* in *IG* 7.31. The appearance of this title on some of Megara's third-century coins suggests that the *grammateus* may have had responsibility for the Megarian mint. See Hanell, *Studien,* p. 146.

CHAPTER 3

Contraction at Home—
Expansion Abroad

If someone were to join together the two sites so that the walls of
Megara joined those of Corinth, they would still not be one polis;
not even if they established rights of intermarriage with each
other.

—Aristotle, *Politics* 1280b. 13-17

ARISTOTLE makes the above statement to illustrate one of the
distinctive characteristics of the Greek polis. It drives home his
point that the polis is an especially exclusive form of political society, based on kinship ties that are not easily manipulated to
accommodate merger or assimilation even with others of its type.
Summing up this aspect of the polis, he writes:

It is clear from this that a polis is not merely a society sharing a
common locale, restraining its members from committing injustice
against each other, and exchanging goods. While these are essential
elements for the existence of a polis, even if they are all present there
is no polis unless there is a genuine partnership of households and
clans for the good life, whose goal is prosperity and independence.[1]

The truth of Aristotle's observation will be evident to all students
of ancient Greece; the tribal and genetic roots of Greek particular-
ism—that intense devotion to the preservation of local independence at all costs—are well established, though, paradoxically, the
supposed purity of the Greeks' genetic strains will not stand up to
critical scrutiny. But to make this point, why does Aristotle choose
Megara and Corinth rather than any other pair of adjacent poleis?

[1]*Pol.* 1280b. 30-35.

59

The choice is not accidental. His fourth-century audience would have been conscious of the traditional hostility between these neighboring states, an enmity which stretched back further than reliable history itself. The suggestion of a voluntary union between Megara and Corinth would have struck Aristotle's contemporaries as preposterous, despite the contiguity of their territories and their common Doric origins.

In this chapter we will examine the origins of hostility between Megara and Corinth, a subject that takes us back to the period when the two states were first consolidating out of smaller village settlements. The process was fluid, and for a considerable period there must have been great uncertainty regarding the final size and shape of the emerging states. Though territorial definitions of poleis eventually became rigid, there was often a stage in the formative process when border settlements could join with any of several coalescing states. This stage in the development of the Isthmian poleis occurred in the second half of the eighth century and possibly the early decades of the seventh. During that period Corinth challenged the Megarians' claim to the western districts of the Isthmus and threatened Megara's very existence as an independent state. The Megarians succeeded in averting complete absorption by Corinth, but lost irretrievably a large proportion of their domain. Relations between the two states were poisoned for centuries to come.

No connected account of the struggle survives, but our scattered literary record, now somewhat augmented by the discoveries at Perachora, allows us to see its broad outlines.[2] In the previous chapter we examined the tradition of a war among the five Megarian komai, as preserved by Plutarch.[3] According to this story, the strife was provoked by Corinth: "for the Corinthians were ever plotting to get Megara under their control." Plutarch conveys the impression of a prolonged effort by Corinth to gain control of the Megarid, and her instigation of a war among the Megarian komai is portrayed as one episode in this long-term strategy. Another phase

[2]Important recent discussions will be found in Dunbabin, "Early Corinth"; Hammond, "Heraeum"; and Salmon, "Heraeum." I am most persuaded by Hammond's view, but I have learned a great deal from all three papers.
[3]*Quaest. Graec.* 17.

of the struggle is preserved in a series of references to the origins of two phrases, *Dios Korinthos* (Zeus-born Corinth), and *Megareion dakrua* (Megarian—crocodile—tears). The main elements of this story, preserved in ancient scholia and lexica and traceable to the late fourth-century atthidographer Demon, are as follows:[4]

The Megarians were originally a Corinthian colony, (*apoikia*) but they were treated arrogantly by the Corinthians. Among other, unrecorded indignities to which they were subjected, the Megarians were obliged to send youths and maidens to Corinth to participate in the public mourning whenever a member of the ruling Bacchiad aristocracy died. This compulsory show of grief gave rise to the expression "Megarian tears." Eventually, the Megarians were emboldened to defy Corinth's demands for this and other services, whereupon Corinthian envoys were dispatched to Megara to complain of this neglect. They appeared before the Megarian people and issued a solemn warning that *Dios Korinthos* would be mightily displeased unless the Megarians mended their ways. The people greeted this pompous declaration with jeers and a hail of stones, and the ambassadors, shielded by some in the crowd, were lucky to escape with their lives. A short time later, the Megarians attacked the Corinthians, whom they defeated and pursued, urging each other on to strike *ho Dios Korinthos*.

A different but obviously related explanation of "Megarian tears" is given by Zenobius.[5] In this version an otherwise unknown king of Megara by the name of Clytius is alleged to have married his daughter to a Corinthian rather suspiciously named Bacchius. When Bacchius' Megarian spouse died, Clytius forced some Megarian youths and maidens to travel to Corinth to mourn her. Diogenianus makes even less of the story, for in his explanation of "Megarian tears" they were merely the tears shed by the Megarians when their own kings died.[6]

Any of these explanations can be made to convey something of the notion of insincerity behind the phrase, but the concept is most in tune with the custom described in the dominant tradition. I am

---

[4]Demon, fr. 19 in *FGrH* 3B suppl.; Schol. Pind. *Nem.* 7.155; Schol. Ar. *Ran.* 439; Schol. Pl. *Euthd.* 292e; Suidas, *s.v. Dios Korinthos* and *Megareion Dakrua*.
[5]5.8.
[6]6.35.

inclined to believe that the tradition summarized above preserves historical elements; yet there are signs that these elements have been intertwined with fiction. Thus, as noted in the last chapter, the assertion that Megara was a Corinthian colony is surely to be rejected. In fact, the relationship described between Corinth and Megara in this tradition makes Megara more of a subject territory than what the Greeks normally meant by a colony. Even the symbolism of "Megarian tears" and "Zeus-born Corinth" may have been grafted onto the basic story. The kernel of this tradition seems to be that at an early date Megara was for a time subject to Corinth, and that she ultimately threw off the Corinthian yoke by force of arms. The story fixes these events between the mid-eighth and mid-seventh centuries, since they are said to have occurred while the Bacchiads controlled Corinth, a state of affairs which ended with the rise of Cypselus sometime during the second half of the seventh century.

We may be able to date this series of events more precisely if the career of the Megarian hero Orsippus is associated with the early conflict between Megara and Corinth. A surviving inscription bears Orsippus' epitaph:

To warlike Orrippos [Orsippus] of Megara I dedicate this famous, magnificent memorial, urged on by the divine utterance of Delphi. When a great number of his country's boundary markers had been seized, he recovered many by force of arms, and he was also the first Greek to win a crown at Olympia competing naked, winning the footrace.[7]

Pausanias visited Orsippus' tomb in Megara:

Near the grave of Coroebus is the grave of Orsippus, who won the race at Olympia running naked, whereas according to an ancient custom athletes had previously worn girdles in the games. They say that afterwards Orsippus as general annexed part of the neighboring territory.[8]

[7]IG 7.52. The date of the surviving inscription is many centuries later, but the stone probably records a much earlier (albeit not contemporary) epitaph. See L. Moretti, *Olympionikai* (Rome, 1957), p. 61.
[8]1.44.1.

Orsippus appears also in the traditional list of Olympic victors as the winner at the fifteenth Olympiad, in 720.[9] It is reasonable to assume, as Pausanias may well have done, that military advancement came after Olympic glory. The foot race was a young man's sport, and if Orsippus was in his twenties or younger when he won it, the military command is likely to have come ten, twenty, or even more years later—that is, sometime between 710 and 680.

It is frustrating that neither Pausanias nor the epitaph on which he evidently relied indicates the name of the enemy Orsippus vanquished. Since the war in question was clearly fought with a neighbor, there are only three possibilities—Attica, Boeotia, and Corinth. Boeotia can be eliminated: there is no supporting evidence of any kind for a dispute between the two states prior to their taking opposing sides in the Persian Wars. Attica cannot be dismissed so easily. The dispute between Athens and Megara over possession of Salamis was still several generations away, but the consolidation of Attica, incorporating Eleusis circa 700, could have initiated the dispute over rights along the border, a dispute that heated up several times in the fifth and fourth centuries.[10] But the territory at issue between Megara and Athens covered a relatively small area, while Orsippus' exploits are portrayed as involving a great deal of Megarian land. Hence the most plausible case can be made for Corinth as Megara's opponent in the border war. There is, as we have seen, in the quarrel among the Megarian komai and in the stories of *Dios Korinthos* and "Megarian tears," some evidence for early conflict between these two states involving a large amount of land, perhaps even the entire Megarid.

Pausanias is unlikely to have had authority independent of the epitaph for describing Orsippus' campaign as one of annexation rather than reconquest, as in the inscription. The nuance might not have seemed important from his point of view, but in our effort to relate Orsippus' career to the larger picture of Megarian-Corinthian conflict, it could mislead. Taking the epitaph as the more reliable guide, it seems that a large part of the Megarid had fallen into Corinthian hands by the time Orsippus took up arms, and that he was responsible for regaining part of the lost territory.

[9]Moretti, pp. 61-62.
[10]See below, Chapters 9, 11.

One further literary reference may be relevant. In describing the Megarian treasure house at Olympia, Pausanias mentions having seen

> a shield suspended above the pediment [which] says that the Megarians dedicated the treasury out of Corinthian spoils. I believe this victory of the Megarians occurred when the archon at Athens was Phorbas, who served to the end of his life, since annual archonships did not yet exist, nor had the Eleans yet begun to keep records of the Olympiads. They say that the Argives contributed to the Megarian success over Corinth. The Megarians built the treasury at Olympia . . . years after the battle, but they seem to have kept the offerings from early times, since these were made by Dontas(?) the Spartan, a student of Dipoinos and Skyllis.[11]

Recent study of the treasury and the surviving fragments of its pediment sculpture (Plate 2) suggest a date circa 500 for construction of the building.[12] This makes any connection with a war at the beginning of the seventh century most unlikely, and if the spoils of a war with Corinth were at all responsible for the Megarian treasury, a sixth-century war must be sought. But Pausanias appears to have coupled the story of the treasury's origins with another which told of a war between Megara and Corinth before the ten-year and annual archonships were introduced at Athens. The traditional dates for these changes were 752/1 and 682/1 respectively. Without entering into the complexities of the development of the Athenian archonship, we can postulate that Pausanias has recorded a distorted memory of a war no later than the end of the eighth century, arguably a phase in the conflict we have been trying to elucidate. I am not suggesting, however, that much weight can be attached to this confused and vague source.[13]

---

[11]6.19.12-14. Dipoinos and Skyllis were brothers. Pliny (*HN* 36.9) puts their floruit c. 580. The name "Dontas" is widely regarded as a textual corruption for Medon, a mid-sixth-century sculptor.

[12]See P. C. Bol, "Die Giebelskulpturen des Schatzhauses von Megara," *AM*, 89 (1974), 64-75.

[13]It is possible that the Phorbas named here is identical with Theseus' legendary contemporary. Pausanias' reference here to Argive intervention on Megara's behalf may also relate to the early war. It could have taken place during the reign of Pheidon, when Argive power was expanding and there is some evidence that she fought against Corinth. Will, *Korinthiaka*, pp. 343-44, supports this hypothesis,

2. A detail of the pediment sculpture from the Megarian treasury at Olympia, executed ca 500. Olympia Museum. Reproduced by courtesy of the Greek Ministry of Culture and Science.

The final element, though by no means the least significant, which should be considered is the archaeological record of Hera's cult at Perachora.[14] The significance of the physical record uncovered by excavation in the 1930's is still undergoing evaluation as our comparative understanding of sites in Corinthia, the Argolid, the islands of the Saronic Gulf, and the early western colonies is brought to bear on this material.[15] The more recent studies challenge fundamental premises of the earlier ones—for example, in minimizing Argive involvement in Hera's cult at Perachora. It now appears that the earliest temple built here was a limestone apsidal chamber dedicated to Hera Acraea circa 800. The date depends on the dates assigned to the oldest pottery and metal objects found on the site, rather than on architectural or engineering features. The artifacts have been placed in the Middle Geometric II period, circa 800-775, and are either of Corinthian manufacture, or under the strong influence of Corinthian technique. There may be a few isolated examples of Middle Geometric I cups, which could push the date of the temple back by as much as a quarter of a century, but nothing found in the Geometric temple of Hera Acraea suggests a date prior to 825. This structure stood at the water's edge on a tiny cove on the south coast of Perachora near the tip of the peninsula (see Plate 1). Here, pilgrims came with offerings that were either deposited in the temple or tossed into the water. The apsidal temple remained in use until circa 725, when, judging from the pottery record, it seems to have either collapsed or gradually become derelict. Only a scattering of finds from the seventh and early sixth centuries have been found near the cove. An archaic temple of Hera Acraea was built circa 550 on a site overlapping that of the original temple, but there is no trace of an intermediate building. During this intermediate period, however, a sanctuary was con-

---

placing Argive intervention in a war between Corinth and Megara before the Battle of Hysiae (trad. 669). But this case rests in part on acceptance of direct Argive involvement in the cult of Hera at Perachora, which the most recent considerations of the extant remains do not support.

[14]The major publications are Payne, *Perachora*, Vol. 1: *Architecture, Bronzes, Teracottas* (Oxford, 1940), and T. J. Dunbabin, *Perachora*, Vol. 2: *Pottery, Ivories, Scarabs, and Other Objects* (Oxford, 1962).

[15]For recent work bearing on these issues, see J. N. Coldstream, *Greek Geometric Pottery*, London, 1968; Salmon, "Heraeum"; and J. Boardman and F. Schweizer, "Clay Analysis of Archaic Greek Pottery," *BSA*, 68 (1973), 267-83.

structed about two hundred meters east of the cove and dedicated to Hera Limenia. Late Geometric pottery dates this structure circa 750-730, and for the following few centuries it was the repository of ever more abundant pottery dedications, mostly Corinthian.[16]

This physical record raises a number of questions. Were different cults and cult practices involved in the worship of Hera Acraea (Hera on the Promontory, or on the Height) and Hera Limenia (Hera by the Shore), or were these titles merely descriptive of the buildings' locations? Was the worship of Hera Acraea abandoned circa 725 at Perachora? If so, why? If not, why was it necessary to build a new sanctuary, rather than expand the structure on the cove? Does the presence of pottery necessarily signify Corinthian control of the site? These questions are interesting in themselves, but they take on added significance because of the light which a correct interpretation of the finds at the Heraeum promises to shed on the problem of Megarian versus Corinthian control of Perachora in the ninth and eighth centuries.

Currently, there are two opposing views on this issue. One maintains that while Megara may have controlled Perachora in the tenth century (to account for the Megarian Heraeis), Corinth was in possession of the peninsula before the first temple was built.[17] Proponents of this view emphasize the Corinthian character of all the pottery at Perachora. Salmon has ingeniously explained the sanctuary of Hera Limenia as intended to handle the overflow of dedications to Hera, which the small temple of Hera Acraea could not handle. The alternative position is that the creation of the sanctuary of Hera Limenia and the neglect of Hera Acraea reflect a shift in control of the Heraeum and Perachora itself circa 750-725, the period in which the Corinthians took over from the Heraeis and Piraeis of Megara.[18] The second approach implicitly holds that the introduction of a new cult name, neglect of the original temple, and construction of a new sanctuary reflect a significantly different mentality—that is, a new population. The presence of Corinthian-type pottery in the earlier Geometric temple of Hera Acraea is not

---

[16]J. N. Coldstream, *Geometric Greece* (London, 1977), p. 174, puts the building of the temple c. 740.

[17]See esp. Salmon, "Heraeum," followed by Coldstream, *Geometric Greece*, pp. 85-86 and 105 n.

[18]See esp. Hammond, "Heraeum."

regarded as a serious objection to Megarian control at that stage, since no Megarian tradition of Geometric pottery has thus far been established. It remains possible that the Megarians, lacking their own potters, chose to dedicate Corinthian ware. It is even more likely that the Megarians, adhering to an older tradition, long continued to make perishable offerings to Hera, rather than dedicate ceramics. It is generally acknowledged that the flat ceramic votive cakes found at the Heraeum evolved from real cakes that were dedicated at an earlier stage in the history of the cult.[19] By analogy with cults elsewhere, these cakes may have been cast on the water. But, whereas this suggestion has been made by Salmon in order to show how the Megarians might have worshiped Hera before the first temple was built, without leaving a trace of their presence, it can be used with equal force to argue that they were present at a later date. This practice could explain the survival of a modest quantity of Corinthian ware from a period before she had control of the shrine, and the paradoxical absence of a physical record of the principal worshipers, the Heraeis of the Megarid. (Fibulae and other metal objects found in the Geometric deposit could indeed be Megarian as easily as Corinthian, as they are more difficult to localize than the pottery.)[20] Those who argue for Corinthian control of the Geometric temple of Hera Acraea explain the far greater quantity of votive offerings in the later shrine of Hera Limenia as a result of growing Corinthian prosperity, but this may also reflect Corinth's peripheral involvement in the worship of Hera at Perachora prior to circa 750 and her absolute control thereafter.

Thus the archaeological evidence from Perachora can be made to harmonize with either view of the issue of Megarian versus Corinthian control. In these circumstances, the relationship between this evidence and the literary sources we have already examined becomes crucial, and I believe that the conjunction between the two argues strongly for a Corinthian take-over at Perachora in the third

[19]Payne, pp. 67-69, and Salmon, "Heraeum," p. 167. Cf. the practice at the Epidaurus Limenia, described by Pausanias (2.23.8), where barley cakes were cast into Lake Ino and omens were regarded as favorable if the cakes sank to the bottom.
[20]See Coldstream, *Geometric Greece*, pp. 174-77. On p. 175 he observes that "the Perachora fibulae are a mixed lot [in terms of style], lacking in any obviously local characteristics."

quarter of the eighth century. The loss of Heraea and Piraea cannot have occurred before the Megarian synoikism, and the theory of a ninth-century conquest of Perachora by Corinth would therefore require us to push the creation of the Megarian polis back to the mid-ninth century or earlier.[21] Such an early synoikism, while theoretically possible, is unprecedented and highly improbable. The far likelier course of development was the emergence of Megara and Corinth as poleis in the first half of the eighth century. At this stage Perachora and the surrounding area would have comprised roughly two fifths of the land mass of the Megarid and accounted for two of its five political divisions. The shrine of Hera, which had existed for some time under the care of the Heraeis, would have become Megarian with the synoikism, though the neighboring Corinthians continued to make occasional offerings. From the period of synoikism, the Corinthians had designs on the Megarid, or at least on the western komai. In the mid-eighth century the Bacchiad aristocracy of Corinth attempted to realize these ambitions by provoking a war among the five Megarian komai. The Bacchiads succeeded in weakening Megara sufficiently to take control of Perachora and probably other Megarian territory as well, and they appear to have reduced the entire Megarid to a subject status. The Heraeis and Piraeis were expelled from their homes and took refuge in the remaining Megarian districts, while the Corinthians put their own stamp on the Heraeum and its cult. Megara endured tributary status for a generation or more, but circa 710 to 680 she rebelled under the leadership of Orsippus and regained independence for the central and eastern Megarid. Perachora, however, remained in Corinthian hands. Although no specific claims are made for Orsippus in our meager account of his exploits, the tradition may exaggerate the extent of his success. It is impossible to say whether he led the decisive phase of the conflict,

---

[21]Will, *Korinthiaka*, p. 358, makes the sensible observation that a border dispute between Megara and Corinth would have been impossible prior to synoikism. Thus the theory of early Corinthian conquest of Perachora would have to be coupled with an early date for Corinthian synoikism. Salmon avoids the problem by neglecting to differentiate between the founding of Corinth, which he puts c. 900, and the synoikism of Corinthia. For a thorough and balanced discussion of the evolution of early Corinth, which is consonant in its essentials with the view adopted here of the evolution of both Corinthia and the Megarid as Dorian communities, see Carl Roebuck, "Some Aspects of Urbanization in Corinth," *Hesperia*, 41 (1972), 96-127.

or whether the fighting continued a good deal longer. We know that at some date before the mid-sixth century Corinth took Crommyon on the south coast from Megara,[22] but we cannot say whether this was a result of the same war.

The outcome of the struggle was not fatal to Megara, but it is no exaggeration to say that it ended any prospect she might have had of becoming a major power in Greece. It also confronted her with serious immediate problems, since the loss of her western districts must have led to the influx of a large number of refugees into her remaining territory. Economic opportunities for these refugees were extremely limited. Megara possessed only a small proportion of arable land, which had been fully occupied by the Dorian settlers of the eastern komai for generations by the time the displaced Heraeis and Piraeis arrived. Their opportunities to establish themselves as farmers must have been negligible. If, however, as suggested earlier, the Perachoran economy was always largely pastoral, it is more than likely that a substantial number of the refugees reestablished themselves as shepherds on the slopes of the eastern mountains and in the Vathikhoria. Others may have migrated to the still small towns, especially Megara. While we can only imagine the extent of the economic and social strains that resulted from this sudden contraction of Megarian territory, it can scarcely be doubted that the Heraeis and Piraeis raised their voices in favor of armed resistance against the encroaching Corinthians, and that their compatriots were hopeful of solving the crisis by recapturing the lost territories. Proximate solutions, however, either through reconquest or resettlement, were to prove insufficient, and the Megarians were forced to turn to colonization to alleviate the pressures created by Corinthian aggrandizement in the western Megarid. I believe that this externally induced population crisis had more to do with Megara's extraordinary colonial activity than any internal demographic factors or economic ambitions.[23]

---

[22]Strab. 7.22.

[23]The only scholar who seems to have made this suggestion previously is C. Roebuck (above), p. 108, where it is limited to the founding of Megara Hyblaea. As argued below, the same factor may help to explain Megara's seventh-century colonial activity.

The colonization movement that began in the middle of the eighth century was to transform the Greek world geographically, economically, and politically over the next two hundred years, and Megara, despite (or perhaps in part because of) her modest size, was to play an important role.[24] Her first colonial venture was the settlement of Megara Hyblaea on the small plain above a deep bay on the eastern coast of Sicily, about twenty kilometers north of the site of Syracuse. Thucydides relates the founding of this colony in his account of the origins of the Greek states of Sicily at the beginning of Book 6. He names the Chalcidean colony of Naxos as the earliest on the island. The *oikist*, leader of the expedition, was Thucles. Thucydides puts the foundation of Syracuse by the Corinthians, under the leadership of Archias, one year after the establishment of Naxos. Five years after that, he says, Thucles and some of the Chalcidean settlers from Naxos founded Leontini and Catana. Then the Megarian expedition enters his story:

> About the same time, Lamis brought another group of colonists to Sicily from Megara and established a settlement at a place called Trotilus, which lies beyond the Pantacyas River. Later he left and for a short time joined the Chalcidean settlement at Leontini. Being driven out by them, he settled Thapsos, where he died. His followers, having been expelled from Thapsos, were offered some land by Hyblos, the king of the native Sicels, who led them to it. This colony they called Megara Hyblaea. After having lived there for 245 years, they were driven from the town and its territory by Gelon, the tyrant of Syracuse.[25]

Herodotus relates the eventual siege and destruction of Megara Hyblaea by Gelon in a context that places the event between 484 and 480, though probably nearer the later date.[26] If we compute backward from the date of the colony's annihilation, Thucydides' 245 years puts the settlement of Megara Hyblaea circa 729-725. It has been usual to place the foundation of Naxos circa 735 and Syracuse circa 734, relying on the Eusebian chronology,[27] but Euse-

---

[24]For a recent overview of Greek colonization, see J. Boardman, *The Greeks Overseas*, 2d ed. (Harmondsworth, England, 1977). Cf. C. G. Starr, *The Economic and Social Growth of Early Greece, 800-500 B.C.* (New York, 1977), esp. chapter 3.

[25]6.4.1-2.

[26]7.56.

[27]See H. F. Clinton, *Fasti Hellenici*, Vol. 1 (Oxford, 1834), 164.

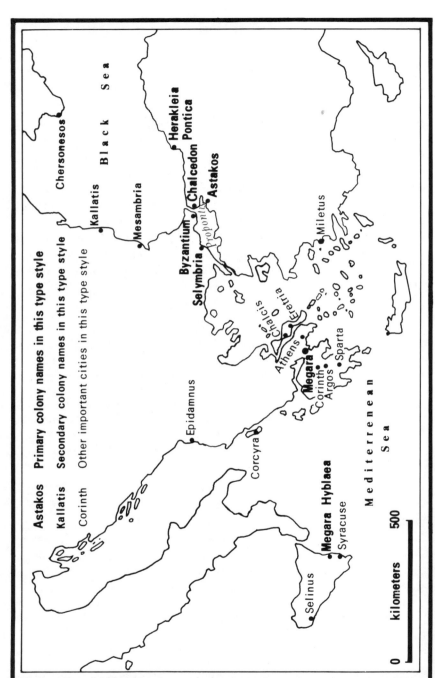

Map 4. Megara's colonies.

bius may only be calculating these dates on the basis of Thucydides' and Herodotus' statements, which we have just examined. This is a reasonable procedure if one accepts Thucydides' *relative* chronology for the Sicilian colonies; but his account is directly contradicted by another tradition, which can be traced to the fourth-century Athenian historian Ephorus. Strabo preserved most of this rival account:

> . . . [Naxos and Megara Hyblaea] were the first cities the Greeks founded in Sicily in the [tenth] generation after the Trojan War. . . . Theocles of Athens, who had been forced to Sicily by the winds, brought home stories of the weakness of the island's inhabitants and the richness of the soil; he was unable to convince the Athenians to go back, and it was the Chalcideans of Euboea above all whom he took with him as well as some Ionians and Dorians, of whom the greater number were Megarians. The Chalcideans, says Ephorus, founded Naxos, the Dorians, Megara, first called Hyblaea; these cities no longer exist.[28]

Further elements of this tradition, though preserved in Strabo,[29] are related more clearly in the late verse history known as the Pseudo-Scymnos. After describing the mixed expedition of the Chalcideans, Ionians, and Dorians, which set out for Sicily under the command of the Athenian Theocles, Pseudo-Scymnos continues:

> . . . conflict arising between them, the Chalcideans founded Naxos, the Megarians founded Hyblaea, and the [other] Dorians took refuge at Cape Zephrion in Italy. The Corinthian Archias took them on his expedition and, with these Dorians, founded the city of Syracuse. . . . Following these events, the city of Leontini was founded by the inhabitants of Naxos.[30]

There are common elements in the two traditions, but there are also significant differences. Thucles and Theocles are certainly one

---

[28]6.2.2.

[29]6.2.4: "Archias, sailing from Corinth, founded Syracuse at about the same time that Naxos and Megara were established. . . . pursuing his route, (Archias) met with certain Dorians at Zephyrium who had come from Sicily after quitting the company of those who had founded Megara; these he took with him, and together they founded Syracuse."

[30]5.270-82.

and the same person, but Ephorus makes him an Athenian, while Thucydides implies that he was Chalcidic. An even earlier authority, Hellanicus, explicitly calls him a Chalcidean.[31] Ephorus, or at least the surviving portion of his account, omits all mention of Lamis, whom Thucydides identifies as the leader of the Megarian expedition. But since Lamis is said to have died at Thapsos before the founding of Megara Hyblaea,[32] his omission from Ephorus' account need not mean that Ephorus denied his historicity, merely that he did not associate Lamis with Megara Hyblaea. Both versions record acrimony between the Megarian and Chalcidean contingents, but Thucydides introduces this factor only when a separate Megarian party seeks to join the Chalcidic colony at Leontini, while Ephorus pictures the two groups as participating in a joint venture from the beginning and parting company shortly after landing in Sicily. Finally, Ephorus records the sequence of Sicilian colonies as Naxos, Megara Hyblaea, Syracuse, and Leontini (omitting mention of Catana altogether), whereas Thucydides gives Naxos, Syracuse, Leontini, Catana, and Megara Hyblaea. In both lists Naxos stands unchallenged as the first Greek foundation on the island, but the relative dates of Syracuse and Megara Hyblaea cannot be reconciled.

Faced with these contradictions, most historians have rejected Ephorus in favor of Thucydides, relying on the latter's greater authority on most questions and on a reasonable skepticism regarding the element of Athenian chauvinism which Ephorus injects—that is, the improbable Athenian origin of Theocles, which gives Athens a basis to claim involvement in the settlement of Sicily. Yet Thucydides' authority on such remote events should not be accorded the reverence that his masterful contemporary account of the Peloponnesian War inspires. In this case he may be the victim of local sources that were as chauvinistically motivated as Ephorus or his authorities, for the Syracusan chroniclers on whom Thucydides' account depends may well have put forward an unhistorical claim to Syracuse's primacy over the despised and by

[31]Hellanicus, fr. 82, *FGrH*. 1.

[32]The single Geometric Period grave thus far discovered at Thapsos has been labeled the Tomb of Lamis. See P. Orsi, "Thapsos," *Monumenti Antichi,* 6 (1895), cols. 90-150, esp. tomb no. 8 in cols. 103-4.

then defunct Megara Hyblaea.[33] In fact, the Geometric pottery found at Megara Hyblaea antedates by a generation any thus far discovered at Syracuse.[34] The settlement of the Megarian colony must be placed close to 750, according to the most recent archaeological studies. This date is further bolstered by the remains of ancient Selinus, the colony that Megara Hyblaea is reputed to have established a hundred years after her own foundation.[35] Rather than a date in the 620's, which would be consistent with Thucydides' chronology, the archaeologists believe Selinus was settled circa 650.

Consideration of the implications of the two traditions gives additional grounds for preferring at least some elements of the Ephoran version. Thucydides would have us believe that Megara was capable of launching a colonial expedition to Sicily entirely on her own in the early 720's. Ephorus, on the other hand, asks us to believe only that a decade or two earlier the Megarians joined a mixed company of Ionians and Dorians dominated by a large Chalcidic contingent. I suggest that this is by far the more plausible alternative. Neither literary nor archaeological evidence suggests that Megara had achieved a level of naval development commensurate with the demands of an independent colonial venture to so distant a land at this early date, while the Chalcideans' role as pioneers on the seas is well known. We may also doubt whether the number of Megarians prepared to participate in such an expedition was sufficiently large to risk going it alone. I am therefore inclined to believe that a small party of Megarians, perhaps fewer than a thousand, mostly recent refugees from the Corinthian seizure of Perachora, possibly under the leadership of a certain Lamis, joined Theocles and his Chalcideans and a number of smaller contingents in an expedition to Sicily. Once there, this diverse company split up, either by prearrangement or because of internal

[33]G. Vallet and F. Villard, "Les dates de fondation de Mégara Hyblaea et de Syracuse," *BCH*, 76 (1952), 322, suggest that Thucydides may have relied on the work of Antiochus of Syracuse.

[34]Ibid., pp. 328-47.

[35]Ibid., pp. 325-28, and, in more detail, Vallet and Villard, "La date de fondation de Sélinunte: les données archéologiques," *BCH*, 82 (1958), 16-26. For the gap of 100 years between the founding of Megara Hyblaea and Selinus, see Thuc. 6.4. Diodorus (13.59.4) gives 650 as the date of Selinus. The chronographer Hieronymus gives 654.

differences in the Greek camp. The Megarians went their separate way and, after several abortive attempts, found a home at Hyblaea. I do not have much confidence in various attempts to fix a precise date for this or any other early Sicilian colony, but it seems reasonably certain that Hyblaea was settled within the third quarter of the eighth century, the same period during which Megara lost Heraea and Piraea. We know that a temple of Hera was built by the Megarians on the shore at Hyblaea, and it is tempting to see this as the special contribution of the displaced Heraeis of Perachora.[36]

Megara appears to have maintained good relations with her Sicilian colony. When Megara Hyblaea launched what was to prove the more important and enduring colony of Selinus in western Sicily circa 650, Megara in Greece was invited to send an oikist, Pammylos, and may have sent settlers too.[37] The two Megaras may have moved in step culturally. It is perhaps indicative of this relationship that both states laid claim to the invention of comedy.[38] Economic cooperation between the two is also likely, though impossible to confirm, given the state of the evidence. Hyblaean grain may well have been exchanged for the varied produce of the Megarid as time passed. The earliest Geometric pottery found at Megara Hyblaea and in a single contemporary grave at Thapsos, which has been called "the tomb of Lamis," has been differentiated from the Corinthian pottery that predominated everywhere in Greek Sicily by the end of the eighth century.[39] This so-called Thapsos class of Late Geometric ware is chemically different from the bulk of Corinthian ceramics, and though it shows signs of Corinthian influence, Athenian and Boeotian stylistic tendencies are also exhibited. The connection of this distinctive class of pottery with the Megarid has not been positively established (although the clay may have come from the slopes of Gerania, it could as well be the product of many other localities), but if this hypothesis is correct, it could confirm early exchange between the two Megaras and lend support to the view adopted here of a rift in relations between Megara and Corinth after the middle of the eighth century. As

[36]Diod. 20.32.4.
[37]Thuc. 6.4 and Diod. 13.59.4.
[38]Arist. *Poet.* 1448a.
[39]See J. Boardman's review of Coldstream, *Greek Geometric Pottery,* in *Gnomon* (1970), p. 496, and Boardman and Schweizer (above, note 15), pp. 278-80.

Boardman suggests, "Mid-century differences with Corinth might well have stimulated independent pottery production at Megara."[40] Yet even if the Thapsos class is shown to be Megara's attempt at an independent pottery industry, the effort seems to have petered out before 700, when this class disappears in Sicily. What significance should be attached to the ultimate predominance of Proto-Corinthian and Corinthian ware at Megara Hyblaea? Did Hyblaean trade ultimately fall to the Corinthians, or did the Megarians, despite their political differences with Corinth, revert to the use of Corinthian pots in their commercial dealings with the Sicilian colony? I am inclined to believe that both alternatives are at least partly true. The number of Thapsos class vessels found thus far does not suggest any great volume of trade in the eighth century, and I believe that Megara's trade with her lone western colony was never more than modest, any ambitions Megara might have had along these lines being largely preempted by the phenomenal growth of Corinthian naval power and trade in the West in the seventh and sixth centuries.

The foundation of Megara Hyblaea antedates the establishment of distinctive local scripts in Greece, but the later inscriptions of archaic Megara Hyblaea exhibit letter forms closer to those of Corinth and Syracuse than to those of Nisaean Megara.[41] This may be taken as an indication that Megara ceased to be the dominant influence over the practical and business affairs of her colony at a fairly early date. Apart from her possible contribution of settlers to the founding of Selinus, Megara made no further colonizing efforts in Sicily or anywhere in the West, despite her early involvement with the region and her considerable colonial activity elsewhere. For the next two centuries the West was a Corinthian preserve.

Heraeis and Piraeis probably accounted for the majority of Megarian emigrants to Sicily in the second quarter of the eighth century, but many more must have remained in the Megarid, eking out livings as best they could and hoping for the eventual return of their homeland. Megara's limited success in the war with Corinth circa 710-680 fell short of satisfying the needs of the ref-

[40]Boardman, *Gnomon*, p. 496.
[41]L. H. Jeffery, *The Local Scripts of Archaic Greece* (Oxford, 1961), p. 134.

ugees. Once resigned to the permanent loss of their lands in Perachora, many more of them were prepared to undergo the trauma of emigration to a distant colony. It is no coincidence that the second quarter of the seventh century witnessed Megara's most active period of colonization.

The Hellespont, Propontis, and the coasts of the Black Sea were first being opened to Greek settlement at the beginning of the seventh century, most notably through the efforts of the most powerful of the Ionian states, Miletus.[42] By concentrating their efforts at the eastern end of the Propontis, where the Milesians had not yet established themselves, the Megarians were able to play a major role in this new development. Megara's primary and secondary foundations in this region and along the coasts of the Black Sea, ultimately included Chalcedon, Selymbria, Byzantium, Astakos, Herakleia Pontica, Mesambria, Kallatis, and Chersonesos.[43]

The predominantly agrarian concerns of the Megarian colonists in the early stages of Megarian activity in this area are revealed by the choice of sites. From the outset, the magnificent point on the European coast of the Propontis, which was to become Byzantium and later Constantinople, cannot have been unfamiliar to Greek sailors. Here, where the Bosphorus leading from the Black Sea joins the Propontis, the prevailing winds and currents drive sailing ships toward the European coast, where the calm waters of the Golden Horn offer safe and commodious shelter. The peninsula that divides the Propontis from the Golden Horn is the natural center of naval traffic between the Black Sea states and Greece.[44] Yet at a time when the entire Propontis was open to them, the Megarians chose instead to settle on the Asiatic coast at Chalcedon,

[42]For a survey of Milesian colonial activity, see C. Roebuck, *Ionian Trade and Colonization* (New York, 1959), chapters 7, 8.

[43]The ancient testimony regarding Megarian colonization and that of her daughter states is most fully treated by Hanell, *Studien*, pp. 116-36.

[44]Polybius (4.38) gives the following description of the virtues of the site from the perspective of a later era: "As far as the sea is concerned, Byzantium occupies a position the most secure and in every way the most advantageous of any town in our quarter of the world; while in regard to the land, its situation is in both respects the most unfavorable. By sea it so completely commands the entrance to the Pontus that no merchant can sail in or out against its will" (tr. E. S. Shuckburgh, *The Histories of Polybius*, Vol. 1, London, 1889, p. 313.) The Romans were to reduce dramatically the town's early vulnerability to land attack, further enhancing the strategic value of their eventual eastern capital.

within sight of the future Byzantium.[45] Chalcedon possessed an ample plain, significant copper deposits (hence the name), and a decent harbor, though the harbor was in no way comparable to that of Byzantium. Here was a colony that was ideally suited to a self-supporting existence, based on agriculture, mining, and a modicum of trade. Given the virtual absence of metals in the Megarid, the Megarians might have considered Chalcedon's copper of greater significance at first than any grain surplus she might ultimately produce for export, if, indeed, Megarian commercial needs played any conscious role. Control of trade for its own sake, however, is unlikely to have been a major consideration of either the mother state or the colonists.

Herodotus tells us that the Persian general Megabazus called the settlers of Chalcedon "blind" when he learned that their city had been settled before Byzantium, and the Delphic Oracle later took credit for this remark.[46] But the Chalcedonians had probably found what they were looking for. The epithet might have been more appropriately applied to the inhabitants of Megara's second Propontic colony, Selymbria, which was founded only a short time before Byzantium.[47] By this time, perhaps fifteen years after the founding of Chalcedon, the Megarians and their early colonists in the region had first-hand knowledge of geography and sailing conditions of the Propontis; yet they ignored Byzantium and chose to settle on the modest plain of Selymbria some 70 kilometers further west along the European coast. Here another agricultural settlement was successfully established.

According to Herodotus, Byzantium was settled seventeen years after Chalcedon.[48] Even then it is likely that the fishing waters of the Golden Horn were a greater attraction than the site's potential

[45]Thuc. 4.75.2; Strab. 12.4.2; Pompon. 1.101. I follow Hanell, *Studien*, pp. 120-22, in regarding Astakos, on the Asiatic coast near Chalcedon, as a later Chalcedonian offshoot, possibly founded with Megarian support, rather than an even earlier Megarian settlement. The evidence is contradictory, however, and we cannot entirely reject the possibility of an early Megarian foray into the Propontis, a generation before the founding of Chalcedon. Eusebius gives 712/11 for the founding of Astakos.

[46]See Hdt. 4.144 for Megabazos' remark. This comment is attributed to the Delphic Oracle in Strab. 7.6.2 and Tac. *Ann.* 12.63. Apollo is supposed to have advised the Greeks to plant a colony opposite "the land of the blind men."

[47]Ps.-Scymn. 715 f.

[48]Hdt. 4.144. An interval of nineteen years is specified by Hsch. *Pat. Constan.* 5.3.

as a port.[49] Commerce between Greece and the Northeast was only gradually developing in the course of the seventh century and had not yet reached a volume that would permit settlements based primarily on trade to succeed. The Milesians, after all, were at least as responsible for ignoring Byzantium as the Megarians had been. The Greeks in the early seventh century could not envision the future importance of Byzantium. Still, the Megarians were most fortunate to have developed the site, and were to reap benefit in later times from their association with this vital emporium.

The ancient chronographers give dates in the mid-680's for the foundation of Chalcedon and in the early 650's for Byzantium.[50] No specific date is assigned to Selymbria, which is merely said to have preceded Byzantium. These dates are not consistent with Herodotus' statement that Byzantium was settled seventeen years after Chalcedon, and the date of the latter has sometimes been lowered by ten years in order to conform to the historian's interval.[51] The issue need not trouble us here, since our main interest is Megarian development and either date for Chalcedon puts her foundation into close proximity with the last phase of the war between Megara and Corinth—for which we have no firm date in any case. There is, however, one late source, John of Lydia, who dates Byzantium to 628—that is, thirty years after the more common date.[52] The expedition, which John describes is sometimes treated as supplemental to the initial settlement[53] or, alternatively, as the actual foundation date,[54] though it is most often ignored altogether. Regrettably, the archaeological records of early Chalcedon and Byzantium are so meager, that it is impossible to demonstrate the occupation of either site much before 600, but I am strongly inclined to accept the earlier dates and to regard the settlers of 628, if

---

[49]The abundance of tunny fish in the waters of the Golden Horn is noted by Pliny *HN* 9.20; Tac. *Ann.* 12.63; and Strab. 7.6.2.

[50]Eusebius (*Hieron.*) gives 685 for Chalcedon and 659 for Byzantium. For variant dates, see Hanell, *Studien*, p. 126.

[51]Clinton, p. 186.

[52]3.70.

[53]Clinton, p. 208.

[54]See, e.g., Burn, *Lyric Age*, pp. 113-14, where Chalcedon is moved down to 645 and Byzantium to 628. Burn himself earlier accepted the more commonly held dates in his article on "Greek Sea Power, 776-540 B.C. and the Carian Entry in the Eusebian Thalassocracy List," *JHS*, 47 (1927), 171.

John's authority is to be trusted, as an additional force. A further thirty years of neglect of Byzantium is difficult to imagine unless one is prepared to bring down the dates of all the Hellespontine, Propontic, and Bosporan colonies. If, then, we tentatively accept circa 675 and 658 for Chalcedon and Byzantium, a hundred years would pass before the Megarians launched another primary colonial expedition, to Herakleia Pontica. Smaller contingents may have been sent to join colonists from Megara Hyblaea at Selinus circa 650, to reinforce Byzantium in 628, and possibly to augment the colonial efforts of Chalcedon and Byzantium, but the extreme pressure created by the Perachoran refugees appears to have eased by the middle of the seventh century. In fact, the Megarians may have had to augment their expedition to Byzantium through the inclusion of settlers from other states.

The Megarian claim to Chalcedon and Selymbria was never seriously challenged in antiquity,[55] but a great many states claimed credit for having played some role in the founding of Byzantium. The list includes the Athenians, Spartans, Argives, Corinthians, Arcadians, Boeotians, Milesians, and, by inference, the Chalcedonians, in addition to the Megarians.[56] This is hardly surprising in view of the importance Byzantium eventually attained, but it must also reflect the absence of an early and unequivocal tradition regarding her foundation. Megara's primary role is substantiated by a number of considerations. She is the most frequently mentioned colonizer, even where the involvement of the states is noted, and there is a close correspondence between the cults, alphabets, and calendars of Megara, Byzantium, and the other Megarian colonies.[57] The political institutions of later Byzantium

[55]Hsch. (*Pat. Constan.* 1.9) mentions settlers from Euboean Chalcis at Chalcedon, but this statement probably derives from an erroneous etymological inference, based on the apparent similarity of name between the two states rather than from any independent evidence.

[56]For Megara as sole founder, see Ps.-Scymn. 717; Strab. 7.6.2; Philostr. *VS* 24; Jo. Lyd. 3.70. For Megara as the principal founder, see Dion. Byz. 7, 15 (with the Corinthians), 17, 19 (with the Arcadians), and 22 f. For Argos first, with Megara afterward, see Hsch. *Pat. Constan.* 5.3, 6.3. For Megara together with Athens, Boeotia, and Sparta, see Amm. Mar. 22.8.8. For Miletus alone, see Vell. Pat. 2.7.7. For King Pausanias of Sparta as founder, see Just. *Epit.* 9.13 and Oros. 3.13.2.

[57]Hanell, *Studien,* pp. 161-204, reviews the evidence concerning the calendars and religious cults of the Megarian colonies and Megara herself. On the alphabet, see Jeffery, pp. 134-35 and 366. These more recent studies should remove any doubt

present, however, a more mixed picture. Some elements, such as the division of the populace into "hundreds," parallel the practice in Megara and other related communities, but there are anomalies, the most serious of which is that the Byzantine council is not called the aesymnatae in any surviving document. The names of two official bodies are preserved, the "fifteen," and a committee of thirty, called the *Boiotoi*.[58] The single reference to the latter in Diodorus' account of fourth-century affairs has been challenged as a corruption of the text. It is a rather odd choice, and lends credence to the participation of Boeotians at Byzantium, as they were to be involved a hundred years later at Herakleia Pontica. The claims of some other states—for example, Athens and Sparta— may relate more to their subsequent roles in Byzantine affairs; and the story that Pausanias of Sparta founded the city is an obvious confusion based on his having expelled the Persians in 479 and returned the city to the Byzantines, constituting the second founding of Byzantium. But if the Boeotians could have contributed manpower to the settlement of Byzantium, so might others on the Greek mainland who were not actively involved in colonization themselves—for example, the Arcadians and Argives.

The roles of Chalcedon and Miletus may have been different. It is hard to imagine that Chalcedon would not have played some part in the settlement less than 2 kilometers distant across the Bosporan straits and sponsored by her own founder, Megara. The only evidence for her involvement comes, however, in a late account of her assistance to Byzantium when the Scythians attacked the colony, presumably shortly after its foundation.[59] The Chalcedonian leader, Dineos, is said to have played a major role in saving Byzantium, and was later made general there, the next after Byzas, the eponymous founder of the colony. Hanell's suggestion is attractive: since Byzas is clearly a non-Greek name, Dineos may have been the actual oikist of Byzantium; but that Chalcedon does not figure at all in the foundation legends is disturbing, to say the least. I believe it is highly likely that Chalcedon was an important

about Megara's role in the founding of Byzantium. For an earlier dissenting view, one may consult J. Miller, "Ist Byzanz eine megarische Colonie?" *Philologus*, 56 (1897), 326-33.

[58]See Ditt. *Syll.*[3] 645 for the *pentekaideka* and Diod. 14.12.3 for the *Boiotoi*.

[59]Hsch. *Pat. Constan.* 20.9 and 22 f. Cf. Hanell, *Studien*, pp. 124-28.

factor in the new settlement, but I hesitate to shift the leading role from Megara to her. The case for Milesian participation rests on Velleius Paterculus' statement that Miletus founded Cyzicus and Byzantium at the same time. That is scarcely sufficient grounds for rejecting Megara's role. Given the active colonial policy of Miletus along the entire northeastern passage between the Aegean and the Black Sea, however, many historians have been tempted to credit her with partial responsibility or, at the least, sympathy and support for the Megarian venture, though even the latter view, which is certainly reasonable, may grant Miletus a greater proprietary interest in the commercial route to the Euxine than she is likely to have felt circa 660. In the absence of any record of conflict between Megara and Miletus at this time or later, it seems highly probable that the two states most actively involved in opening the Black Sea and the Propontis to Greek settlement and commerce were on terms of friendship. They may even have taken steps to coordinate their policy in the region.

The evident good relations between Megara and Miletus in the second quarter of the seventh century have been stressed in attempts to link Megara with the Lelantine War, which broke out sometime in the last third of the eighth century.[60] Thucydides tells us that this was the earliest general war in Greece, but he does not supply a list of the allies on either side.[61] The initial *casus belli* was a dispute between the Euboean states of Chalcis and Eretria over control of the Lelantine Plain, which lay between them, but the conflict expanded to involve other states and, presumably, wider issues. Herodotus specifically implicates Samos in support of Chalcis, and Miletus in support of Eretria,[62] but it has been left to modern historians to infer the allegiance of other states from signs of affinity or hostility between them and one or more of these central four. In this fashion, Corinth has been tied to the Chalcidic coalition, and Megara—at odds with Corinth, hostile to the Chalcidians in Sicily in the second quarter of the eighth century, and friendly with Miletus in the seventh century—has been assigned to the

[60]The most persuasive treatment of the Lelantine War is that of W. G. Forrest, "Colonization and the Rise of Delphi," *Historia,* 6 (1957), 160-75. See esp. p. 164 for his remarks on the role of Megara.
[61]1.15.3.
[62]5.99.

Eretrian camp. The case for Megarian involvement is inconclusive. The border war with Corinth needed no external stimulus; the issue was purely local. Chalcis and Megara had begun by cooperating in Sicily, and there is no extended evidence that the rift that developed within their joint expedition extended to the parent states. The relationship with Miletus is purely a matter of inference, and we are in no position to say how it developed or to describe its terms. It might further be objected that the dates do not easily fit our picture of the Lelantine War. If the chronological suggestions made here are accepted, Megara's differences with Corinth and Chalcis probably antedate the war and her accord with Miletus may only have developed after the war had ended. Still, if Megara was at all involved in this conflict, the overwhelming likelihood is that she stood with the Eretrians and Milesians. What is far less plausible, however, is that the Lelantine War was a struggle for the control of trade routes and that the combatants were linked in rival trade leagues.[63] This view, though less fashionable than it once was, still has its adherents; but it is in clear opposition to our understanding of commerce in the eighth and early seventh century and of Greek trading practices altogether.[64] At the time of the Lelantine War, the volume of trade was minute and its organization haphazard. Conditions were to change gradually in the course of the archaic period, and Megara was to play an important role in that process, but those developments took place after the Lelantine War, whatever its true causes and extent, had faded into history.

The hundred year period covered in this chapter saw events of the greatest importance in Megarian history. Hemmed in at home by the expanding power of Corinth, the Megarians were forced to turn early to colonization to alleviate the plight of their refugees. At first, this colonial policy was dependent upon the logistical support of the seafaring Chalcidians, but by the early seventh century Megara was capable of mounting her own naval expeditions to the

[63]This view is most fully developed by Burn in his article on "The So-Called Trade Leagues in Early Greek History and the Lelantine War," *JHS*, 49 (1929), 14-37. It appears most recently in L. H. Jeffery, *Archaic Greece: The City-States, c. 700-500 B.C.* (New York, 1976), pp. 64-67.

[64]See the discussion in chapters 2 and 3 of Starr, *Economic and Social Growth.*

Propontis. She successfully spawned a series of colonies that were to play a major part in the growing economic and strategic importance of the Northeast. Megarian commitment to the sea was to grow further under the stimulus of her gradually developing economic interdependence with the grain and mineral rich states of the Propontus and Euxine, and especially with her own colonies. These developments and their impact on the internal affairs of Megara are the subjects of subsequent chapters.

CHAPTER 4

Commerce, Social Change, and Tyranny

Cyrnus, the *polis* still survives, but the people are different, men who formerly knew neither its laws nor customs, but wore goat-skins to cover their nakedness and grazed like deer beyond the city. And now they have become worthy men, O son of Poly-paus, and they that were once noble are now base. Who can endure to see such things?

—*Theognidaea* 53-58

IN THE course of the seventh century, Megara began the gradual transformation from a purely agrarian economy to one more dependent upon imports and exports.[1] Her colonies, particularly those in the Propontis, had access to metals, timber, and other natural resources that were either totally absent or in very short supply in the Megarid. These are likely to have been the initial stimuli to commerce, and a few enterprising individuals doubtless made their fortunes plying the waters between Megara and the friendly havens of her northeastern colonies. But as the Propontic colonies prospered and began to produce agricultural surpluses, and as the Greeks advanced into the Black Sea and began to tap the grain resources of the non-Greek hinterland there, basic foodstuffs increasingly became the predominant object of Megarian commercial activity. Byzantium must have served as the chief entrepôt of this trade. Megarian grain importation may have begun by the latter part of the seventh century, although archaeological confirmation

---

[1]For the most detailed recent treatment of this period of Megarian history, see Oost, "Theagenes and Theognis." I find myself in agreement with most of what Oost has to say about Theagenes, though some differences are noted below.

of the grain trade does not become abundant until the later sixth century, and, even then Megarian participation cannot be confirmed.[2] Again, the absence of pottery may create a false impression regarding the trade of a state that produced little or no pottery for export but may have traded in other commodities.[3] I do not suggest, however, that Megara soon became greatly dependent upon imported grain, or that the search for a source of supply was a conscious motive behind the establishment of her early colonies.

Considering their meager resources, it may well be asked what the Megarians could offer in exchange for grain and other commodities from the Northeast. It is possible that some of the specialty crops that were a regular feature of their trade with Athens in the fifth century, such as onions, garlic, apples, and pomegranates, were earlier shipped as far as the Black Sea. Small quantities of wine and oil may have been exported before they were driven from the market by superior products from Athens and elsewhere. The distinctive, strong salt of the Megarid may also have been in demand among the Megarian colonists. But the major export items seem to have been woolen garments and perhaps wool itself. The earliest explicit references to this trade, it is true, come in the late fifth and early fourth centuries.[4] By then, the Megarians were

---

[2] The case for the establishment of a grain trade between the grain-poor states of Greece and the European coast of the Black Sea is well stated by C. Roebuck, "The Economic Development of Ionia," *CP*, 48 (1953), 9-16, and in his book, *Ionian Trade and Colonization*, New York, 1959. This view has been disputed on the basis of reports of Soviet archaeology on the north coast of the Black Sea. See T. S. Noonan, "The Grain Trade of the Northern Black Sea in Antiquity," *AJP*, 94 (1973), 231-42, who argues that this trade did not reach significant proportions until the later sixth century. The two positions are not as far apart as first appears, since there is no agreed-upon definition of what volume of traffic merits the designation "grain trade." Noonan and others do not categorically deny that some grain was shipped out of the Black Sea in the seventh century, and may simply be applying a more rigorous standard than Roebuck. Furthermore, Noonan is exclusively concerned with specific sites along the northern coast of the Black Sea, which later came to supply a substantial proportion of Greece's cereals, while the arguments for an earlier grain traffic are concerned with a much wider supply area, including regions settled earlier by the Greeks and also the non-Greek hinterland. In fact, there is evidence that Greeks traded with the natives in the interior earlier than on the coasts themselves. See Boardman, *The Greeks Overseas*, pp. 238-39.

[3] This point is made persuasively and at length by G. Vallet and F. Villard, "Céramique grecque et histoire économique," in *Études Archéologiques*, ed. P. Courbin (Paris, 1963), pp. 205-17, esp. p. 212.

[4] Ar. *Ach.* 519, *Pax* 1003, Xen. *Mem.* 2.7.6.

famous for the coarse but serviceable woolen tunics they produced for export. These *exomides* or *chlaniskia* were the Greek equivalent of ready-to-wear clothes, within the means of ordinary folk who might otherwise wear homespun garments. Their price might actually compare favorably with homespun in regions where domestic wool was in short supply. Given the high proportion of Megarian land that was suitable for little else than pasturage, it is hardly surprising that more sheep were raised and more wool produced than could be absorbed in the domestic market. Megara's association with the rearing of sheep is reflected in a reported remark of the fourth-century Cynic philosopher Diogenes.[5] When he saw Megarian sheep wearing leather coats and the children wearing none, he is supposed to have said that it was better to be a Megarian's ram than his son. But do we have any reason to presume that the Megarians produced wool or woolen garments for export more than two centuries earlier than any of the evidence cited thus far? Woolen cloaks, unlike pots, do not survive to be unearthed by the archaeologist's spade.[6] One hint, however, may be seen in Pliny the Elder's statement that the art of fulling was invented by a certain Nicias of Megara.[7] It is highly improbable that the invention of techniques of bleaching and cleaning woolen cloth could actually be traced back to Nicias (or to any single individual), but the tradition on which Pliny draws must have fixed on a Megarian because of Megara's early association with the production of textiles. In a passage to which we will shortly return, Aristotle tells us that the seventh-century Megarian tyrant Theagenes won popularity when he attacked the livestock (*ta ktēnē*) of the wealthy.[8] The livestock in question are more than likely to have been either predominantly or exclusively sheep, and the natural implication of Aristotle's statement is that sheep were abundant and controversial in seventh-century Megara. Finally, we have already noted Perachora's likely concentration on the rearing of sheep, and the probability that the Perachoran refugees brought their flocks with

[5] D.L. 6.41.
[6] See Starr's comments on the textile trade in *The Economic and Social Growth of Early Greece, 800-500 B.C.*, pp. 65-66.
[7] *HN* 7.196.
[8] *Pol.* 1305a.

them into the eastern Megarid when they were expelled from their homeland.

By the fourth century large numbers of slaves were employed in workshops turning out Megarian tunics, but this must have been the end of a long process of evolution. The earliest cloth was doubtless produced in a cottage industry that supplemented the income of farming and laboring as well as sheep-rearing house-holds. Yet even in the earliest stages of this activity, there would have been some specialists, such as fullers, and the various steps of production from the collection of the wool through to the sale of the finished product were probably coordinated and financed by an emerging class of entrepreneurs. Thus a small but significant number of Megarians were freed from directly agrarian pursuits. An even larger number of men must have been absorbed by Megar-ian naval activity in the seventh century, the captains and crews of the commercial vessels, and the laborers and craftsmen of the ship-yards. The activity of shipbuilding must have increased in the course of the century. Megarians built the ships that carried their colonists to the Propontis and that continued commercial and cultural interchange with them thereafter. By the end of the cen-tury, if not much earlier, the Megarians were building warships too. They probably inflicted a naval defeat on the Athenians late in the century, and they lost a large-scale sea battle with the Samians in the Propontis circa 600.[9] A. R. Burn has gone so far as to suggest Megarian naval supremacy in the Aegean between circa 660 and circa 600 as the solution to a corrupt passage in the Eusebian thalas-socracy list.[10] Although this is improbable, particularly in view of Corinth's naval power at this time,[11] it is equally unreasonable to doubt that Megara was a significant naval power in the second half of the century and later. The episodes noted above do not estab-lish Megara as a leading naval power, but they show that she had sufficient confidence in her fleet to use it as an instrument of policy in dealing with rival states.

[9]See below, Chapter 5.
[10]See Burn, "Greek Sea Power, 776-540 B.C.," pp. 165-71.
[11]See W. G. Forrest's response to Burn in "Two Chronographic Notes," CQ, 63 (1969), 95-110.

The number of people who were directly engaged in the various aspects of commerce and shipping in the seventh century may have reached the hundreds rather than thousands, but their impact on the economic and social life of Megara was immense. It is obvious that the sheep-raising element of the populace was directly affected, as were the households that supplemented their incomes with spinning, weaving, etc. But even the subsistence farmer may have felt the effects of the woolen industry. What was once mediocre farmland might now be seen as prime pasture and, as such, under pressure from a mounting demand for pasturage. This pressure may have taken the form of increasing prices for such land, if it was treated as alienable, but it is equally possible that the impact in a hierarchical society was arbitrary exploitation and expropriation. Abuses of this sort could have prompted Theagenes' sheep raids. Toward the end of the century, grain prices may have fallen in the face of imports, and the small Megarian farmer may have encountered increasing difficulty selling the surplus on which he depended to pay for the few items he could not produce for himself. The interplay of these pressures probably meant that more and more marginal land was taken out of grain production in favor of cash crops and pasture, though every farmer must have continued to plant sufficient grain to meet the needs of his own family.

A concomitant of Megara's changing economy was urban growth. Some day archaeology may be able to trace the stages in the physical expansion of the town of Megara, but there can be little doubt that it experienced a boom in the middle decades of the seventh century. Prior to this time, it had been almost entirely parasitic on the countryside. Early Megara's residents were the great landlords, laborers, and slaves who catered to their needs, and the destitute. But in the course of the seventh century a self-sustaining population of skilled workers, sailors, entrepreneurs, and merchants gradually filled the gap between the rich and poor urbanites. The city began to serve as a magnet attracting many of those who had insufficient land, or no land at all, with the promise of greater opportunity. The major achievement of Theagenes was provision of a secure and convenient water supply for the city—by means of his famous conduit and fountainhouse.[12] The scale of this project, which was probably unprecedented in Greece, is a clear reflection of Megara's increased population and of the town's prior inability to supply the needs of its inhabitants. Connected with the growth of the city was the establishment or expansion of the port at Nisaea. Because of its proximity to the main urban center, a distance of under 2 kilometers, its constricted area, as well as the marshy, insalubrious conditions along the coast, Nisaea never attracted a large residential population, and workers from the city probably walked to the coast and back each day.

The diversity of the expanding town was at once a reflection of Megara's economic vitality and a source of social and political friction. The majority of the ruling aristocracy did not enjoy the prospect of regular contact with their social inferiors, or even with those commoners who had achieved wealth comparable to their own. Their scorn for the ignorant savages from the countryside who had invaded *their* city is expressed in the lines of the Megarian poet, Theognis, which stand at the head of this chapter. By the time he penned these verses, probably near the end of the century, many less hide-bound aristocrats had made their peace with the upstarts. This accounts, in part, for Theognis' venom. It is only natural that the snobbery of Megara's traditional elite rankled among the socially ambitious, but their resentment of the aristocracy's monopoly of political power was far more serious. Many of the newly prosperous had both the time and the means to play an active role in political affairs, which was denied to them by the established order. Their claim was undoubtedly strengthened by their expanded military role as well, for the seventh century saw the introduction of the hoplite phalanx as the dominant tactical formation of the Hellenic armies.

This new style of fighting was based upon a massed formation of heavy-armed foot soldiers, and its effectiveness was directly related to its breadth and depth—that is, to the number of troops participating. The skills required of the hoplite were not of the same high order as those needed to survive individual hand-to-hand combat, and anyone who could afford the hoplite panoply

---

[12]Paus. 1.40.1 and 41.2.

and the time to drill could become proficient. Under these conditions, the practical necessity to admit all men of moderate means
into the phalanx overcame the aristocracy's reluctance to share its
traditionally central military role; a role that was one of the chief
rationales for the social and political hierarchy of the early polis.
These developments occurred first among the Dorian states of the
Peloponnese, and the earliest pictorial confirmation of the phalanx
comes from Corinthian vases of the mid-seventh century.[13] It is
likely that the phalanx was introduced in Corinth sometime in the
first half of the seventh century and possible that she used it for the
first time in her war with Megara circa 700, and that the Megarians
were obliged to adopt the mass formation in response to the danger posed by the restructured Corinthian army. In any case, it is a
virtual certainty that the Megarians would have had to adopt the
phalanx by the middle of the seventh century, and with it the
enhanced prominence of the middle class. As elsewhere, the new
hoplites, urban and rural, were probably not slow to press their
demands for admission to the magistracies and the *aesymnatae* as
well as for a share in the aristocracy's other prerogatives. Only
effective leadership was needed to turn their grievances into active
opposition to the regime.

The poorer elements of Megarian society may have been less of
an immediate threat to the established regime, but their discon-
tentment may also have increased as the general level of prosperity
rose in the course of the seventh century. In part this would have
been an example of the familiar pattern of rising expectations, but
it is also likely that urbanization and commercialization were leading to the gradual breakdown of the paternalistic role of the hereditary elite. Labor may have been exploited more ruthlessly, justice
dispensed more impersonally, and debts collected mercilessly. The
flashpoint for mounting popular feeling was likely to be the city,

[13]There is an extensive literature on the date, purpose, and effect of the introduction of the phalanx in archaic Greece. Major works dealing with the subject include
recent books by P. A. L. Greenhalgh, *Early Greek Warfare* (Cambridge, 1973), esp.
pp. 70 ff., and A. M. Snodgrass, *Early Greek Arms and Armour* (London, 1967), esp.
pp. 49-60. Two important articles appeared in *JHS*, 97 (1977): "Hoplites and Heroes:
Sparta's Contribution to the Technique of Ancient Warfare," by P. Cartledge, pp.
11-27, and "Political Hoplites?" by J. Salmon, pp. 84-101. I am persuaded by Salmon's case for the introduction of hoplite tactics early enough in the seventh century to have influenced the rise of the first tyrants.

rather than the countryside. Here, rich and poor, privileged and deprived, were closely juxtaposed. Here, too, the poor could assemble more readily and dare to transform the docile popular assembly into a political weapon.

The Megarian aristocracy survived the disastrous contraction of Megarian territory at the hands of the Corinthians, partly by sponsoring a series of distant colonies for the displaced citizenry of the western komai and partly by promoting the diversification of the Megarian economy, but it was unable to preserve itself from the consequences of having made Megara a more dynamic society. Colonization, commercial development, and urban growth had led to a new political consciousness and mounting demands by the middle and lower classes. This pressure would ultimately have undone the aristocratic monopoly on wealth and power, but the process was accelerated by the emergence in Megara of one of the earliest Greek tyrannies, that of Theagenes. The dates of his regime cannot be absolutely determined, but he appears to have attained power around 640. This date is suggested by the one sequence of events in his reign to which an approximate date can be attached: his association with the Athenian Cylon. Cylon had won a footrace at Olympia in the thirty-fifth Olympiad, about 640. According to Thucydides, Cylon married the daughter of the Megarian tyrant and, with Theagenes' support, attempted to make himself tyrant in Athens during a subsequent Olympic year.[14] Since Cylon was still a

[14]Thuc. 1.126.3-11, quoted later in this chapter. The link with late seventh-century events in Athens has been sufficient grounds for most historians to date Theagenes' tyranny in the last third of the seventh century, but several have attempted to move him down into the sixth century, most notably Beloch, *Gr. Gesch.* 1², pp. 308-09, and T. Lenshau, "Forschungen zur griechischen Geschichte im VII. und VI. Jahrhundert v. Chr., I, Die Tyrannis in den Isthmosstaaten," *Philologus*, 91 (1936/7), 286-89. Their arguments are aimed at bringing Theagenes into closer relation with a supposed late sixth-century date for the poet Theognis (discussed in the following chapter), and rest on an *a priori* picture of slower political evolution in Megara. As I hope will emerge from the treatment of sixth-century Megara below, these assumptions are not necessary and do not merit rejection of our only direct evidence bearing on Theagenes' date. Nor do I accept Lenshau's down-dating of the Olympiads, based on the argument that the festival was annual, rather than quadrennial for a considerable period of time.

Approaching the problem from an entirely different perspective, however, M. Lang, "The Kylonian Conspiracy," *CP*, 62 (1967), 243-49, argues that the omission of Theagenes in Herodotus' brief treatment of the Cylonian conspiracy (5.71) calls into

young man, supported by other young men, at the time of his abortive coup, it can scarcely have occurred later than 628, and may have taken place four or even eight years earlier.[15] If, as is argued below, Theagenes attained power prior to his liaison with Cylon and held it until sometime after Cylon's failure, the 640's would be the earliest reasonable date for the Megarian tyranny.

Thus the Megarian tyranny is roughly contemporary with those in nearby Corinth and Sicyon.[16] Broadly speaking, by the middle of the seventh century, tyranny was proving to be the most effective means of challenging entrenched aristocratic regimes, though its results were variable and it often failed to resolve the grievances of elements of society which were prepared to support a strongman against established authority. We know considerably more about such tyrants as Cypselus and Periander of Corinth and Cleisthenes of Sicyon than we know about Theagenes, but it could be seriously misleading to flesh out our picture of him and his regime by borrowing elements from other tyrannies; local conditions and issues

---

question the validity of Thucydides' testimony on the point. Yet while it is arguable that Thucydides may have introduced into his account a bit of anti-Megarian propaganda (rife in Athens after 446), it is equally possible that Herodotus suppressed or merely ignored a point that was damaging to Megarian-Athenian relations, writing at a time when the two states were still allies—i.e., before 446. I cannot imagine that the story of Cylon's marriage to the daughter of Theagenes was an invention, though the degree of Theagenes' involvement in Cylon's coup might have been exaggerated or distorted by tradition.

[15]Herodotus' account, though not Thucydides', creates the impression that Cylon began preparing his coup in the afterglow of his Olympic glory—a matter of years, not decades.

[16]Orthagoras of Sicyon is usually thought to have gained power c. 657 (based on arguments for the collapse of this supposedly 100-year tyranny c. 557). See, e.g., A. Andrewes, *The Greek Tyrants* (London, 1956), pp. 57-61; N. G. L. Hammond, "The Family of Orthagoras," *CQ*, 50 (1956), 45-53; and D. M. Leahy, "Chilon and Aeschines Again," *Phoenix*, 13 (1959), 31-37. A minority, however, have argued for a later dating, c. 615, most recently M. White in "The Date of the Orgathorids," *Phoenix*, 12 (1958), 2-14. Opinion is similarly divided on the date of Cypselus' coup in Corinth. The traditional dating c. 657 is most recently defended by J. Ducat, "Note sur la chronologie des Kypsélides," *BCH*, 85 (1961), 418-25. See Will, *Korinthiaka*, pp. 363-440, for an exhaustive review of the problem and a defense of down-dating Cypselus to c. 620. I have no desire to enter either of these controversies here, and either the high or low datings of these neighboring regimes would be compatible with a date in the 640's for Theagenes' rise to power. The main issue affected, though at present insoluble, is the sequence in which the Isthmian tyrannies developed—i.e., did Megara take the lead, or was she following a pattern already established in surrounding states?

always played a decisive role in the rise of tyrants and the policies they followed, and their individual character and ambition could also differ sharply.

Although nothing is directly known about Theagenes' background or station in life prior to his becoming tyrant, it has sometimes been argued that he was himself an aristocrat, since his daughter was judged a suitable match by an Athenian Eupatrid.[17] But since their marriage is likely to have taken place subsequent to Theagenes' establishment of his tyranny, his acquired power and prestige could have compensated for any deficiency in his pedigree. Nevertheless, it is probable that Theagenes belonged to the privileged class in Megara from birth, to judge from the context of Aristotle's comments about his rise to power:

> In early times, when a single individual become both leader of the *demos* and general, the state became a tyranny; . . . in those days the leaders of the *demos* emerged from the men who served as generals. . . . Furthermore, since cities at that time were not large and the *demos* lived in the countryside fully engaged in making their living, when the leaders of the *demos* became warlike, they grasped for tyranny [rather than, as later, democracy]. They used to do all this when they had gained the trust of the *demos*, which was won by a show of hostility toward the rich as . . . Theagenes of Megara did by slaughtering the flocks of the wealthy which he caught grazing by the river.[18]

Thus Aristotle includes Theagenes among the tyrants who parlayed legitimate political and military office within a preexisting aristocracy into absolute rule. Since public office in the aristocratic regimes was undoubtedly restricted to members of the elite, Theagenes would seem to have enjoyed this status in Megara.

The passage from Aristotle just quoted leads us directly into consideration of the issues and tactics that brought Theagenes to power. He appears to have slaughtered the flocks of the wealthy, which he surprised while they were grazing by a river. One is at a loss to identify a river in the Megarid where this incident might

[17]See, e.g., Oost, "Theagenes and Theognis," p. 188, and F. Schachermeyer, "Theagenes," *RE,* 5A2, col. 1341.
[18]*Pol.* 1305a.

have occurred, although there were seasonal torrents. Leaving this puzzle aside, however, it may be inferred that Theagenes made this attack in his official capacity, probably on the grounds that the owners of these animals had no right to graze them on this land— or possibly to water them at this "river." These owners are termed *euporoi*—men of substance—by Aristotle, rather than *aristoi*, which may indicate that they were both noble and common in background; but the tenor of the passage as a whole points to the established order as being the target of Theagenes' action. It is not unreasonable to detect tension between the powerful owners of the larger flocks and the poorer shepherds and farmers of the Megarid.[19] That was a natural development in light of the growth of the woolen trade in Megara, on which we have already speculated. But it would be too extreme to see in Theagenes' action a thorough hostility toward sheep grazing on his part or that of his followers. Rather, it was squarely aimed at the class that was attempting to monopolize this growing activity and to displace or expropriate others from the limited pasturage available in the Megarid. On the other hand, it would be anachronistic to suggest, as was once fashionable,[20] that Theagenes sought to establish his own monopoly on the woolen industry by eliminating the flocks of his competitors.

Aristotle makes one further reference to Theagenes' rise to power, including him in a list of tyrants who had been granted public bodyguards which they used to seize control of their states.[21] No details or surrounding circumstances are supplied by Aristotle, and it is left for us to imagine how Theagenes might have justified the bodyguard or used it against the Megarian government. On the first point, it is tempting to speculate that Theagenes may have endangered his personal safety through his punitive raids on the livestock of the rich.[22] However justified the step may have been, it

[19]Burn, *Lyric Age,* p. 188, suggests a background of "strife over land between cattlemen and crofters."

[20]See, e.g., P. N. Ure, *The Origins of Tyranny* (Cambridge, 1922), p. 267.

[21]*Rh.* 1357b.

[22]So, e.g., Meyer, "Megara," col. 184. Others put Theagenes' acquisition of a bodyguard before his livestock raids, e.g., Oost, "Theagenes and Theognis," p. 189, because he would not have dared offend the nobility without this protection. Either view is arguable, but I prefer to see the bodyguard as a consequence rather than a cause of Theagenes' boldness.

must have caused a tremendous stir and earned Theagenes the hatred of many of his aristocratic peers. Retribution was not an unlikely possibility. Under these circumstances, if Theagenes was granted his guard to protect him from retaliation for his livestock raids, the Megarian council is unlikely to have sponsored the measure. Many of its members would have been unsympathetic, and few were so naive as to play into the hands of an ambitious peer: a public bodyguard, unlike a troop of private retainers, was an armed force that could be brought into the city without raising suspicion of treason. Such a force could be used to capture the citadel and intimidate, disperse, or murder the members of the aesymnatae. Like Pisistratus' in the next century, Theagenes' bodyguard was probably granted him by the popular assembly in a gesture of defiance to the regime.[23] No source describes the actual coup, which may indicate that it was a relatively bloodless affair; a bloody one is likelier to have left a historical trace. Perhaps the tactics of Cylon in Athens paralleled the recent example of his father-in-law—namely, armed seizure of the acropolis (Alcathoa, in the Megarian case) and a public declaration.

Little is known of Theagenes' style, policies, and achievements once in power. We cannot say whether he tolerated, reshaped, or disbanded the aesymnatae or the other state machinery. His one outstanding accomplishment was, as noted above, the construction of an aqueduct and fountainhouse for the city.[24] The fountainhouse was one of the earliest, possibly the earliest, such structure in Greece, and together with the water conduit may have established Megara's reputation for hydraulic engineering.[25] The house was centrally located in the town of Megara, a short distance above the agora, in the saddle between Caria and Alcathoa. It provided the urban populace with a convenient and abundant source of fresh water, and it is a clear reflection of urban growth. The project is far more likely to have been a response to existing conditions than an anticipation of future development. One could push this line of reasoning a bit further to suggest that Theagenes' concern

[23]See Hdt. 1.58 f. for Pisistratus' bodyguard.
[24]Paus. 1.40.1 and 41.2.
[25]Herodotus (3.60) credits the Megarian engineer Eupalinus with one of the greatest of Greek building feats—a tunnel more than one kilometer long—which was dug c. 530 to bring water to the city of Samos.

for the urban water supply is a manifestation of his sympathy with the growing urban populace and with the economic diversification of seventh-century Megara. Another aspect of this undertaking may not be irrelevant here, since the construction of both the conduit and the fountainhouse must have provided employment for a considerable number of laborers over a period of years. Thus it speaks to the availability of such a labor force and the funds with which to pay it. We are at a loss, however, to identify the source of these revenues, whether from the normal duties and taxes of an increasingly commercialized state or from the confiscated wealth of Theagenes' opponents.

We are as much in the dark concerning other elements of his domestic policy. Were his benefactions to the rural poor comparable to his improvement of urban life? As tyrant, he must have continued his protection of the poor from the excesses of the powerful, but did he attempt major reforms such as land redistribution or protection for debtors? We cannot even say whether Theagenes had an overall policy or was primarily an ambitious opportunist. It is fairly certain, however, that his reforms, if any, were moderate, and that he stopped short of sweeping changes in the order of things; it was left to the popular regime which came to power shortly after his downfall to adopt extreme measures.[26] Unlike some other tyrants, Theagenes was not a revered or heroic figure in the popular imagination of later generations of Megarians, if we may judge by his virtual absence from surviving Megarian tradition. Theagenes is probably best understood as a popular reformer who raised the expectations of the lower classes, but whose measures failed to respond fully to the needs of his supporters and were soon reversed by the resurgent aristocracy.

Our evidence for Theagenes' efforts on the diplomatic front is equally poor. Here, his already noted association with Cylon is the only solid fact. Our only source for this connection is Thucydides, since Theagenes is not mentioned in Herodotus' briefer account of the Cylonian conspiracy.[27] Thucydides reports:

[26]These reforms are discussed in the next chapter.
[27]5.71; cf. Plut. *Sol.* 12.

In the early times there lived an Athenian Olympic victor by the name of Cylon, well-born and powerful. He had married the daughter of Theagenes the Megarian, who at that time held tyranny over Megara. Cylon went to Delphi to consult the oracle, and the god advised him to seize the Athenian acropolis during the great festival of Zeus. Having obtained troops from Theagenes and having persuaded his friends to support him, Cylon seized the acropolis when the Olympic festival in the Peloponnese came round, intending to make himself tyrant. For he presumed that the great festival of Zeus was that held at Olympia and also that he had a special connection with it because of his victory there.[28]

After speculating as to whether Cylon had correctly interpreted the god's advice, Thucydides continues:

When the Athenians learned what Cylon had done, they all came in from the countryside to oppose him and laid siege to the acropolis. As time passed, the Athenians grew weary of the siege and the majority went home, assigning the vigil to the nine archons and giving them full powers to resolve the issue as they saw fit. For at that time the archons held the greatest political power. Meanwhile, Cylon and his party were in dire straits from lack of food and water. Therefore, Cylon and his brother escaped while the others, in great distress, some actually dying of hunger, sat down before the altar on the acropolis as suppliants. When the Athenians who had been assigned to maintain the siege saw these men dying in the temple, they got them to leave the sanctuary, promising not to harm them, and then led them away and put them to death. Some they even killed at the altar of the dread goddesses when they sought refuge.[29]

Thucydides' interest in the affair, no less than that of our other ancient sources, is in its ramifications for Athenian politics, and many questions that arise from the perspective of our interest in Megarian involvement go unanswered. We may safely infer that Theagenes lost some troops in the fiasco. It seems probable, too, that if Cylon himself escaped (Herodotus numbers him among the casualties), he sought refuge with his father-in-law. A further practical point that might be inferred from Thucydides' account relates

[28]1.126.
[29]Ibid.

to the likely absence of a large proportion of the Athenian nobility in Olympia at the time of the coup. Not only did this enhance Cylon's chances of initial success, but his ally Theagenes was in a position to block or impede the return of pilgrims to Athens when they got wind of what was happening at home. Yet there is no indication in Thucydides' version that Theagenes interfered with these returning Eupatrids, nor that he tried to rescue the Cylonians when they were trapped on the Acropolis. It is possible that events moved too quickly, that the Athenians' stout resistance came as a complete surprise to Theagenes, or that his meddling in Athenian affairs was too unpopular at home for him to risk further involvement. (Cylon's use of foreign troops may well have cost *him* popular support.)

No elaborate theory is needed to account for Theagenes' complicity in the Cylonian coup. He saw an opportunity to help establish a friendly and even somewhat dependent regime in a neighboring state, thereby extending his (and Megara's) influence, and, perhaps, broadening his power base. Athens in the 630's was still a predominantly agrarian, inward-looking state, and despite her size, population, and future greatness, it is far from ludicrous that seventh-century Megara could have taken the leading role in their relations. It is possible, of course, that Theagenes was influenced to intervene in Athenian affairs by some immediate issues between the two states, seeing a prospect of resolving them in Megara's favor. One such issue might have been the status of land along the border between Megara and Eleusis, which caused considerable friction in the fifth and fourth centuries and might have been a bone of contention between Megara and Athens at any time after Eleusis became a part of the Athenian polis, about 700. The only possible allusion to this issue which might go back as far as the seventh century or earlier is in Herodotus' account of Solon's meeting with the Lydian king Croesus.[30] Here Solon declares Tellus of Athens to have been the happiest of men, having died in a battle fought between the Athenians against their neighbors at Eleusis (*pros tous astygeitonas en Eleusini*). But a less strained interpretation of this passage is that it concerns a battle between the Athenians

[30]1.30. See Highbarger, *Megara*, p. 132, for this view.

and the Eleusianians themselves—that is, the Eleusinians rather than the Megarians were the neighbors in question.

A more probable issue in this period was the dispute over possession of the island of Salamis, which was to be the major preoccupation of Megarian-Athenian relations in the first half of the sixth century. Salamis was situated in the northwestern corner of the Saronic Gulf, facing the shores of both western Attica and the eastern Megarid. The island's resources were meager, but its location was well suited to monitor and harass the shipping of either state. During the Dark Ages, Salamis was probably a pirate haven,[31] and it may have continued to shelter freebooters until the Megarians and Athenians took an active interest in suppressing piracy. Concern for this problem would have developed first in Megara, given her colonial and commercial activities in the seventh century. At some point the Megarians invaded the island, expelled the inhabitants, and introduced new settlers. There is no way to pinpoint this development in time, though it obviously occurred before Solon's involvement, which cannot have taken place before the closing years of the seventh century. That there is not a single mention of Theagenes in the ample and conflicting testimony on the Salamis dispute cannot be lightly dismissed, but we must consider the possibility that if the Megarian conquest took place before or during his regime, this could explain his particular interest in influencing Athenian politics.[32] The Athenians were determined to expel the Megarians from the island and made repeated attempts to do so. It would therefore have been extremely desirable from the Megarian standpoint to install a friendly or subordinate regime in Athens.

Be that as it may, the failure of Cylon's coup must have badly shaken Theagenes' regime. Athenian enmity had been provoked or heightened, troops had very likely been sacrificed, and nothing had been accomplished. I doubt that Theagenes survived the Cylonian fiasco by many years. And when he was ousted, it is likely

---

[31]See Hesiod, *Cat.* 68.55 ff., where Salaminian Ajax is described as preying on the sheep and oxen of Troezen, Epidaurus, Aegina, Corinth, Hermione, and Asine, as well as Megara. Athens' absence from this list of victims has often been cited as evidence for the early association of Salamis with Athens.

[32]The case for this connection is argued at length by A. French, "Solon and the Megarian Question," *JHS*, 77 (1957), 238-46, esp. 241.

that the Eupatrid regime in Athens lent his opponents sympathy or support. Regrettably, the coup that unseated him is described only in a single sentence in Plutarch's *Greek Questions*.[33] He tells that Theagenes was expelled and replaced by a *sophrosynē* regime. This term, which has no exact equivalent in English, may be translated in a political context as "moderate" or "balanced." It is possible to interpret Plutarch's use of it here as a reference to the *composition* of the government which took power after Theagenes—that is, a moderate oligarchy including prosperous non-nobles. But I believe he intended it as a comment on the *conduct* of this regime as contrasted with the violence and irresponsibility of the government which soon replaced it and which was the main focus of Plutarch's attention in this passage. There are, however, other reasons to infer that Theagenes was unseated by a coalition of the propertied classes, noble and non-noble alike. These reasons will be made clear in the next chapter, where the politics of the subsequent period will be discussed in detail.

Surviving testimony, therefore, does not indicate the reasons for Theagenes' fall from power. As already noted, the failure of his Athenian policy may have been a contributing factor, but we cannot determine whether his support had seriously eroded or he simply fell victim to a new coalition of the prosperous classes. It is equally impossible to say whether Theagenes and his remaining followers put up a fight or the tyrant left without a struggle. The later hostility of the poor to the *sophrosynē* regime suggests that they, at least, may have looked back on the tyranny as a relatively good period. Perhaps they had stuck with Theagenes to the end. On the other hand, it is worth keeping in mind that he was not elevated to the status of a popular hero by later Megarian tradition.

Altogether, Theagenes' tyranny probably lasted between ten and twenty years, ending before 620,[34] and left little permanent imprint on Megarian history. Yet this brief reign proved long enough to move Megara beyond narrow aristocratic rule, opening

---

[33]*Quaest. Graec.* 18.

[34]It may be significant that Aristotle makes no mention of Theagenes in his list of the longer tyrannies (*Pol.* 1315b 11-39), although that list omits some lengthy tyrannies of the fifth and fourth centuries and might not be comprehensive for the archaic tyrannies.

the door to further change. Although Theagenes does not seem to have inaugurated sweeping reforms, he may well have played a key role in setting the stage for radical reform within another generation.

CHAPTER 5

The "Unbridled Democracy"

Never yet, Cyrnus, have good men destroyed a *polis*, but when bad men run riot, lead the *demos* astray, and turn the law over to the unjust for the sake of their own profit and power, do not expect such a *polis* to remain peaceful for long, even if it be quite placid for the moment.

—*Theognidaea* 43-48

IN CHAPTER 18 of his *Greek Questions*, Plutarch offers an explanation of the term *palintokia* (return-interest):

Having thrown out the tyrant Theagenes, the Megarians observed moderation (*esophronesan*) in their political affairs. But later, as Plato puts it, when the leaders of the *demos* gave them a taste of unrestrained freedom, they were completely corrupted. Among other licentious acts they committed against the rich, the poor would enter their homes and demand to be wined and dined lavishly. And if they were not satisfied, they would ransack everything. Finally, they passed a decree which required the interest formerly collected by their creditors to be paid back, calling this act the "return-interest."[1]

Plutarch's reference to Theagenes as well as the *sophrosynē* regime suggests a relatively rapid transition from tyranny to conservative government to mob rule. The popular regime thus appears to have taken power within a few years of Theagenes' fall and sometime before 600 at the latest. Later in the same work, Plutarch refers to this as the period of "unbridled democracy" (*akolastou demokratis*) in Megara,[2] a time of "political disorder" (*ataxian tēs politeias*), rather than of any duly constituted government.[3]

The credibility of Plutarch's references to this unruly era in

[1]Plut. *Quaest. Graec.* 18.
[2]Ibid. 59.
[3]Ibid.

Megarian history is enhanced by the widespread view that he drew upon Aristotle's lost *Constitution of the Megarians,* one of the many local histories compiled in preparation for the writing of the *Politics.*[4] Indeed, several passages in the *Politics* appear to deal with this same period of democratic rule in Megara,[5] and the collapse of this movement is attributed to its "disorder and anarchy" (*ataxia kai anarchia*),[6] terms that are strikingly similar to those Plutarch later employed. It has sometimes been argued that these are references to Megara's democratic regime in the 420's which is discussed by Thucydides.[7] But Thucydides' detailed account of the collapse of the later democracy cannot be reconciled with Aristotle's comments.[8] Furthermore, Aristotle's belief in a much earlier period of democracy in Megara can be independently established from a passage in the *Poetics* where he reports the tradition that the Megarians invented comedy under their democracy.[9] This claim was advanced against the Athenian tradition of primacy in comedy. Since the earliest Athenian comic poets known to Aristotle were dated from the second quarter of the sixth century, the Megarian case would have been substantially weakened if there had been no democratic regime in Megara prior to that time. Aristotle neither affirms nor rejects the Megarian claim, but his silence on this point implies his acceptance of an early Megarian democracy.

Plutarch and Aristotle convey the impression that this "democracy" was actually a corruption of the *sophrosyne* regime that ended in anarchy and mob rule. The picture may be based on hostile sources which could see no redeeming features in this period of

[4]See Halliday, *The Greek Questions of Plutarch,* pp. 92, 95, 99-100, and 219. Halliday regards all the references to early Megarian history in the *Greek Questions* as derived from Aristotle.

[5]1300a 15-19; 1202b 31-32; 1304b 35-40.

[6]1302b 31-32.

[7]See, e.g., Meyer, "Megara," col. 185, and T. Hudson-Williams, "Theognis and His Poems," *JHS,* 23 (1903), 1-23. Oost, "Theagenes and Theognis," p. 194; A. A. Trever, "The Intimate Relation between Economic and Political Conditions in History, as Illustrated in Ancient Megara," *CP,* 20 (1925), 127; Highbarger, *Megara,* p. 139; and others regard these as references to the popular regime described by Plutarch.

[8]4.66 ff. See below, Chapter 10.

[9]1448a 30 ff. Cf. above, Chapter 2, for a discussion of this claim in relation to the nature of the Megarian komai. Megarian comedy was the subject of ridicule by Aristophanes and other Athenian comic poets. A Megarian joke was supposed to be especially vulgar and crude.

popular government, but it is the only picture we have. I believe
that the Megarian poet Theognis was one of those hostile sources
and that many of his surviving poems reflect various stages of
these revolutionary developments. But before we can use Theognis' verses in this context, we must address some of the fundamental problems of Theognid scholarship.[10]

The *Theognidaea* is a body of 1,388 elegiac verses that come down
to us under the poet's name,[11] but even a cursory examination of
the corpus in its present form shows it to be a late compilation. It
consists of two very unequal books, the first containing more than
1,200 lines and including several invocations that read like pream-
bles to separate works.[12] There is no apparent order or continuity in
the corpus, and many poems recur once with only slight
variations.[13] The only theory claiming to detect overall continuity
and unity in the collection as it stands which ever gained currency
has long since been abandoned.[14] It was based on the almost in-
finitely flexible principle of word-association links between succes-
sive poems and, even if it had proven correct, the device could as
easily have been employed by a later editor as by the poet himself.

In fact, however, the poems included in the *Theognidaea* cover
too great a chronological span to have been the work of any single
artist. In lines 891-894 the poet curses the Cypselid rulers of
Corinth, still evidently in power, while in lines 773-782 he contem-
plates Xerxes' impending invasion of the Megarid. Even if we
accept the later chronology that has been proposed for the Cypselids, which ends their rule in the 550's rather than at the traditional
date in the 580's, three quarters of a century still separate the latest
possible date for a contemporary reference to them and one concerned with the Persian invasion of 481/80, and a gap of decades
longer is probable.[15] An active career of this duration is incredible,

[10]C. M. Bowra's chapter on Theognis in his *Early Greek Elegists*, Martin Classical
Lectures, Vol. 7 (repr. New York, 1969), is the best general introduction to the poet
and the problems surrounding his career.

[11]There are, in addition, a few lines ascribed to Theognis by later writers which do
not appear in the *Theognidaea*, including several addressed to Cyrnus.

[12]1-26 and 757-68.

[13]Cf., e.g., 853-54 with 1038a-b, or 877-78 with 1070a-b, or 39-42 with 1081a-2b.

[14]A convenient statement of the so-called "catch-word" theory may be found in
Hudson-Williams, pp. 12-22, where it is also convincingly refuted.

[15]Some commentators have identified these Persian references with Cyrus' con-

and one is forced to conclude that the two poems in question were written by different men.

Another blow to the integrity of the collection is the inclusion of nearly fifty scattered lines that appear elsewhere as the work of other Greek poets, such as Tyrtaeus (lines 935-938 and 1003-1006), Mimnermus (795-796 and 1020-1022), and Solon (227-232, 315-318, 585-590, and 1253-1254).[16] Theognis or a compiler may have borrowed some of this material, and some may have been borrowed from him by these other noted poets. It is even possible that many more lines are derivative but cannot be detected because their models no longer survive independently. This sort of plagiarism (or flattery) was common in early Greek literature, making it difficult to gain a clear impression of many individual poets, including Theognis.

If, then, it is reasonably certain that Theognis was responsible for only a portion of the verses included in the *Theognidaea*, the problem is to determine which poems and sentiments are most likely to be his own. This problem has long occupied Theognid scholarship despite the poet's attempt to anticipate and resolve the question of authenticity for posterity. In the long preamble that opens the collection, Theognis addresses his friend Cyrnus, the son of Polypaus, as follows:

> Oh Cyrnus, I place my shrewdly contrived mark on these verses, they can never be stolen, nor can anyone substitute inferior lines, and everyone shall say, "These are the works of Theognis the Megarian, renowned among all mankind."[17]

Unfortunately, Theognis' meaning in this passage is open to several interpretations and has fueled rather than quelled controversy

---

quest of Lydia c. 550; see, e.g., Hudson-Williams, pp. 4-6. Others connect them with Harpagus' conquest of Ionia a short time later—e.g., Bergk, *G. Literaturgesch.*, Vol. 1, p. 301. These solutions eliminate the enormous time span otherwise covered by the collection, but the verses in question fit the events of the 480's so well and the earlier circumstances so poorly that it is hard to avoid the obvious conclusion. Cf. below, Chapter 7, for a discussion of Megara's attitude toward Xerxes' invasion.

[16]See A. R. Burn, *Lyric Age*, pp. 258-64, for a full discussion of all the borrowed lines in the *Theognidaea*. Cf. the comments of Bowra, pp. 139-42, on this issue.

[17]19-23.

over the authenticity of particular poems.[18] One view is that he is simply announcing himself at the beginning of his work, as, indeed, many ancient writers did. But if this was his intention, he has chosen an indirect way of doing it. He speaks of a mark or seal that will enable the reader to detect genuine Theognis from counterfeit, which is something quite different from a blanket declaration of authorship. The seal should be something evident throughout the authentic works of Theognis. Two suggestions have been put forward regarding the identity of this seal. One is that Theognis relied on the reader being able to identify his unique poetic style. The other is that some word or clue is incorporated in each of the genuine poems, and the obvious choice here is the name of Cyrnus, which, together with his patronymic, son of Polypaus, appears more than seventy-five times in the collection. I favor the last of these alternatives as a working hypothesis. It is the narrowest, and therefore the most conservative, interpretation of Theognis' meaning; it validates approximately 20 percent of the collection; and, significantly, none of the borrowed lines occurs in Cyrnus' poems. We must recognize the possibility that Theognis did not use this seal consistently throughout his career, and that the collection may include authentic poems that do not bear the name of Cyrnus. But his friend's name does appear in verses penned at various stages of the poet's career. In these circumstances, the soundest approach is to rely primarily on the Cyrnus poems, turning to other poems in the corpus when they elaborate themes and views that are well established in this reliable core. A less cautious approach would have the attraction of offering considerably more material for analysis but would also confront us with many contradictions and inconsistencies, which vanish if we concentrate on the message of the Cyrnus poems.

A few words about Cyrnus, the son of Polypaus, may be in order before we proceed to examine other problems connected with the work of Theognis. Cyrnus, who is known to us only through these poems, emerges as a man of aristocratic birth, as was Theognis himself, and somewhat younger than the poet. Theognis affects to teach the young man what he has learned of life. The bond be-

[18]See B. A. Van Groningen's commentary on lines 19-23 in *Theognis: Le premier livre édité avec un commentaire* (Amsterdam, 1966) for a recent discussion of rival theories as to Theognis' meaning.

tween them in the early stages of their relationship stands out as a prime example of pederasty in Greek aristocratic society. Yet there are no explicitly homosexual references in the Cyrnus poems. Many of the verses in the brief second book are, on the other hand, openly homosexual,[19] suggesting that the natural implication of Theognis' bond with Cyrnus encouraged a later compiler to append such material to the famous poet's opus. Eventually, Theognis denounced Cyrnus as his betrayer, but it is impossible to tell whether there was any legitimate basis for this accusation, or whether Cyrnus merely ran afoul of the poet's mounting cynicism and paranoia.

The second major problem connected with Theognis is in some ways even more fundamental than the first. Up to this point I have treated him as if there were no doubt that he was a native of Nisaean Megara. This is, in fact, the view of the great majority of historians, but the reader should be aware that two other Megaras have been proposed as Theognis' birthplace. Only one ancient writer, Plato, dissents from the *communis opinio* regarding the poet's native land, placing him in Megara Hyblaea in Sicily.[20] Plato's high standing as a scholar and his first-hand familiarity with the affairs of Sicily have encouraged some scholars to take his view seriously and look for evidence in the poems which is more consistent with conditions in Sicily than on the Isthmus of Corinth. Nothing solid has been found, but it has been argued[21] that a solitary reference to the use of cavalry is incompatible with the military resources of Nisaean Megara in the archaic period:

> A silent messenger, shining from a distant lookout point, rouses sorrowful war, Cyrnus. Bridle the swift-footed horses, for I think they must soon face their enemies. The journey to this rendezvous will not be long, unless the gods deceive me.[22]

Yet other historians find it credible that Nisaean Megara could have maintained an elite cavalry force down to the sixth century,

---

[19]See, e.g., 1259-74, 1283-98, and 1335-72.

[20]Pl. *Leg.* 630a. The scholiast to this passage takes exception to Plato's view, as do Didymus and Harpocration, *s.v. Theognis*.

[21]See, e.g., K. J. Beloch, "Theognis Vaterstadt," *Neue Jahrb. für Class. Phil.*, 11 (1888), 733.

[22]551-54.

while still others find it as difficult to believe in knights at Megara Hyblaea as at the mother city. This has led to a third position, unsupported by any ancient authority, associating Theognis with the obscure Macedonian town of Megara in a region where continued reliance on cavalry is beyond question.[23]

While neither alternative to the majority view seems well founded, it is quite difficult to find corroboration of Theognis' attachment to Nisaean Megara within the corpus. No references to locale appear in the Cyrnus poems. The mention of a *visit* to Sicily in a non-Cyrnus poem may eliminate Megara Hyblaea from contention, but it might only mean that a later editor saw nothing inconsistent with his picture of Theognis in this poem, and therefore placed it among the poet's works.[24] The same doubts must attend our interpretation of the previously mentioned lines dealing with Xerxes' invasion and praying for divine protection of Alcathoa's citadel—that is, the western acropolis of Nisaean Megara. This late poem, which I cannot accept as the work of Theognis, was very likely placed in his corpus by a compiler who had no doubt about the poet's ties to Nisaean Megara. Without significantly more evidence to the contrary than exists, I believe we must concur with this judgment. In the end, the case for Nisaean Megara as Theognis' birthplace and home rests on the weight of ancient opinion and the consistency of the Cyrnus poems with our other evidence for developments there in the late seventh and early sixth centuries. The affairs of the alternate Megaras are so little known as to make similar corroboration impossible.

A third subject of dispute is the dating of Theognis' life and career. The ancient chronographers placed his floruit in the fifty-seventh to fifty-ninth Olympiads—that is, in the late 550's and 540's.[25] But these authorities may have based their conclusions on little more than their understanding of the internal evidence of the *Theognidaea*, treated as the work of a single author. Working from this dubious premise and believing that the Cypselids fell from power in the 580's, they may have reasoned that the poet was

[23]See G. F. Unger, "Die Heimat von Theognis," *Philologus*, 45 (1890/1), 18-33.
[24]783 ff. Harpocration was the first commentator to draw the inference that Theognis was not from Hyblaean Megara on the basis of this poem.
[25]Paschale puts his floruit in Ol. 57 = 552; Eusebius and Cyril give Ol. 58 = 448; Suidas gives Ol. 59 = 444.

active that early and continued writing down to the time of Xerxes' invasion over a hundred years later. This, in turn, would suggest a birth date before 600 and death about 480, giving a floruit in the 540's. Once one recognizes the composite nature of the *Theognidaea*, there is no longer any reason to postulate this extravagant lifespan for Theognis. Modern scholars have therefore come to widely different conclusions about Theognis' actual dates. My own inclination is to place Theognis in the first half of the period assigned him by the chronographers. Some of my grounds will emerge when we return to the events of the late seventh- and early sixth-century Megara, but one point in favor of an earlier career can be made here. The only reference to Theognis' dates outside the chronographers occurs in Isocrates, who makes him a contemporary of Phocylides.[26] This seems confirmed by the Suda, which gives 544 as the floruit of both poets. But the Suda's date for Phocylides may well be based on nothing more than the presumed date for Theognis and Isocrates' statement, rather than on independent evidence placing Phocylides in the mid-sixth century. Nor should it be overlooked that a reference to the fall of Nineveh in 612 in one of the fragments of Phocylides suggests that he was writing in the late seventh century.[27] One might therefore argue that if Isocrates' pairing of Theognis with Phocylides is valid, Theognis too ought to be dated in the late seventh century. I would provisionally suggest a birth date of about 630 for him, during the tyranny of Theagenes. While recognizing that our evidence does not admit of certainty on this point, I believe that the succeeding decades provide the most convincing context for the poet's undisputed works.

If we return now to the period immediately following Theagenes' fall, a reconstruction based on Theognis' evidence may be attempted. There is no mistaking his own position in the political and social spectrum of his society. Theognis was the landed aristocrat par excellence.[28] He deplored nothing so much as the venal sacrifice of their exclusive social standing by many of his fellow aristocrats:

[26]*Ad Nic.* 43.
[27]Fr. 4.
[28]See lines 1200-01, which refer explicitly to Theognis' farmlands: "my blossoming fields," where "mules silently pull the plow."

In rams, asses, or horses, Cyrnus, we seek the purebred, and a man wants to possess the issue of good stock. But a nobleman thoughtlessly marries the base daughter of a bad man, if the man rewards him richly. Nor does a woman refuse marriage to a bad man if he be wealthy; indeed she prefers wealth to goodness. People honor money above everything, and good men marry of bad stock while bad men marry of good. Wealth confounds breeding. Therefore, do not be surprised, son of Polypaus, that the race of your fellow citizens grows feeble, because good is mixed with bad.[29]

For Theognis and many like him, men were judged good (*agathos*) or bad (*kakos*) according to their birth and lineage, rather than by any personal qualities; goodness was an inherited attribute of the nobility.

Theognis perceived the most serious threat to his class as coming from the rich but low-born elements of Megarian society who were successfully buying their way into the chief families. The insinuation of these inferior outsiders into politics also aroused the poet's ire:

Cyrnus, the *polis* still survives, but the people are different; men who formerly knew neither its laws nor customs, but wore goatskins to cover their nakedness and grazed like deer beyond the city. And now they have become worthy men, O son of Polypaus, and they that were once noble are now base. Who can endure to see such things? And while they smile sweetly, they cheat one another, for they are incapable of recognizing either good or evil.[30]

Theognis deplored the rise to positions of power of men who did not share the ingrained political traditions of the nobility. That such men might overcome their backgrounds as humble shepherds and farmers who had dwelt in the countryside and worn rough clothing was inconceivable to hidebound aristocrats like Theognis.

Given the prejudice of at least that portion of the old Megarian aristocracy represented by Theognis, it is understandable that the non-noble elements of the *sophrosyne* government might have cast about for support beyond the governing classes in order to maintain their position. It is in this context that I believe the poem which

[29]182-92.
[30]53-60. Cf. 1109-14.

opens this chapter should be interpreted. The good men, *hoi agathoi*, says Theognis, never ruin a city, but the bad, *hoi kakoi*, corrupt the common people and destroy the internal harmony of the state. The bad men in question here must be the non-noble members of the political coalition, since they are distinguished from the demos itself, to whom they appeal. I suggest that they are the demagogues whom Plutarch blames for inciting the popular revolution which caused the downfall of the sophrosynē regime. This poem closes with a warning of the consequences of the short-sighted tactics of these bad men: "such things lead to civil strife (*stasis*) and internecine slaughter and then to tyranny; may it never happen to this *polis*!"[31] A similar, but more succinct warning is contained in these lines: "O Cyrnus, the *polis* is in labor and I fear lest she give birth to a man who will suppress our evil arrogance. For though the townfolk are even yet sensible, their leaders are nurturing great evils."[32] And an even more apocalyptic warning is to be found in this couplet: "I am afraid, son of Polypaus, that this *polis* will be destroyed by licentiousness, like the flesh-eating Centaurs."[33]

These sentiments and observations, albeit distorted by Theognis' social and political values, fit the picture of the collapse of the sophrosynē regime we have drawn from the comments of Plutarch and Aristotle. It is a picture of a government after the fall of Theagenes, in which, to the great displeasure of conservatives like Theognis, prosperous elements beyond the aristocracy played a major role. The cooperation of these groups may have been necessary to get rid of Theagenes, but it is obvious that many aristocrats were not reconciled to sharing their traditional political preeminence. Nor, perhaps, were the newly enfranchised satisfied with their role as junior partners in government. Thus, for reasons of

[31]51-52. Neither here nor elsewhere does Theognis make any reference to Theagenes. Hammond, *HG*, p. 150, suggests that the omission implies Theognis' approval of the earlier tyrant "who did not upset the autocratic privileges of the Dorian community." But the corpus is as lacking in positive as in negative allusions to Theagenes' regime. We ought not to expect Theognis to have immortalized Theagenes by name, yet his complete silence on this significant episode in Megara's recent political history is puzzling on any interpretation of the poet's own political views or his date.

[32]39-42.

[33]541-42. Cf. 1103-04.

insecurity and personal ambition, some among them turned to demagogy, giving voice to popular grievances and winning the backing of the poor. The expectations of redress they aroused led to the outbreak of violence, and members of their own class were not spared. This picture may be accurate to a point, but it is based on conservative sources and we must make allowance for the possibility that the grievances of the poor were legitimate and that the emerging popular leaders were at least partly inspired by higher ideals.

It is likely that Theognis was himself active in Megarian politics during the period of this mounting crisis, and was not merely commenting from the sidelines, as might appear from the poems thus far cited. Some historians have dated Theognis' years of political activity to the period after the fall of the "unbridled democracy," when, they presume, he returned from exile to become one of the mainstays of a new oligarchy.[34] But I find the high-minded sentiments of the passages that suggest direct political involvement to be more in keeping with the poet's years of youthful idealism than with the cynicism and disillusionment that pervade what I take to be his later work. Consider these verses, in which he trumpets his political moderation—despite his often proclaimed conservative views: "Do not be too distraught when your fellow citizens are in an agitated state, Cyrnus, but take the middle of the road, as I do."[35] And: "Cautiously walk the middle of the road, as I do, Cyrnus, and never give one man what belongs to another."[36] (Though moderate in tone, this last piece of advice hints at Theognis' uncompromising position on the economic issues that were to culminate in passage of the *palintokia*.) In another passage: "I must judge this case by ruler and square, Cyrnus, and give equal justice to both sides. [. . .] On the other hand [paying heed to] prophets, the flights of birds and burnt offerings, lest I be condemned for doing wrong."[37] Possibly this reference to a suit is only metaphoric, but in light of the other references to political involvement, we cannot dismiss the possibility that it is a literal description of

---

[34]See, e.g., Oost, "Theagenes and Theognis," pp. 194-95.
[35]219-20.
[36]331-32.
[37]543-46.

Theognis' personal experience as a magistrate, analogous to Solon's somewhat similar poems.[38] Here, though a lacuna of uncertain length interrupts his thought, it seems that he is expressing the need to weigh evidence on the one hand and observe ritual niceties on the other in judging a case. One later poem may reflect bitterly on this early political activity: "The noble man who serves as acropolis and wall to an empty headed people, little honor is his lot."[39] But Theognis may only have in mind here the Megarians' disregard of his advice rather than their lack of appreciation of his direct political role. In either case the tone is understandable in a man who saw his personal and political fortunes collapse as the schism in the sophrosynē regime deepened.

Plutarch's description of the movement that led to the enactment of the palintokia and the period of "unbridled democracy" makes clear that the basis of popular discontent upon which the demagogues built was economic, rather than political in the narrow sense. The focus of popular animus was the upper classes, not the government *per se*, although the latter was in actuality an extension of the former. Beginning with sporadic attacks on the wealthy and their property—for example, mob occupations of the homes of the rich—it led eventually to sweeping debt-reform—the "return-interest" legislation. Doubtless, the government's inability to quell mob violence emboldened the demos and its leaders to mount a more direct challenge to the power and legal status of the old guard.

The palintokia, whose passage signals the effective end of the sophrosynē regime, invites comparison with Solon's more famous *seisachtheia* (shaking-off-of-burdens) in Athens. In fact, the Megarian reform, which I am inclined to place shortly before 600, antedates Solon's law by from ten to forty years, depending on when one dates the seisachtheia.[40] Both measures reflect conditions of

---

[38]A more explicit reference to direct political involvement is found in a non-Cyrnus poem (947-48): "I will rule my splendid native city neither favoring the demos nor being won over by unjust men." The moderate position espoused here is consistent with that expressed in 331-32 and 543-46.

[39]233-34.

[40]For a recent statement of the case for dating the *seisactheia* and Solon's other reforms to the 570's and a review of other opinions, see S. S. Markianos, "The Chronology of the Herodotean Solon," *Historia*, 23 (1974), 1-20. Cf. R. Sealey, "Zum Datum der solonischen Gesetzgebung," *Historia*, 28 (1979), 238-41.

mounting debt among the poor, usurious practices on the part of wealthy creditors, and harsh prosecution of defaulting debtors. Such conditions might have resulted as much or more from a breakdown of the social contract between rich and poor as from any sudden deterioration of economic conditions. In the case of Megara, Theagenes may have prevented creditors from exploiting the poor unrestrainedly and may have blocked the accumulation of increasingly valuable grazing land through foreclosure on loans. (His attack on the herds of the rich early in his career, as already noted, was very likely a response to their monopolization of pasture land.) Once Theagenes was out of the way, the dispossession of marginal farmers and herders might have gained momentum once more. It is a natural inference from Theognis' advice against giving one man's goods to another that the issue of property was at the center of political controversy in the years before the collapse of the sophrosynē regime. This dispute ended in revolution.

Plutarch describes the palintokia as forcing creditors to pay back interest they had collected, but it is not clear whether outstanding debts were totally abolished and foreclosed property was returned to its original owners. (A similar problem exists in interpreting the effect of the seisachtheia in Athens.) Without explicitly mentioning the palintokia, Aristotle describes the policy of this regime in terms which suggest that its economic reprisals were extreme: "The leaders of the *demos*, in order to have goods (*chremata*) to seize in the name of the people (*demeuein*), continued expelling many wealthy citizens, until they had turned the exiles into a formidable force."[41] This policy of expropriation and expulsion of the rich and the redistribution of their property is a logical extension of the cancellation of debts and the return of foreclosed land by the earliest recorded measure of the new regime.

Theognis himself was a victim of the policies of the "unbridled democracy." He appears to have suffered the confiscation of his estates and been forced into exile abroad:

I have heard the piercing cry of the bird, O son of Polypaus, who comes to announce the season for plowing; and the sound has broken

[41]*Pol.* 1304b 36-38.

116

my heart. For other men possess my blossoming fields, nor do the mules silently pull the plow on my behalf, because of this most hateful voyage (*nautiliēs*).[42]

A further comment on exile may be autobiographical in inspiration: "Cyrnus, never befriend an exile in expectation of repayment, for no one is the same once back home."[43] Some have thought this an indication that Theognis lived to return home and was disappointed in friends he had made while in exile, but it is equally possible that the poet is merely reflecting on the exile's need (perhaps his own need?) to dissimulate in order to survive, in which case it would be impossible to gauge his true character and beliefs.

Theognis' outspokenness may have made him an early target of the democratic movement, or prompted even his noble compeers to disown him to save their own skins. Some experience of this sort may provide a legitimate basis for the frequent accusations of personal betrayal in his poems. One example will suffice to convey the flavor of these verses:

Cyrnus, something I have suffered which is not as bad as death, perhaps, but more evil than anything else; my friends have betrayed me. Now I am delivered up to my enemies, and I shall learn what plans they have for me.[44]

Even the beloved Cyrnus does not escape accusations of betrayal. How much of this is justified and how much is the poet's paranoia is impossible to say. But in either case, the sense of having been played false contributes to the cynical tone of Theognis' later works. Compare the following lines with his urgings of honesty, consistency, and political moderation, which we have noted in his earlier elegies:

Cyrnus, adjust your temper to the liking of everyone, blending with the disposition of each man in turn; now imitate this fellow, then alter

[42]1197-1202.
[43]333-34.
[44]811-14. Cf. 69-92.

your character to suit others. This knack is better even than great virtue.[45]

The poet's bitterness was undoubtedly increased by the unaccustomed poverty he had to endure in exile. Penury and its effects form one of the major themes of his opus.[46] One couplet recommends a seafaring life as the last refuge from poverty, suggesting that Theognis may have become a sailor while in exile: "One must strive alike to deliver oneself from cruel poverty, Cyrnus, whether on land or on the broad back of the sea."[47] There is, however, no mistaking how undesirable an occupation this was in the eyes of the landed aristocrat. Indeed, this piece of advice is wedged between two poems which advise suicide if all else fails to relieve poverty.[48]

No Cyrnus poem reveals where Theognis spent his years of exile, although several other poems in the corpus suggest logical havens for a Megarian expatriate:

I travelled once to the land of Sicily, I visited the vine-covered fields of Euboea, and also the splendid town of Sparta by the reed-bearing Eurotas, and everywhere I went I was received most kindly. But none of them brought joy to my heart, for truly, no place is as dear as one's homeland.[49]

Visits to Euboea and Sicily are consistent with the hints of a seafaring period during Theognis' exile which we find in the Cyrnus poems; and a visit to Sicily, where he might well have found refuge in Megara Hyblaea or Selinus, would help to explain the later confusion over the poet's birthplace. Another verse proclaims: "I am descendant of Aethon, but I dwell in well-walled Thebes, denied my native land."[50] Thebes was certainly a likely place for

---

[45]1071-74.
[46]See, e.g., 145-48, 173-82, and 1161-62. Poverty is a major theme of the non-Cyrnus poems as well. See, e.g., 351-54, 383-92, and 667-82.
[47]179-80.
[48]173-78 and 181-82.
[49]783-88.
[50]1209-10. It has been pointed out that Aethon is a name assumed by Odysseus in one of his many disguises (Od. 19.183), and may only be intended to suggest Theognis' experience as a wanderer. For a radically different view of this allusion, see K. J. McKay, "Studies in Aethon, II," Mnemosyne, 14 (1961), 16 ff.

Megarians to seek refuge in any period. As we shall see, Aristotle's description of the exiles' eventual triumphant return suggests that most of them were living within easy striking distance of their native land while waiting for their opportunity to destroy the "unbridled democracy." Yet despite the plausibility of the inferences to be drawn from these two poems, we must not forget that they lack sure signs of authenticity and might have found their way into the collection only because some later editor was tempted by their possible relevance to to Theognis' experience.

The constitutional basis of this unprecedented regime was probably not very well developed. It seems to have represented the triumph of the Megarian assembly over the aesymnetae, which, I presume, regained its leadership role after the fall of Theagenes. Under the influence of popular leaders, the demos enacted the palintokia, may have provided a legal basis for later expropriations and expulsions, and possibly lent its support to foreign policy initiatives we have yet to consider. But day to day control of this radical regime may well have remained in the hands of a small group of leaders. The purged council may even have continued to meet and annual magistrates to be chosen from among the demagogues themselves. None of this necessitated any fundamental constitutional changes any more than had the imposition of tyranny. In particular, the power of the assembly was a latent force in the early city-state, and at any time that body could cease to be the rubber stamp of aristocratic or oligarchic rule and become an effective instrument of government. It would be anarchronistic to suppose that such phenomena as popular courts, a large bureaucracy, and payment for public service were instituted under this regime; nothing so formal or expensive is suggested by our sources. To the contrary, they suggest that a state of near anarchy prevailed. Nor would these features associated with fifth-century Athens and a handful of other classical states be at all appropriate to conditions in late seventh- and sixth-century Greece. But while acknowledging that we must scale down the implications of the term "democracy" as it applies to archaic Megara, we should not fail to note that the movement which overthrew the sophrosynē regime there may be the earliest one anywhere to which later writers applied the term.[51] It would be a mistake to ignore this phase of Megara's political evolution in charting the development of popular government in the Greek polis.[52]

We turn next to consideration of Megarian foreign policy during the period of "unbridled democracy." Several episodes are known through Plutarch's *Greek Questions*. The more intelligible of these tales concerns conflict between Megara and Samos over the Samian colony of Perinthos, which was established around 600 on the north coast of the Propontis.[53] This region held several Megarian colonies and had been virtually a Megarian preserve throughout the seventh century. Perhaps the chaos in Megara encouraged the Samians to establish themselves on the Propontis, but the Megarians roused themselves to respond, despite their internal preoccupations. The security of their colonies and commerce appear to have transcended internal political differences. Though no date can be assigned to the clash, it seems likely to have occurred very soon after the establishment of Perinthos, when the Megarians' concern and indignation would have been at their height. According to Plutarch, the Megarians sent a fleet against Perinthos, to bring the interlopers back in chains (*pedetes*).[54] The Samians responded to this threat by sending a fleet of twenty-eight ships to defend Perinthos. A sea-fight ensued in which the Samians were victorious, taking six hundred Megarian prisoners. In an age of penteconters, with approximately sixty men per ship, the Samians had managed to capture the equivalent of ten complete crews. If we take into account the likelihood that some Megarians drowned

---

[51]I believe that Oost, "Theagenes and Theognis," pp. 193-94, is too cautious in regarding this democracy as merely "an oligarchy in which the oligarchs, for purely selfish reasons resulting from their struggle among themselves, acted to benefit wider circles of the state in order to win support." When members of an oligarchic class break away from their peers to lead a popular movement and an attack on property rights, they can no longer be regarded as oligarchs.

[52]See, e.g., the comments of Busolt-Swoboda, *Gr. Staats.*, pp. 417 and 437, where Megara is listed—together with Chios and Solonian Athens—as a pioneer democracy. Samos, too, should be included in this list (see below), but the precise chronology of all these popular movements is in doubt, as is their relationship to one another. As we shall see, it can be argued that the Megarians influenced the Samians, and it is entirely possible that their experience affected the course of political development in nearby Athens.

[53]For the foundation of Perinthos, see Strab. 7 fr. 56, and Ps.-Scymn. 714 f. Cf. A. J. Graham, *Colony and Mother City* (Manchester, 1964), p. 74.

[54]*Quaest. Graec.* 57.

and others escaped, it is hardly conceivable that the Megarian fleet consisted of fewer than twenty ships, and it may well have equaled or exceeded the size of the Samian armada.[55] Thus even from the scant evidence of a naval defeat, we gain some idea of Megara's substantial investment in sea power. This defeat was a serious blow to Megara's maritime interests and ambitions, and it may have encouraged the Athenians to believe that the time was ripe to challenge her once again for possession of Salamis. But at least some of the sting of this reverse was assuaged by its improbable sequel.

Plutarch places the sea-battle at the time when Samos was governed by an oligarchy of wealthy landholders, the *geomoroi*.[56] After the victory at Perinthos, the nine Samian admirals resolved to overthrow the oligarchy when they returned home, and they persuaded their Megarian prisoners to lend themselves to a ruse with this object in mind. Ordered by the oligarchs to bring back the prisoners in their own chains, the admirals provided the six hundred Megarians with weapons and rigged their bonds so as to be readily unfastened. Thus prepared, the admirals

> sailed back to Samos, disembarked their prisoners and led them through the agora to the council house, where all the geomoroi had assembled. Then, the signal being given, the Megarians attacked and killed them. And when the city had been liberated in this fashion, those among the Megarians who desired it were granted citizenship.[57]

The rest of the prisoner-conspirators were presumably set free to return home. The Samian admirals may have used the Megarians in their plot to avoid the stigma of blood guilt,[58] but the more obvious purpose was to introduce a large armed force into the assembly of the geomoroi without arousing suspicion.

---

[55]Burn, *Lyric Age*, p. 218, judges the Samian fleet to represent only a fraction of Samos' total naval strength, possibly a "relief squadron." If he is correct, we should probably postulate a substantially larger Megarian fleet as well. But there is no evidence for a larger Samian fleet prior to the 540's, under Polycrates, who, Herodotus says in one place (3.44), had forty triremes, and in another (3.39), 100 penteconters.

[56]*Quaest. Graec.* 57.

[57]Ibid.

[58]As suggested by Burn, *Lyric Age*, p. 219.

Plutarch relates all this by way of explaining how one of the public buildings of Samos came to be called the Fetters (*Pedetes*) and one suspects there was a good deal more to be told about the incident. Some have suggested that the contact of the Megarian veterans with the Samians planted the idea of democratic revolution in their minds,[59] but I think it more likely that the reverse was actually the case—that is, the Megarian prisoners, coming from a state that had recently overthrown its oligarchy, aroused similar ambitions in the Samian fleet. At all events, I would place both coups close to the year 600. With both Megara and Samos under popular rule in the early years of the sixth century, and especially with the Megarians having played a part in the creation of the Samian regime, it seems likely that for a time relations between the two states were good. Perinthos may have seemed less menacing to Megarian interests under these circumstances, but the fact remains that Megara's relative power in the Northeast was declining.

In the same period, Megara was shaken by the loss of Salamis to Athens. As described, the Megarians had taken control of the island during the seventh century, probably out of a desire to suppress piracy which preyed on their southern coast and on their ships. The inhabitants of the island had been expelled, and Megarian settlers were introduced. The dispossessed Salaminians had probably taken refuge in Attica, since the Athenians claimed rightful possession of Salamis. Athens fought with Megara over control of the island for a considerable period of time, but without success. Plutarch notes that before the time of Solon "The Athenians had worn themselves out in a long and difficult war against the Megarians for possession of Salamis."[60] A distorted recollection of this struggle may lie behind a story Pausanias tells in connection with a trophy he saw in the Temple of Zeus at Megara:

> There, the bronze beak of a trireme is dedicated. They (the Megarians) say that this ship was taken off Salamis in a sea battle with the Athenians, and the Athenians agree that for some time they relinquished the island to the Megarians.[61]

[59]E.g., Burn, ibid.
[60]Plut. *Sol.* 8.
[61]1.40.5.

If, indeed, what Pausanias saw was the prow of a trireme and not that of an earlier type of warship, it could not have come from the seventh century, but even if the trophy itself was bogus, the tradition of a naval victory over Athens in the early stages of the struggle for Salamis remains. That Megara was able to control the seas around Salamis in the seventh and, as we shall see, the early sixth century should come as no surprise. Athens was a relative latecomer in maritime affairs, and there was as yet no hint of the preeminence she would achieve in the Aegean by the fifth century. That Athens even tried to challenge Megara in a sphere to which the smaller state had heretofore made a far greater commitment is an indication of the depth of feeling in Athens over the Salamis issue.

Despite this feeling, however, the Athenians eventually recognized the futility of continuing the war: "they passed a law prohibiting anyone from urging the *polis* to renew its claim to Salamis in either written or oral form, on pain of death."[62] The law Plutarch describes here is probably the same measure which Pausanias' Athenian sources had in mind when they spoke of Athens' temporary ceding of Salamis to the Megarians; it is highly unlikely that any formal agreement was reached in which Athens relinquished her claim. The Salamis law was directed not toward the Megarians, but toward those in Athens who were demanding that the war continue. I suspect that the families that had been driven from Salamis were the most ardent supporters of the war and that the resolution was meant to silence them. We cannot say whether the law achieved its purpose for a substantial period of time, but the familiar story of Solon's challenge to it is at the beginning of Plutarch's account of his political career, which indicates that it was put aside by the 590's:

> Solon, finding this disgrace unbearable, and observing that there were many young men who wished to see war initiated but who did not dare lead the movement because of the law, pretended he was insane. His relations spread the word that he was out of his mind. Secretly writing some elegiac verses and practicing them so that he could recite them from memory, he suddenly marched into the agora wearing a felt cap on his head. When a throng of people had gathered

[62]Plut. *Sol.* 8.

round he mounted the herald's platform and sang his verses, which begin:

I am a herald come from lovely Salamis with a well-ordered song, not a harangue.

This is the poem *Salamis*, which consists of a hundred verses, graceful throughout.[63]

Plutarch does not quote the poem any further, but six additional lines of *Salamis* are preserved by Diogenes Laertius:

I wish I were from Pholegandros or Sicinos in the Sporades rather than Athens, denying my fatherland. For when I am among strangers they jibe: "This is one of those Athenians who gave up Salamis."

And:

Let us sail to Salamis, fight for the lovely island, and shake off our bitter shame.[64]

Plutarch continues:

When Solon finished his song, his friends began to congratulate him, and Pisistratus above all urged and stirred up the people to follow Solon's advice. They repealed the law on the spot and embraced war, making Solon the commander.[65]

Mention of Pisistratus in this context may result from confusion about the stages of the war over Salamis, which we will try to clear up a little later on, but Solon's role in renewing the struggle is not to be doubted—though, of course, other factors may help to explain why many Athenians were encouraged to challenge Megara in the 590's. They may well have taken heart from Megara's internal troubles and her recent defeat at the hands of the Samians. As we shall see, there may even have been Megarian exiles urging them on and offering assistance, oligarchic refugees from the popular regime. Then, too, Athens may have gained sufficient confidence in her naval strength to mount another challenge. Toward the end of the seventh century the Athenians launched their

---

[63]Ibid.
[64]D.L. 1.47 = Bergk, Solon fr's. 1 and 2.
[65]*Sol.* 8.

first significant naval expedition. They captured the port of Sigeion at the entrance to the Hellespont, near the site of ancient Troy.[66] The town had previously belonged to the Mytileneans, and the seemingly unprovoked Athenian attack triggered a long, sporadic war between the two states, which was ultimately arbitrated in Athens' favor by Periander of Corinth. The Athenians appear to have treated Sigeion as an outpost rather than as a free-standing colony, which suggests that they were more interested in the site's commercial potential than in finding homes for large numbers of colonists.[67] The commercial importance of the route from the Black Sea to the Aegean through the Propontis and the Hellespont had grown steadily in the course of the seventh century as a result of Greek expansion, and we have seen that Megara played a significant role in this development. Now Athens was apparently attempting to gain a foothold in this region. Sigeion was well placed to serve as an entrepôt for much of the northeastern trade and as a safe haven for Athenian merchantmen, whose belated entry into the field might not be welcomed by the established trading states. Indeed, Athens' bold stroke suggests that the use of force was necessary to promote and protect her developing interest in the Euxine trade. The capture of Sigeion points as well to an emerging Athenian commitment to the development of a navy, since this distant possession could be defended only through naval power. It might therefore have seemed that the time had come to take back Salamis by force.

The course and chronology of the war over Salamis, once renewed at Solon's urging, are open to a variety of interpretations, because our evidence, though relatively abundant, is contradictory on a number of central points. The reconstruction offered here is an attempt to resolve the tradition into four sequential stages, which can be summarized briefly. The first stage is Solon's agitation, leading to a renewal of the war.[68] The second is Solon's campaign, resulting in the reconquest of Salamis by Athens.[69] The third

---

[66]See Hdt. 5.95; Strab. 13.1.38; D.L. 1.74; Steph. Byz., s.v. Sigeion.

[67]See H. Bengtson, "Einzelpersönlichkeit und Athenische Staat," Sitz. Bayr. Acad. (1939), p. 216. I accept his view over that of Graham, pp. 32-33.

[68]Plut. Sol. 8; Paus. 1.40.5; D.L. 1.46-47; Polyaenus Strat. 1.20.1; Just. Epit. 2.7.

[69]Arist. Ath. Pol. 17.2; Plut. Sol. 8-9 and Comp. Sol. et Publ. 4; Polyaenus Strat. 1.20.2.

is Pisistratus' seizure of the Megarian port of Nisaea several decades later, as the conflict dragged on.[70] The fourth is the final resolution of the dispute in Athens' favor through Spartan arbitration, in the course of which the aged Solon participated in a debate over the ancient associations of Salamis.[71] We have already dealt with the first of these stages and must now turn to the second, which immediately ensued (most likely in the 590's, as noted previously). Plutarch narrates Solon's Salamis campaign before his treatment of Solon's role in the First Sacred War, about 585, or his archonship, usually dated 594/3. Further support for an early date in Solon's career may be drawn from Aristotle's rejection of the tradition linking Pisistratus with the young Solon. Noting that Pisistratus died thirty-three years after first seizing power (circa 561), he observes: "Therefore it is apparent that those who say Solon and Pisistratus were lovers and that Pisistratus was a general in the war for Salamis are talking nonsense."[72] The sense of this passage is that Pisistratus, whom Aristotle elsewhere says "attained great distinction in the war against the Megarians,"[73] could not have been involved in the stage of the conflict which saw Solon's capture of Salamis, because it took place before Pisistratus reached manhood—that is, in the early part of the century.

Turning to Solon's military campaign, we must choose between several conflicting versions of how he wrested control of Salamis from the Megarians. One version, recorded by Plutarch, is identical in its essentials with our only detailed account of how Pisistratus took Nisaea a generation later.[74] Both stories relate how the Megarians attempted to carry off the aristocratic matrons of Athens by ship as they celebrated the Eleusinian Mysteries, unprotected, at Eleusis. Instead, the Megarians fell into a trap and were captured, along with their vessels. The Athenians then sailed the Megarian ships home, with Athenian youths impersonating the supposedly captured women of Athens. The ruse took the unsuspecting Megarians by surprise, resulting in a quick Athenian victory. The major differences between the two stories are that Solon is the tactician in

[70]Hdt. 1.59; Arist. *Ath. Pol.* 17.2; Aen. Tact. 4.8-11; Just. *Epit.* 2.8.
[71]Plut. *Sol.* 10; Arist. *Rh.* 1375b 29-30; Strab. 9.1.10; D.L. 1.48.
[72]*Ath. Pol.* 17.2
[73]*Ath. Pol.* 14.1.
[74]Plut. *Sol.* 8 and Polyaenus *Strat.* 1.20.2 versus Aen. Tac. 4.8-11.

one and Pisistratus in the other, and that the military objective of the former was the town of Salamis and of the latter, Nisaea. I very much doubt that the same trick was used twice. The ploy seems far more appropriate to the problem that faced Pisistratus—namely, the capture of the chief harbor of a navally superior power—than to the mission of overwhelming an outpost on Salamis. It must also be borne in mind that although we have several alternative accounts of Solon's capture of Salamis to choose among, this is the only tradition surviving with reference to Pisistratus' capture of Nisaea.

Plutarch himself gives an alternate account of Solon's campaign immediately after the one already summarized:

> Others deny that the capture [of Salamis] was accomplished in this manner, but rather that first the god at Delphi proclaimed to him [Solon]:
>> With sacrifices propitiate the heroes who once ruled this land and are now gathered to the bosom of the Asopian plain, with their faces turned toward the setting sun.
>
> Then Solon sailed by night to the island and made sacrifice to the heroes Periphemus and Kychreus. Afterward, he chose 500 Athenian volunteers, a decree having been passed to the effect that those who conquered the island should be its political leaders (*kyrious einai tou politeumatos*). They set sail in a number of fishing boats accompanied by a triaconter and anchored off Salamis at a breakwater looking toward Euboea. Unable to get a reliable report of what was happening, the Megarians on Salamis excitedly marched there under arms, and launched a ship to spy on the enemy. When this ship arrived, it was overpowered by Solon's forces and the Megarians were detained. Then he embarked his best Athenian troops on the ship and instructed them to sail to the city, concealing their identity as best they could. Simultaneously the rest of the Athenians occupied the Megarians with a land assault, and while this battle was going on, the men on the ship arrived (at Salamis) unexpectedly and captured the city.[75]

Plutarch himself seems to credit this version more than the first, and he cites later Athenian ceremonies as lending support to it. I find it more plausible as well. Five hundred troops might well have been sufficient to overcome the Megarian settlers. If this version is

---

[75]*Sol.* 9.

close to the truth, the modest ruse employed by Solon could easily have been confused with the more elaborate trap Pisistratus set later. The account becomes still more credible if we assume that the decree in question gave the 500 volunteers the right to settle on Salamis with their families, rather than having singled them out for political privileges among a considerably larger body of settlers. The volunteers and their families, perhaps a total of roughly two thousand people, would have been sufficient to repopulate the island after the expulsion of the Megarians. A tempting conjecture is that many original Salaminian families responded to Solon's call.

In this connection it is noteworthy that Solon himself is called a Salaminian in the ancient tradition. According to Diogenes Laertius and Diodorus of Sicily, Solon was born on Salamis.[76] If true, he and his parents were evidently among the refugees of the Megarian conquest. The silence of our major sources, Herodotus and Plutarch, and others, on Solon's birthplace neither supports nor refutes this tradition, and references to him as Athenian could have applied to someone of Salaminian birth in light of the assertion that Salamis was a part of Attica. While Plutarch says that Solon's father, Execestides, dissipated his fortune, leaving his son poorly off,[77] it is arguable that if he had been forced to abandon his property in Salamis, he had little more than an aristocratic name to bequeath. If, indeed, Salamis was Solon's ancestral home, it goes without saying that his motives for risking so much to regain the island become far more understandable in personal terms. On the other hand, the view that Solon's family was Salaminian may be no more than an ancient inference, based on such factors as his role in the reconquest of the island, the reverence of his memory among later Salaminians, who raised a statue to him,[78] the "widely reported tradition" that he was cremated there,[79] and too literal an interpretation of ambiguous lines of his poem *Salamis*—for example, "I come as a herald from lovely Salamis." From the standpoint of Megarian history this is a minor point, and I do not wish to push it too far. Solon's origins, like so much else in his life and work,

[76]See D.L. 1.45 and Diod. 9.1.
[77]*Sol.* 2.
[78]See Aeschin. 1.25.
[79]So characterized by Plutarch (*Sol.* 32), who, however, rejects this view.

remain problematic despite, or perhaps because of, the attention paid to him by a number of ancient writers.

There is still a third tradition regarding the reconquest of Salamis. Pausanias reports that the Megarians had a distinctly different explanation: "The Megarians assert that exiles from Megara, whom they name Dorycleans, went to the colonists in Salamis, and betrayed the island to the Athenians."[80] Unfortunately, no detail is supplied as to how such an act of treason was carried out. With a bit of imagination, we might work this element into either of the versions reported by Plutarch. But it is also possible that Plutarch has this tradition in mind when he reports in his comparison of the lives of Solon and Publicola that Daimachus of Plataea denied Solon's role as leader in the war against Megara altogether.[81] Then again, Daimachus' assertion may have been merely one more reflection of the confusion surrounding the relative roles of Solon and Pisistratus in the protracted struggle with the Megarians.

The mysterious Dorycleans might have been oligarchs who had been exiled by the "unbridled democracy" and had come to Attica. Their support of Athenian plans to take Salamis could have been the price for their continued protection by the Athenians, or even for assistance in overthrowing the popular regime in Megara. All of this is possible but can hardly be proven on the basis of a single reference to "Dorycleans." The story may be no more than a surviving trace of an accusation leveled against the oligarchs by the demagogues of Megara casting about for some excuse for the loss of Salamis. At a time when Megara's naval power was still greater than Athens', public anger over this calamity may well have occasioned the most desperate efforts of the popular leaders to exonerate themselves and place the blame on their enemies.

At all events, Salamis was now in Athenian hands, but the dispute continued. The final stages were not to come for another generation, and will be treated in the next chapter. Modern scholars have sought to understand this long and bitter conflict over a small and meagerly endowed island largely in terms of its strategic importance.[82] They emphasize the value of its location for the con-

---

[80]1.40.5.
[81]*Comp. Sol. et Publ.* 4.
[82]This view is most fully stated by French, pp. 238-46. But some authorities, while

trol of shipping in and out of the harbors of Athens and Megara. The argument, in essence, is that either state was in a position to disrupt, or even to entirely shut off, the commercial and strategic shipping of the other through possession of Salamis, and that control of Salamis was a precondition of naval development and prosperity for either state. Hence, Megarian control of the island in the seventh century is seen as constituting a serious obstacle to Athens' budding ambitions in the Aegean, and Athenian control in the sixth century and later is regarded as relegating Megara to the status of a minor sea power. This view is less than convincing. True, Salamis was well suited to serve as a pirate base during unsettled periods, but established states could not use it routinely to prey on one another's ships without an endless series of provocations to full-scale war. Permanent use of the island for this purpose would indicate a perpetual state of war between Athens and Megara, and we have no reason to believe that condition existed, once the issue of possession of Salamis itself was resolved.

It is likely that under normal circumstances both Athenian and Megarian ships sailed the Saronic Gulf without molesting one another. But even if we were to grant that these rival sea powers intended to use Salamis to interdict one another's shipping, it would not have been easy to make such a strategy effective. During the Peloponnesian War in the late fifth century, the Athenians attempted to blockade Megara, but found that lookout points and bases on Salamis and frequent patrols of the Megarian coast were insufficient.[83] They eventually seized the island of Minoa, which stood virtually inside the harbor of Nisaea, and even then, Megarian ships managed to slip through the noose. Bear in mind, too, that fifth-century Athens was an incomparably greater naval power than contemporary Megara and had far greater resources at her disposal than either state possessed in the archaic period. In fact, the Athenians' use of subterfuge rather than frontal attack at various points in the sixth-century naval war with Megara suggests that Megara still held the edge in naval strength through all or most of the struggle over Salamis. In these circumstances, it is

noting the strategic and commercial value of Salamis, give at least some weight to its potential as a colonial settlement. See, e.g., Trever, p. 122.

[83]See below, Chapters 9, 10.

hardly likely that the Megarians would have seen Athenian control of Salamis in the sixth century as spelling the end of Megara's career as a naval state. Conversely, Athens' Saronic Gulf harbor in this period was not the Piraeus, which lies about the same distance from the nearest points on Salamis in one direction as Nisaea does in the other, but the beach of Phaleron, which is further east and largely obscured from surveillance from Salamis by the Akte Peninsula. If it would have been impossible for archaic Athens to restrict Megarian shipping, it would have been even more problematic for Megara to interdict Athens' modest naval activity from a base on Salamis.

In sum, Salamis was in a position to harass but not to disrupt the naval enterprises of either state fatally, and even this harassment could only be undertaken at the risk of general war. Possession of the island, once the freebooting ways of the early settlers had been stamped out by Megarian action, was primarily an emotional, patriotic issue for both sides, involving marginal land and rival groups of settlers, each regarding themselves as the true Salaminians. Ultimate control of the island did not determine the long-term naval superiority of Athens over Megara, but was itself determined by the gradual growth of Athenian military power on the sea as well as on land. In the course of the sixth century, tiny Megara watched the advantages of her early and rapid development disappear as her larger neighbor steadily matured. Both states were committed to Salamis; the stronger was bound to win out in the end. The outcome of this dispute was symptomatic of the growth of Athenian power and Megara's inability to keep pace.

The last episode of which we have any detailed information concerning Megara's relations with the rest of the Greek world during the period of "unbridled democracy" is, at first glance, bizarre. Plutarch, who is again our only source, as in the war with the Samians, explains why some Megarians—probably those living in a particular district of the Megarid—are known as the "wagon-rollers":

> During the period of the unbridled democracy, which was responsible for both the palintokia and the temple robbery [an incident otherwise unknown], a Peloponnesian delegation to Delphi which, as it hap-

pened, had brought along their wives and children in wagons, stopped by Aegeiri by the lake on their way through the Megarid. The boldest of the Megarians in a drunken state wantonly and cruelly pushed the wagons into the lake so that many of the pilgrims drowned. Then, since the Megarians took no action against the wrongdoers, the Amphictyones, in view of the fact that religious emissaries were involved, punished the guilty by invading the region and exiling some and executing others. The descendants of these people were called the "wagon-rollers."[84]

This affair, as related by Plutarch, is an illustration of anarchic conditions in Megara: For unexplained reasons, a drunken mob attacked a party of religious pilgrims passing through Megara, and when the popular government proved unwilling or unable to punish the culprits, the states of the Amphictyonic League took matters into their own hands, violating Megarian sovereignty in the process.

The Delphic Amphictyony had only been formed around 600, and its first known act was the destruction of Cirrha, near Delphi, for its alleged harassment of pilgrims.[85] This was the First Sacred War, circa 595-590. Could the undated reprisal raid against the "wagon-rollers" have been a contemporaneous and related measure? Is it significant that Athens was one of the leading members of the Amphictyony and that Solon was her representative?[86] He is credited with a major role in persuading the Amphictyons to declare war against Cirrha. Given his (and Athens') animus toward Megara because of the Salamis dispute, did he seize upon the "wagon-rollers" crime as a means of bringing the military might of the league to bear on the hated Megarians? Another possibility, though less likely, is that the conservative regimes of the Amphictyonic states saw an excuse to strike a blow against a threatening new kind of popular regime. The magnitude of the crime may well have been blown out of proportion by Megara's enemies.

But why did the "wagon-rollers" murder the pilgrims in the first place? Even if they were drunk, they must have been angry about something. One possibility is that the travelers had refused to pay

---

[84]*Quaest. Graec.* 59.
[85]See H. W. Parke, The Delphic Oracle, Vol. 1 (Oxford, 1956), pp. 103-04.
[86]Plut. *Sol.* 11.

a toll on the road through Megara. Although Aegeiri has not been positively identified, Hammond has suggested that it was in the valley of the Vathikhoria, through which the Road of the Towers made its way toward southern Boeotia, and where the Megalo Vathikhori was probably turned into a lake for much of the year.[87] The Road of the Towers was the preferred route through the Isthmus for wheeled traffic and for all traffic heading for Boeotia and points west. It must have been the path used by southern visitors to Delphi from time immemorial. The Vathikhoria, where a number of lesser tracks converged on the main route, was the likeliest place along the route at which to control traffic and levy tolls, if there were any. The policy of the Amphictyons toward Cirrha suggests that they were in general opposed to pilgrims being taken advantage of on their way to worship or consult Apollo.[88] It is possible, therefore, that the unfortunates who were drowned at Aegeiri were traveling under the protection of the new League and refused to pay what was customary. Our ignorance about ancient tolls in general, and not merely in the case of Megara, however, makes this an extremely hazardous speculation. It is also possible that the people of Aegeiri were acting more out of hostility toward the oracle than toward the people they attacked. Both from Plutarch's account of Solon's conquest of Salamis and from references to the later debate over the original affinities of the island,[89] it appears that Delphi took a pro-Athenian stance. As the Salamis issue was very likely hot during the time of the incident at Aegeiri, it is possible that the Megarians were venting their anger and frustration with Delphi through this rash act. It would also be useful to know where the pilgrims had come from, in order to see whether their treatment reflects Megara's relations with particular Peloponnesian states. These various suggestions may all be wide of the mark, but without more evidence, I do not believe we can get closer to the truth.

Looking back over the foreign policy record of the "unbridled

[87]Hammond, "Main Road," pp. 118-20. His further identification of this seasonal lake as the Lake Gorgopis, the "staring-eyed lake," of Aeschylus' *Agamemnon* (302), is one of the more attractive solutions to this geographic puzzle.

[88]N. G. L. Hammond, *OCD*[2], p. 943, suggests that the issue in the First Sacred War was the collection of tolls. Cf. Hammond, *JHS*, 57 (1937), 44 ff.

[89]See below, Chapter 6.

democracy," it is difficult to find positive achievements. The regime seems to have tried to defend Megara's traditional interests in the Northeast and on Salamis, but with a notable lack of success. The incident of the "wagon-rollers" suggests that Megara was treated as something of an outlaw during this period. Surely, these developments must have shaken the popular regime and contributed to its eventual downfall; but I wonder whether any government might have averted these setbacks entirely. Time had begun to operate against Megarian interests, as states which had developed more slowly, but which had greater natural wealth and larger populations—Athens, in particular—began to eclipse this enterprising but tiny state.

Aristotle is the only writer to record the fall of the popular government. We noted earlier a passage in which he describes how the demogogues continued exiling the wealthy in order to have largess to distribute to their supporters. He goes on to say that eventually so many were expelled in this way that "the exiles were turned into a formidable force, and they returned and defeated the demos and established an oligarchic regime."[90] He fixed no date for this coup, though one might infer from the apparent participation of the original exiles that it took place less than a generation after the expulsions began. If popular government took hold in Megara in the years just before 600, it is safe to say that it collapsed by 580, and possibly a good deal sooner. Considering the disastrous record in foreign relations which the "democrats" compiled in the 590's, it would not be surprising to find that they lost enough internal support to be vulnerable shortly thereafter.

The returning exiles established a narrow oligarchy. Aristotle reports this in his description of the various criteria which oligarchies used to establish eligibility for public office: "at Megara only those were eligible who had returned together from exile and fought together against the *demos*."[91] Undoubtedly, the returning oligarchs reclaimed their confiscated property and exiled or executed, at the very least, the leaders of the popular regime who

[90]*Pol.* 1304b 35-40.
[91]*Pol.* 1300a 15-20.

had not immediately fled. Though considerable support for popular rule may have remained beneath the surface, Megara now entered a period of conservative government which lasted more than a hundred years.

CHAPTER 6

Oligarchy, Symmachy, Prosperity

> May the strong right arm of Zeus who dwells in heaven always preserve this polis unharmed, and the other blessed immortal gods too. Further, may Apollo guide our speech and thoughts, and may holy sounds come from the lyre and the flute; let us pour a libation to the gods and drink together, talking with one another in friendly wise, not fearing the war with the Medes in the least. This surely is better, to live united in spirit, carefree, joyfully, and to keep at a distance evil spirits, destructive age, and ultimate death.
>
> —*Theognidaea* 757-768[1]

THE WAR over Salamis was continued by the narrow oligarchic regime that gained power in Megara in the early sixth century. If members of the ruling clique had betrayed Salamis to the Athenians while in exile—the alleged treason of the Dorycleans—they now reversed themselves. But it would not be unique in Greek political history for a faction to behave differently in and out of power. In either case, it is apparent that the new government was determined to pursue Megara's interests in the Saronic Gulf and the Aegean. The course of the war in this period, however, is as obscure as in its earlier stages. Plutarch, intent on reconciling rival traditions, inserts Megarian reconquest of Salamis and Nisaea—which neither he nor any other source suggests was conquered by Solon—between the victories of Solon and Pisistratus.[2] This is an unnecessary complication if one simply credits Solon with conquest of Salamis and Pisistratus with conquest of Nisaea some thirty years later. The latter Athenian success was achieved through the elaborate ploy summarized in the last chapter. The incident is described in detail by Aeneas the Tactician:

[1]These lines are not the work of Theognis himself. See the discussion of authenticity in the previous chapter.
[2]*Sol.* 12.

Word was brought to Pisistratus, when he was general at Athens,[3] that the Megarians would come in ships, and attempt a night attack upon the Athenian women while they were celebrating at Eleusis the festival of Demeter. On hearing this, Pisistratus set an ambush ahead of them, and when the Megarians disembarked, in secrecy as they supposed, and were some distance from the sea, he rose up and overcame those who had been trapped, killed most of them, and captured the ships in which they had come. Then after quickly filling the ships with his own soldiers, he took from among the women those best fitted to make the voyage, and late in the day landed at Megara at some distance from the city. Now many of the Megarians, officials (*synarchai*) and others, when they caught sight of the ships sailing into the harbor, went out to meet them, wishing, no doubt to see as many women as possible brought in as captives . . . [lacuna— evidently describing Pisistratus' orders for the Athenian attack] and disembarking with daggers in their hands to strike down some of the Megarians, but to bring back to the ships as many as possible of the most prominent men; and this they did.[4]

The harbor into which the Athenians sailed was undoubtedly Nisaea, and though Aeneas does not say so, this must be the same campaign which Herodotus speaks of as resulting in the capture of Nisaea by Pisistratus.[5] If Herodotus is correct, the Athenians now had several powerful bargaining counters to force Megara to give up all claim to Salamis—that is, hostages who were members of the ruling oligarchy and, even more significantly, control of Megara's chief port. Although the loss of Salamis was not a fatal blow to Megarian shipping, even temporary hostile occupation of Nisaea meant the complete disruption of Megara's naval activity. This was an intolerable situation, and the Megarians must either have retaken Nisaea by storm—which no source confirms—or agreed to some settlement of the war within a few years at most.

It is tempting to suppose that it was these considerations which persuaded the Megarians to accept arbitration of the Salamis dis-

---

[3]I.e., prior to his having become tyrant for the first time, c. 561, though probably not long before.

[4]Aen. Tac. 4.8-11, tr. members of the Illinois Greek Club, *Aeneas Tacticus, Asclepiodotus, Onasander* (Cambridge, Mass., 1948), pp. 41-43. Cf. Just. *Epit.* 2.8, whose source was probably Ephorus.

[5]1.59. Herodotus is the only authority who explicitly credits Pisistratus with the capture of Nisaea, but his word is generally to be preferred to that of the substantially later authorities on whom we are otherwise dependent.

pute by a third party, Sparta.[6] The tradition that it was Solon who put Athens' case before the Spartan arbitrators also points to a date in the 560's or early 550's at the latest. Some historians have doubted whether Sparta's prestige and influence were sufficiently developed for her to have become involved in such a dispute until much later.[7] She was still not absolute master in the central Peloponnese, her struggle with the tenacious Tegeans was probably in mid course, and her conclusive victory over Argos at Thyreatis was yet to come. But Sparta was already one of the major powers of the Greek mainland, and she was sufficiently remote from the two contestants in both distance and strategic interests to be seen as an impartial arbiter. If, on the other hand, we attempt to date the Spartan arbitration in a substantially later period, when Megara had been drawn into the network of Spartan alliances, Solon's role would be impossible and Athens is unlikely to have agreed to this choice of mediator.

Plutarch gives the fullest picture of the circumstances of Spartan arbitration:

> [After Solon's conquest of Salamis] the Megarians persisted and both committed and endured many evils in the course of the war, until they made the Spartans mediators and judges [of the dispute]. Most authorities say that Homer's teachings supported Solon's position. For at the trial he read this verse which he himself had interpolated into the Catalogue of Ships:
>> Ajax led twelve ships from Salamis and stationed them where the Athenian forces stood.[8]
> But the Athenians themselves regard this as nonsense, and say that Solon convinced the judges that Philaeus and Eurysaces, the sons of Ajax, became Athenian citizens, turned the island over to them, and settled in Attica . . . They also say that in his desire to thoroughly disprove the Megarian case, he insisted that corpses on Salamis were not buried in the same orientation as those in Megara, but like those in Attica. For the Megarians bury their dead facing the east, while the Athenians bury theirs facing the west. But Hereas of Megara rebuts

[6]See Plut. *Sol.* 10; Strab. 9.1.10-11; D.L. 1.48; Arist. *Rh.* 1375b. 29-30.
[7]See, e.g., Beloch, *Gr. Gesch.* 1², pp. 312 f.
[8]*Il.* 2.557-58. The Megarians quoted an alternate couplet here, according to Strabo (9.1.10): "Ajax conducted ships from Salamis, Polichna, Aegirussa, Nisaea, and Tripodes." See my comment above, Chapter 2, note 25. Neither the Athenian nor Megarian couplet inspire confidence.

that the Megarians too turn their corpses to the west, and, more important still, he says every Athenian has a separate tomb, while the Megarians (like the Salaminians) bury three or four together. However, they say that Solon was also supported by several Delphic oracles in which the god referred to Salamis as Ionian.[9] The case was judged by five Spartans, Kritolaidas, Amompharetos, Hypsechidas, Anaxilas, and Kleomenes.[10]

Curiously, Plutarch does not say in so many words in whose favor the arbiters decided, but the context of his remarks—a record of Solon's achievements—leaves little doubt about the outcome. Athens was awarded the island and Megara must have regained Nisaea and the hostages, if they had not already been returned as a precondition for arbitration.

Modern scholarship has spent a great deal of effort in attempting to adjudicate the rights and wrongs of the Salamis dispute. In fact, if as was judged likely in Chapter 2, above, Megara and Attica were ethnically and politically linked in the sub-Mycenaean period, the question may be moot or meaningless. The Spartan decision may have been more heavily influenced by the fact that Athens currently held the upper hand in the struggle (and in Salamis itself) than by an objective weighing of the evidence. A decision in favor of Athens was the one likeliest to put a permanent end to the conflict. By now the balance of power between Megara and Athens had begun to tilt decisively in favor of the larger state. True, Megara's long-standing naval superiority, which may have necessitated Pisistratus' brilliant stratagem at Nisaea, had been only temporarily neutralized. She was soon to regain her naval poise and launch yet another major colony, but she never again raised the Salamis issue or challenged Athens' growing role in the Aegean. Coexistence rather than confrontation on the seas became the keynote of Megarian foreign policy for the next century and longer. As we shall see, this pacific policy coincided with a period of unprecedented prosperity for her. Whether or not they appreciated it at

[9]It might be observed, parenthetically, that this seems to be one of a number of instances in which Megara did not enjoy the favor of the Delphic Oracle, from the incident of the wagon-rollers to the resolution of rival Athenian and Megarian claims to borderland in the mid-fourth century.
[10]*Sol.* 10.

the time, the resolution of the Salamis dispute lifted a great burden from the shoulders of the Megarians, a burden that had drained their energies away from more profitable pursuits.

Nothing is known of the internal policies of the Megarian oligarchy in the decades before or after the war with Athens ended. The exclusiveness of the new regime must have given way in time to either a hereditary or, more likely, a property criterion for participation. The revolutionary comrades in arms did not live forever. Whether the oligarchy mellowed in other respects is less certain. The apparent longevity of the oligarchy could be evidence of moderation and consequent internal stability—for example, through the restraint of usury. But it might equally imply effective political repression. That there were malcontents in Megara during the last stages of the war for Salamis may be hinted in Aeneas' remark that Pisistratus received advanced warning of the Megarians' surprise raid on Eleusis. The most suggestive occurrence, however, was the founding of Herakleia Pontica—Herakleia on the Black Sea—by the Megarians and the Tanagrans of Boeotia, around 559.[11] This foundation, so close to the lastest possible date for Spartan arbitration, could have been a response to the political and social consequences of Megara's permanent loss of the island. If so, Megara's Salaminian refugees probably bulked large among the settlers at Herakleia. But that the colony either began as a democracy or soon became one, later mirroring the struggle between democrats and oligarchs in the early decades of the sixth century in the mother city, suggests that democratic sympathizers and critics of the regime were also deported to Herakleia. According to Aristotle:

> The demos at Herakleia was overthrown soon after the settlement was founded on account of the demagogues' behavior. For the no-

[11]See Ps.-Scymn. 972 ff.; Paus. 5.26.7; Ephorus fr. 44 in *FGrH* 2A.56; Ap. Rhod. 2.846 f. Other sources credit Megara alone with the foundation. See Xen. *An.* 6.2.1; Arr. *Peripl. M. Eux.* 18; Diod. 14.31.3; *Geog. Gr. Min.* 1.383. Strabo (12.3.4) names Miletus as founder. As Hanell, *Studien,* pp. 128 f., and most others have concluded, the weight of the evidence points to a joint foundation by Megara and Tanagra, with Megara probably taking the leading role. The responsibility for transporting the colonists to the Black Sea must certainly have fallen on the Megarians.

tables (*gnorimoi*) were unjustly expelled by them, but later these exiles, joining together and returning, toppled the democracy.[12]

Some historians have inferred that Herakleia was intentionally founded as a democracy from this passage, and a few have even based a later dating of the democracy in Megara on a presumed connection between the two regimes.[13] But the presence of "notables" makes it likelier that Herakleia was launched as a hierarchical, oligarchic state, mirroring Megarian conditions after the overthrow of the "unbridled democracy." It appears, however, that there were enough disgruntled democrats among the rank and file colonists to effect a short-lived democratic coup in the colony's early days. The Megarian oligarchs may well have sent many of their political opponents on the expedition to Herakleia—a sensible precaution against the danger of revolution at home, especially in the wake of such setbacks as the loss of Nisaea and Salamis. Thus Megara exported her troubles and the colony at Herakleia got off to a very shaky start, which it managed to survive. Ultimately, Herakleia was able to found a succession of her own colonies.[14] It is worthwhile to note in passing that the settlement of Herakleia, Megara's last known colony, at a time when the Black Sea was beginning to assume major proportions, demonstrates Megara's continued vitality as a naval state after the loss of Salamis.

Sometime during the second half of the sixth century, Megara entered her first formal association with another Greek state, concluding a bilateral treaty, a symmachy, with Sparta. Since the middle of the century, Sparta had been working out such treaties with one after another of the Peloponnesian states, beginning with

[12]*Pol.* 1304b 31-34. It is possible that Aristotle is here referring to Herakleia in Trachis, rather than to the Megarian colony, but the case for Herakleia Pontica is stronger. See W. L. Newman's note on this passage in his edition of the *Politics*, Vol. 4, p. 337. That Aristotle might have referred to Herakleia Pontica simply as Herakleia is confirmed by *Pol.* 1306b.1ff., where the same events are described as in 1305b.33-36, where Herakleia Pontica is specified. Nor is there even one unequivocal reference to Herakleia in Trachis in the *Politics*.

[13]See, e.g., Jeffery, *Archaic Greece*, p. 157.

[14]Herakleia's foundations included Chersonesos in the Crimea and Kallatis on the Thracian coast of the Euxine.

Tegea.[15] These agreements to have "the same friends and enemies" served two major purposes for the Lacedaemonians. First, Sparta gained some protection against the ever-present danger of a revolt by the Messenian helots. With Laconia and Messenia ringed by states loyal to Sparta's interests, the possibility of external support for a helot revolt was greatly reduced. Second, Sparta's alliances enabled her to isolate and encircle her only rival in the Peloponnese, Argos. For the lesser partners in these pacts, the only alternative to agreement was war with the feared Spartan hoplites, and there were often tangible advantages to alliance with Sparta. Prime among these was independence and protection from their own local enemies, many of whom would themselves be allies of Sparta. General peace was another potential benefit, for when the Spartan alliance system had spread far enough, the possibility of war within the Peloponnese was greatly reduced. Finally, since the Lacedaemonians posed as enemies of tyranny and other deviations from oligarchic government, and backed or helped to establish oligarchies in all the states to which they were allied, like-minded factions in the other states might see greater security for themselves under Spartan hegemony than otherwise. This policy meant that the Spartans had relatively pliable and predictable regimes to deal with among their allies, since these governments were to some extent indebted to Sparta for their continued stability in the face of internal opposition.

The political dependence of the allies contributed to Sparta's ability to dominate them, but there were other factors as well. One was certainly the disparity in size and power between Sparta and each of the allied states. By keeping these alliances separate, Sparta could overawe her partners individually and prevent them from acting in concert to counterbalance her own disproportionate influence. Thus the earliest hegemonal system of Greek poleis took shape. It has long been called by historians the "Peloponnesian League," a term that was not used in antiquity, when the association was referred to as the Lacedaemonians and their allies. No

[15]For a recent overview of the growth of the Peloponnesian League, see K. Wickert, *Der peloponnisische Bund von seiner Entstehung bis zum Ende des archidamischen Krieges*, Erlangen, 1961. Wickert adopts a sensible, not overlegalistic approach to the organization. Cf. the excellent treatments of the league in de Ste Croix, *OPW*, pp. 96-124, and Kagan, *Outbreak*, pp. 9-30.

terrible injustice is done by retaining what has become common modern usage, so long as we do not make the mistake of assuming the same sorts of formal relations within the Spartan hegemony as characterize modern leagues, or, indeed, ancient ones. Whether the Peloponnesian League eventually developed the procedures we commonly associate with leagues is a subject to which we shall return.

In the course of the second half of the sixth century, Sparta's alliance system spread steadily northward, making it likely that the Isthmian states were not drawn into her net until relatively late. Megarian involvement, in fact, cannot be explicitly confirmed until the period of Xerxes' invasion of Greece in 481. On the other hand, we can be certain of the inclusion of Corinth by 507, when the Spartans were bent on destroying Cleisthenes' regime in Athens. The nature of that operation and of the Spartan Cleomenes' interference in Athenian affairs for the previous few years make it extremely likely that Megarian as well as Corinthian allegiance had been secured by the Spartans before 510. The only recorded instance of Spartan presence in force at the Isthmus prior to 510 was an expedition led by this same King Cleomenes in 519. That was the date at which, according to Thucydides, the Boeotian state of Plataea allied itself with Athens to avoid absorption by Thebes.[16] Herodotus, in relating the background of that alliance, reports that the Plataeans appealed first to Cleomenes, who "happened to be in the neighborhood with a Spartan army."[17] To have been in the vicinity of Plataea, Cleomenes would have had to march through Corinthia and the Megarid, and he may actually have been in Megara at the time, since it was less than a day's journey over the Road of the Towers from Plataea to Megara.

Though Herodotus says nothing of Cleomenes' purpose in having brought an army this far from Sparta, his treatment of the Plataean appeal and Cleomenes' response may give us a clue:

Hard pressed by the Thebans, the Plataeans first offered themselves to Cleomenes . . . and the Spartans who were with him. But he declined

[16]3.68.5. Thucydides says Plataea fell to the Spartans in 427, ninety-three years after the alliance with Athens was concluded.
[17]6.108.2.

143

to accept them, saying, "We live too far away and our protection would be of no avail. For, you could be enslaved before we ever heard of it. We recommend that you give yourselves to the Athenians, a neighboring people whose aid is not to be despised." The Spartans did not give this advice out of good will toward the Plataeans, but out of a desire to set the Athenians against the Boeotians.[18]

The Plataeans had requested an alliance with Sparta which would protect them from Theban domination. I suspect that they were encouraged to make such an appeal because Sparta's hegemony had been extended almost to their borders by the inclusion of Corinth and Megara at this date or earlier. While at first glance the Spartans' refusal and their stated reason suggest that they would have felt almost equally out of touch with Isthmian affairs, we have not only Herodotus' word that this answer was disingenuous, but the fact of Spartan military presence in the region at that very moment. The Spartans were already active on the Isthmus and were shortly to become involved in Athenian affairs too.

Going one step further, it is not impossible that Sparta was in the midst of an armed intervention between two allies, Megara and Corinth, when the Plataeans made their overture. Though her allies did not have formal treaty relations with one another, Sparta usually tried to prevent or resolve conflict between them. We know that border wars between Corinth and Megara had taken place in the past, and one in the later sixth century is a distinct possibility. One hint of more recent differences may be seen in Plutarch's comment that the Corinthians were not "prevented from joining the Greek side" in the Persian Wars by "their dispute with the Megarians."[19] The nature and timing of this quarrel are not specified, and Herodotus makes no mention of conflict between the two states in his detailed treatment of events after 500. The only possible point in his narrative with which Plutarch's remark might be associated is Cleomenes' military presence on or near the Isthmus in 519. It is also possible that the Corinthian spoils, which helped to build the Megarian treasury at Olympia in the last years of the sixth or the first years of the fifth century, came from a relatively

[18] 6.108.2-3.
[19] *De Mal. Hdt.* 35.

recent clash, rather than the remote war with which Pausanias or his informants associated them.[20] This would certainly seem more plausible than that the Megarians transferred to Olympia about 500 B.C. trophies and treasure taken from Corinth two hundred years earlier. If, indeed, Cleomenes intervened in a war between Megara and Corinth around 519, it would seem that Megara had enjoyed some success in the conflict up to that point—hence, the spoils. But it is hard to imagine the smaller state prevailing if the struggle had been allowed to continue. Corinth's pique at being restrained by the Spartans in this instance might well have affected her attitude toward Sparta's later adventures north of the Isthmus. This episode might also help to explain the war between Corinth and Megara about 461, at a time when their hegemon was too busy at home to prevent it; Corinth may have seen an opportunity to achieve aims that had been frustrated sixty years earlier. The issue around 461 was the border between these uneasy neighbors, and it is hard to imagine any other issue at the root of the sixth-century war.[21] Still, it is surprising that a war between two major Greek states in the latter part of the sixth century left no clearer traces in the historical record, and the suggestions made above must therefore remain a hypothesis. The only conclusion of which we can be fairly confident is that Megara had been drawn into the Spartan orbit by 510, and that 519 is the most plausible date for this to have occurred.

The first known crisis involving the Spartan hegemony after Megara had joined it arose from the Spartans' intervention in Athenian affairs. In league with Athenian exiles, led by Cleisthenes the Alcmaeonid and urged on by the Delphic Oracle, the Lacedaemonians launched two expeditions against the Athenian tyrant Hippias in 510.[22] The first, a seaborne raid on Phaleron, met defeat. The second, which marched through the Isthmus under the command of King Cleomenes, forced Hippias and his supporters to take refuge on the Athenian Acropolis. (The sources are silent on the

[20]Paus. 6.19.12-14. See above, Chapter 3 for a discussion of the earlier conflict between Megara and Corinth. If a war between the two states did occur c. 520, we can only speculate about the issues, but dispute over borderlands is once more the most likely cause.

[21]See below, Chapter 8, on the conflict c. 461.

[22]See esp. Hdt. 5.62-65; Thuc. 6.59; Arist. *Ath. Pol.* 19.

145

question whether Sparta's allies contributed to this army.) When one of Hippias' sons was captured soon after the siege of the Acropolis had begun, he accepted the offer of a safe conduct out of Attica for himself and his family.

This campaign was of a piece with Spartan policy as it developed throughout the sixth century, though it probably brought them further from home than ever before. A tyranny had been overthrown, oligarchy was expected to replace it (and actually did, for a time), and another state had been drawn into the Spartan sphere, although the sources are silent on the matter of an immediate treaty between Sparta and Athens. Soon afterward, however, a struggle for influence developed within the moderate oligarchy that had come to power in Athens, pitting the revolutionary leader, Cleisthenes, against the conservative Isagoras, who had the personal support of Cleomenes.[23] Isagoras appears to have held the upper hand until 508, when Cleisthenes successfully outbid his adversary by promising to share power with the demos. Isagoras appealed to Cleomenes to intervene once more, and the Spartan king obliged by demanding the explusion of Cleisthenes from Athens on the basis of the ancient blood-guilt of the Alcmaeonids. Cleisthenes withdrew, and Cleomenes assumed matters were well enough in hand to risk a journey to Athens with only a token military force. Once there, on the advice of Isagoras, he attempted to exile seven hundred families and to dissolve the Athenian council, but the council defied him, and their resistance sparked a general uprising that caught both the Spartans and the faction of Isagoras unprepared.[24] Cleomenes had to negotiate an embarrassing retreat from Attica, and Cleisthenes was brought back in triumph to implement his reforms.

Cleomenes began plotting his revenge at once.[25] He set about gathering the forces of the Peloponnesian League and arranged for the Boeotians and Chalcidians, neither of whom enjoyed good relations with Athens, to attack her simultaneously. Up to this point, no more than tacit acceptance of Sparta's Athenian policy

[23]See Hdt. 5.66-73; Thuc. 1.126.12; Arist. *Ath. Pol.* 20.
[24]It is uncertain which council is meant, the Areopagus, the Boulē of 400 (if it ever existed), or the Boulē of 500 (if it had already begun to function).
[25]See esp. Hdt. 5.74-78.

had been demanded of her allies. Spartan forces had marched through the Peloponnese and the Isthmian states into Attica and back again several times, but there is no evidence that the allies contributed to these expeditions. Now, however, their treaty obligations were being invoked. As described by Herodotus, the Spartan summons appears to have been issued without specifying the nature of the campaign to be fought, but in the light of recent events, few could have been surprised when Athens proved to be the target. When the army was led into Eleusis and its purpose became clear to all, the Corinthians withdrew their contingent, and a split developed between the two Spartan kings, Cleomenes and Demaratus. This, in turn, led to the departure of all the other allied forces, no doubt including the Megarians, and the Spartans themselves had no choice but to return home. The Athenians were thus free to meet and repulse the Boeotian and Chalcidian armies with their entire might.

Herodotus' account of this familiar episode is too compressed (and remote) to record fully the political maneuvers which led to the collapse of this Peloponnesian League campaign; it is seldom the case that our sources adequately expose the subtle interplay of power and influence in the highest councils. It seems a safe conclusion, however, that Corinth was unhappy with Sparta's Athenian policy and seized the first real opportunity to oppose it, as she later opposed Sparta's plan to restore Hippias to power. It is doubtful that Corinth's opposition stemmed from any enthusiasm for Cleisthenes' political movement. Likelier motives were unhappiness with Cleomenes' readiness to become so deeply involved in the internal affairs of another state, and concern about the future spread of Spartan influence north of the Isthmus. Both developments could have been seen as threatening to circumscribe Corinth's freedom of action in the future. Other states probably felt the same way, but Corinth's size, strength, and key location made her the logical leader of any resistance to Sparta's will within the hegemony. Megara, on the other hand, like the other allies, complied with the Spartan call to arms and marched her troops home when the expedition was dissolved. We can only speculate about the true feelings of the Megarian oligarchy toward this expedition. As the league member closest to Athens, this issue must have been

147

of greater concern to Megara than to most of the other allies. If intervention was successful, the Megarians could anticipate the establishment of a compatible oligarchic regime in neighboring Attica—one, furthermore, that would be under the sway of the same hegemon as they themselves. Then, too, the influence of Corinth in the region might be further reduced, a possibility that may have been as attractive to the Megarians as it was to the Corinthians. On the other hand, if intervention led to a protracted war, Megara would find herself on the front line, and this could be no welcome prospect. But the quiet acceptance of a democratic, anti-Spartan regime in Athens had both positive and negative consequences too. It might prolong the half-century of peaceful relations between Megara and Athens since the resolution of the Salamis dispute, but it would flaunt the example of a popular regime before the Megarian demos, which had once before attacked the oligarchs and might do so again. Given these conflicting pressures and prospects, it may be that the oligarchs were content to bend with the prevailing winds, rather than put their modest weight wholeheartedly behind a single policy.

Several years later, the Spartans, who had not given up hope of re-establishing their influence in Athens, decided to float the idea of putting Hippias back in power there before a gathering of their allies.[26] The Corinthians were again the first to speak out against this proposal, conveniently basing their opposition on the immorality of imposing tyranny on any state, and the other allies rose, one after another, to second the Corinthian remarks and urge Sparta not to interfere in the internal affairs of other states. Faced with a chorus of criticism, the Spartans abandoned this plan also. Perhaps the Megarians were among those who spoke up, but none of the others is identified by Herodotus.

The conference at Sparta around 505 has been seen by some historians, most notably Jacob Larsen, as a critical turning point in the development of the Peloponnesian League.[27] Their argument, in

[26]Hdt. 5.90-93.

[27]See esp. J. A. O. Larsen, "Sparta and the Ionian Revolt: A Study of Spartan Foreign Policy and the Genesis of the Peloponnesian League," *CP*, 27 (1932), 136-50, and "The Constitution of the Peloponnesian League," *CP*, 28 (1933), 256-76, and *CP*, 29 (1934), 1-19.

essence, is that after the fiasco at Eleusis two years earlier, Cleomenes recognized the need to gain the prior assent of the allies for any future joint expedition, and that from this point forward decisions on such matters were put to the vote, with majority rule deciding the league's policy. Thus the bilateral treaties initially worked out by Sparta gave way to a genuinely mutual alliance. Herodotus' account, however, cannot bear the weight of this interpretation. There is no hint of a vote having been taken at this gathering, nor did any action follow which might indicate that a minority was acting in compliance with the policy of the majority. Pragmatic politics could as easily or more easily account for the Spartans' backing down from their proposal than defeat in a parliamentary sense. What those who argue for the introduction of constitutional formalities into the Spartan hegemony at the end of the sixth century need but cannot find is an instance in which the opinion of the allies was divided, a vote was taken, and all joined in carrying out the policy supported by the majority. Nothing happened in 505 except that the Spartans tried to rally support among their allies for a dubious enterprise, which they anticipated would be unpopular. The project was Cleomenes' pet, and opinion in Sparta was probably as divided as at the time of Demaratus' opposition two years earlier. Outspoken Corinthian criticism set off an avalanche of denunciations, which persuaded Cleomenes and his supporters not to press the issue. As a practical matter, the Spartans could not lead where their allies would not follow.

The case for formal organization and majority rule within the Peloponnesian League at that time is, therefore, unproven. We shall return to this issue several times, since Megara's membership in the league renders it of more than passing interest. It should be clear already, however, that I stand with the historians who have placed relatively little faith in the effort to define a formal structure and clear-cut stages in the evolution of the Spartan hegemony.[28] I prefer to believe that we are dealing with a set of relationships that were constantly shifting under the pressures of *realpolitik*. Neither

---

[28]See, e.g., Wickert, Kagan, *Outbreak*, and de Ste Croix, *OPW*. There is still considerable latitude for disagreement within the middle ground, as detailed analysis of these authorities would show.

Sparta nor her allies ever accepted any fixed definition of the extent or limits of their obligation to one another. The behavior of the league in any news crisis was unpredictable.

The second half of the sixth century was a period of considerable prosperity for Megara, to judge from the record of public building and artistic patronage she left behind. Recent excavation has shown that the fountainhouse ascribed to Theagenes reached its final form toward the end of the century.[29] The expanded fountainhouse attests to Megara's need for a larger urban water supply, which, in turn, points to an expanded urban population, the result of growing commercial and manufacturing activity. It also points to Megara's access to the most advanced technology of the period. The building is a rectangular structure, approximately 14 by 21 meters, containing two reservoirs side by side (Plate 3). These had separate sluices and basins, from which the townsfolk could draw their water. The roof was supported on five rows of octagonal pillars in Doric style and the solid exterior walls. The central row of pillars was connected by a solid wall below water level, serving to divide the two reservoirs. A modern building crowds what was the front of the fountainhouse, making it impossible to draw firm conclusions about the exterior appearance, but the presence of some sort of porch is likely.

I suspect that the redesigned fountainhouse was part of a total overhaul of the urban water supply. The career of the Megarian engineer Eupalinus, the son of Naustrophus, may indirectly support this suggestion. According to Herodotus, he was responsible for one of the most impressive technological achievements in the Greek world: he supervised the burrowing of a tunnel and an aqueduct through a mountain on the island of Samos. The tunnel was more than one kilometer in length and better than two meters in width and height, with a deeper furrow one meter wide to carry water into the town of Samos.[30] This project was undertaken by the tyrant Polycrates, and is usually dated around 530. It is reasonable to infer from this that Eupalinus gained his experience and reputation on similar projects at home, though none was on quite this

[29]See Gruben, pp. 37-41.
[30]3.60.1-2.

. The fountainhouse of Theagenes. Visible remains are from the structure erected circa
. Note the octagonal columns and the central wall, which separated the two reser-
:s.

scale. The fountainhouse, then, which may also have been his work, could have been the final stage of a water-supply scheme that had been carried out over several decades.

The last years of the sixth century also saw the construction of the Megarian treasury at Olympia. This date is suggested by recent restoration of the pediment sculpture that adorned the front of the building and now occupies a place of honor in the new museum at Olympia (see Plate 2).[31] The scene represented is the familiar battle between the gods and giants; according to specialists, it "represents an important stage in the development of Greek pediment and group composition."[32] In a passage to which we have several times referred, Pausanias says that this treasury was built from the spoils of a victory over the Corinthians, but it is doubtful that such spoils sufficed in this case or in many others to erect an entire building.[33] The treasury, like the fountainhouse, must stand as a testament to Megara's resources in the late sixth century.

Further support for this picture of a thriving Megara can be drawn from the discovery of several large *kouroi,* sculptures in the round of young men.[34] These works, which seem likely to have been produced in the Megarid, where they have been found, have been classed as part of the Melos Group, dating from the period of roughly 555 to 540.[35] These finds are noteworthy in a region which, as we have observed, has left such a sparse archaeological record. No examples of Megarian kouroi have been found from either earlier or later periods, in contrast to Athens and other states, which produced them in a succession of styles over long periods of time. What is still more worthy of our notice is the fact that the

[31]See P. C. Bol, "Die Giebelskulpturen des Schatzhauses von Megara," and K. Hermann, "Die Giebelrekonstrucktion des Schatzhauses von Megara," *AA,* 89 (1974), 65-83 and plates 31-39.

[32]Bol, p. 74.

[33]6.19.13. See Starr's sober assessment of the probabilities of financing of temples and other public buildings in *The Social and Economic Growth of Early Greece,* pp. 36-37.

[34]See G. M. A. and I. A. Richter, *Kouroi: Archaic Greek Youths,* 3d ed. (New York, 1970), pp. 90, 99, 155, and figs. 297-301 and 609-11. The finds consist of two torsos and a head which does not belong to either. The larger and better preserved torso is on display at the National Museum in Athens (Exhibit no. 13 = Richter no. 92). The smaller (near life-size) is in the Eleusis Museum (Richter no. 93).

[35]These dates are not firmly fixed. The National Museum dates its specimen c. 540.

largest of these Megarian kouroi, prominently exhibited in the National Archaeological Museum at Athens, is probably the finest surviving example of the entire Melos Group (Plate 4).[36] Whoever made it must rank as a leading figure among the sculptors of archaic Greece.

The same level of excellence characterizes another product of Megarian art in the later part of the archaic age. This is a bronze miniature, a statuette of Herakles, dated circa 500 (see frontispiece).[37] Payne offers the following appreciation of this piece: [it] "has few rivals in the series [of bronze Herakles'] and few in the whole company of contemporary bronzes. I doubt if there is in existence a figure more characteristic of the archaic conception of Herakles."[38] He was able to identify its origin as somewhere in the northeastern Peloponnese on the basis of style. The attribution to Megara is based on the spelling and letter forms of the name "Herakeas" etched on the left leg, which point unmistakably to that state.[39]

It is possible in the case of both the bronze Herakles and the National Museum kouros that the artists were not themselves Megarian. Even if this were true, however, it seems beyond argument that the Megarians were patrons of the arts in this period, and sophisticated patrons at that, able to appreciate and willing to pay for the finest workmanship. It remains possible, of course, that the workshops of Megara actually produced these fine objects.

Given the vagaries of archaeological survival in the Megarid, this brief catalogue of achievements in the period circa 550 to 500 is very significant. Yet the absence of one feature usually associated with prosperity in this period and later—namely, coinage—must be mentioned. Megara lacks an authenticated coinage earlier than the fourth century. It was suggested by Svonoros in the last century that some coins which had been subsumed in the *Wappenmünzen* of Athens, with four spoke wheels on their obverse and incuse punch-

---

[36]The Richters call it "an impressive work of individual style" and "one of the finest works of the period" (p. 90).

[37]See H. G. Payne, "A Bronze Herakles in the Benaki Museum at Athens," *JHS*, 54 (1934), 163-74 and plate 7.

[38]Ibid., p. 163.

[39]This is the conclusion of the leading authority on archaic Greek scripts, L. H. Jeffery, in "Comments on Some Archaic Inscriptions," *JHS*, 69 (1949), 31-32.

153

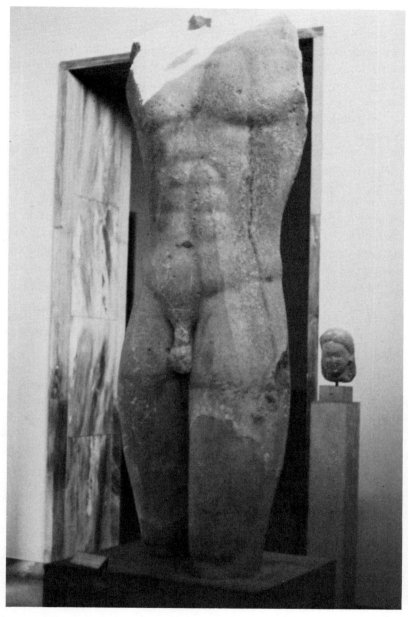

4. Megarian *kouros*, circa 540. National Archaeological Museum, Athens.
Reproduced by courtesy of the Greek Ministry of Culture and Science.

es on the reverse, were in fact archaic Megarian coins.[40] This hypothesis has been either abandoned or neglected in more recent work on archaic Greek coins, and having examined at first hand some of the coins in question, I see no basis for reviving it now. Several distinct styles are apparent among the wheel coins, but whether this reflects different mints, different artists, or different periods of production cannot be determined from the surviving coins. If, then, we accept the likelihood that early Megara produced no coins, an explanation must be sought. One possibility would be that despite the evidence of Megarian prosperity and the case for her development as a commercial state as outlined in the preceding chapters, Megarian trade was of extremely modest proportions; for coinage is associated with many of the major commercial states of the archaic period—though we are not entirely sure how it functioned in the area of interstate exchange.[41] It should be kept in mind, however, that Megara possessed no native source of silver or of any other precious metal, and that she was surrounded by the leading minting states of the era—Corinth, Aegina, and Athens. Under these circumstances, the decision not to issue coins may have been both practical and economic, signifying nothing about Megara's status as a trading power. As we shall have occasion to note in Chapter 11, even in the fourth century, when Megarian trade is unquestioned, she issued only small-denomination coins, continuing to rely on the larger issues of the major minting states—as she apparently had been doing since the sixth century.

If, as argued in this chapter, Megara was a flourishing state in the closing decades of the sixth century, with a growing urban population and substantial overseas trade, there is both irony and an important lesson in that fact.[42] For this prosperity came after

[40]See Svonoros' views as stated by B. V. Head, *Historia Numorum: A Manual of Greek Numismatics* (Oxford, 1911), p. 393, and E. Babelon, *Traité des monnaies grecques et romaines*, Pt. 2, Vol. 1 (Paris, 1901), 778-82. C. Seltman, "Aegean Mints," *NC*[5] 6 (1926), 139-43, proposed that some supposed early Aeginetan coin types depicting dolphins were really Megarian, but this suggestion has won no adherents.

[41]My view is that coins were first introduced to facilitate wholesale exchange in the marketplace, and to enable states to collect duty on these transactions without having to deal directly with a wide variety of merchandise. Of published views, mine is most in accord with that of C. H. V. Sutherland, "Corn and Coin; A Note on Greek Commercial Monopolies," *AJP*, 64 (1943), 129-47.

[42]It must be observed that this was a period of rising prosperity in other commer-

Megara had lost Salamis, and it continued, perhaps even increased, when she surrendered some of her autonomy by joining
the Spartan hegemony. Evidently peace, security, and internal stability were more critical to Megara's material well-being than any
ultimately quixotic efforts to match her larger neighbors militarily,
or to maintain absolute independence at all costs. It is too early,
however, to discount Megarian military power altogether. She was
still able to supply twenty triremes and three thousand hoplites at
the time of Xerxes' invasion, and according to Diodorus, the Megarians, together with the Aeginetans, were "generally considered to
be the best seamen after the Athenians."[43] We ought not to expect
less from a prosperous state with a long seafaring tradition.

---

cial states as well, including Athens, Aegina, and Corinth, but Megara's involvement in this trend is highly significant, nonetheless.
[43]11.18.

CHAPTER 7

The Persian Wars

Lord Phoebus, who raised the battlements of the city's acropolis
to please Alcathoös, the son of Pelops, may you ward off the
violence of the Median army from this city, so the rejoicing people may honor you with wonderous hecatombs at the return of
springtime . . . For I am filled with alarm when I see foolishness
and discord destroying the Hellenic race. But you, O Phoebus,
propitiously defend this city of ours.

—*Theognidaea* 773-782[1]

MEGARA appears to have entered the fifth century prosperous
and at peace. She seems, for example, to have avoided any involvement in the naval war that raged intermittently after 507 between her Saronic Gulf neighbors, Athens and Aegina.[2] This is the
more noteworthy in view of the role played by other states in the
region. Aegina initiated the conflict in cooperation with Thebes,[3]
and the Corinthians lent twenty triremes to Athens for use against
Aegina at some stage.[4] Even Sparta ultimately became involved in
the early 490's, when Cleomenes stepped in to prevent the
Aeginetans from inviting Persian intervention.[5] He called a temporary halt to the war by turning Aeginetan hostages over to
Athens, and in the process he seems to have mended Sparta's
relations with the Athenians. It would be out of place to attempt a
complete reconstruction and analysis of this complex affair here,
nor can we stop to consider such puzzling questions as whether

---

[1]Once more these lines cannot be the work of Theognis unless we move him
down into the fifth century. But whoever wrote them must have been associated
with Megara, as the reference to the acropolis of Alcathoa makes clear.

[2]Hdt. 5.79-81, 89; 6.49-50, 73, 87-93; and 7.145.

[3]Hdt. 5.79-81, 89.

[4]Hdt. 6.88-89.

[5]Hdt. 6.49-50, 73.

157

Aegina was allied to Sparta at the time of Cleomenes' and the Corinthians' intervention in support of Athens, or to deal with the considerable chronological difficulties.[6] Still, it is striking that Megara played no role in a conflict that was waged virtually on her doorstep and that promised to affect the balance of naval power in the Saronic Gulf and the Aegean, a matter of no little consequence to herself. There is always the possibility that Herodotus has merely neglected to mention Megarian involvement, but it is not difficult to cite reasons why Megara might well have steered clear of this struggle deliberately, although she possessed both the means and the opportunity to have affected the outcome. Her seeming neutrality could reflect the good relations she maintained with both of the principals, a calculated policy of allowing her naval competitors to weaken one another or, indeed, any number of considerations, including mere lassitude. Rather than look for specific motives in this instance, it may be more significant that with the possible exception of a border war with Corinth around 520, the Megarians appear to have avoided warfare altogether for the better part of a century, from the end of the Salamis dispute to the time of Xerxes' invasion. This is an appropriate note on which to begin our discussion of Megarian policy during the Persian Wars, since the Megarians seem in this instance also to have adhered to a pacific policy, at least until they were overtaken by events.

The vast Persian Empire first loomed on the Greek horizon with Cyrus' conquest of the Lydian Empire in western Anatolia in the mid-540's. This led to Persian hegemony over many of the Greek states on or near the coast of Asia Minor in Ionia and Aetolia, though Miletus, the most powerful Ionian state, was able to maintain relative independence.[7] The others transferred their tribute payments from an independent Lydia to the satrapies that now governed the same region, and the Persians installed subservient tyrannies in their Greek dependencies. Because of military crises elsewhere and chronic power struggles within the Median-Persian aristocracy, Persia's foothold in the Greek world was not im-

---

[6]For a detailed discussion of Aeginetan foreign policy in this period, see M. Amit, *Great and Small Poleis* (Brussels, 1973), pp. 9 ff. He assumes (p. 25) Aegina's membership in the Peloponnesian League.

[7]In general, see Hdt., Books 1, 5, 6, on Persian-Ionian relations.

mediately used as a base for further expansion in the west. But by 520 or shortly thereafter, King Darius I was able to turn his attention to the western frontier. He organized an expedition to subdue the Scythian tribes of Thrace, the first Persian operation in Europe.[8] Although frustrated in his main objective and forced to retreat, Darius extended Persian control over the eastern Greeks to include those along both shores of the Hellespont and Propontis. When Darius' hasty departure from Thrace emboldened some of his recent Greek acquisitions to throw off the Persian yoke, he left his generals Megabazus and later Otanes, son of Sisamnes, behind with a military force in order to consolidate Persian control of the cities along the European and Asian coasts of the route to the Black Sea.[9]

Any illusions the Greeks might have nurtured that the Persians would be content with Asia should have been shattered by the Scythian expedition. Darius' embarrassing withdrawal from the interior of Thrace promised only a temporary respite before the Persian juggernaut continued its relentless expansion into Europe. Most Greeks were not anxious to hasten the day of their own reckoning with the eastern giant, and when one considers the disparity in size, population, and wealth between the Persians and the Greek poleis, it is not difficult to understand why. In the aftermath of the Scythian expedition, many Greek states, especially in the north, closest to the danger, made some accommodation with the Persians, while almost all the rest, including the Megarians, were inclined to let the future take care of itself. Though no one knew at the time, the final reckoning with Persia was not to come for more than a generation. The outcome of that confrontation was to prove that time had worked to the advantage of the Greeks, and it is therefore unwise to be very critical of them for not precipitating an earlier showdown, for who is to say how that might have turned out?

Megara was among the handful of mainland Greek poleis whose interests were directly affected by the Persians' first foray into Europe. Their oldest and most important eastern colonies were drawn into the Persian orbit by the time of the Scythian expedition.

[8]Hdt. 4.143-44.
[9]Hdt. 4.143-44 (Megabazus) and 5.25-27 (Otanes).

Herodotus records that Darius and his army crossed into Europe from Chalcedon,[10] which implies the town's previous submission to Persia. Herodotus also identifies Ariston of Byzantium as one of the Persian-backed tyrants who voted against Miltiades' proposal to abandon Darius to the Scythians.[11] But there is no way to determine whether Ariston had been in power a number of years, or only since Darius' arrival on the European shore of the Propontis. Though not mentioned at this stage of Herodotus' narrative, it is a virtual certainty that nearby Selymbria as well had become subject to Persia. Herodotus names Byzantium and Chalcedon prominently among the states that rebelled from Persia during or after Darius' retreat from Thrace.[12] Otanes captured them around 510, but there is no record of how severely they were punished or what form of government they were given in order to forestall future rebellions.

These developments could not have been matters of indifference to the Megarians, but there is not the slightest hint in Herodotus' narrative that they played any role whatsoever. Though we cannot entirely dismiss the possibility that they lent moral or even material support to their colonists' revolt from Persia, Herodotus' silence makes this doubtful. Nor can we ignore the fact that Megara was not singled out by the Persians as a target for revenge, either now or later. In all likelihood, the Megarians, though distressed by the plight of their relations overseas, made no move to interfere and so call down the wrath of Persia on themselves.

Even so, they could not have avoided completely the practical consequences of war in the Propontis. There must have been at least temporary disruption of Megarian trade in the region while the states that had traditionally welcomed Megarian ships were under siege. But these disruptions were probably of short duration, and Megarian prosperity appears to have continued through this period. The Persians certainly showed no inclination to impede Greek commerce during peacetime.

When Aristagoras of Miletus traveled to Greece in 499 to seek support for the newly begun revolt of the Ionian Greeks, he does not seem to have made any direct appeal to the Megarians, though

[10] 4.85 ff.
[11] 4.138.1.
[12] 5.26.

his unsuccessful efforts to persuade Cleomenes may have been a bid for the support of Sparta's naval allies, Corinth and Megara, as well.[13] Only Athens and Eretria were prepared to be drawn into the Ionian conflict, and even they appear to have withdrawn after a single campaigning season which witnessed the burning of Sardis.[14] Though by 497 the Ionians had been left to their fate by their fellow Greeks, they, or at least their anti-Persian leaders, had little choice but to carry the rebellion forward as energetically as possible. Taking advantage of the considerable time-lag before the Persians could concentrate their land and naval forces on the Aegean coast, the Ionians liberated additional states from Persian control. Herodotus reports that "they sailed to the Hellespont and got control of Byzantium and all the other towns thereabouts," including, no doubt, Chalcedon and Selymbria.[15] There is no suggestion that there was stout resistance to joining the revolt; pro-Persian governments in this region seem to have been as unpopular, and to have fallen as easily, as those in the Ionian cities.

Megara's colonists and trading partners were now committed once more to war with Persia, but there is still no evidence that Megara allowed herself to be drawn into open hostility to Persia. For several years the existence of a state of war along the access route to the Black Sea made little practical difference to commerce. The Phoenician fleet had not yet challenged Greek control of these waters. But shortly before the decisive sea-battle at Lade in 494, traffic to and from the Black Sea was impeded by the activities of Histiaeus of Miletus. He had been a guest *cum* hostage in Darius' court at Susa since the closing years of the sixth century, and, according to Herodotus, he had instigated the Ionian revolt partly to extricate himself from the Great King's clutches. But by the time he made good his escape, his nephew Aristagoras, who had acted as his surrogate in Miletus, was dead, and the Milesians had no wish to readmit their former tyrant.[16] Histiaeus managed, however, to persuade the Mytileneans to accompany him to the Propontis

---

[13]Hdt. 5.38, 49-54.

[14]Hdt. 5.97-103. Though Herodotus does not specifically say that the Eretrians withdrew their support after the burning of Sardis, it is reasonable to assume that they did so, as there is no further mention of their involvement.

[15]5.103.2.

[16]6.1 ff.

with eight warships. They were admitted to Byzantium, which they used as a "base for the seizure of *all ships* bound out from the Black Sea, except those whose crews promised to obey his [Histiaeus'] orders."[17] Herodotus later refers to Histiaeus' policy of "seizing *Ionian* merchantmen outward bound from the Black Sea," which suggests that ships returning to the Greek mainland were not interfered with.[18] There is no certain way to resolve the contradiction between these two passages, but at the very least a new hazard had been added to the voyage from Greece to the Euxine. If Histiaeus needed money, men, ships, and supplies to carry on the war with Persia and to restore his own position in Miletus, he was not one to draw fine distinctions between Ionians and mainlanders.

Worse was to follow. In the spring of 493, having already destroyed the Ionian fleet at Lade, the Persians advanced on the remaining pockets of resistance along the Hellespont and Propontis both by land and sea.[19] Towns along the Asian coast were retaken by the Persian army, while those on the European coast were reduced by the fleet. Selymbria, Byzantium, and Chalcedon, as well as many others, were burned to the ground, but Herodotus says that the Byzantines and Chalcedonians managed to escape before the Persians arrived, settling themselves at Mesambria on the Black Sea.[20] This migration may, in fact, represent the establishment of Mesambria. It is doubtful that the Persians would have allowed so strategic a site as Byzantium to have remained unoccupied for long, but there is no indication that the original inhabitants (or their descendants) returned until around 478, when Pausanias liberated Byzantium from the Persians.[21] (As previously suggested, this circumstance likely gave rise to the story that Pausanias actually founded Byzantium.) Thus for approximately fifteen years the Megarians lost their special relationship with the Propontis, and the course of political development after 478 prevented the com-

---

[17]Hdt. 6.5.3.
[18]6.26.1.
[19]Hdt. 6.31 ff.
[20]6.33.
[21]Thuc. 1.94. See below, Chapter 9. It is not clear whether repopulated Byzantium and Chalcedon contributed to the total of 100 ships from the Hellespontine and Bosporus districts in Xerxes' armada in 480 (Hdt. 7.95.2).

plete restoration of those ties, since Athens rather than Megara was to become the chief protector of Greek interests in this region.

It is not clear whether the Persians took advantage of their renewed control of the Hellespont and Propontis after 493 to cut off trade between the Black Sea states and mainland Greece. As late as 481, however, Xerxes saw Aeginetan grain ships sailing down the Hellespont and, against the advice of his staff, allowed them to continue toward home unmolested. Was this an exceptional act of restraint, an abrogation of the usual practice—or does the presence of these ships in the Hellespont in the very midst of Xerxes' preparations to invade Greece suggest that Greek traders continued to ply these waters throughout the late 490's and the 480's, despite the risks? I suspect that the latter was in fact the case. If, as seems likely, Greek commerce with the Euxine states continued after 493, it is highly probable that the Megarians continued to be active in it.[22]

Megara's apparent passivity in relation to the growing Persian menace is illustrated once more by the events of 490.[23] Though her immediate neighbor, Athens, was threatened with conquest and the installation of a pro-Persian tyranny, the Megarians did nothing.They watched the destruction of Eretria and the invasion of Marathon, and when Sparta sent her army to relieve the Athenians, the best the Megarians could manage was not to get in the way. This was most likely the result of a conviction that resistance to Persia was futile and would serve only to hasten the day of Megara's conquest and the severity of the resulting Persian settlement, though it is possible that some Megarians still believed Persia's assurances of friendly feeling toward the majority of the Greek states were sincere and that their own conquest was far from inevitable. These are the attitudes seemingly reflected in the poem that opens Chapter 6, above: let us enjoy the pleasures of life and hope that war with the Medes never reaches us. If, indeed, the

---

[22]See Hdt. 7.147.2-3 on the Aeginetan ships. *Pace* H. Merle, *Die Geschichte der Städte Byzantion u. Kalchedon* (Kiel, 1916), p. 14, who states confidently that "the seizure of the Bosporus by the Persians closed off all Greek commerce with the Black Sea states, so vital to Greek nourishment," but presents no evidence to substantiate this point. Given the *de facto* state of war between Persia and Athens, the Athenians may, however, have encountered some difficulty or been subject to a ban.
[23]Hdt. 6.94 ff.

poet was Megarian, I suggest for this lyric a date in the late 490's, sometime between the destruction of Byzantium and Chalcedon and the invasion of Attica.

Though Megara can hardly be said to have shown any initiative in the movement to save Greece from Persian conquest up to this time, neither had she reached an accommodation with the Persians at the expense of other Greek states, as others had done or would do in the next few years. And once Darius' successor Xerxes began his massive preparations for the subjection of all Greece, the Megarians lent wholehearted support to the defense of Hellas. They became active participants in the coalition of anti-Persian states which took shape in the late 480's and which came to be known as the Hellenic League. The major organizational meeting took place in 481.[24] It was attended by representatives of a great many poleis, including some who were shortly to go over to the Persians. The membership of the Peloponnesian League formed the core of the new alliance, with Phocis, the Boeotian states who were at odds with Thebes, and, most important of all, Athens constituting the remainder. The allies swore an oath to resist the Persians and to punish any Greek states who voluntarily supported the enemy. They also pledged themselves to put aside internal disputes, a decision that ended the hostilities between Athens and Aegina, though it did not make them friends.

When the league congress met, as in 481 or at the Isthmus in the following year, the members determined policy by majority vote, although commanders in the field seem to have exercised considerable discretionary powers. By general consent, these commanders, both on land and sea, were Spartan. No one could dispute Sparta's right to lead the army, and the naval states, particularly Athens and Aegina, were so jealous of one another that they found Spartan leadership more palatable than one another's. The Athenians, who had built a fleet of unprecedented size in Greece during the previous years, thereby eclipsing all the other naval powers of Greece,[25] certainly deserved the naval command, but they con-

---

[24]Hdt. 7.145-46. See P. A. Brunt, "The Hellenic League against Persia," *Historia,* 2 (1953), 135-63, for a persuasive reconstruction of the Hellenic League's organization and development.
[25]Athens had at least 180 triremes in 480, but only fifty during her war with

tented themselves with influencing the strategy of a Spartan admiral.

The story of Xerxes' expedition is widely known, thanks to Herodotus and a vast modern literature on the subject, and to repeat it here would take us beyond the scope of our inquiry.[26] Attention must focus on Megara's contributions to the war effort, her views on the major strategic decisions of the war, and the impact of this struggle on her material and political fortunes.

Megara aligned herself with Athens and against many of the Peloponnesian states on the issue of where to meet the Persians. Understandably, she favored the defense of northern Greece and later the Saronic Gulf rather than the Isthmian strategy that would have delivered Attica and the Megarid into Persian hands without a fight.[27] Fortunately for both, the Spartans also supported the northern strategy, although this was surely due more to their desire to retain the cooperation of the Athenian fleet than to protect the Megarians.[28] Again, after the Persian fleet had been defeated at Salamis and had sailed home, leaving a streamlined army under the command of Mardonius in northern Greece to carry on the war, the Megarians joined the Athenians in urging the allies to march north to intercept Mardonius in Boeotia, rather than allow him to occupy their land unopposed. The Megarians also joined the Athenians and Plataeans in a direct appeal to Sparta in 479, after Mardonius had occupied Boeotia.[29] They pressed the case for a military stand in Attica, and gained Sparta's consent. The campaign that followed culminated in the decisive engagement at Plataea.

The Megarians' military commitment was commensurate with their diplomatic efforts. Megara sent twenty triremes to take part in

---

Aegina in the 490's (Hdt. 6.89). This represents a fourfold or greater increase in little more than a decade. In comparison, Megara's twenty triremes may have constituted a significant force prior to the late 480's, but had diminished in importance as a result of Athens' unprecedented buildup.

[26] A good starting point is C. Hignett, *Xerxes' Invasion of Greece*, Oxford, 1963.

[27] Hdt. 8.49 ff., esp. 8.74.

[28] Hdt. 8.63.

[29] Hdt. 9.7 ff. Hignett, pp. 282 ff., regards as improbable the details of this story, but the idea that Megara joined Athens in a move to bolster Spartan resolve to fight north of the Isthmus is not at all unlikely. A. R. Burn, *Persia and the Greeks* (London, 1962), pp. 503-07, accepts the embassy as authentic.

the Greeks' first naval operation at Artemisium, and the same number to Salamis.[30] The only larger fleets at Artemisium were the Athenian (127 triremes plus another twenty manned by the Chalcidians) and the Corinthian (forty triremes). Even Aegina was represented by only eighteen triremes. At Salamis, the Aeginetans increased their contribution to thirty triremes, with reserves being held back, and Chalcis is listed as providing twenty ships, though these may be the ones lent earlier by the Athenians.[31] Additionally, the Athenians had rasied their own fleet to 180, and many of the smaller contingents had been modestly augmented. These figures suggest two things: First, that Megara's twenty triremes must have comprised her entire navy, since she was unable to expand her fleet at Salamis when nearly every other state did. Second, that a fleet of this size made her the fourth ranking sea power among the states of central and southern Greece. This last observation, however, should not impress us unduly. By 480 the Athenian fleet overshadowed Megara by a factor of ten, the Corinthians and Aeginetans outstripped her 2:1, and a host of states we scarcely think of as naval were able to put a respectable number of ships into the water—for example, Sparta (sixteen) and Sicyon (fifteen). The only hint that the Megarians were regarded as a significant naval power at the time comes not from our main narrative source, Herodotus, but from Ephorus, the fourth century historian, by way of Diodorus. He contradicts Herodotus by placing the Aeginetans and Megarians on the right wing at Salamis:

> These were judged to be the most outstanding sailors after the Athenians and the most desirous to acquit themselves honorably, since they alone among the Greek allies had nowhere to flee if the naval engagement ended in defeat.[32]

This favorable comment on Megarian naval skill may be accepted, even if we are inclined to follow Herodotus in placing the Athenian fleet on the right.[33] In 479, when the Greeks sent their fleet across

---

[30]Hdt. 8.1. No Megarian troops are mentioned as having taken part in the land and sea operations at Thermopylae and Artimesium.

[31]Hdt. 8.45.

[32]11.18.

[33]8.85.

the Aegean to harass the Persians and liberate the eastern Greeks from Persian control, a Megarian contingent of undetermined size took part. The conclusive evidence on this point comes from the inscription on a monument raised to honor Megara's war dead.[34] (Neither Thucydides nor Diodorus mention the Megarians by name as participants at the battle of Mycale, although they note Peloponnesian contributions of twenty and fifty ships respectively.)[35] Megara's interest in restoring Greek control of the entire Aegean and, particularly, of the access route to the Black Sea needs no explanation.

The Megarians made a substantial contribution to the land war as well, turning out 3,000 hoplites for the decisive Plataea campaign.[36] This figure compares with 8,000 for Athens, 5,000 for Corinth, 3,000 for Sicyon, and 500 for Aegina, in an army that included nearly 39,000 hoplites. Some historians have doubted that Megara could have supplied nearly 8 percent of the Greek army.[37] It is possible that the figure is partly distorted by Herodotus' obvious rounding off of all figures (upward in this case?) and may include marines stationed with the Megarian fleet at Mycale. But I believe that the total of 3,000 is not a significant exaggeration of Megarian strength at the beginning of the fifth century. There is no better ground for rejecting it than to doubt Herodotus' entire numerical scheme, which seems far more reliable in calculating the strength of the Greeks than that of their enemies.

Herodotus' military statistics for the Persian Wars give us a rare opportunity to estimate Megarian population, if we assume that these figures represent total mobilization at the height of the conflict. With 200 men per trireme, the Megarian fleet carried 4,000 sailors, and Megara fielded 3,000 hoplites in addition, yielding a total of 7,000 men under arms. It is possible that Herodotus' figure of 3,000 represents Megara's total hoplite strength, including the marines, who would have been men of hoplite status, though sailing with the fleet. Because in this period it was typical to have

---

[34]M. N. Tod, *GHI*, Vol. 1, 20, which is discussed below.
[35]Thuc. 1.94.1; Diod. 11.44.2.
[36]Hdt. 9.28, 31.
[37]See, e.g., Meyer, "Megara," col. 188, and H. Munro, "The Campaign of Plataea," *JHS*, 24 (1904), 152. Munro regards Herodotus' figures as total manpower estimates.

30 marines per trireme, the error could amount to 600 men, and 6,400 may be closer to Megara's actual military manpower. Taking these figures, between 6,400 and 7,000, to approximate Megara's male citizenry between the ages of roughly 20 to 55 or 60, the total population except for slaves should be about four times greater, 25,000 to 28,000. In the early fourth century, Xenophon describes the slave population as quite large,[38] but there is no basis for estimating its size a hundred years earlier. A rough approximation of Megara's total population around 480 can be put in the range of 30,000 to 40,000.

The Megarid was untouched during the 480 campaign, though the Persians could have swept over it after the Greek retreat from Thermopylae had they chosen to do so. After their defeat at Salamis, however, invasion of the Megarid became too risky. In the following year, when Mardonius marched south, he continued the devastation of Attica until he received word that the Peloponnesians were marching north. The Persian general decided to make his stand in the Boeotian plain, near friendly Thebes, after briefly considering the deployment of his forces in Megarian territory:

> When he had already set out [for Thebes], he received intelligence that an advance force of 1,000 Lacedaemonians had reached Megara. When he learned this, he hoped it might be possible to overcome these troops, and, turning his army around, he marched against Megara, while his cavalry raced ahead and overran the Megarian countryside. This was the furthest west that the Persian army ever reached. Meanwhile, news reached Mardonius that the main Greek force was at the Isthmus. He therefore retreated by way of Decelea.[39]

Thus the main body of Mardonius' army probably never set foot on Megarian soil, since they would most likely have taken the Road of the Towers into the Boeotian plain, had they begun their retreat from inside the Megarid. But the Persian cavalry raiders must have done some damage.

Most historians doubt the interpretation that Herodotus places on this brief episode.[40] It is unlikely that Mardonius would have

[38]Xen. Mem. 2.7.6. Cf. Plut. Demetr. 9. This evidence is discussed below in Chapter 11.

[39]Hdt. 9.14-15.1.

[40]See, e.g., Hignett, pp. 291 ff., for a full discussion of this episode and various modern interpretations.

thought he could destroy the 1,000 Spartan troops in the vicinity of Megara. Surely they could have retired inside the city walls and held out until the main force arrived; it would have been foolhardy for Mardonius to pin his troops down in front of Megara, in terrain ill suited to his purposes. Still, it is barely possible that he thought a lightning cavalry raid would catch the Spartans off guard. Other, more promising, suggestions include the possibility that this was merely a reconnaissance maneuver which Herodotus has blown out of proportion, or that the Persian cavalry was being sent to harass and delay the Greek advance, giving Mardonius additional time to prepare his army in Boeotia.

Pausanias reports a local tradition that appears to deal with the fate of the Persian horse in the Megarid, though the troops in question are not specifically called cavalry. The story is as follows:

> They say that men from Mardonius' army, having raided the Megarid, afterward wished to return to Mardonius at Thebes, but, by the contrivance of Artemis, night descended on them while they were en route, and, missing the road, they veered into the mountainous part of the country. Trying to determine whether a hostile force was in the vicinity, they let fly some arrows, and when these struck a nearby rock, it moaned, whereupon they renewed their barrage more vigorously. In the end, they exhausted their supply of arrows shooting at imaginary enemies. When day began to break, the Megarians attacked them, and their hoplites, fighting against men without either armour or missiles, slaughtered most of them. In memory of this [victory], they made a statue of Artemis the Saviour.[41]

Pausanias elsewhere records the location of the rock at which the Persians are alleged to have fired their arrows:

> A short distance off the highway leading to Pagae, a rock is shown completely studded with arrows, it was this rock at which the Medes shot in the night.[42]

Some skepticism of the exotic elements of this tale may be forgiven: the curious arrow-covered rock shown to Pausanias was more than

[41] 1.40.2-3.
[42] 1.44.4.

169

likely a battlefield trophy.[43] But that the Megarians inflicted a defeat on some Persian cavalry as the latter attempted to find their way into Boeotia is believable. The site of the trophy, above Pagae, suggests that the Persians were trying to make their way to the Road of the Towers, or along the northern coast toward Aegosthena and beyond. The Persian foray into the Megarid was probably too brief to have caused extensive damage. Still, Megara had had direct experience of the Persians, and the incident was to be noted in local tradition.

Herodotus records Megarian involvement in several phases of the Plataea campaign that followed. First, the Megarian contingent was subjected to an assault by the Persian cavalry shortly after Pausanias led the allies through the Cithaeron passes into Boeotia.

> It chanced that Megarians were stationed in the most exposed part of the battlefield. Vulnerable to cavalry as a consequence, they were attacked by the enemy horse. The Megarians were hard pressed and sent a messenger to the commanders of the Hellenic army. When he reached them, the herald delivered this message from the Megarians: "Allies, we are unable to hold back the Persian cavalry by ourselves, or to maintain our original position on the battlefield. So far we have held our ground through perseverance and courage, hard pressed though we be. But now, unless you send others to relieve us, we shall have to abandon our position." When he [the herald] had delivered this message, Pausanias [the commander-in-chief] asked if there were any among the Hellenes who would volunteer to go to that quarter of the battlefield and relieve the Megarians. But when none of the others were willing, the Athenians undertook the mission with 300 picked men. . . . and they took the archers too.[44]

When the Athenians succeeded in killing the Persian cavalry commander, Masistius, a general melee ensued in which the Greeks eventually gained the upper hand.[45] The Megarians were saved. It may have been only coincidence that placed the Megarians in a more exposed position than the other Greek troops, as Herodotus

[43]Frazer gives a different explanation of this passage: "there rises on the south side of the road [between Megara and Pagae, near Tripodiscus] a height now called Karydi ('walnut-tree'), in the rocky summit of which there are many holes. These holes in the rock probably gave rise to the fable which Pausanias here relates." Cf. Bursian, *Geogr.* 1, p. 381. But where were the arrows?
[44]9.21-22.1.
[45]Hdt. 9.22-25.

says, but perhaps the Persian cavalry were seeking revenge for the recent slaughter of their comrades in the Megarid.

A generation later, in the 450's and early 440's, when Athens and Megara were allied against the Peloponnesian League, Herodotus' largely Athenian audience might have warmed to the story that of all the Greek allies, only their forebears were willing to come to the Megarians' rescue that day. In fact, many historians detect a strong pro-Athenian bias in these chapters of Herodotus' narrative and doubt whether the Athenians actually volunteered or the other Greeks refused. It has been suggested that the presence of archers in the Athenian ranks made them better able to deal with a cavalry charge, and that Pausanias ordered their intervention.[46] This may be true, but it would not be surprising if the Athenians were more eager than others to assist the Megarians. As we have noted already, their vital interests coincided closely during the period of the Persian invasion, and they had more to lose than virtually anyone else if the Greeks failed to drive Mardonius from central Greece. Perhaps Pausanias' decision to assign the Megarians a place on the left wing, next to the Athenians and Plataeans, also reflects their mutual support during this crisis.

In the event, Pausanias was unable to draw his troops up in their assigned places for the decisive engagement. It took place while he was in the process of executing a tactical retreat from the southern bank of the Asopus River to the Cithaeron foothills, where the Persian and Boeotian cavalry would be ineffective.[47] The Spartans, Tegeans, and Athenians—the forces on the right and left flanks respectively—were the last to withdraw, and the only ones to be caught by the pursuing Persian forces.[48] The rest of the Greeks became aware that the battle had begun only when it was already under way and the Greeks had gained the advantage:

> When they learned what was taking place, they rushed forward in disorder, and those in the Corinthians' quarter set off across the

[46]Hignett, p. 300. W. W. How and J. Wells, *A Commentary on Herodotus* (Oxford, 1912), Vol. 2, p. 294, reasonably suggest that the Athenians may have been under obligation to come to the aid of those next to them in the Greek line—i.e., the Megarians. Hignett doubts this.
[47]Hdt. 9.51 ff.
[48]Hdt. 9.59-61.

foothills (of Cithaeron) . . . while those in the Megarian and Phliasian quarter took the level road through the plain. When the Megarians and Phliasians came near the enemy, the Theban cavalry, seeing them advancing in complete disorder, charged against them. . . . Falling upon them, they (the Thebans) killed 600 of them and chased the rest of them up Mt. Cithaeron. This is the last that was heard of them.[49]

From this description, it appears that the left-center contingents were hurrying to the sector of the battlefield where the Athenians were facing the Boeotian hoplites. The Theban cavalry intercepted the reinforcements before they could reach the Athenian lines and cut them to pieces. Perhaps, as some historians suggest, the Theban cavalry's preoccupation with these easy targets diverted it from its primary role in support of the Boeotian infantry, thereby enabling the Athenians to complete their rout of the enemy.[50] But if the Megarians, Phliasians, and others had played some part in the overall Greek victory, they had paid a very heavy price. Megarian casualties alone out of the 600 dead may well have exceeded 250, since the Megarian hoplites accounted for more than 40 percent of all left-center troops. Compare this figure with Sparta's losses of ninety-one men, Athens' of fifty-two, and Tegea's of sixteen.[51] Megara and Phlius had suffered devastating blows in relation to their population bases. Each of the states which had lost a significant number of men at Plataea dug a mass grave for its dead on the battlefield, except that the Megarians and Phliasians buried their dead in one grave.[52] Their tomb must have been the largest by far.

Megara's contribution to the war effort was duly credited on the Serpent Column later erected at Delphi.[53] At home, the Megarians

[49]Hdt. 9.69.

[50]Modern commentators are fairly unanimous in judging the charge of the left-center troops as a major contribution to the Greek victory at Plataea. See, e.g., Hignett, pp. 338-39; Burn, *Persia and the Greeks*, pp. 537-38; and W. J. Woodhouse, "The Greeks at Plataiai," *JHS*, 18 (1898), 51.

[51]Hdt. 9.70.3.

[52]Hdt. 9.85.

[53]Meiggs and Lewis, *GHI* 27. Cf. Hdt. 9.81; Thuc. 1.132.2-3; Paus. 5.23.1-3; Plut. *Them.* 20.3. Plutarch (*Arist.* 20.1-2) records another tradition regarding the aftermath of the Greek victory at Plataea: "When the battle was over, the Athenians were not willing to concede the prize of valor to the Spartans, nor permit them to erect a trophy. Then the cause of Greece might have been completely lost in a clash of arms, if Aristides (of Athens) had not persuaded the other generals with copious pleas and admonitions to submit the issue to the Hellenic League. When the Hellen-

raised a monument of their own. Though it was unusual to inter the dead inside the city walls of a Greek polis, the Megarians built a tomb for their Persian War dead (apart from those who fell before the Theban cavalry at Plataea) in the town, crowned it with a cenotaph bearing an epitaph by Simonides, and made annual sacrifices to these latter-day heroes. Pausanias saw this monument when he visited Megara six hundred years later,[54] and a late-Roman period copy of the epitaph shows that the memory of these heroes was kept alive for centuries more.[55] The inscription on the re-erected cenotaph is worth quoting in full:

> The epigram of those who died in the Persian War and are buried here as heroes, being lost in the course of time, the chief priest, Helladios has caused to be inscribed in honor of the dead and of the polis. Simonides wrote it.
>
> To sustain the freedom of Hellas and Megara we willingly accepted death as our fate, some under Euboea and Pelion, where stands the precinct of the chaste archeress, Artemis, some at Mt. Mycale, some before Salamis . . . [one line missing][56] some on the plain of Boeotia, who dared to fight against men on horseback. Our fellow citizens accord us the privilege (of burial) around the center of the busy agora of the Nisaeans.
>
> Down to our own day, the polis sacrifices a bull (to their memory).

ic council assembled, Theogeiton the Megarian proposed that the prize of valor be granted to another polis, unless they wanted to stir up internecine war. Then Cleocritus the Corinthian rose . . . and, to the delight and surprise of everyone, spoke in favor of the Plataeans . . ." The story concludes with the Spartans and Athenians accepting this compromise.

This tradition may be a confused version of the allies' charge to the Plataeans to maintain the memorials of the battle in their territory (Thuc. 5.58-59), but there may be some truth in a story that preserves the identities of so many participants. The gist of Theogeiton's role is at least consistent with the Megarians' policy during this crucial phase of the Persian Wars, i.e., a policy of conciliation with the various members of the Hellenic League in the interests of presenting a united front to the Persians.

[54]1.43.3.

[55]M. N. Tod, *A Selection of Greek Historical Inscriptions to the End of the Fifth Century B.C.*, 2d ed. (Oxford, 1946), no. 20, which was found in Palaeochori, in the northeastern Megarid.

[56]Could this have been a reference to the cavalry clash near Pagae (Paus. 1.40.2-3)?

CHAPTER 8

Between Two Hegemonies

The Megarians attached themselves to the Athenians as allies, having broken with the Lacedaemonians because they (the Megarians) were being hard pressed by the Corinthians in a border war. As a result, the Athenians gained possession of Megara and Pagae and built long-walls for the Megarians from the city to Nisaea which they themselves garrisoned.

—Thucydides 1.103.4

THE EXPANSION of the Athenian navy in the years immediately preceding the Persian War and during the war itself altered the balance of power in Greece. The implications of this development for Greek politics were partially obscured during the period of Xerxes' invasion by Athens' willingness to accept Spartan leadership as the price for Peloponnesian support in her struggle to survive. But with the victories at Salamis and Plataea and the return of peace in mainland Greece, Athens was inclined to regard herself as Sparta's equal—as dominant on the seas as Sparta was on land. Given the narrow loyalties of polis-oriented Greeks, competition rather than cooperation was the natural relationship between Athens and Sparta when there was no longer an external threat to drive them together. It took several decades for the effects of wartime camaraderie to wear off completely, and there were always some political leaders in the rival states who sought to maintain friendly relations, but their efforts did not prevent the steady polarization of the Greek world around its two most powerful states. The result was a succession of debilitating wars in which Greece as a whole, at the height of its cultural and political powers, was the loser.

Megara occupied a particularly exposed and uncomfortable position in this struggle, since her geographic situation made her territory the border zone between the two power blocs, and control of her roads and ports was of vital concern to both sides. Megarian history during this period provides an interesting counterpoint to the story of relations between the great powers, for while Spartan and Athenian strategists saw Megara as little more than a pawn in their contest for dominance in Greece, the Megarians were simultaneously engaged in the pursuit of their own vital interests, which never entirely meshed with those of either power. At several critical stages in the larger struggle, Megarian policy played a decisive part in the course of events. Thus investigation from the Megarian perspective can make a significant contribution to our understanding of the complexity of inter-state relations in this period.

The Megarid had not been extensively wasted during the Persian invasion, but the Megarians had suffered a great many casualties. Their losses, as indicated in the previous chapter, may well have totaled five or six hundred—that is, as much as 10 percent of the free male citizenry. Few other states, if any, had sustained losses proportionately as great as Megara's decimation. Under the circusmtances, Megarians must have welcomed the return of peace and the opportunity to regain their lost strength. The immediate prospects were encouraging. Megara probably felt as secure from attack as at any time in her history. Her hegemon, Sparta, was at the height of her prestige and could be expected to keep any of Megara's potential enemies in check. This was especially important in terms of her relations with Corinth, who, as we shall see, coveted more Megarian territory than she had already taken. The Spartan shield was, for the time being, less essential on Megara's eastern borders. Athens was well disposed toward the Megarians as a result of their support for the Athenian naval strategy during the period of Xerxes' invasion, and the Boeotians were in disgrace and disarray after their disastrous pro-Persian stance in the war. It would be decades before they would pose a threat to anyone.

The only cloud on the horizon was Persia's continuing presence in the eastern Aegean and the lands flanking the route to the Black Sea. For two reasons this was particularly troubling to Megara. First, it meant that most of her colonies were still in Persian hands. As suggested earlier, the majority of Byzantines and Chalcedonians may have been living in exile at Mesambria since the 490's.[1] Though her colonies had been independent of her in every sense, the Megarians had maintained friendly relations with them and must have been distressed at their plight. A second concern, somewhat related to the first, was about prospects for the revival of Megarian commerce, which I believe was customarily channeled through her colonies, and which was in a state of suspense as long as hostilities continued in the northeast. For these reasons, I suspect that Megara was more willing than most Peloponnesian states to see the war carried into the eastern Aegean and beyond. At the conference on Samos in 479, after the Greek victory at Mycale, the Peloponnesians initially opposed the admission of the Ionian states into the Hellenic League and the corresponding obligation to defend their interests.[2] They proposed instead that the Ionians be removed to Greece, where the lands of the Medizers would be turned over to them. In Herodotus' compressed account of this conference, the attitudes of individual Peloponnesian states are not differentiated, and reversal of the initial response to the Ionians is attributed largely to Athens' strong protest. This, however, is unlikely. Sparta and *some* of her Peloponnesian allies must have been more inclined than others toward the liberation of the eastern Greeks. There is no state more likely than Megara to have stood against the majority Peloponnesian sentiment and in favor of driving the Persians out of the Aegean altogether.

While the Megarians apparently sailed home at the end of the summer of 479 along with the other Peloponnesian contingents, leaving the Athenians and the eastern states already liberated to conduct the siege of Sestos during the winter of 479/8,[3] they must have contributed to the modest-sized fleet which sailed east in the following spring under the command of the Spartan regent Pausanias.[4] Thucydides numbers this Peloponnesian squadron at only twenty ships, with the Athenians contributing another thirty, with some additional support from the eastern states. The numbers seem small compared to the forces assembled at Salamis, but

[1]See above, Chapter 7.
[2]Hdt. 9.106.
[3]Hdt. 9.114 ff.; Thuc. 1.89.1-2.
[4]Thuc. 1.94.1.

there is no basis for preferring Diodorus' figure of fifty Peloponnesian triremes.[5] The Greeks were evidently aware that the main Persian fleet had pulled back to Phoenicia and that they were unlikely to encounter stiff naval opposition. This, indeed, proved to be the case, even when the Greeks were so bold as to invade Cyprus, dangerously close to the Phoenicians' home ports.[6] The size of Megara's contribution to the fleet of 478 can only be guessed. If her contingent was proportionate to her forces at Salamis, she may have sent as few as three triremes, but it is possible that Peloponnesian states not deeply committed to the war in the east sent little or no support. In that case, the Megarians may have sent as many as five or six triremes—perhaps a thousand men—but probably no more. Even this level of involvement would have represented a major effort in light of her losses in the previous two years.

After the successful assault on Cyprus, Pausanias' fleet turned its attention to the Propontis and Bosporus, the Persians having already been forced back from the Hellespont.[7] The objective of clearing the passage to the Black Sea was of importance to many states, but as we have noted, Megarian interest was as keen as any. The first target was Byzantium, where the Persian garrison soon surrendered. Given Byzantium's key position, it is likely that the other Greek settlements in the Bosporus and eastern Propontis fell shortly thereafter, though our sources make no specific mention of when and under what circumstances these were freed from Persian control. Refugees at Mesambria may have returned to their homes at this time.

Despite the success of the expedition, relations within the Greek fleet were far from harmonious. Major responsibility for this state of affairs is assigned by our sources to the behavior of Pausanias, and there is no doubt that his conduct was at least a contributing factor.[8] But the rapidity with which Athens and her Ionian friends capitalized on Pausanias' disgrace to take charge of the war suggests that his crimes may well have been exaggerated in order to

[5]Thuc. 1.94.1; Diod. 11.44.
[6]Thuc. 1.94.2.
[7]Ibid.
[8]Thuc. 1.95, 128-34; Diod. 11.44-47.

177

establish a pretext for challenging Spartan leadership. He was accused of acting more like an eastern potentate than a Greek general and of being especially harsh toward the Ionian forces under his command. At Byzantium he had placed Gongylus of Eretria (a personal adherent?) in charge and had instructed him to return valuable Persian captives without ransom or conditions.[9] It was further alleged that Pausanias' friendly gesture toward the Persians was part of a larger plot. Gongylus was supposed to have delivered a letter to Xerxes in which Pausanias offered to betray Greece in exchange for the hand of the king's daughter in marriage. When these charges reached Sparta, Pausanias was ordered to return home. He probably took the Peloponnesian fleet with him, since the Spartans sent no substitute commander at the time they recalled Pausanias. Only after he had stood trial and been convicted of minor offenses (though acquitted of the more serious allegation of treason) did the Spartans send out another admiral, Dorcis, together with a small fleet, probably to replace the vessels withdrawn earlier.[10] But during the hiatus between Pausanias' departure and Dorcis' return, the Athenians and their supporters had begun to shape a new alliance. When Dorcis arrived, the allies refused to recognize him as commander-in-chief. He therefore sailed home, no doubt taking with him the Megarians and any other Peloponnesian ships in the Propontis.

The new Athens-centered alliance, which we know as the Delian League, was able to take shape without further involvement or interference by Sparta and the other Peloponnesians.[11] Ostensibly, the new organization was not a threat to other Greeks. Its stated purpose was to punish the Persians for their attack on Greece, a pledge which in practice meant the continuation of the war in the east, liberating Greek states still under Persian control, looting Persian territory, and, in general, keeping the enemy on the defensive. This policy effectively precluded a renewal of Persian efforts

[9]Thuc. 1.128. It is striking that Pausanias did *not* appoint a Megarian to govern Byzantium, as was done by the Spartans in 412 (see below, Chapter 10). The practice of employing a citizen of the founding state in this capacity was probably not uncommon.

[10]Thuc. 1.95.3-6.

[11]The most recent and authoritative study of the Delian League is R. Meiggs, *The Athenian Empire* (Oxford, 1972).

to control the Aegean, thereby serving the interests of Greece as a whole and of those who remained outside the new league, as well as those who joined. Even Sparta seems to have raised no protest to the rebuff she had suffered at the hands of the fledgling alliance.[12] Few Peloponnesians, after all, had their hearts in this expanded war, and probably none foresaw how successful and powerful the Delian League would become in a few short years. Only gradually were they persuaded that the league posed a serious danger to the prosperity and independence of nonmembers, or that it might ultimately undermine the whole of Sparta's land-based hegemony.

These dangers were especially acute for Megara. Her colonies, through whom she seems to have conducted a profitable trade with the Black Sea, were now members of a league which was led by the fastest growing commercial power in the Aegean, and to which Megara herself did not belong. While the 470's must have seen the resumption of Megarian trade and other contacts with Byzantium, Chalcedon, and the rest of her colonial connections, these states now looked to Athens and the Delian League for support, protection, and patronage. The bond between them and Megara was certain to weaken. Given Megara's impotence in the face of Persian expansion in the northeast during the sixth century and her small size and limited manpower relative to other Aegean states, this trend was probably inevitable, with or without the creation of the Delian League. But the assimilation of her colonies by the Delian League must have accelerated the process. In the long run, Megara might have had to face the question whether her commerce could survive without her own political realignment, but in the 470's and for some time thereafter this developing problem may not have been clearly perceived. Athens was several stages away from using her naval hegemony to restrict free trade, and Megara does not seem to have been tempted to exchange the security her attachment to Sparta provided for a greater role in the Aegean under Athenian hegemony.

The Delian League grew rapidly during its early years, as the

---

[12]Diodorus (11.50) contradicts the tenor of Thucydides' account somewhat by reporting that the Spartans in fact considered but ultimately rejected the idea of challenging Athens' assumption of naval hegemony.

allies forced Persia to release her grip on the coasts of Anatolia. Before long, the league boasted of several hundred members, most of them quite small, and an annual tribute on the order of 460 talents, which, in effect, swelled Athens' war chest and enabled her to continue expansion of her naval forces. Within a few years of its inception, the Persians seemed to many Aegean states only a distant threat, and Athens had to face the first of the attempts at secession which were to plague the league.[13] These revolts usually involved larger and therefore bolder member states whose political, economic, and, sometimes, ethnic makeup were in conflict with the hegemonal state. The result was always the same: The revolts were suppressed and Athens' grip on the league tightened still more. Compliant democratic regimes that were superficially modeled on that of Athens steadily displaced oligarchies, and open opposition to Athenian policy initiatives was repressed.

Sparta and the other Peloponnesian states may have been distressed at these developments, but I doubt that they would have done anything about the situation for some time to come had not Athens attempted to extend her hegemony to the mainland, thereby challenging the Peloponnesian League directly. Thucydides reports that when Thasos revolted from the league in about 465, Sparta was prepared to attack Athens in response to the Thasians' appeal for aid, though a domestic crisis is supposed to have prevented her from honoring this pledge.[14] The story may be true, but it is hard to reconcile with Sparta's request for Athenian assistance in putting down a helot rebellion during the same period.[15] The year in which this insurrection began is in dispute,[16] but for our purposes it is sufficient to point out that the request for Athenian help postdates an earthquake in Laconia in 464, which caused numerous Spartan fatalities, threw Spartan affairs into chaos, and either sparked or aggravated the helot rebellion. Perhaps the story of Sparta's promise to Thasos was only a later attempt to excuse Spartan acquiescence during the early stages of Athens' policy of repression within the Delian League.

[13]Thuc. 1.98.
[14]1.101.
[15]Thuc. 1.101-02; Diod. 11.64; Plut. *Kim.* 16; and others.
[16]For a recent review of the evidence and various modern opinions, see P. Deane, *Thucydides' Dates, 465-431 B.C.* (Ontario, 1972), pp. 16-30, 99-106.

Ironically, the onset of hostilities between Athens and the Peloponnesians was triggered by a chain of events which followed Athens' favorable response to the Spartans' appeal for aid against the helots. Sparta had taken the extreme step for so xenophobic a state of calling for assistance not merely from her close allies, but from states as tenuously tied to her as Athens—still technically a member of the Hellenic League. Thucydides says that the helots had established themselves on Mt. Ithome in Messenia, and that the Athenians were noted for their skill in the type of siege warfare tactics which were needed to dislodge the rebels.[17] But whatever the practical and diplomatic basis of the request, it is some measure of Sparta's desperation that she felt compelled to appeal to a state whose policies she deplored. In fact, there may well have been several calls for Athenian aid, since it appears that the Athenians sent two expeditions into the Peloponnese in the later 460's.[18]

We cannot date the first Athenian expedition with any precision, but it must have occurred between 464 and 462. Kimon, the conservative, pro-Spartan general, whose prestige was responsible for Athens' assent to the Spartan request, led an army of 4,000 Athenian hoplites, according to Plutarch. This expedition is of interest to us in the context of Megarian history because it provides our earliest reference to a fresh outbreak of border violence between Megara and Corinth. Plutarch reports that when Kimon, on his way home, was passing through Corinthian territory (which was as impossible to avoid as to skirt the Megarid), the Corinthians complained that he had not asked permission to do so. His sharp reply was:

> You Corinthians . . . didn't so much as knock at the gates of Cleonae or Megara, but simply burst them open and entered by force of arms, believing that every place should be open to those possessing greater power.[19]

The implication of this statement, that both Megara and Cleonae had been stormed by the Corinthians, surely goes too far. Perhaps

[17]1.102.2.
[18]This, at least, is the implication of Plutarch's account (*Kim.* 17), accepted by Gomme, *HCT* 1, p. 301. Cf. Diod. 11.64.
[19]*Kim.* 17.1.

the tiny town of Cleonae on the border between Corinthia and Argolis had actually been overrun by the Corinthians, but it is difficult to conceive that so striking an event as the breaching of Megara's walls could have left no trace in Thucydides. Perhaps Kimon's remark, genuine or apocryphal, maliciously confounds Corinth's rough handling of Megara in the 460's with the more extreme fate of Cleonae; alternatively the reference to "gates" could be nothing more than a rhetorical exaggeration meant to connote some form of intrusion into the territory of another state.

At all events, Kimon's alleged rebuke and the challenge that prompted it suggest that relations between Athens and Corinth had seriously deteriorated by the later 460's. This is hardly surprising in the light of what we have already said regarding mounting Peloponnesian resentment toward Athens over her Delian League policies. Corinthian interest in this issue was undoubtedly affected by membership in the league of Potidaea, her lone Aegean colony. But at least a modicum of antipathy between Athens and Corinth can be traced to the period of Xerxes' invasion, when the Corinthians showed themselves extremely reluctant to defend Attica. Based on the Persian War experience, Athens' sympathy in any quarrel between Corinth and Megara was likely to favor the latter. The sequel shows that this dispute was seized upon primarily by anti-Spartan elements in Athens, which saw it as a means of launching a challenge to Spartan hegemony in Greece, but it is not impossible that, as Plutarch's story implies, even pro-Spartans like Kimon expressed support for Megara at an earlier stage. The Corinthians had evidently revived their ancient border dispute with Megara at a time when Sparta was preoccupied with a revolt of the helots and therefore was unable to fulfill her traditional responsibility as hegemon to mediate quarrels among her allies. This can hardly have been accidental. Corinth had chosen her opportunity carefully, hoping to have her way with the smaller state without hegemonal interference. Her action could have been seen as a challenge to Spartan authority as much as an attack on Megara. In all likelihood, the Megarians had appealed to Sparta in vain when the quarrel first broke out, and even Athenians who had no wish to anger Sparta might have felt justified in opposing the Corinthians in some fashion, acting as Sparta's surrogate.

The helots at Ithome were still holding out in 462, when Kimon was returned to the Peloponnese with another Athenian army.[20] This time he seems to have passed through the Isthmus without incident. None, at any rate, is recorded. On his arrival in Messenia, however, the Athenians, alone of all the contingents, were asked by the Spartans to leave.[21] This rebuff was a crushing blow to Kimon's pro-Spartan policy and to his personal career. He soon fell victim to ostracism, and his radical democratic opponents embarked on a foreign policy that was openly hostile to Spartan interests. One of the first steps they took was to conclude a bilateral treaty with Megara, who simultaneously severed her ties with the Peloponnesian League.[22]

The immediate purpose of the alliance from the Megarian standpoint was to discourage Corinth from pressing her military advantage in the border war. (The situation is strikingly analogous to Corcyra's aim in seeking an alliance with Athens in the 430's.[23] In both cases Corinth was the *bête noire*, frightening the weaker state into Athens' arms.) It has sometimes been suggested that democratic sympathies in Megara, or even the advent of a democratic regime, drew Megara to Athens at this time, since it would have been awkward, and potentially destabilizing, for an oligarchic Megara to abandon the supportive climate of the Peloponnesian League.[24] But there is virtually no evidence for Megara's internal politics in this period, and the suggestion remains pure speculation. I regard it as extremely doubtful. Megara's military predicament and Sparta's unwillingness or incapacity to intervene were not merely the most pressing issues in the Megarian decision, but seem entirely sufficient to justify it. Contamination by the Athenian political system

[20]If Plutarch is in error, this may have been the only Athenian expedition to aid in the suppression of the helot revolt, which, in turn, would push the likely date of the outbreak of hostilities between Megara and Corinth down a year or two from the date I have proposed.

[21]Thucydides (1.102.3) cites the Spartans' fear of Athenian daring and unconventionality and suspicion of their secret sympathy with the helots as the basis for the rebuff. Perhaps Athens' treatment of the Thasians and her Delian League policies in general were also contributing factors.

[22]Thuc. 1.103.4; Diod. 11.79.1-2.

[23]Thuc. 1.14-44, esp. 28.3 and 31-32.

[24]See, e.g., L. Whibley, *Greek Oligarchies* (London, 1896), p. 84, n. 2. Highbarger, *Megara*, p. 160 n., is more cautious: "democrats were influential in making this alliance with Athens."

could easily have been judged an acceptable risk by Megarian oligarchs under these circumstances. The Athenians, doubtless, were only too willing to give the Megarian regime whatever assurances of nonintervention in the domestic affairs of Megara were necessary in order to seal the agreement. If further reasons for Megara's liaison with Athens need be sought, they are more likely to be found in the realm of naval affairs and commerce, where the Megarians might have seen advantages in tying themselves to the dominant Aegean power, thereby benefiting their commerce and colonial connections. But direct evidence of these concerns also is lacking.

From the standpoint of Athenian policy, the treaty with Megara is part of the aggressive pattern that rapidly took shape after Kimon's disgrace and the rise of Ephialtes and Pericles in the late 460's. Under the radicals, Athens began to forge a mainland coalition with the obvious aim of taking over the leadership of Greece. The moment was opportune. The Thasian revolt had been suppressed, and the Delian League was once more secure. Sparta was preoccupied with a bitter struggle against the helots and was in no position to respond to Athenian provocations on the perimeter of her sphere of influence. Also the mood of the Athenian populace was right. The common people were caught up in the euphoria of their now unrestrained control of policy. In a matter of months, the Athenians were to conclude alliances with Argos and Thessaly and seize upon the opportunity to detach Megara from the Peloponnesian League.[25] Soon, they would commit themselves to many more ventures, including assistance in Egypt's revolt from the Persians.[26]

The connection with Megara significantly improved Athens' strategic position in the contemplated struggle with the Peloponnesian states. Pagae was less than two days' march from Athens through friendly territory, thus providing Athens with a naval base on the Corinthian Gulf which could be maintained without stationing thousands of men abroad on a year-round basis. The Athenians probably acquired Naupactus at the strategically vital narrows of the gulf after, rather than before, their pact with Megara,[27] but in either case control of Pagae made Naupactus a

[25]Thuc. 1.102.4, 103.4.
[26]Thuc. 1.104.
[27]Thuc. 1.103.1-3.

more valuable asset than if it could have been resupplied only by circumnavigating the Peloponnese. Another attraction for the Athenians was the prospect of controlling the passes through the Megarid, which might discourage the Peloponnesians from attempting to invade Attica in the event of full-scale war. Finally, possession of Megara brought Athens closer to a complete monopoly of naval power in the Aegean, since Megara was one of the few states with a substantial naval tradition which had remained outside her sphere. The possibility of a naval response by the Peloponnesians thus became even more remote. In sum, there was hardly a more valuable prize for Athens in all of Greece than Megara.

In reporting the alliance struck between Megara and Athens, Thucydides notes that the Athenians came into possession of the ports of Nisaea and Pagae, and built and manned long-walls connecting Nisaea to Megara itself. These consequences of the treaty are likely to have occurred over a period of years, as military and political circumstances justified them, rather than in the months immediately following the conclusion of the pact.[28] That is but one example of the chronological compression in Thucydides' *Pentakontaetia*. The long-walls, for example, probably took a year or two to build, and we have no idea when they were begun. Nor have we any solid basis for estimating the size of Athenian forces manning these long-walls, or stationed in Megara, Nisaea, and Pagae. But it is clear at least that the Athenians developed a substantial physical presence in the Megarid during the 450's, and that the Megarians became heavily dependent on Athenian military might. Megara's commercial ties to Athens may also have increased during this period, since it is likely that all traffic with the Peloponnese was cut off by the state of belligerency between Megara and Corinth. As we shall see, the course of the conflict can only have further heightened Megara's dependence on Athens. Given Athens' record elsewhere, it is probable that her relationship would have begun to undermine the political system of the smaller state, but we have no direct confirmation of this. It would be interesting to know, for example, whether Athens tried to communicate and dispense patronage in Megara through local *proxenoi* who were secretly or

[28]Contra Meyer, "Megara," cols. 188-89.

openly democrats, rather than through influential members of the oligarchic regime. That device can be traced in some of the Delian League states, but no comparable evidence exists for Megara.[29] We shall have more to say on the subject of political divisions in Megara later in this chapter.

When we examine the military situation created by the new alliance, it becomes evident that Athens lived up to her pledge to defend Megara in the years following the agreement. Fighting along Megara's western border may have continued, possibly with the involvement of some Athenian troops, but the first large-scale Athenian enterprise was a naval expedition along the Aegean coast of the Peloponnese in 459, which carried the war to Corinth and her supporters in the northeastern Peloponnese.[30] The Athenians landed at Haliae and fought an engagement against the Corinthians, Epidaurians, and other unspecified Peloponnesian troops—Troezen and Sicyon are likely participants. (Corinth was apparently successful in drawing support from her neighbors without the sanction of a general Peloponnesian congress.) Although the Athenians lost at Haliae, they may have succeeded in temporarily relieving pressure on the Megarid. Later in the same campaign, the Athenians won a sea-battle against the Peloponnesian fleet off Cecryphalia. The clash must have involved Aeginetan ships, among others, leading to the Athenian attack on Aegina, which Thucydides next recounts.[31] There is no mention of Megarian participation in this naval campaign. Since Megara had twenty triremes at the time of the Persian Wars and at least as many in the early years of the Peloponnesian War, it is a virtual certainty that she possessed a war fleet in 460, and Thucydides' omission may be only an oversight, understandable in the context of his Athens-oriented treatment in the *Pentekontaetia*. But it is also possible that Megarian manpower was fully occupied patrolling the Corinthian border, or attempting to regain territory while the enemy was preoccupied with the Athenian assault.

Later in the same summer, the Megarian-Athenian alliance faced a major challenge, when the Corinthians and their allies launched

[29]See my article "Megara and Mytilene," *Phoenix*, 22 (1968), 204 ff.
[30]Thuc. 1.105.1-2.
[31]Ibid.

an invasion of the Megarid.[32] Previous campaigns in the border war may have been confined to the districts in dispute along the border, but now the Corinthians seized the heights of Gerania and marched into the Megarian plain. This attack threatened the complete devastation of the Megarid and possibly of Attica as well, if a later characterization of this campaign by the Athenian orator Lysias is to be believed.[33] As Thucydides describes Corinth's reasoning, this was an opportune moment to attack, since the Athenian fleet and army were engaged in Egypt and the siege of Aegina. Athens would either be unable to relieve Megara or would have to abandon the attack on Aegina in order to do so.

Be that as it may, the Corinthians were given a rude shock, when, contrary to expectations, they were quickly met and thrown back. The role of Megarian troops in this memorable victory is totally eclipsed in our sources by the fact that this episode was treated as a prime example of the triumph of the Athenian spirit. For instead of recalling troops from Aegina, the Athenians raised a fresh army to meet the Corinthian challenge:

> The Athenians marched to Megara with a force made up of those who remained in the city, consisting of the oldest and youngest men, led by Myronides. After an evenly fought battle with the Corinthians, the two forces disengaged, each side believing that it had not suffered the worse. When the Corinthians withdrew, the Athenians, who actually had the better of the fighting, erected a trophy. But when the older men in the city berated them for cowardice, the Corinthians readied themselves and marched back twelve days later, and set up a rival trophy of their own as if they had won the battle. The Athenians sallied out of Megara, slaughtered those who were setting up the trophy, and, attacking the rest, vanquished them. As the defeated force retreated, not a small number of them were harassed, lost their way, and fled onto some private property which was surrounded by a trench and had no way out. When the Athenians realized what had happened, they placed their hoplites so as to block the entrance and surrounded the enclosure with light armed troops who stoned all the trapped men to death. This was a great misfortune for the Corinthians, but most of their troops managed to reach home.[34]

[32]Thuc. 1.105.3–106.2; Diod. 11.79. Athenian casualties at Haliae, Aegina, Egypt, Cyprus, and Phoenicia, as well as the Megarid, all within a single year, are memorialized on a single stone: Meiggs and Lewis, *GHI* 33.
[33]2.49 ff.
[34]Thuc. 105.4–106.2.

The absence of any mention of Megarian participation in this sequence of events, either in Thucydides' account or any other, is both extraordinary and improbable in the extreme. But it is easy to see how the Megarian role might have been overlooked in an Athenian-oriented tradition, particularly in view of Athens' later hostility toward Megara.

One immediate result of the Corinthians' deep penetration into the Megarid may have been the initiation of a project to safeguard Megara's access to the sea: the construction of the long-walls already mentioned. These walls, which were dismantled during the Peloponnesian War, reconstructed in the 340's, and stood well into the Hellenistic period, have disappeared without a trace, though their route and length (under 2 kilometers) have been reasonably well determined. The project was contemporaneous with the construction of Athens' long-walls, a far larger and more ambitious undertaking. The logic behind this means of defense is familiar from the more famous Athenian example. The Greeks were not particularly effective in the conduct of siege warfare. A strongly walled town with a secure water supply could hold out against superior forces for as long as its food reserves lasted, usually one to two years, unless betrayed from within. But if the besieged town could maintain access to the sea, it could, in theory, resist a land attack as long as it had money or friends enough to keep fresh supplies arriving by ship. For an inland city to withstand a siege in this manner, obviously it was not sufficient merely to control the sea lanes; a secure corridor to the sea was necessary. Long-walls linking metropolis to port satisfied the requirement, rendering an inland city as invulnerable to siege as any on the water's edge. But the strategy was not without drawbacks. Reliance upon long-walls violated one of the cardinal principles of Greek warfare—one defended one's land at all costs. The new strategy demanded that the natural inclination to meet the enemy at the border in a do-or-die effort to protect farms, orchards, and homesteads from looting and burning be suppressed in favor of waiting patiently and securely behind the walls while the invader spent his fury, realized the futility of his methods, and went home. This approach to war demanded total commitment and iron discipline. If the stakes were high enough, as they may have been for

Athens in her fifth-century wars against the Peloponnesians, when
the stake was supremacy in Greece, perhaps the internal division
and demoralization that would inevitably result from passive en-
durance of an enemy invasion could be borne without causing a
fatal rupture of the political and social fabric of the state—although
this is far from evident, even in Athens' case. But if the state under
attack was primarily concerned with territorial security, as was
unquestionably true of Megara, reliance on long-walls meant capitulation on the very issues that were being fought over and would
be all the harder to bear or justify in terms of some long-range goal.
For Megara the issue was border lands, and though the long-walls
might protect her from total destruction at the hands of the Corinthians, they were not likely to have a direct effect on the fate of the
disputed territory. Thus while the long-walls may have helped
guarantee Megara's capacity to survive, they were more an effective means of maintaining a foothold in the Megarid for the Athenians than a decisive factor in the Megarian effort to hold or regain
lands on the border with Corinth. Furthermore, the walls rendered
Megara hostage to Athens, through the continual presence of an
Athenian garrison force as well as the policy of reliance on supplies
arriving by sea. Athens' apparent act of generosity, in fact, served
Athenian interests best, binding Megara to Athens and discourag-
ing invasion of Attica by strengthening the ability of the town of
Megara to survive as a base behind enemy lines.[35] It is no wonder
that the Athenians were willing to build defensive works for
Megara which one might have expected her to provide for herself,
though it is difficult to believe that Megarians did not perform a
substantial share of the labor the project required.

One obvious though unanswerable question is whether Megarian leaders saw the implications of the long-walls clearly when
they agreed to the undertaking. If they did, they might have given
their assent anyway as a price for obtaining what they sought most
from Athens: direct military support in their struggle with Corinth.
For those who choose to date a change from oligarchy to democracy at the time of Megara's pact with Athens, it might even be
argued that a high degree of dependence on Athens was precisely

[35]Meyer, "Megara," col. 189, says that Megara "had actually become Athenian."

what the *new* Megarian leaders wanted. But as has been noted, there is no evidence whatsoever for such a political shift. I am persuaded that the potential effects of the long-wall strategy were probably not understood by the Megarians (if, indeed, even the Athenians grasped them fully). The ploy was, after all, new and untested. It may well have seemed to the Megarians tangible evidence of Athens' commitment to her new ally, to be understood in the context of other forms of military assistance on land and sea. Years may have passed before it dawned on many Megarians that the long-walls had transformed Megara into an outpost of Athenian power.

Athens was successful in defending Megarian interests as long as Sparta chose to remain outside the conflict; but the helot revolt appears to have ended by 457, and in that year Sparta became militarily active. Having put her own house in order, she embarked on a campaign to reverse the erosion of her position elsewhere in Greece. Slippage had occurred in regions apart from Megara, and the Spartans chose to move first against Phocis in central Greece, which had attacked and taken territory from the neighboring state of Doris, the Spartans' legendary homeland.[36] A force of 1,500 Spartiates and 10,000 allies under the command of Nicomedes sailed across the Corinthian Gulf, apparently reluctant to march through the Megarid, where Athenian and Megarian troops undoubtedly had been occupying the Isthmian passes since the time of Myronides' victory. It seems reasonable that the choice of Phocis rather than Megara as the initial target was at least partly based on the anticipated difficulty of gaining access to the Megarian plain. The Athenian fleet in the Corinthian Gulf, stationed at either Pagae or Naupactus, or perhaps at both, was evidently caught napping when the Peloponnesian force slipped by, probably sailing from Lechaeum in Corinthia to some point on the Crisaean Gulf. Nicomedes quickly brought the Phocians to terms, but the expeditionary force was unable to return as it had come. The Athenian fleet was now alerted, and a naval crossing was too risky.[37] The Spartans were aware that their retreat by land through the Megarid was also being blocked by Athenian forces in the

[36]Thuc. 1.107.2; Diod. 11.79.4-6.
[37]Diodorus (11.80.1) puts Athenian naval strength in the Corinthian Gulf at fifty ships.

mountain passes. This intelligence may have reached the Peloponnesian army through a disaffected faction in Athens, which, according to Thucydides, was plotting the overthrow of the democracy and the abandonment of the long-walls under construction there.[38] We will not pause to consider whether this plot was genuine or a fiction concocted by the radicals to strengthen their hold on the government; but alarm over internal instability may account for the Athenian democrats' decision to force the issue by sending their army into Boeotia, where Nicomedes was camped, awaiting developments.[39] The Athenian force, augmented by contingents from Argos and other allied states (probably including Megara) actually outnumbered the Peloponnesian troops, and this fact, coupled with recent successes against the Corinthians, may have emboldened the Athenians to take the step.

Battle was joined at Tanagra in Boeotia. Both sides suffered heavy casualties, but the Peloponnesians were victorious.[40] Nicomedes could now make his way home unopposed: "Then the Spartans came into the Megarid and after cutting down some trees returned home through Gerania and the Isthmus."[41] Nicomedes made no attempt to destroy the Megarian long-walls, as he probably would have done had they been only partially erected. Evidently, the populace of Megara watched the destruction wrought by his troops from the safety of their fortifications. Perhaps the beginnings of disillusionment with the Athenian alliance should be dated from this point.

Megara seems to have been the main loser in the clash with Nicomedes' forces in 457. The Athenians rebounded quickly from their defeat at Tanagra, triumphing against both the Boeotians and Aeginetans before the year was out and soon forging a chain of alliances which stretched along the northern coast of the Corinthian Gulf as far as Locris.[42] In succeeding years, Athenian war fleets could more easily sail around the Peloponnese to harass her

[38]1.107.4.
[39]Thuc. 107.5–108.1.
[40]Diodorus (11.80.6) says the battle ended in stalemate, and that the Spartans returned home under a four-month truce. In this and other instances where Diodorus directly contradicts Thucydides, I generally follow the latter, but I use Diodorus to supplement and expand the Thucydidean narrative where the two appear consistent or at least not directly contradictory.
[41]Thuc. 1.108.2.
[42]Thuc. 1.108.3.

enemies, since safe portage was available in the west and most of the sailors could furlough in Athens during the winter, returning to their vessels at Pagae in the spring.[43] In the summer of 454, however, news reached Athens of a distant defeat, which significantly altered the military situation.[44] The Athenian fleet in Egypt had been destroyed, and though scholars disagree as to the size of this force and therefore the magnitude of the catastrophe, there is no doubt that Athens' naval supremacy in the Aegean was in jeopardy for the first time in a generation. One consequence was that the fleet at Pagae, fifty ships at this stage, according to Diodorus, one hundred in Plutarch's account, had become vital to Athenian security.[45] Pericles himself set off for Pagae with a thousand men to bring these ships home.[46] This small force must have consisted of marines or reinforcements, since ten to twenty thousand men would have been necessary to man the entire fleet. Even after this large-scale withdrawal, Athens doubtless maintained a military presence at Pagae, but she had surrendered the initiative in the Corinthian Gulf. The significance of her retreat was not lost on the states of central Greece, however, and they gradually fell away from their allegiance to Athens. When it appeared that the Persians might attempt to reenter the Aegean, and Sparta began threatening to invade Attica, the Athenians were ready to strike a bargain. In 451 they concluded a five-year truce with the Peloponnesians, which enabled them to concentrate their forces against the Persian menace and to shore up the Delian League, which was restive after Athens' recent setbacks.[47]

Athens' desire to extricate herself from the war with the Pelo-

---

[43]The best attested of these expeditions took place c. 456 under the command of Tolmides. His forces consisted of fifty triremes and 4,000 hoplites (Diod. 11.84.6). Tolmides wreaked havoc along the Laconian coast and later in Sicyonia and Corinthia (Thuc. 1.108.5), and possibly captured Zacynthos and Cephallenia (Diod. 11.84.6-8). Diodorus also dates the occupation of Naupactus by the helot refugees from this expedition. Cf. Pausanias (1.27.5), and the scholiast to Aeschines (2.75), who improbably adds the island of Cythera to Tolmides' conquests.
[44]Thuc. 1.109-10.
[45]Plut. *Per.* 19.2; Diod. 11.85.1.
[46]Thuc. 1.111.2-3. Cf. Diod. 11.88.1-2; Plut. *Per.* 19.2-4. No source describes this expedition as a direct consequence of the Egyptian disaster, but this seems a reasonable inference. Diodorus may have made two expeditions out of one; cf. 11.85 and 11.88.
[47]Thuc. 1.112.1-4.

ponnesians was a troublesome development from Megara's point of view. True enough, the truce released the Megarians as well as the Athenians from fear of immediate invasion, but the future looked bleak. Should war resume, it was inevitable that Megara would face another invasion, and it was far from certain that Athens would be either willing or able to defend her. Yet Megara's prospects looked equally poor in the event that the truce led to a permanent peace. Athens was in no position to dictate the terms of such a peace, and Sparta was bound to demand the return of Megara. Might not Athens make this concession in the interests of her own security? What treatment could Megara expect from her erstwhile allies if she were forcibly returned to the Peloponnesian fold? How, then, would Sparta regard Corinth's designs on Megarian territory? What punishment would be dealt the political leaders who had brought about the alliance with Athens? If, on the other hand, Megara were to anticipate events by voluntarily repudiating the Athenians, with all the risks inherent in such a move, might she be able to salvage some status and bargaining power within the Peloponnesian League? Megarian politicians must have considered questions like these—albeit quietly, in view of the Athenian military presence in the Megarid. Then, too, it is possible that the Megarian oligarchs were growing more uncomfortable in the hands of their democratic protectors, judging by the behavior of Athenian partisans like Pythion (to be discussed shortly).

The years between 451 and 446 were doubtless a time of quiet diplomacy, with various parties to the conflict exploring the likely terms and conditions for peace and the possibilities for attracting new allies. It is in the nature of such contacts that they are usually hidden from the view of both ancient and modern historians. For example, a Spartan army which appeared at Delphi in 449, probably marched out and back through the Megarid.[48] These occasions might well have provided opportunities for both direct negotiation and psychological pressure. In any event, contacts between

[48]Thuc. 1.112.5. de Ste Croix, *OPW*, p. 191 n., suggests that the Spartans may have gone to Delphi by sea under the terms of the truce, but the truce could as easily have permitted them to travel overland. In light of Sparta's moves in 457, Thucydides would probably have taken note of the fact if the Spartans had been obliged to sail across the Corinthian Gulf in this later instance.

Megara and the Peloponnesians would not have been difficult to arrange in the succeeding few years. Though we cannot trace the steps, it is clear that Megara negotiated the terms of her reentry into the Peloponnesian League during the latter stages of the truce, and must have received guarantees that she would be taken back without reprisals or loss of status. Her repudiation of Athens must also have been planned at this stage. It was to be coordinated with a series of moves designed to bring maximum pressure to bear on the Athenians on the eve of the truce's expiration.

This plan was set in motion when the island of Euboea revolted from the Delian League in 446.[49] Pericles crossed over to Euboea with the Athenian army to suppress it, but soon after he arrived in Euboea, he received news that:

> Megara had revolted, the Peloponnesians were about to invade Attica, and the Athenian guards, except for those who flet to Nisaea, had been destroyed by the Megarians. The Megarians had succeeded in the revolt by inviting in Corinthians, Sicyonians, and Epidaurians. Pericles hurriedly brought his army back from Euboea. After this, the Peloponnesians invaded Attica advancing as far as Eleusis and Thria under the command of Pleistoanax, the son of Pausanias, the king of Sparta, but, sparing the rest of the land, they marched home again. Then the Athenians returned once more to Euboea under Pericles' command.[50]

Pleistoanax's precipitate return home, which enabled the Athenians to suppress the Euboean revolt, infuriated the Spartans. He and his adviser, the ephor Cleandridas, were accused of accepting a bribe from Pericles.[51] Pleistoanax paid a fine and Cleandridas chose voluntary exile. But historians are more inclined to believe that Pericles secured the Spartans' withdrawal by a pledge to negotiate terms of peace in addition to, or in lieu of, any monetary bribe.[52] At all events, the contending parties were able to work out peace terms over the next few months.

---

[49]Thuc. 1.114.1. de Ste Croix, *OPW*, p. 197 n., believes that a plan coordinated with Sparta was being put into effect, but dates its implementation after the expiration of the truce. I doubt the plotters were so circumspect.
[50]Thuc. 1.114.
[51]Plut. *Per.* 22-23. Cf. Schol. Ar. *Nu.* 858-59.
[52]See, e.g., Kagan, *Outbreak*, pp. 124-25.

Diodorus, probably relying on Ephorus, gives a quite different picture of events following upon Megara's revolt. He fails to mention the attack on the Athenian garrisons, or Pleistoanax's invasion, and he places the revolt in 448, but he also adds something that is not to be found in Thucydides' account or any other—namely, an Athenian military response to the revolt:

> The Athenians were distressed and sent an army into Megarian territory, looting their property and taking their goods. When those in the city tried to protect their lands a battle took place in which the Athenians were victorious and drove the Megarians back inside their fortifications.[53]

Although Diodorus' version as a whole does not inspire confidence, it must at least be said that an Athenian attack on Megara when Pericles returned from Euboea and before the Spartan invasion is neither impossible nor out of character.

The possibility that a large Athenian force entered the Megarid after the Megarian revolt is strengthened by the description of an Athenian retreat from Pagae in a surviving inscription. The document is the epitaph of a Megarian expatriate who lived out his days in Athens:

> [This] memorial [is] placed over the body of the bravest of men. Pythion of Megara killed seven men in battle and left seven broken spears in their corpses. He embraced a life of bravery, bringing glory to his father among his fellow citizens. This same man, who saved three Athenian tribal regiments, leading them from Pagae through Boeotia to Athens, brought fame to Andocides with his 2,000 slaves [or prisoners—*andrapodoisin*]. Not a single man on earth did he injure, and he died admired by everyone. The tribes he saved were: Pandionis, Kekropis, and Antiochis.[54]

Pythion's claim to have rescued these troops and the circuitous route by which he led them back into Athenian territory suggest that they were in danger of being trapped by Pleistoanax's advancing army. (Pythion must have conducted Andocides and his men

---

[53]12.5.2.
[54]*IG* 1².1085. Cf. the comments of Meiggs and Lewis, *GHI*, 137 ff. and Gomme, *HCT* 1, pp. 340 f.

over the cliffs to Aegosthena, or over one of the lesser tracks that joined the Road of the Towers.) The epitaph does not make clear what these tribal regiments were doing in the vicinity of Pagae. At least a few possible reasons could support Diodorus' account of an Athenian army in the Megarid after the fall of Megara. Thucydides gives the impression that all Athenian garrisons in the Megarid had been destroyed at the time of the Megarian revolt except for the soldiers who managed to escape to Nisaea. That would seem to include the troops in Megara itself, those inside the long-walls, others at Pagae, and any that might have been guarding the Gerania passes. But we know from the ensuing peace negotiations that after the Megarian attack, the Athenians retained possession of Pagae as well as Nisaea. One possibility is that Thucydides did not mean to give the impression that Pagae had fallen to the Megarians; another is that the Athenians swiftly retook the town. In the first case, Andocides and his men might represent a portion of the garrison at Pagae which retired, leaving a smaller force to hold it against the Peloponnesians. In the second case, these troops might have participated in Pagae's recapture, either alone or as part of a larger Athenian force operating in Megarian territory. The present state of our evidence makes it impossible to choose among these alternatives.

Another tantalizing point in the epitaph is the mention of 2,000 *andrapoda*, "captives" or "slaves." The number seems too large for them to have been prisoners of war in the hands of only three tribal regiments, though admittedly we do not know how many troops Andocides commanded. Although the possibility exists that these were Megarian and/or Boeotian prisoners taken by force, they are more likely to have been runaway slaves who saw an opportunity to gain their freedom. If such is the case, their loss, assuming that at least a substantial proportion were Megarian, would have been a serious economic blow to Megara.

Finally, the career of Pythion himself, as set forth in his memorial, is worthy of comment. Recognizing that his misdeeds, if any, are unlikely to have found a place in his epitaph, and that his career is portrayed in the most favorable light possible, we can nevertheless learn a great deal from the objective facts cited and the manner in which they are treated. Pythion seems to have begun as a genuine Megarian hero. He can hardly have killed seven men during the retreat from Pagae; these exploits must have occurred during the war between Megara and Corinth, perhaps stretching back as far as the 460's. Hence, he notes that they brought honor to his father in Megara. But the obvious implication of his assistance to Andokides in 446 and his subsequent residence in Athens, where he died and was interred, is that he became an Athenian partisan in Megara and opposed Megara's return to the Peloponnesian camp, lending material support to the Athenians against his own countrymen. Pythion's choice must be judged treasonable by conventional definitions, and the oligarchic regime's connivance against Athens in 446 must be called patriotic. But these categories are far too arbitrary to fit the complexity of Megara's relations with the hegemonal states and the self-interest of her political leaders. There was no public discussion of Megara's planned abandonment of the Athenian alliance, no attempt to gauge popular feeling or win popular support for the move. Such behavior would have been uncharacteristic of oligarchic rule in general and impossible in the circumstances, under the watchful eye of Athenian garrisons. The decision reflected the will of the ruling oligarchic faction, no more. It is little wonder that pro-Athenians were less than willing to accept this sudden reversal of policy, though few probably carried their opposition as far as Pythion. The claims of bravery, justice, and honorable behavior are those of a man who was reviled in his own land but refused to accept the label of traitor.

Pythion's pro-Athenianism probably identifies him as a democrat. There is no hint in his epitaph that he ever held public office in Megara or had any connection with the ruling oligarchy. His career points to the emergence of a democratic faction during the period of Megara's association with Athens. This group (of unknown size) had not yet moved to seize power, hence was both ignorant of the plan to abandon the Athenian alliance and powerless to prevent it. Had Megara remained in the Athenian camp much longer, men like Pythion might have come to power, overthrowing the oligarchic regime. As noted earlier, the oligarchs' anticipation of such an eventuality may have been a factor in their decision to return Megara to the oligarchicly inclined Peloponnesian League. Their success crushed any immediate prospects for democracy in Megara, but a legacy of democratic aspirations fostered by the Athenian connection may have remained beneath the surface of Megarian politics, ready to burst forth at a future time.

When we attempt to add up the gains and losses for Megara which resulted from the reversal of her foreign policy in 446, the result is mixed in the extreme. The oligarchy had managed to preserve itself, and there was probably nothing further to fear regarding Corinthian incursions on the western border. But the Athenians had managed to retain vital footholds in the Megarid. They still held Megara's two principal ports, Nisaea and Pagae— Megara's "two legs," as Aristophanes called them.[55] Neither was as valuable to Athens without the active support of the Megarians and safe passage through their territory, but Athens was at least able to deny Megara access to the sea, and could use them as bases from which to launch raids on the farms and fields of the Megarid. It is almost a certainty that Megara's navy and commercial fleet fell into Athenian hands too, since these vessels were normally stationed at Nisaea and Pagae. Perhaps some that were at sea were salvaged by the Megarians, but any wholesale movement of Megarian ships in the period just before the attack on the Athenian garrisons would have tipped the Megarians' hands.

Thus in the months after their repudiation of Athens, the Megarians were unable to import foodstuffs by sea or to carry on normal agricultural activities at home. Had the war continued for even a few years longer, Megara would have faced extreme deprivation, with the growing possibility of collapse and capitulation. The situation was not very different from that which took shape in the early years of the Peloponnesian War. Apart from these grim prospects, Megara may already have suffered serious material loss. If we accept the burden of Diodorus' account and Pythion's epitaph, Megarian territory had been plundered and Megarian slaves carried off. Any hope the oligarchs had nurtured that their move might prevent Megara from becoming a battleground once more may have been dashed in a matter of weeks. Finally, if we assume that there were other pro-Athenians in Megara, the danger of the

[55]*Lys.* 1170.

town being betrayed to the Athenians at Nisaea was very great. The Megarian regime was in a very precarious position, and every day that the war continued, their plight worsened. The consequences of their only partly successful maneuver were about as disastrous as their continued hostility to Sparta would have been.

Fortunately for the Megarians' gamble, Athens, for her own reasons, was anxious to see the conflict end. Pleistoanax may have extracted a promise of peace from the Athenians, but even if this had not occurred in any formal sense, his invasion was a warning they were well advised to heed. The roads through the Megarid were now open to Peloponnesian armies, and the next invasion of Attica might do far more extensive damage than the first. The Athenians seem to have realized that their mainland policy had been a failure, and they were prepared to surrender their remaining footholds in the Peloponnese to secure peace. In the winter of 446/5 the two sides agreed to a peace of thirty years duration, and one clause of the agreement obligated Athens to return Nisaea and Pagae to Megara.[56] Thus Sparta redeemed the pledges which helped to bring Megara back into the Spartan hegemony, and Megara averted disaster. But the return of peace in no way lessened the legacy of bitterness between Athens and Megara. In particular, the Athenians would long remember Megara's betrayal in 446 as a key element, if not the decisive factor, in the collapse of her mainland ambitions in the middle decades of the fifth century.

[56]Thuc. 1.115; Diod. 12.7; Paus. 5.23.

CHAPTER 9

The Megarian Decree

No one should think we would be going to war for a trifle, if we do not rescind the Megarian Decree, which they (the Spartans) stress above all, saying there need not be war if we remove it. Do not put the blame on yourselves, as if we went to war over a small issue. For this trifling thing represents nothing less than the firmness and conviction of your resolution. If you give in on this demand, you will immediately be faced with a greater one, as if you conceded the first one out of fear.

    —Pericles' speech to the Athenians, Thucydides 1.140.4-5

THE THIRTY YEARS PEACE ended the immediate threat of general war in Greece, but it did no reconcile the contending powers. The Greek world remained divided into hostile camps, with most states tied, to a greater or lesser degree, to one of the two superpowers. Athens controlled nearly all the seaboard states of the Aegean and the eastern colonies as far as the Black Sea. Sparta dominated the Peloponnese and portions of central Greece, and had close links with the dominant states in western Greece and Magna Graecia through Corinth. Megara occupied a key position within this divided world. I refer here not to her continuing importance as the land frontier between the two power blocs, but to her role as a naval state. We do not know whether Athens returned captured Megarian ships at the time of the Thirty Years Peace, or whether the Megarians were forced to build new ones, but in either case Megara assumed unprecedented importance in the Aegean after 445. With Aegina now a part of the Delian League, Megara had more extensive commercial and political contacts in the east than any other Peloponnesian ally, and the Megarian fleet had become the largest squadron available to the Spartans in the Aegean.[1] This is not to

---

[1] See, e.g., the remarks of O. Murray, *G&R*, n.s. 20 (1973), p. 205. There is no evidence that Athens returned the Megarian ships which were in her hands at the time of the Thirty Years Peace, but the Megarians were in possession of a fleet—

dispute the fact that Corinth was Sparta's most powerful naval ally, but in my view Corinth's naval power and commercial shipping were largely confined to the west by this time.[2] In a protracted crisis the Corinthians might be prepared to haul their triremes across the *diolchos* and into the Saronic Gulf, or to sail their merchant ships around the Peloponnese and into the Aegean, but normally it was Megara who maintained a significant Peloponnesian presence there. She therefore constituted both a symbolic and a practical obstacle to Athens' ambition to turn the Aegean into an Athenian lake, though she was obviously incapable of mounting any serious threat to Athenian strategic or commercial dominance. Megara's status in this regard was bound to aggravate the bitterness already felt in Athens regarding Megara's stab in the back in 446.

The revolt of Byzantium from the Delian League in 440 can only have made relations between Athens and Megara worse. This rebellion seems to have been part of a chain reaction set off by the revolt of Samos.[3] The Athenians had intervened in a territorial dispute between Samos and Miletus on behalf of the latter, taking the opportunity to install a democratic regime in Samos. As soon as the Athenians went home, the oligarchs seized power again, renewed their contest with Miletus, and openly broke with the Delian League. Thucydides is silent about Byzantium's motives for joining the revolt, but they can hardly be identical with those of the Samians. The issue between Miletus and Samos was local, and if there is any basis to the legend of Milesian involvement in the founding of Byzantium,[4] the Byzantines may well have been sympathetic to Miletus. Then, too, Byzantium had probably long since been converted to democracy, and there is no hint of an oligarchic

---

whether or not as the result of new construction—by 435 at the latest, when they fought at Leucimne, and they doubtless had restored their commercial fleet as well.

[2] The case for Corinth's concentration on the western sea lanes is summarized in my article "The Megarian Decree and the Balance of Greek Naval Power," *CP*, 68 (1973), 164-65. Cf. C. Roebuck, *Ionian Trade and Colonization*, pp. 128-29, where it is argued that *Aegina* had replaced Corinth in the Black Sea trade by the mid-fifth century. But after 457 Aegina was not free to pursue her trade independently of Athenian interests.

[3] See Thuc. 1.115-17 on the Samian and Byzantine revolts. For a recent discussion of this episode, see Kagan, *Outbreak*, chapter 10, esp. pp. 172-73, on Byzantine involvement. Cf. Busolt, *Gr. Gesch.* 3¹, pp. 544-45, for hints that still other league members were involved in this revolt.

[4] See above, Chapter 3.

uprising in connection with her secession from the league. Nor do we have evidence of differences between Byzantium and Athens in this period. Nevertheless, it is tempting to see some relationship between the deterioration of Megarian-Athenian relations and the revolt of Megara's greatest colony from Athens.[5] The nature of that relationship, if any, remains purely speculative. At the extreme, we might picture Megara inciting the rebellion. On a more subtle level, both Megara and Athens might have put pressure on Byzantium to alter her ties to the other party. At the other extreme, Athens might have adopted discriminatory or repressive measures against the Byzantines out of suspicion of their contacts with Megara, and these policies could have sparked an anti-Athenian movement. We are unlikely ever to know the truth of the matter, but some link is more than likely.

According to Thucydides, the Corinthian embassy to Athens in 433 claimed that the Peloponnesians held a synod in 440 to discuss the possibility of supporting the Samian rebellion by invading Attica.[6] (There is no explicit mention of support for Byzantium, but the effect of a Peloponnesian invasion would have aided her as well.) Opinion seems to have been divided on the issue, and the Corinthians later tried to take credit for preventing Peloponnesian interference. It would be interesting to know what position the Megarians took. On the one hand, they must have been eager to support the Byzantine revolt, but they may also have felt constrained by the likelihood of warfare in their own territory if the Peloponnesian states made an assault on Attica. Lacking outside support, the Samians were obliged to surrender in 439, and the Byzantines followed suit, apparently having put up little fight, if any.[7] In the aftermath, Byzantium's tribute was raised and a garrison force was placed in the town.[8] Perhaps her contacts with Megara were restricted or cut off, but there is no evidence one way or the other.

It is small wonder that the period after 440 was one of great tension between Megara and Athens and was filled with incidents

---

[5]See, e.g., Meiggs, pp. 189-90.
[6]1.40.5.
[7]Thuc. 1.117.3.
[8]Her tribute was raised from fifteen to eighteen talents per annum. Cf. the tribute lists for 442, 441, and 432. The presence of a garrison at Byzantium is established by Ar. V. 235-37.

and provocations on both sides, culminating in the famous Megarian Decree. Though Thucydides notes that the Megarians held many grievances against Athens apart from the decree, he fails to mention any.[9] He is more helpful regarding some of the Megarians' offenses against Athens. Two of these emerge in Pericles' *post hoc* justification of the decree.[10] One was the allegation that the Megarians had "encroached on sacred land (*hiera gēs*) and unmarked borderland." The charge of cultivating land consecrated to Demeter and Persephone on the border with Eleusis (the *hiera orgas*) also appears in Plutarch and in some minor sources, but there is no other reference to unmarked borderland.[11] No source spells out the Megarian response to this accusation, but the general character of boundary disputes suggests that there could have been a legitimate difference of opinion at the root of this one. The issue of the *hiera orgas* became a bone of contention in Megarian-Athenian relations again in the mid-fourth century,[12] and it may have existed long before Pericles raised it in 432. I doubt it was ever as clear-cut as it appears in our Athenian-oriented sources. Quite possibly the dispute became inflamed as a result of hostility between Athens and Megara in the 430's, and it may have been deliberately blown out of proportion by the Athenians merely to serve the purpose to which Pericles evidently put it—namely, to justify passage of the Megarian Decree.

The second accusation recorded by Thucydides is that the Megarians were harboring runaway Athenian slaves. No surviving provision of the Thirty Years Peace obligated the signatories to return runaways, as treaties sometimes did. This must have been a perpetual sore point between unfriendly neighbors in the Greek world. It may well have been another two-sided issue in the present case, with Megarian slaves finding asylum in Athens as well. The Athenians may, in fact, have helped as many as 2,000 Megarian slaves to escape in 446, a short time before the peace was signed.[13] This could have set in motion the acts of which the Athenians com-

[9]1.67.4.
[10]Thuc. 1.139.2.
[11]*Per.* 30.2. Cf. Paus. 1.36 and Harpocration, *s.v. Anthemocritus.*
[12]See below, Chapter 11. K. Völkl, "Das megarische Psephisma," *RM*, 94 (1951), 330-36, argues unconvincingly, I believe, that Corinth instigated Megara to provoke Athens into a declaration of war.
[13]See above, Chapter 8.

plained. Though we may deplore the slave system itself, we cannot ignore the seriousness of an issue which might have caused considerable economic disruption in both states.

Aristophanes mentions several more issues between Megara and Athens as preliminary to the passage of the Megarian Decree. While he is our most nearly contemporary source, it is extremely hazardous to use his treatment of political matters as historical evidence.[14] It is no easy task to find the truth amid his deliberate exaggerations, distortions, absurdities, and outright inventions. Perhaps the only point on which historians can agree is that Aristophanes' comments cannot be taken at face value. In the *Acharnians*, produced in 425 with the Peloponnesian War well under way, he makes a plea for peace by questioning whether the war was justified in the first place, and by extolling the benefits of peace. Dicaeopolis, the play's protagonist, is an Athenian citizen who resolves to conclude his own peace with the Peloponnesians and open a market for their goods. When the old farmers of Acharnae, who had made great sacrifices in the war, threaten to kill him for his treason, Dicaeopolis defends himself in a mock trial. We shall return to his defense for its picture of the Megarian Decree itself, but at this point we are concerned with what he describes as the decree's antecedents:

> Some of us—I don't say the polis; be sure to remember that; I do not say the polis, but some no-account villains, frauds, despicable men, counterfeits and half-breeds, impeached the Megarians' little cloaks, and whenever they saw a cucumber, a hare, a swine, a garlic, or a speck of salt anywhere, these were branded Megarian and seized on the spot. But these were minor incidents and of only local interest. Next, however, some drunken youths went to Megara and abducted the whore Simaetha. The Megarians, aggrieved and fortified with garlic, stole two of Aspasia's whores in retaliation. Then war among all the Greeks was unleashed on account of three harlots.[15]

---

[14]See de Ste Croix's excellent discussion of the problems of using Aristophanes as an historical source (*OPW*, pp. 232-36); cf. his perceptive exposition of the comedian's political views (pp. 355-76). I find myself in general agreement with de Ste Croix's approach, though not always with his specific inferences from the plays.
[15]*Ach.* 514-29.

The two issues presented here, an official or unofficial boycott and the abduction of a few prostitutes, hardly seem of the same degree of importance. Yet Aristophanes says the denunciation of Megarian goods was a small matter in comparison to this woman stealing! This ludicrous juxtaposition is probably only one of the jokes of the passage, along with the jibes at garlic-smelling Megarians— repeated in many comedies—and at the disreputable occupation of Aspasia, Pericles' inamorata. To dispose of the more frivolous accusation first, other sources confirm the existence of *hetairai* in Megara, the so-called "Megarian Bracelets."[16] Aspasia was a genuine personality; perhaps Simaitha was too. But the real incident(s), if any, behind this curious allegation seem hardly the sort which fifth-century poleis went to war over. Aristophanes may well have twisted some episode beyond recognition in order to have an excuse to parody Herodotus' discussion of woman-stealing as the basis for the Trojan and Persian Wars.[17]

Clearly, Aristophanes' suggestion of a boycott is the more serious matter. If he has described this affair with any degree of fidelity, there is likely to have been some legal basis for the denunciation and confiscation of Megarian goods—for example, an anti-Megarian enactment earlier than the Megarian Decree. There are no adequate precedents for such a move, but that circumstance does not rule it out.[18] Athens was certainly angry enough with Megara to have taken some extraordinary step. But what are we to make of Dicaeopolis' insistence that the polis was not responsible for the denunciation of Megarian goods? Some historians have felt that this inconsistency is sufficient ground for dismissing the entire affair.[19] Other ways can be found out of this difficulty, however. One possibility is that a law barring Megarian goods had been passed earlier (perhaps at the height of Athens' rage against Megara in 446), had become a dead letter, but was revived in the

[16]There are many ancient references to the presence of *hetairai* in Megara. See, e.g., Dem. 59.35 ff.; Luc. *Catapl.* 6; Plaut. *Pers.* 139. They were often called "Megarian bracelets." See D.L. 6.35 and Hsch., Suda, and Phot., *s.v. Megarikai Sphinges.*
[17]Hdt. 1.1-4.
[18]One remote and partial parallel might be seen in the earlier Thasian law prohibiting boats from sailing to Thasos or the Thasian peraea with foreign wine (*IG* 12 suppl. 347.2). But here it was particular merchandise, rather than a particular nationality of trader, which was barred.
[19]See, e.g., Beloch, *Gr. Gesch.* 2².1, p. 293, and Kagan, *Outbreak*, pp. 254-56.

430's by malicious individuals.[20] Another, related solution would be that a law had indeed been passed, but there had been no real intention of enforcing it, as has been the case with some boycotts of more recent memory. Yet another explanation could be that Megarian goods were being denounced on the basis of general customs regulations, having entered Athens without the payment of duty.[21] This last approach would eliminate the need to hypothesize a specifically anti-Megarian law. It is equally possible that Dicaeopolis' exculpation of the polis was not seriously intended at all. Aristophanes could be trying to protect himself from prosecution, or poking fun at the assembly's tendency to blame failed policies on various scapegoats rather than accept responsibility itself—"half-foreigners"—the very men whom Pericles' citizenship law had struck from the citizen rolls—might be a particularly apt target of such accusations.[22] Another joke might be directed against the Athenian courts, where the defendant was well advised to appear friendly to the demos, just as it was a wise precaution to dress in rags like those Dicaeopolis borrows from Euripides to gain the jurors' sympathies. It is difficult to choose among all these conflicting options, but we cannot rule out the possibility that Athens adopted a milder economic sanction against Megara prior to the passage of the Megarian Decree. To the trade implications of both acts, it has been objected that Athens would have been foolish to deprive herself of Megarian goods, but there is an element of *self*-denial in all boycotts, else they are pointless.

An open clash between the Athenians and Peloponnesians had been averted in 440, but a mounting crisis in the Ionian Sea in the 430's was to lead to the resumption of full-scale war between the two hegemonies. Again, Megara was to play a significant role, first through her direct participation in the Ionian Sea confrontation, and secondly through the Megarian Decree, its attendant circumstances, and the Peloponnesian response to it. Sometime after 440, Corinth seized an opportunity to increase her influence in northwestern Greece at the expense of her long estranged colony, Cor-

[20]See, e.g., Busolt, *Gr. Gesch.* 3.2, pp. 810-11 and F. A. Lepper, "Some Rubrics in the Athenian Quota-Lists," *JHS*, 82 (1962), 51-55.

[21]De Ste Croix, *OPW*, pp. 383-86, where most of the counterarguments to this suggestion may be found.

[22]For Pericles' citizenship law, see Arist. *Ath. Pol.* 26.3 and Plut. *Per.* 37.3-5.

cyra, by injecting herself into a debilitating civil war in Epidamnus, on the coast of Illyria.[23] Her pretext was that she had been involved in the foundation of Epidamnus, though Corcyra had been the principal sponsor of the colony. Delphi sanctioned Corinthian intervention. The Corcyraeans rightly perceived Corinth's move as a threat to their position, and they reacted with force. We cannot here consider the course of this struggle in detail, but it is important to note that Megara energetically supported this Corinthian initiative from the beginning. When the Corcyraeans blockaded the original Corinthian expeditionary force in Epidamnus, the Megarians responded to Corinth's appeal for ships to convoy a larger force to the area by contributing eight fully manned triremes.[24] This was the largest contingent sent by any member of the Peloponnesian League, apart from Corinth's own thirty triremes and three thousand hoplites. In comparison, Epidaurus sent five ships, Troezen two, Hermione one, and Elis some unmanned hulls and money. Phlius and Thebes, neither a naval state, also sent cash, while several independent states in western Greece which were interested parties to the dispute—Leucas, and Ambracia together with Cephallenia—supplied ten and eight triremes respectively. Some of Corinth's allies, most notably Sparta, made no contribution whatever. In this context Megara's role must be judged substantial. Her differences with Corinth seem to have been completely settled, or at least the Megarian oligarchs had decided to cast their lot with Corinth wholeheartedly.

The armada that Corinth assembled was decisively beaten by the Corcyraean navy at Leucimne in 435, and no relief got through to Epidamnus. Thucydides does not itemize the losses of the Corinthian fleet, saying merely that the Corinthians lost fifteen ships; but Megara and the others may have shared in this defeat.[25] Leucimne was a serious embarrassment to the Corinthians. Their naval prestige had suffered, they had lost ground in the northwest, and their forces already at Epidamnus were placed in grave danger. As I have argued in greater detail elsewhere, Corinth was

[23]The major source for this affair is Thuc. 1.24-55. Two recent, detailed treatments will be found in Kagan, *Outbreak*, pp. 205-50, and de Ste Croix, *OPW*, pp. 66-79. Cf. my comments in "The Megarian Decree," pp. 161 ff.
[24]Thuc. 1.27.2.
[25]1.29.5.

determined to reverse the decision at Leucimne whatever the cost. She therefore undertook a major ship-building program, which enabled her to launch a fleet of ninety triremes for a rematch against the Corcyraeans a scant two years later.[26] It is probable that Megara and Corinth's other supporters in this conflict also augmented their fleets during these years.[27] Largely because of the naval build-up it had prompted, the Athenians soon became concerned about this seemingly remote war between Corinth and Corcyra. As the Corcyraeans stressed in their appeal to Athens in 433, the expanded Corinthian fleet constituted a danger to Athenian security, particularly if it were allowed to defeat and absorb Corcyra's considerable navy.[28] In fact, the combined fleets available to the Peloponnesians would then exceed the three hundred triremes Athens normally commissioned each year. Doubtless, Athens would still have held the edge in reserves, capital for further expansion, and skill in naval warfare, but she would have lost so much of her advantage over her rivals that they might be encouraged to support dissidents within the Delian League in the future, or to challenge Athens in other ways. A series of measures that stopped short of open violation of the Thirty Years Peace provided the Athenians with the means to block this development. They did not wish to appear responsible for a new war which, if we may believe Thucydides, they were convinced was coming anyway.[29] Thus as a first step they concluded a purely defensive alliance with Corcyra.

When the Athenians learned in 433 that a Corinthian armada had set sail for Corcyra, several Athenian squadrons were quickly dispatched to honor the terms of Athens' new treaty. Megara again figured prominently among the contributors to the Corinthian forces, this time sending twelve ships, though the increase in her

[26]Thuc. 1.31.1 and 46.1; Diod. 12.32.1-2.

[27]The contribution of Corinth's allies rose from forty-five ships at Leucimne to eighty-five at Sybota. It is impossible, however, to gauge what proportion of their total naval strength this represented, although it is safe to assume that it was a lesser proportion than the Corinthians supplied from their own armory. The fight, after all, was primarily Corinth's affair.

[28]Thuc. 1.36.3. Thucydides affirms that the Athenians were persuaded by this argument (1.44.2), and he even makes the Corinthians concede its validity in their speech at the first gathering of the Spartan allies in 432 (1.68.4).

[29]1.44.2.

support or that of Corinth's other allies was not proportionate to the Corinthians' own expanded effort.[30] Sparta once more stayed on the sidelines. When battle was joined at Sybota, the Megarian and Ambraciot squadrons were assigned the right wing.[31] This would normally have been the place of honor, but the Corinthians deliberately chose the left wing for themselves in order to face the ten Athenian ships on the Corcyraean right. Thucydides says that in the early stages of the battle, a squadron of twenty Corcyraean ships routed the enemy right wing, which we know was held by the Megarians and Ambraciots.[32] Meanwhile, the Corinthians were beating the rest of the Corcyraean fleet, as the Athenian squadron watched. In their pursuit of the Corcyraeans, the Corinthians "unwittingly killed some of their own allies, unaware that they had been worsted on the right wing."[33] These unfortunates were, of course, survivors of the beaten Megarian and Ambraciot ships. When the Corcyraeans had been driven to the shore, the Corinthians began towing off disabled vessels. Eventually, the Athenians intervened to prevent a total Corinthian victory and a landing on Corcyra, and at this critical juncture twenty more Athenian triremes appeared on the horizon.[34] The Corinthians wisely chose to break off the engagement as these reinforcements approached. Thucydides gives the figure of thirty triremes as the total losses of the Corinthian armada.[35] As few, if any, were lost on the left wing, the majority must have been from the right. We know that the Megarian and Ambraciot ships totaled thirty-nine, not many more than the round thirty mentioned by Thucydides. These two squadrons had apparently come close to being entirely destroyed, and we can be reasonably certain that a substantial proportion of the 2,400 Megarians who came to Sybota died there.[36]

[30]Thuc. 1.46.1.
[31]Thuc. 1.48.4. Megara probably earned her position on the wing by the size of her squadron, but her reputation for naval prowess may also have been a factor.
[32]1.49.1-5.
[33]Thuc. 1.50.1.
[34]Thuc. 1.50-51.
[35]1.54.2.
[36]Perhaps the Corinthians made good the lost Megarian and Ambraciot ships by awarding these allies a large proportion of the captured Corcyraean triremes, but there is no proof of this, nor do we understand Greek practice in the distribution of booty sufficiently. For the little that is known about the subject, see W. K. Pritchett, *The Greeks at War* (Berkeley, 1971), Vol. 1, pp. 82-84.

In a narrow sense, the battle at Sybota had been a stand-off, with the Corinthians in fact inflicting heavier casualties than the Corcyraeans. But in most respects the clash must be judged a victory for the Corcyraeans and their Athenian allies.[37] Corinth had failed to win control of the Ionian Sea lanes or to relieve Epidamnus. But as serious a defeat as Sybota was for the Corinthians, it was a tragedy for Megara. It would not be surprising if this debacle, the result of the oligarchy's zealous support for Corinth, fueled opposition to the government itself. The fortunes of Megara over the next few years raised even more questions about the wisdom of her policies and of the men who shaped them.

Sybota had brought members of Sparta's symmachy into direct conflict with Athens and left the Thirty Years Peace hanging by a thread. Corinth began applying pressure on Sparta to declare war.[38] Other issues fed this crisis, and among these was a *psephism* (decree) passed by the Athenian assembly affecting relations with Megara and known to modern historians as the Megarian Decree.[39] The decree may have been passed even earlier than the alliance between Athens and Corcyra was approved, but all we can say with any confidence is that it was in effect when Megara lodged a complaint about it at a synod of the Peloponnesian allies at Sparta in the summer of 432. Thucydides describes the issue raised on this occasion as follows:

> the Megarians . . . brought forward not a few other issues, but above all that they were barred from the harbors (*limenon*) of the Athenian empire (*archē*) and from the Athenian marketplace (*agoras*), contrary to the treaty.[40]

He uses virtually the same language to describe the gist of the decree on two other occasions. A Spartan embassy to Athens is said to have declared that the Athenians "could avert war only by

---

[37]Thucydides (1.54) lists the grounds for the rival claims of victory.

[38]This pressure became public after the crisis had been compounded by Athens' siege of Potidaea (Thuc. 1.56 ff.), and a meeting of the Spartan symmachy took place (Thuc. 1.66 ff.).

[39]There is a vast literature on the decree. Most views are summarized by Kagan, *Outbreak*, pp. 251-72, and de Ste Croix, *OPW*, pp. 224 ff., and 381-83. The latter's own views have already stirred a fresh avalanche of opinions; see note 51, below.

[40]1.67.4.

rescinding the decree concerning the Megarians, in which they were commanded not to have dealings with the harbors of the Athenian empire or in the Athenian marketplace."[41] And Pericles is reported to have urged the assembly to respond to this threat as follows:

> regarding the Megarians . . . we will let them use the marketplace and the harbors, if the Spartans will cease expelling foreigners (*xenelasia*) as far as concerns us and our allies; for nothing in the treaty prohibits our policy or theirs.[42]

The treaty in question is the Thirty Years Peace. That agreement can hardly have anticipated so unprecedented an act as the Megarian Decree, but the Megarians argued that it was a hostile act which violated the fundamental commitment to peace. Pericles was surely correct in the narrow legal sense that the enactment was not prohibited by Athens' treaty with the Peloponnesians.

Plutarch's description of the decree itself accords in large measure with Thucydides', while adding several nuances that may not be altogether insignificant. In describing the same meeting at Sparta as gave rise to Thucydides' first reference, Plutarch writes:

> and the Megarians went with them (the Corinthians), complaining they were barred and driven from all the market places and harbors which the Athenians controlled, contrary to common justice and the oaths the Greeks had sworn to each other.[43]

Three points seem worthy of note here. First, Plutarch gives the impression that the decree had involved the actual expulsion of Megarians abroad at the time of its enactment. Secondly, Plutarch speaks of "all the agoras" (*pasēs agoras*) rather than the Athenian agora, as specified by Thucydides.[44] Finally, in Plutarch's version the fragile basis of the Megarian claim regarding the decree's illegality is somewhat clearer.

---

[41]1.139.1.
[42]1.144.2.
[43]*Per.* 29.4.
[44]De Ste Croix, *OPW*, pp. 388-91, tries to refute the obvious meaning of Plutarch's statement, suggesting "the whole agora," rather than "every agora." The argument is inconclusive, and de Ste Croix's alternative presents other difficulties for his view of the decree (discussed later in this chapter), since "the whole agora" would seem to encompass the Athenian marketplace as well as the civic agora.

Aristophanes is the third major source to be considered. Dicaeopolis' defense in the *Acharnians*, which we have had occasion to cite earlier in this chapter, goes on to describe the passage of the Megarian Decree as the culmination of the chain of events in which the boycott of Megarian goods and the abduction of prostitutes had played a part:

> Then war among all the Greeks was unleashed on account of these harlots. Next Pericles, the Olympian, becoming enraged, lightened, thundered, threw all Greece into confusion, and drafted laws that sounded like drinking songs, as: The Megarians shall not be allowed on land, in the market place, on the sea, or in heaven (*en ouranoi*) [the manuscripts read *en ēpeiroi*—"on the continent"]. Then the Megarians, slowly starving, appealed to the Spartans to have the law of the prostitutes repealed. But we chose not to do so, though asked repeatedly. Next came the din of shields.[45]

Here, Pericles is made responsible for proposing the Megarian Decree. Thucydides and Plutarch say only that he vigorously fought against its repeal. Aristophanes also seems to make the decree virtually an act of war, rather than a mere provocation.[46] His description of the central clause, which we have seen in several guises already, is extravagant and pompous. This may reflect in part the tone of the actual *psephism*, but it is also a parody of a popular ballad of the time:

> O blind Plutus, you ought not to show yourself either on land, or sea, or on the continent [emended by de Ste Croix: *en ouranoi*, "in heaven"], but remain in Tartarus and Acheron (Hades); for men suffer every kind of evil through you.[47]

Aristophanes' clever adaptation has the Megarian Decree in effect banish the Megarians to Hades, having declared land, sea, agora, and, for good measure, heaven itself, off limits.[48] Too literal an interpretation is obviously out of place here, but the agreement of

---

[45] *Ach.* 528-39. Cf. *Pax* 608 f.

[46] Some modern historians follow him in this view—e.g., E. Meyer, *Forschungen,* Vol. 2, p. 303, and Beloch, *Gr. Gesch.* 2², p. 293.

[47] Schol. Ar. *Ach.* 532 = Timocreon fr. 5.

[48] De Ste Croix, *OPW,* p. 241, turns the usually assumed relationship between the Timocreon song and Aristophanes' jest on its head, suggesting that Aristophanes'

this other contemporary source with Thucydides in noting a single agora may be decisive in rejecting Plutarch's alternative wording. Finally, Aristophanes' comment about the Megarians slowly starving is undoubtedly an exaggeration if it is meant to describe the short-term effects of the decree, but it may at least point the direction in which to look for an effect better than our other sources.[49]

There has long been disagreement among scholars regarding the Athenians' motives in passing the decree, its effects on Megara, and its significance as a cause of the Peloponnesian War. But until recently there has been virtual unanimity on the meaning of the central provision of the decree: It cut off Megarian trade with Athens and her allies. This rare instance of consensus has now been shattered by G. E. M. de Ste Croix, who presented a radically different interpretation of the decree in 1972.[50] He argues that the exclusion applied only to Megarian citizens, not to the Megarian state or to the resident aliens (metics) and foreigners who he believes shouldered the main burden of Megarian commerce; that it barred Megarians only from entering the harbors of the Delian League states (*not* including Piraeus), allowing them to land on the coasts of league states or even to make their way on foot to the local marketplaces; that in Athens only the clearly demarcated civic and religious agora was off limits, giving the Megarians continued access to the sprawling commercial market which overflowed the bounds of the agora proper. He concludes that Athens' purpose was to humiliate the Megarians for their sacrilegious violation of the *hiera orgas,* and that any economic or strategic hardship inflicted by the decree was an incidental, though acceptable, side effect which, in any case, has been grossly exaggerated by historians.

This thesis, if correct, not only revises our understanding of the Megarian Decree, but affects all the other long-debated issues surrounding the decree. As it is set forth in nearly one hundred pages

---

alteration of Timocreon's "in heaven" to "on the continent" led the scholiast to misquote the original passage from Timocreon. It is an attractive hypothesis.

[49]Minor sources touching on the decree, but adding nothing of substance, include And. 3.8; Diod. 12.39; schol. Ar. *Ach.* 527, 532, and *Pax* 246, 483, 605, 609; Suda, *s.v. Aspasia;* Aristodem. 16.1-3; Ael. *VH* 7.12.53; Gell. *NA* 7.10; Lib. *Or.* 16.50.

[50]*OPW,* pp. 225-89, 381-99. The argument pervades much of the rest of this detailed survey of the causes of the Peloponnesian War.

213

of text and appendices, it would be impractical to attempt a thoroughgoing critique here. But enough must be said to indicate why this picture of the Megarian Decree should be rejected, as it has been in virtually all the responses to de Ste Croix's case which I have been able to consult.[51] It is possible that this signifies nothing more than the reflexive response of historians long accustomed to regard the decree in a certain way, but de Ste Croix's thesis has been persuasively challenged on many grounds. Few would accept his distinction between the civic and commercial agora of Athens, or between Megara and the Megarians, for example. Yet even if we concede these points, exclusion from the civic agora would have placed Megarian traders outside the protection of Athenian law, making it hazardous, if not impossible, for them to do business in Athens.[52] And if only Megarian citizens fell under the ban, it is still not proven that they played no significant part in Megarian commerce. De Ste Croix relies heavily on an analogy with Athens, where a substantial proportion of trade was in the hands of metics and foreigners.[53] Yet while we can confirm the existence of some resident aliens in Megara,[54] there is no basis for assuming that their numbers were proportionately as high as they were in Athens, or, indeed, that Megarian commerce was organized along the same lines. Certainly the crews of Megarian ships would have been at least partly citizen, even if most merchant ships were owned or captained by metics, and the presence of a few Megarians aboard would have been sufficient grounds to invoke the terms of the decree and bar these ships from the harbors of the empire.

Nor is it as obvious as de Ste Croix makes it seem that Megarian

[51]See, e.g., the following reviews and review articles: G. L. Cawkwell, *CR*, 25 (1975), 260-61; W. R. Connor, *Phoenix*, 28 (1973), 401-03; W. den Boer, *Mnemosyne*, 27 (1974), 437-38; V. Ehrenberg, *JHS*, 95 (1975), 242; W. G. Forrest, *Times Literary Supplement*, 72 (1973), 541-42; N. G. L. Hammond, *EHR*, 88 (1973), 870; D. Kagan, *AJP*, 96 (1975), 91-93; O. Murray, *G&R*, n.s. 20 (1973), 205; R. Sealy, "The Causes of the Peloponnesian War," *CP*, 70 (1975), 103 ff.; J. D. Smart, *CW*, 68 (1974), 180; C. G. Starr, *AHR*, 78 (1973), 663. P. Oliva, *Eirene*, 12 (1974), 143-45, gives a summary of the argument without comment. A. French, *Historia*, 25 (1976), 245-49, accepts de Ste Croix's criticism of earlier economic and strategic interpretations of the decree but rejects de Ste Croix's thesis.

[52]De Ste Croix concedes this point himself (pp. 280-82). Cf. Connor (note 51 above).

[53]See de Ste Croix, *OPW*, pp. 264-65.

[54]See below, Chapters 10 and 11, on the career of Hermon and others.

trade would have been swiftly transferred to other carriers, if Megarians could no longer conduct it. Nearly all the possible substitutes or surrogates were citizens or residents of states subject to Athens, and we ought not to assume that they were free to act on Megara's behalf with impunity. No one would argue any longer that Athens was thinking in terms of profit and commercial monopoly, but the possibility that she regarded control of commerce as a *strategic* weapon cannot be so easily dismissed.[55] An Athenian decree concerning the league town of Methone about 426 permitted her to import grain directly from Byzantium, suggesting that other grain-poor states in the Athenian domain were obliged to buy at the Athenian emporium or to seek a similar dispensation.[56] Admittedly, the Methone decree was a wartime measure, but the general policy behind it may well have applied in peacetime too. We also know that Athens was prepared to have league sailors who hired out to the Peloponnesians barred from their own states.[57] Again, it is unclear whether this restriction applied only in time of war—though the example cited certainly did. I suspect that the mysterious Athenian punishment of Aegina before the outbreak of the Peloponnesian War is traceable to the role of Aeginetan sailors in the expanded Corinthian fleet.[58] None of these considerations is unimpeachable or decisive on the question at hand, but they suggest that Athens might have been prepared to restrict the activities of her allies vis-à-vis Megara beyond the terms

[55]*Pace* French, *Historia*, 25 (1976), 245, who asserts: "Perhaps few historians are nowadays likely to defend what de Ste Croix believes to be still the 'standard view' of the decree's purpose and scope, namely to damage Megara's trade by an empire-wide embargo, and by such economic pressure to force Megara to change sides and ally herself to Athens, as she had done in 461." But this statement unnecessarily loads the issue by linking the notion of an embargo with one particular view of Athens' motives. The Athenians might have had any number of reasons for initiating such an embargo. If we remove French's specific attribution of motive, I believe that most historians would still prefer to interpret the decree as an embargo of some sort, rather than as an insult (de Ste Croix) or an element of psychological warfare (French).

[56]Meiggs and Lewis, *GHI* 65.34-36. Cf. the comments of Meiggs in *The Athenian Empire*, pp. 264-65. For a sensible discussion of the issue of Athenian economic imperialism, see M. I. Finley, "The Fifth Century Athenian Empire: A Balance Sheet," esp. pp. 117-21, in P. D. A. Garnsey and C. R. Whittaker, *Imperialism in the Ancient World* (Cambridge, 1978).

[57]Thuc. 1.143.1-2.

[58]Corinth had hired sailors from many parts of the Greek world prior to the Battle of Sybota (Thuc. 1.31.1).

of the Megarian Decree under the cold war conditions of the 430's. We cannot assume that she would have tolerated the resumption of Megarian commerce through the involvement of intermediaries who were within the reach of Athenian law, if her purpose had been to block that commerce in the first place.[59]

De Ste Croix's argument that exclusion from the harbors in the Athenian empire did not mean exclusion from these states themselves is even more questionable. The "harbors" prohibition is most naturally interpreted as forbidding entry into communities that could be reached only by sea; the decree added the Athenian agora, because the Megarians could gain access to Athens by land, rendering exclusion from the harbor at Piraeus insufficient to banish Megarian traffic from Athens itself.[60] It is as hard to believe that Megarians barred from the harbors of overseas states were permitted and expected to gain entry by beaching their ships along the shores, etc., as it is to believe that individuals prohibited from entering the gates of a city would be entitled to climb over or burrow under the walls![61]

As for the religious basis of the decree, it is far likelier to have been a pretext or rationalization meant to obscure Athens' real motives for her action, and possibly a *post hoc* justification at that, intended to put off the Spartans and to stiffen resistance to repeal. De Ste Croix can produce evidence for the exclusion of polluted individuals from the boundaries of the civic agora, but there are no cases of whole classes of individuals or entire populations being so excluded. In effect, he posits a purpose behind the decree which is as unprecedented as the one he attacks. Furthermore, there is no apparent basis for connecting exclusions from *harbors* with sac-

[59]See the *Old Oligarch* 2.11-12 (discussed later in this chapter) on the extent to which Athens was prepared to restrict trade in strategic commodities.

[60]I believe that Piraeus was one of the harbors closed to the Megarians by the decree. De Ste Croix has no grounds for maintaining that Piraeus was open to them, apart from his highly disputable view that the Megarians were free to do business in Athens itself (*OPW*, pp. 287-88).

[61]Thucydides (1.144.2) has Pericles compare the decree with the Spartan practice of excluding foreigners—the *xenelasia*. This Spartan custom is not well understood (see H. Michell, *Sparta*, Cambridge, 1964, pp. 152-54), but it probably was meant to exclude aliens from all of Laconia, not merely from the agora or even the town of Sparta. If Pericles' analogy had any merit, it suggests that the Megarian Decree effectively barred the Megarians from Attica and all the allied territories, not only from parts of the city of Athens.

rilege. Nor does it make sense for Pericles to have cited Megarian violation of Attica's secular boundaries and the protection of runaway slaves as partial justification of a punishment designed to deal with sacrilege.

Though all the points above are telling against de Ste Croix's case, the fundamental flaw of his approach is its excessive legalism and literalism. The crucial clause of the decree (which in any case we do not possess in its original form) cannot be entirely understood by an exhaustive analysis of each of the terms of which it is comprised. Athens had taken an unprecedented step and, so far as we can tell, had invented a formula to achieve her purpose. It is entirely beside the point that de Ste Croix can propose more effective (though equally unprecedented) language to achieve a commercial or strategic embargo. Why must we regard the Athenians as perfect legislators? That there were loopholes in the Megarian Decree tells us nothing about its purpose. History is replete with formulas that were less than ideally suited to achieve their objectives (or that were later interpreted in a manner never anticipated by their drafters). The *combination* of harbors and agora has an obvious commercial implication, confirmed by Aristophanes' exaggerated picture of the decree's effect; to treat the two terms independently is tantamount to endeavoring to understand the meaning of an idiomatic phrase by defining the words that make it up.

Returning, then, to the orthodox view of the decree's central clause—namely that its aim was to shut off or at least impede Megarian shipping in the Aegean and along the route to the Black Sea—we must further consider the significance of that shipping in the 430's. To begin with, one ought not to discount the importance of maritime commerce in the Megarian economy, or the damage that its sudden curtailment would cause. If the picture of the Megarian economy presented in the early chapters of this study and in Chapter 11 below is reasonably correct, Megara was a grain-poor state that regularly exported woolens, vegetables, salt, and other products to finance grain imports. Some of the needed grain was purchased in the Athenian market[62] and more may have come from

---

[62]In Aristophanes' *Acharnians*, when a Megarian farmer comes to Dicaeopolis' market in Athens (729 ff.), he trades his daughters for garlic and salt—two tradition-

Boeotia, but the bulk of it must have been imported on Megarian ships plying the route to Byzantium and Chalcedon. An embargo against this shipping may not have meant starvation for Megara, but it would have caused serious disruption and imbalance. A substantial proportion (if not the entire burden) of Megarian social and political contacts with her eastern colonies was borne by Megarian shipping too, and the imposition of the decree threatened to alter Megara's colonial relations. There is, however, another aspect to Megara's maritime activity in this period which has seldom been considered in assessing the possible effects of the decree. As noted earlier, Megara had become the main commercial conduit between the Peloponnesian states and the cities of the Aegean, Propontis, and Black Sea. When Megarian trade was disrupted, all the Peloponnesians were affected, though we should not imagine that many of these states were heavily dependent upon Aegean imports or markets, or that the decree's effects would have been widely felt initially. In fact, however, Corinth had simultaneously run into difficulties in her western trade, because of the war with Corcyra. Thus the Aegean Sea may have assumed added commercial significance for the Peloponnesians in the late 430's, at precisely the time Athens passed the Megarian Decree. When the Corinthians appeared before the gathering of Peloponnesian allies at Sparta in the summer of 432, they warned their landlocked allies that Athens' recent moves would ultimately affect them too:

> Those who dwell further inland and away from the sea lanes should be warned that unless they support those on the coasts, they will find it harder to export the produce of the land and to receive in exchange what the sea provides the mainland; and that . . . if they forsake the coasts, the danger may eventually reach them, and they are no less considering their own problem (than ours).[63]

In this passage, Thucydides may tell us more about the real impact of the Megarian Decree (and Athens' support of Corcyra) than in any of his explicit references.

---

al Megarian *exports*—not daring even to ask for grain, which he needs most. Here is a clear example of comic exaggeration. See further comments on this scene below in Chapter 10.

[63]Thuc. 1.120.2.

The sudden curtailment of Peloponnesian trade in the Aegean, however, may have had a more immediate impact, which the warning of the Corinthians only hints at, for one article of Aegean trade—timber—had great strategic importance to the seaboard states of the Peloponnese in the late 430's. Although a few stands of trees undoubtedly remained in rainier districts, the states of central and southern Greece, had long been dependent upon imported timber, particularly for building ships.[64] Hardwoods suitable for the frames of Greek ships grew in abundance in the cooler climes of northern Greece, in Epirus and Illyria on the Ionian Sea, and in Macedonia and Thrace on the Aegean. The Corinthians, Sicyonians, Eleans, etc. would normally have acquired timber from the northwest, while Athens, Megara, Aegina, etc. would have relied on the Aegean sources. But Corcyraean supremacy in the Ionian Sea after 435 made it extremely hazardous, if not impossible, to convey supplies from Epirus and Illyria to the Peloponnesian shipyards. Trade with Magna Graecia may have continued, though with increased risk, but it is doubtful that the great logs, which were most in need and which had to be carried as a deck load, could be brought so great a distance. Yet between 435 and 433, the Peloponnesians built a great many ships, probably more than one hundred. Thucydides provides the raw numbers that make this inference clear,[65] and he comments: "During the entire year following the naval battle [at Leucimne] and the next year as well, the Corinthians were building ships and outfitting the mightiest fleet they could launch."[66] Diodorus describes this activity more vividly, though one wonders whether Ephorus or any other source provided him with a solid basis for fleshing out Thucydides' comment:

> the Corinthians . . . determined to build a worthier fleet. Therefore, having procured a great deal of timber and having hired shipwrights from other cities, they began building triremes and making weapons and missiles of every type, and some triremes were newly con-

---

[64]See E. C. Semple, *The Geography of the Ancient Mediterranean* (New York, 1931), pp. 275-82, on the Greek states' sources of ship timber. Cf. A. C. Johnson, "Ancient Forests and Navies," *TAPA*, 58 (1927), 199-209.

[65]1.27.2, 29.5, 46.1.

[66]1.31.1.

structed, but they also repaired those which were damaged, and sent for still others from their allies.[67]

Where was this great amount of timber acquired? I suggest that a substantial proportion, perhaps nearly all of it, came from Macedonia and Thrace, and that Megara played a key role in procuring and shipping this strategic material.[68] The effect of the Megarian Decree would have been greatly to reduce the flow of Aegean timber to Corinth and the other naval states of the Peloponnese.

The case thus far presented for this additional effect of the decree, though plausible, is purely circumstantial. Yet while no source explicitly discusses the decree in terms of the timber trade, several near-contemporary comments about Athens' efforts to dominate the Aegean seem to have the decree or measures of this type in mind. Thucydides gives a hint of this type of tactic in the Corcyraean appeal to Athens. The Corcyraeans advise the Athenians that, as the greatest naval power of Greece, "if you had the power, you should strive to prevent anyone else from having ships, but, if you can't, at least try to have as friends those who are best equipped with them."[69] This suggestion, hypothetical in form, that Athens might consider ways to prevent her enemies from having ships at all, may have been made at the very time the Megarian Decree was under consideration—almost certainly within months before or after its passage. Though it was utopian to believe that rival states could be denied ships altogether, the Athenians might prevent them from building many more.

The most important evidence, however, is a passage in the antidemocratic Athenian pamphleteer, known as the Pseudo-Xenophontic *Constitution of Athens*, or, more conveniently, the *Old Oligarch*. The date of this document is a matter of dispute, but most scholars agree in placing its composition at some point during the Peloponnesian War.[70] The *Old Oligarch* describes the tactic sug-

---

[67]2.32.1-2.

[68]This suggestion was first made in my article "The Megarian Decree," pp. 161-71. Cf. the general remarks on strategic concern for timber supplies in D. W. Knight, *Some Studies in Athenian Politics in the Fifth Century B.C.*, Historia Einzelschriften, 13 (Wiesbaden, 1970), 4-12 and n. 18.

[69]1.35.5.

[70]On the case for a post-431 date for this tract, see W. G. Forrest, "The Date of the

gested by the Corcyraeans as an established facet of Athenian policy:

> The wealth [gained from seafaring] belongs to them (the Athenians) alone among the Greeks and barbarians. For if some polis is rich in timber for shipbuilding, where will it dispose of it without the consent of the ruler of the sea? Or if any is rich in iron, bronze, or flax, where will it dispose of it without the consent of the ruler of the sea? These, however, are the very things I need (to build) my ships, timber from one, iron from another, copper from a third, linen from a fourth, wax from a fifth. Furthermore, we will not allow anyone to ship these goods to any hostile state on pain of being denied the use of the sea.[71]

There is no suggestion in this passage that the *Old Oligarch* is thinking particularly of wartime conditions or military means. He seems to describe a policy that would be as effective and appropriate in peace.[72] In fact, open warfare would scarcely require such subtleties. Among the acts of fifth-century Athens, none corresponds to the policy outlined by the *Old Oligarch* nearly so well as the Megarian Decree. He asserts that Athens' naval supremacy was unchallengeable, because she could deny her enemies access to the timber and other raw materials necessary to build ships. She accomplished this in two ways: first, by prohibiting the suppliers of these materials from selling to anyone Athens perceived as a threat; secondly, by enjoining the shipping states from freighting these strategic supplies to the port of any rival power by threatening the shippers with being denied the use of the sea altogether. The Megarian Decree denied Megara the use of the sea, or at least tried to do so; and what had been Megara's crime?—transporting strategic goods to Corinth and elsewhere in the Peloponnese. It is regrettable that the *Old Oligarch* refrains from giving concrete historical examples, for if he had done so, he could hardly have avoided mention of the Megarian Decree.

Pseudo-Xenophontic Athenaion Politeia," *Klio*, 52 (1970), 107-16; de Ste Croix, *OPW*, pp. 307-10; M. J. Fontana, *L'Athenaion Politeia del V secolo a. C.* (Palermo, 1968); and A. W. Gomme, "The Pseudo-Xenophontic *Constitution of Athens*," *HSCP*, Suppl. 1 (1940), 211-45. A minority of scholars, however, continue to argue for an earlier date. See, e.g., G. W. Bowersock, "Pseudo-Xenophon," *HSCP*, 71 (1966), 33-55.

[71]2.11-2. Tr. H. Frisch, *The Constitution of the Athenians* (Copenhagen, 1942).
[72]*Pace* de Ste Croix, *OPW*, p. 261.

I doubt that the decree could have been totally effective either in denying Megara any role in Aegean commerce or in completely choking off timber supplies to her and her allies. Even a regular blockade of the Megarian coastline in the early years of the Peloponnesian War failed to halt all Megarian shipping.[73] In addition, there must always have been other merchants willing to take risks, even to violate an Athenian edict, if the price was right. Both enterprising Megarian and non-Megarian traders would have found ways around the embargo, though doubtless the volume of shipping would have been greatly reduced and the cost raised to an uneconomic level.[74] To the extent that the act was a response to the Peloponnesian naval build-up, it may have been a case of closing the barn door after the horses had fled. By 433 the Corinthians commanded a fleet whose size must have taxed the available manpower of the naval states of the Peloponnese. Further expansion, if contemplated, depended on the attraction of sailors from the Athenian sphere, which was no easy matter.[75] But the issue became academic when war broke out shortly afterward. Athens now had an excuse for using more direct and violent methods to frustrate the naval ambitions of her enemies. None of these considerations, it should be stressed, invalidates the notion of what Athens hoped to achieve by passing the Megarian Decree: foreign policy initiatives, both ancient and modern, seldom entirely achieve their objectives; and subsequent assessments of their success or failure are not good gauges of what may have been hoped for when they were devised.

The prospect of disrupting Peloponnesian timber supplies and Aegean trade was probably not Athens' sole motive for enacting the Megarian Decree; policy-making is seldom this single-minded or coherent, particularly in an open society. Men may have supported the measure for a variety of reasons: genuine outrage at Megarian border incursions; more general animus toward the

[73]See below, Chapter 10.

[74]De Ste Croix's suggestions of various ways the Megarians might have attempted to circumvent an embargo imposed on them (esp. pp. 262-63 and 284 ff.) make this point, even if they tell us nothing about Athenian intentions.

[75]We have already noted Pericles' response (Thuc. 1.143.1-2) to this threatened Corinthian tactic (1.121.3-4). Could the provision of sailors to the Peloponnesian fleet be the cause of Aegina's difficulties with Athens prior to the outbreak of the Peloponnesian War?

Megarians, heightened by their participation in the war against Corcyra; and, on the part of some, a desire to provoke a Peloponnesian declaration of war. But the objective proposed here seems to me more practical than any hope of forcing Megara to rejoin Athens through economic pressure, more purposeful than any desire merely to damage the Megarian economy, and more responsible than an act of bravado or defiance—thumbing Athens' nose at Sparta and her allies.[76] When we take the question of strategic supplies into account, the Megarian Decree falls into place beside the Corcyraean alliance, the repression of Potidaea, and the unspecified acts against Aegina, as one of a series of measures intended to forestall a naval challenge by Corinth and her Peloponnesian allies. It was nominally directed against Megara, and she was the likeliest to suffer from it, but it was calculated to cause serious difficulties for Corinth and other Peloponnesian states, and to accomplish all this without technically breaching the Thirty Years Peace.

By itself, the decree would probably not have led to a Spartan declaration of war, or even to Corinthian pressure for such a declaration. But it was part of a pattern of Athenian actions which alarmed the Spartans and fed the war fever. (We cannot stop here to consider some of the broader questions involved in sorting out responsibility for the Peloponnesian War, but it is arguable that these Athenian moves were a rational response to Corinthian and other Peloponnesian measures, rather than a deliberate policy aimed at subjugating the Peloponnese.)[77] The historical significance of the decree was blurred in antiquity by several related factors. First, it became one of the main talking points in the diplomatic exchanges during the year between the Peloponnesians' nominal declaration of war and the time the first "shot" was fired.[78] At one point, the Spartans said that there need not be a war if the decree were repealed,[79] and Pericles' response to the final Spartan embas-

[76]See Kagan, *Outbreak*, pp. 251-72, for a full discussion of the historiography of this problem. I have some sympathy for Kagan's own view (pp. 263-66) that the Athenians did not expect a sharp reaction to the Megarian Decree from the Spartans. But I doubt that the decree was adopted as a consciously moderate alternative to an open declaration of war against Megara in 433/2.
[77]This is one of Kagan's central theses in *Outbreak*.
[78]See Thuc. 1.139 ff. and Plut. *Per.* 29 ff.
[79]Thuc. 1.139.1.

sy suggests that the Megarian Decree was still the chief substantive issue.[80] Pericles urged the assembly not to give in on this point, and this, in turn, gave rise to the second distorting phenomenon— namely, the popular impression, immortalized in the comedies of Aristophanes, that the decree and Pericles' advocacy of it were the main causes of the war.[81] Finally, when Thucydides came to write, a decade or two later, he was at pains to refute this popular assumption, which he believed gave little recognition to the major problem of incompatible, rival powers; he deliberately played down the role of the Megarian Decree.[82]

Why did the Spartans insist on the lifting of the Megarian embargo? Part of the answer must be that she was performing her duty as Megara's hegemon, but Megara could not exert sufficient leverage to force Sparta to go to war, even if she threatened secession once more, and I do not believe that the Megarian oligarchy was remotely inclined to try its luck with Athens again.[83] Another part of the answer was that the decree was a strategic blow against Corinth, the other naval states of the Peloponnese, and, ultimately, against the alliance as a whole. In concert, the states directly affected by the decree might have been able to force Sparta to take a stand. But one further factor was that the Spartans believed they could make progress on this issue more easily than on any of the other grievances of their allies, since Athens could make a concession here without breaching any covenant (such as the Corcyraean alliance) or acknowledging any limits on her sovereignty over the Delian League (as in the Potidaean and Aeginetan complaints). Had Sparta been able to negotiate repeal of the decree, she might have been in a position to resist the pressure for war on the part of her allies. The issue became symbolic. For Sparta it was a symbol of her attempts to protect the interests of her allies and of Athens' willingness or unwillingness to be reasonable. For Athens it was a symbol of her resolve to resist Spartan pressure and to appear strong and

[80]Thuc. 1.140-45.

[81]*Ach.* 524 ff. and *Pax* 500 ff., 604 ff.

[82]For Thucydides' general views on the deeper causes of the war and the danger of overstressing the immediate issues, see 1.23, 88, 118.

[83]I seriously doubt that Megara was in sympathy with the Corinthian threat to seek other allies—i.e., to go over to Argos, or, more likely, to Athens—unless the Spartans declared war against Athens, but then, it is doubtful that even Corinth was sincere in this threat as early as 432.

confident. The quotation from Pericles' final advice to the Athenians, which opens this chapter, is a clear expression of the concern that had come to overshadow the practical significance of the decree. Thus an issue of considerable importance was blown out of proportion in the final hours of peace and left a lasting impression that it had been even more critical than it actually was. When Thucydides tried to set the record straight, he did so at the expense of a coherent picture of the decree, thereby launching a controversy which I doubt will ever be fully resolved.

As if the picture were not confused enough, Plutarch describes several further Athenian enactments concerning Megara in this period. They are reported in his treatment of the negotiations between Sparta and Athens after the Peloponnesian vote for war in 432, and I quote these remarks extensively, since the chronology of the events is a matter of dispute:

> They say that a Spartan embassy came to Athens to discuss this very issue (the Megarian Decree), and Pericles alleged that there was a law prohibiting the tablet on which the decree was inscribed from being taken down. Polyalces, one of the ambassadors, replied, "Then don't take it down, merely turn it toward the wall; there's no law preventing that!" Witty as this answer was, it hadn't the slightest effect on Pericles. It seems that Pericles must have nursed some private grudge against the Megarians, but in public he accused them of expropriating the sacred groves (*tēn hiera orgada*), and he proposed a decree that a herald be sent to them (the Megarians) and the Spartans to denounce the Megarians. This decree, which is certainly the work of Pericles, contains a reasonable and courteous justification (of his policy). But when Anthemocritus, the herald who was sent, was murdered, as it seemed, at the hands of the Megarians, Charinus proposed a decree against them, that there should be implacable and irreconcilable enmity toward them, that any Megarian setting foot in Attica should be put to death, and that when the generals swore the ancient oath of office, they should also swear to invade Megarian territory twice each year. Anthemocritus was buried by the Thriasian gates, which are now called the Dipylon. But the Megarians denied responsibility for the death of Anthemocritus and put the blame (for the dispute) on Aspasia and Pericles, citing those well-known and hackneyed verses from the *Acharnians* [524 ff.]. . . . Therefore, the original grounds for the decree are not easily discovered, but everyone agrees that Pericles was responsible for its not being revoked.[84]

[84]*Per.* 30-31.1.

The opening and closing sentences of this passage clearly seem to frame a treatment of events *subsequent* to the passage of the Megarian Decree, and though one may be inclined to doubt the reliability of Plutarch's account of these events, there are no grounds for revising the sequence he intended to convey, as some have attempted.[85] If Plutarch had given no indication of sequence, one might postulate that a "reasonable and courteous" complaint about Megarian violation of the *hiera orgas* was preliminary to the more drastic action of the Megarian Decree. But Plutarch presents the "reasonable and courteous" decree as a response to the Spartan complaint. It might seem a bit late for such tactics, but only if one chooses to regard the "reasonable and courteous" language as sincere, rather than as the propaganda ploy it probably was.[86] In fact, it is not too different a tack from the offer to rescind the Megarian Decree in exchange for the Spartans' lifting of the *xenelasia*, which Thucydides reports Pericles to have made. Though it cannot be demonstrated beyond question, I would not be surprised if both accounts are traceable to the same stage of diplomatic maneuvering between the two sides.

The murder of Anthemocritus and the decree of Charinus present other problems. Thucydides specifically states that although private travel continued, no heralds were exchanged between the two sides after Pericles' response concerning the xenelasia was given to the last Spartan embassy.[87] One could resolve the apparent contradiction by placing Anthemocritus' mission marginally earlier, or by making it simultaneous with the answer given directly to the Spartan ambassadors, or even by associating his murder and the subsequent Decree of Charinus with the fourth-century dispute over the hiera orgas.[88] Although Thucydides' silence is trou-

---

[85]On this point I cannot accept the arguments of de Ste Croix, *OPW*, pp. 246-51, or C. Fornara, "Plutarch and the Megarian Decree," *YCS*, 24 (1975), 213-28. The same sequence of events is implicit in Thucydides' account, where Pericles' rationalization for the Megarian Decree is only presented in response to Sparta's diplomatic protests against its passage (1.139.1-2).

[86]See, e.g., G. L. Cawkwell's remarks in *CR*, 25 (1975), 261.

[87]1.146. Heralds, however, did carry messages between the two sides once the war had begun (Thuc. 2.1).

[88]The theory that Anthemocritus belongs to the fourth century has been most fully developed by W. R. Connor, "Charinus' Megarian Decree," *AJP*, 83 (1962), 225-46. The most convincing rebuttal to Connor's position has been made by G. L. Cawk-

bling, I believe there are even more problems in moving Anthemocritus down to the fourth century, and I am inclined to connect
him with the diplomatic exchanges after the Megarian Decree was
passed. One could easily imagine the Megarians responding to the
Athenians' hypocritical message by turning against the messenger.
But even if we are prepared to believe this, the questions of how
Anthemocritus died and how the Athenians recovered his body
remain.

One aspect of Charinus' Decree is supposed to have touched on
the burial of Anthemocritus; the rest seems to have been, in effect,
a declaration of perpetual war against Megara. If authentic, it could
not have been enacted prior to the Theban attack on Plataea in 431
without calling into question the most basic elements of Thucydides' account. Yet the terms of this decree correspond to the actual
pattern of Athenian attacks on Megara in the early years of the
conflict.[89] Specific legislation was hardly needed to mandate the
twice-yearly attacks on the Megarid, but the possibility of such a
law cannot be ruled out, and would not be inconsistent with what
Thucydides tells us.

On the eve of the war in 431, Megara was already in some
distress as a result of the Megarian Decree, and she faced the
prospect of once more becoming a battleground. Megara's relations with Athens were as dismal as at any time since the dispute
over Salamis, and the Megarians were, as a result, more dependent
upon the Peloponnesians than ever. The Megarian oligarchy had
led Megara down this path since 446, though doubtlessly popular
feeling against Athens ran high, and there must have been widespread support for this policy. Thus Megara was aligned with the
advocates of war in the late 430's. By most measures, this policy
was to prove disastrous for her: the war it helped to cause was to
ruin Megara, destabilize her internal politics, and lead to a temporary overthrow of the oligarchy. These developments are the subject of the next chapter.

---

well, "Anthemocritus and the Decree of Charinus," *REG*, 82 (1969), 327-35. See
below, Chapter 11, for fuller citation of the relevant bibliography and a discussion of
the issues.

[89]See Thuc. 2.31, 4.66.1.

CHAPTER 10

The Peloponnesian War

War: (*adding some garlic to the brew*) O Megara! Megara! Any
moment you'll be destroyed once and for all and ground
to mincemeat.
Trygaeus: My goodness! What large and bitter tears he has tossed
in for the Megarians.

—Aristophanes, *Peace* 246-249

EARLY in the spring of 431, the Thebans carried out a surprise
attack on Plataea, and at the beginning of that summer, King
Archidamus of Sparta led the Peloponnesian army into Attica.[1] The
first phase of the Peloponnesian War, also known as the Archidamian War, had begun.[2] The Athenians, adhering to Pericles'
strategy, remained safely behind their long-walls while the enemy
spent the summer devastating their land. As long as Archidamus
stayed in Attica, the Athenians confined their response to a naval
expedition around the Peloponnese. But when the enemy had
withdrawn, Athens went on the offensive, and it was Megara who
felt the full impact of Athenian fury and frustration:

> In the autumn of the year (431), all Athens' forces, citizens and metics
> alike, marched into the Megarid under the command of Pericles, the
> son of Xanthippus. And the Athenians aboard the 100 ships operating

---

[1]See Thuc. 2.18 ff. The Peloponnesian army assembled at the Isthmus and entered Attica near Oenoe on the Boeotian border. It later marched through Eleusis,
finally exiting into Boeotia by way of Oropus. It thus appears that Archidamus
marched along the Road of the Towers in both directions, rather than along the
coastal road from Megara to Eleusis. This choice would have made sense during his
advance, since it would have enabled him to join forces with the Boeotians before
entering Attica and minimized any risk of the Athenians attempting to block the
Peloponnesian advance. His purpose in returning the same way is not clear, though
it points to the attractiveness of the Road of the Towers in general. Cf. Gomme,
HCT, 2, pp. 66-69, 80.

[2]For a recent and thorough treatment of this period, see Donald Kagan, *The
Archidamian War* (Ithaca, 1972). The specialized literature is vast.

around the Peloponnese (who happened to be at Aegina while on their way home), when they learned that the entire army was in Megara, sailed across and joined forces with it. This was the greatest Athenian army ever assembled in one place. . . . There were no fewer than 10,000 Athenians . . . and they were joined by at least 3,000 metic hoplites, not counting a sizeable body of light armed troops. After having laid waste much of the country, they returned home.[3]

The Megarians did not attempt to resist this overwhelming force any more than the Athenians had tried to fend off Archidamus. Nor did the Peloponnesian army come to Megara's defense: the Peloponnesians had returned home to bring in their crops.

This Athenian invasion was but the first of many. Thucydides goes on to say: "As the war progressed, the Athenians invaded the Megarid with their cavalry, and the entire army every year, up to the time they captured Nisaea [in 424]."[4] Introducing the events of 424, he is more specific regarding the frequency of these incursions: "the Megarians . . . were being hard pressed in the war by the Athenians, who regularly marched their entire army into the territory twice each year."[5] Megara was virtually defenseless against these attacks, since her allies were obviously not prepared to station a large army permanently in her territory, and the Athenians could strike Megara and retire before the Peloponnesians could react. Eventually a Spartan garrison was installed in Nisaea; though we cannot establish precisely when, it was neither able nor intended to ward off Athenian depredation of the Megarian countryside.[6]

During these same years the Athenians took sterner measures against Megarian shipping than those imposed by the Megarian Decree. They established a fort on Salamis at Budorum, facing the Megarid, and tried to prevent any ships from entering or leaving Nisaea. As the likely sites of the fort are at least six to eight kilometers distant from Nisaea and would have had a poor view of ships entering and leaving it, this blockade must have been less than entirely effective. But it can only have resulted in the further

[3]Thuc. 2.31. Cf. Plut. *Per.* 34.
[4]2.31.3.
[5]4.66.1. Cf. the controversial Decree of Charinus discussed in Chapter 9, above.
[6]Thuc. 4.66 ff. The function of this garrison is discussed below.

drastic reduction of Megara's capacity to import food and other supplies by sea. It is true that Pagae on the opposite coast was still in Megarian hands, but ships embarking from it were restricted to the eastern end of the Corinthian Gulf by the Athenian blockading force at Naupactus. Thus Megara was isolated from the grain rich states of Magna Graecia as effectively as from the Black Sea communities.[7] She was unable either to produce whatever proportion of her foodstuffs she normally provided in peacetime, or to import the same from her usual sources of supply. Nor could she produce accustomed quantities of the export goods that normally paid for grain imports. Her situation was desperate, and she may have survived only by handouts received from Boeotia and the Peloponnesian states.

Thucydides says enough to indicate the gravity of Megara's situation, but he does not expand on it sufficiently for us to measure either the practical or psychological effects of this prolonged state of siege. Pausanias preserves a story which shows that the Megarians remembered this as an extremely difficult time. There has to be a local tradition behind the explanation he offers for the fact that the image of Zeus in the Olympieum at Megara was never completed:

---

[7]Thuc. 2.93-94 (on Budorum) and 2.69 ff. (on Naupactus). In a recent article, "Megara, Athens, and the West in the Archidamian War: A Study in Thucydides," *Historia*, 28 (1979), 1-14, T. Wick interprets the blockade at Naupactus and even Athenian meddling in Sicilian affairs in the early 420's primarily as a means of denying Megara western foodstuffs. Athens' purpose, according to Wick, was to gain control of the Megarid in order to prevent Peloponnesian invasions of Attica. He further argues that this strategy was rendered unnecessary by the Athenian capture of Pylos in 425. With the Peloponnesian army now pinned down in Messenia, it was no longer as vital to control the Megarid; hence, Athenian interest in Sicily waned, and the Athenians did not fight as hard to win Megara in 424 as they might otherwise have done. Wick's thesis has the virtue of emphasizing the effects of various war measures on Megara—an often ignored topic—but it may go too far in this direction. The western blockade and Athenian policy in Sicily had aims beyond bringing pressure on Megara, and Athenian interest in the Megarid continued, as we shall see, well beyond 424. Furthermore, there seem to be good reasons for the collapse of Athens' Sicilian initiative in the 420's, quite apart from altered Athenian ambitions, and it is far from clear that the Athenian effort to win Megara in 424 was half-hearted. On that last point, see the discussion later in this chapter. When all is said, however, we must agree with Wick that Megara was the most vulnerable Peloponnesian target, and that Athens was consciously bringing the full weight of her war effort to bear on the hapless Megarians.

The statue of Zeus was not finished because the war between the Peloponnesians and the Athenians broke out, during which the Athenians annually wasted the land of the Megarians by both naval and infantry attacks, thereby destroying her public wealth and reducing individual households to the most dire poverty. While the face of Zeus' image is of ivory and gold, the rest is made of clay and gypsum. They say it was made by a local sculptor, Theocosmus, with help from Phidias. . . . Behind the temple lie some partly finished blocks of wood; Theocosmus intended to cover these with ivory and gold to finish the statue of Zeus.[8]

This memory of dire poverty, public and private, in the 420's scarcely seems exaggerated, based on what we can infer from Thucydides. Pausanias offers no explanation of why Theocosmus' chryselephantine statue of Zeus was not completed in the fourth century, when prosperity returned and the Megarians sponsored many other public monuments. Had they become used to this strange composite figure as it stood? Or had it become a memorial of sorts to their sacrifices during the war?

A more familiar picture of Megarian suffering in these years is that which emerges from Aristophanes' contemporary comedies, particularly the *Acharnians*. By the time this play was produced in 425, the situation in Megara had further deteriorated as a result of civil war and the Athenian capture of the coastal island of Minoa, events to which we shall shortly turn our attention. But Aristophanes' images appear true to the entire period. Megara had become for him the most dramatic illustration of the suffering the war had brought to Greece. He personifies her abasement in the figure of a desperate Megarian farmer (denied even the dignity of a name), who tries to sell his daughters to Dicaeopolis, disguised as pigs, so that both he and they can avert starvation.[9] The scene is filled with low comedy and double entendres, particularly on the theme of whether the Megarian maidens are being touted for their porcine or sexual attributes. The Megarians are starving, grain is so scarce that it is worshiped rather than eaten. The Athenian invasions haven't left so much as a single onion or garlic to be harvested, nor can the Megarians collect salt from the pans along the

[8]1.40.4.
[9]*Ach.* 719 ff.

coast (although this probably applies only to the period after the Athenians had seized Minoa). In fact, the farmer readily accepts small quantities of garlic and salt, traditional Megarian exports, in exchange for his daughters. He doesn't dream of asking for grain, and he is so delighted with the transaction that he expresses the hope that he may strike a similar bargain for his wife and mother!

Since we are dealing with comic exaggeration, satire, and ridicule, we are hardly to imagine that the Megarians were driven to sell their wives, daughters, and mothers, disguised as piglets or otherwise, but conditions in Megara supplied a solid basis for Aristophanes' extravagant image. In *Peace*, which was staged about four years later, the Megarians play the same role. Their sorry condition is the subject of the comments that open this chapter, and when representatives of the various Greek states pitch in to pull Peace out of a ditch, Trygaeus remarks again on how much they had suffered: "The Megarians aren't getting anywhere; but they keep pulling all the same, slipping and scraping like puppies. By Zeus! they're dying of starvation."[10]

The Megarians were ideally suited to Aristophanes' dual purposes of entertaining and persuading his Athenian audience. The people of Athens would have enjoyed a good belly laugh at the expense of their despised neighbors, portrayed as dull-witted, vulgar, and venal. They might also have taken satisfaction from the depiction of Megarian suffering. It was, after all, proof that the Athenians had been able to inflict worse hardship on at least one of their enemies than they themselves had suffered. At the same time, Aristophanes hoped that the pathetic condition of the Megarians would provide an example of the extremes to which the war had been carried, perhaps helping to soften his countrymen's attitude toward peace. The plays were more successful as comedy, however, than as political propaganda, and they did not alter Athens' policy toward Megara in any measurable way.

The Megarians' mood steadily blackened after the outbreak of war. Many must have felt, with some justice, that their allies, who had been hardly touched by the war, comparatively speaking,

[10]*Pax* 481-83.

were not doing enough to protect them from Athens. As a result, there may well have been a growing sense of alienation from the Peloponnesian League. This rising sentiment would probably have fixed on the pro-Spartan and pro-Corinthian policies of the oligarchic regime as the source of Megara's current difficulties. But the oligarchs were still fully committed to this policy, and all they could do to appease popular discontent was to advocate the most vigorous prosecution of the war against Athens. In addition to Megara's participation in the major military operations mounted by the anti-Athenian coalition in the early years of the war,[11] she is credited with having conceived the boldest exploit undertaken by the Peloponnesians in this period, a surprise raid on Piraeus.

In the fall of 429, after the Peloponnesian fleet had failed to break through the Athenian blockage at Naupactus:

> Before disbanding the fleet (which had retreated to Corinth and the Crisaean Gulf) for the winter, Cnemus, Brasidas, and the other Peloponnesian commanders, at the urging of the Megarians, decided to make an attempt on Piraeus, the Athenian port. It was quite reasonably left open and unprotected, because of (Athenian) naval superiority. The plan was that each sailor, carrying his oar, cushion, and oar loop, should go by foot from Corinth to the sea facing Athens [i.e., cross the Isthmus over the *diolchos*], and from there hurry on to Megara over the Scironian Way and launch the forty ships which were in dock at Nisaea. Having accomplished this, they were to sail at once for Piraeus.[12]

Unfortunately for the Megarians and their allies, the execution of the plan failed to match the boldness of its conception:

> (The sailors) arrived during the night and launched the ships from Nisaea, but they did not sail directly to Piraeus as planned. They were overcome by fear of the risk (and it is said they were also hindered by the winds). Instead, they sailed to the promontory [Budorum] on Salamis which looks toward Megara, where there was an (Athenian)

[11]It is likely that Megarian sailors took part in the campaign against Phormio in the Corinthian Gulf in 429 (Thuc. 2.80 ff.), though no Megarian ships were present, and there can be no doubt that Megarian troops participated in the annual invasions of Attica in the early years of the war.
[12]Thuc. 2.93.1-2. Cf. Diod. 12.49.

fort and three ships were stationed to prevent anyone from sailing into or out of Megara. They attacked the fort, towed away the unmanned triremes, and laid waste the rest of Salamis, falling on the place unexpectedly.[13]

While the Peloponnesians were thus occupied, beacon lights on Salamis warned Athens of the danger, and the element of surprise was lost. A fleet was hastily launched from Piraeus, and:

> When the Peloponnesians became aware that a relief force was on the way . . . they quickly sailed back to Nisaea. For, they were afraid that since their ships had not been afloat for a long time, they were not seaworthy. After they reached Megara, the sailors marched back to Corinth.[14]

Thus, it appears, an important opportunity to inflict damage on the Athenian fleet and shipyards was lost. There would be no second chance, now that Athens was alerted to the danger.

Thucydides mentions the sorry condition of the ships at Nisaea almost as an afterthought, but this may have determined the failure of the expedition as much as any other factor. Their unseaworthiness would have been apparent within a short time after they were launched from Nisaea, forcing the original plan to be aborted in favor of a closer target of opportunity—Budorum (though it is strange that Thucydides does not lay more stress on this obvious explanation). In any case, the deterioration of the fleet at Megara is testimony to the effectiveness of Athens' measures to deny the Megarians access to materials for the construction and repair of ships since the days of the Megarian Decree. The figure of forty ships seems high if we assume that the entire flotilla was Megarian. At no other time are more than twenty Megarian warships attested. In fact, the 8,000 men it would have taken to man forty triremes was probably greater than the entire free adult male population of the state, and Thucydides' account makes it clear that rowers from other Peloponnesian states had to be brought in as crews for these vessels. One possible explanation of this puzzle is that the Megarians attempted to float ships that had

[13]Thuc. 2.93.4.
[14]Thuc. 2.94.3.

long since been taken out of service—not only their active fleet, but retired hulls as well. (If this were the case, their leaky condition would be that much easier to understand.) A more plausible explanation is that ships of other Peloponnesian states were stationed or quartered at Nisaea. Such warships might have been used at some stage to convoy supplies to Megara, past the Athenian blockade. Be that as it may, in 429 there were more triremes at Nisaea than at Cenchreai, Corinth's Saronic Gulf port. As Gomme has pointed out, the Peloponnesian plan for a surprise attack on Piraeus would have been better served if the attack had been launched from a point beyond the watchful eye of the guard at Budorum, and the fact that it was not suggests that there were insufficient ships at Cenchreai.[15] This circumstance accords with the view adopted in the previous chapter that Corinth had concentrated her naval resources in the Corinthian Gulf by the 440's, if not earlier.

In the summer of 427, the Athenians tightened their blockade of Megarian shipping by seizing the islet of Minoa, not far from Nisaea. This episode, described in detail by Thucydides, has already been discussed in Chapter 1 in connection with the problem of locating Nisaea and Minoa.[16] It is sufficient for our purposes here to note that Minoa was situated so as to command at least a partial view and perhaps a full view of the harbor at Nisaea, and was close enough to the shore that the distance could be easily bridged. The first of these considerations meant increased effectiveness for the Athenian blockade of Nisaea, beyond what could be achieved from Salamis, while the second meant that both Nisaea and Megara would be vulnerable to surprise attack (although the Athenian force on Minoa was exposed to the risk of counterattack by the Megarians). The capture of Minoa was, therefore, a catastrophe of no mean proportions for Megara.

Megara's deepening crisis had brought her to the point of revolution by 427, and the loss of Minoa may have been the last straw for those who regarded the oligarchs' policy as bankrupt.

[15]HCT, Vol. 2, p. 238. This inference is strengthened by the necessity for the Corinthians to haul triremes over the diolchos from the Corinthian to the Saronic Gulf in 427 in order to launch a naval attack in the Aegean (Thuc. 3.15).

[16]3.51. Cf. Plutarch (Nic. 6), who telescopes this event with the capture of Nisaea three years later, crediting Nicias with both exploits.

The first hint that a democratic revolution had unseated the Megarian oligarchy comes later in Thucydides' account of events in 427. The tiny Boeotian town of Plataea, which had been under siege since the beginning of the war, surrendered in that summer, and in relating the Spartans' punishment of the Plataeans, Thucydides writes: "They allowed the city to be occupied for about a year by some Megarians who had been expelled in a civil war and to those among the surviving Plataeans who favored the Peloponnesian cause."[17] Who were these Megarian exiles, who so obviously enjoyed Sparta's sympathy? They must be the same group that Thucydides says had taken control of Pagae sometime before the Athenian attempt to capture Megara itself in 424: "the Megarians . . . were being hard pressed in the war by the Athenians . . . and by their own exiles in Pagae, who had been expelled by the majority (*tou plēthous*) for making civil war and whose raids were now wreaking havoc."[18] The most natural connection between these two passages is that after a year's haven at Plataea, the exiles had invaded the northern Megarid and managed to take Pagae, which they used as a base for raiding Megarian territory. The raids probably had the dual purpose of harassing their enemies and supplying some of their own wants.

We cannot pinpoint the date of the revolution (*stasis*) that had overthrown the Megarian oligarchy, but the fall of Plataea provides a safe *terminus ante quem*. I suspect that the oligarchs were newly exiled when the Spartans offered them temporary refuge. This would place the revolution in close proximity to the fall of Minoa, but we will probably never know which event helped to trigger the other. The period from 427 to 424, when the oligarchs returned and the democracy collapsed, is the first clearly attested democratic regime in Megarian history, and possibly the first period of popular government since the fall of the "unbridled democracy" in the early sixth century. Democratic sentiments may have long existed beneath the surface, and were probably given impetus by Megara's close association with Athens in the mid-fifth century, but there is no evidence that they had seriously shaken the Megarian oligarchy prior to the 420's. Now, however, under the extreme stress of the

[17]3.68.3.
[18]4.66.1. My views on this disturbance in Megara were set forth in "Megara and Mytilene," *Phoenix*, 22 (1968), 211-23.

Peloponnesian War, Megara's long-term political stability crumbled.

Little detail survives regarding the short-lived democracy that followed. Though Thucydides refers to the leaders of the demos collectively as the *prostatai,* he does not identify any of the men who led this revolution or held political office under the new regime by name.[19] Nor does he tell us what constitutional or practical changes were involved in the shift from oligarchy to democracy. We cannot judge, therefore, how closely the institutions of Megarian democracy may have been modeled on those of Athens. The possibility that a council similar in function to the Athenian *boulē* was introduced is rasied by Aristophanes' reference to the leaders of Megara as *probouloi* in the *Acharnians,* which was written while the democracy was in power.[20] The term is unattested for Megara at any other time. But Aristophanes may have been using it loosely, perhaps as a term that meant more to his Athenian audience than to the Megarians. We ought to assume at least that Thucydides' description of the regime as a democracy meant that the Megarian assembly was more active than it had been during the centuries of oligarchy. The scholiast to Aristophanes' *Knights* makes reference to the existence of the practice of ostracism in Megara at some unspecified time, and perhaps that is the most likely period, if we give credence to this source.[21] It is even possible that some of the oligarchs at Plataea and later at Pagae were the victims of ostracism.

There is equally little to help us understand the changes in policy discussed or implemented by the democrats prior to their abortive attempt to deliver Megara into Athens' hands in 424. One issue that must have been constantly at the fore, however, was how to treat Megara's oligarchs, both those already in exile and others who were still in the city. Thucydides makes it clear that there were many oligarchic sympathizers who had not been purged, and who eventually grew so bold as to advocate openly repatriation of the exiles.[22] Other than this, the subject that must have been uppermost in the minds of Megarians during this period was Megara's

[19] 4.66.3.
[20] *Ach.* 755.
[21] Schol. Ar. *Eq.* 855.
[22] 4.66.2.

future course in the Peloponnesian War. But this topic could not be frankly and openly discussed, even though Megara was now a democratic state.

There is no reason to believe that the Megarians' repudiation of the oligarchs implied any surge of positive feeling toward Athens. They were still just as bitter against the Athenians. Though they may have expected the new government to prosecute the war more effectively, or to ration Megara's limited supplies more equitably than the oligarchs had done, any talk of treating with the Athenians—much less of going over to them—would have been very unpopular, and could have triggered a fresh bout of stasis. This was something the new and still shaky democratic regime could ill afford, especially in the light of a second factor—namely, the vigilance of their Peloponnesian allies, who had shown open sympathy for the exiled oligarchs and did not trust the democracy. At some point the port of Nisaea "had been entirely garrisoned by [Peloponnesian] troops, in order to make sure of the loyalty of Megara," says Thucydides.[23] The commander of this force was a Spartan, and his presence is sometimes seen as a precedent for the Spartan harmosts installed in many states at the end of the war.[24] The garrison at Nisaea may have been officially present to repulse any Athenian attack on Megara or her port which might be launched from Minoa, but if Thucydides is to be believed, it was really there to prevent collusion between the Megarian democrats and the nearby Athenian base. The Peloponnesians' suspicions were natural enough, and were fully justified by later events. Although the garrison failed in its primary mission when the crisis came, it would have been successful at an earlier stage in inhibiting any open talk in Megara about reaching an accommodation with the Athenians. For the alarm would have been raised, and the Peloponnesians would have intervened in force to prevent the loss of Megara. Thus the democratic leaders had no good opportunity to persuade the people of Megara that a radical shift in foreign policy might be to their advantage.

After 425 the Spartans may have had a further motive for hold-

[23]Thuc. 4.66.4.
[24]Thuc. 4.69.3. See the remarks of H. W. Parke, "The Second Spartan Empire," *JHS*, 50 (1930), 39-40.

ing Nisaea, beyond their suspicion of the Megarian democrats and the threat posed by the Athenians on Minoa. Sparta had suffered a setback that changed the complexion of the war, and she appeared ready to conclude peace, even at the expense of Megara and some of her other allies.[25] The Athenians had seized the headland of Pylos in Messenia, threatening to precipitate another helot uprising, and they had trapped several hundred Spartiate hoplites on the island of Sphacteria, for whose release they would obviously demand no small price. The Spartans pulled back all their military forces in an effort to quarantine the Athenians at Pylos, and they simultaneously began to explore the prospects for peace. They requested and were granted a truce, during which they were to send an embassy to Athens to discuss terms for bringing the war to a close.[26] One might expect the Megarians and others to have been buoyed up by this prospect of ending the conflict, but under these circumstances there was no reason for any of Sparta's allies to rejoice. After all, she was acting unilaterally, without consulting them, and she was not in a good bargaining position.

The Athenians offered the Spartan ambassadors harsh terms; they demanded, in effect, that the Thirty Years Peace be rolled back, and that territory surrendered by Athens at that time be returned to her. This territory included Nisaea and Pagae,[27] Megara's two ports. Thucydides believed that the Athenians took such a hard line because, under the influence of Cleon, they were convinced that their position was strong and likely to become even stronger with the capture of the Spartans on Sphacteria.[28] The Spartan response to these terms is revealing: rather than reject them out of hand, the envoys asked only that they be allowed to discuss them with an appointed committee in private, instead of negotiating in the open forum of the Athenian assembly.[29] This was an ominous sign for Sparta's allies, since the concessions the Athenians were demanding would have come largely at their expense, rather than Sparta's, and their hegemon's request for secret talks implied a willingness to consider granting at least some of Athens'

[25]Thuc. 4.8 ff.
[26]Thuc. 4.15-16.
[27]Thuc. 4.21.3.
[28]4.21.2-3.
[29]Thuc. 4.22.1.

demands. Cleon used the Spartan proposal of private negotiations to discredit the embassy in the eyes of the Athenian assembly, and the peace initiative collapsed.[30] Though the truce expired and fighting resumed, there was no reason for Sparta's allies to feel reassured of her zeal on their behalf. The conditions that had led Sparta to sue for peace still obtained, and she might renew her efforts, openly or in secret, at any time.

The Megarians had more reason to be alarmed over this turn of events than Sparta's other allies. It would have been a simple matter for the Spartans to turn over Nisaea to the Athenians, since it was in the hands of a Spartan-led garrison. Pagae, too, might have been included in Sparta's gift, since the Megarian oligarchs who held it were heavily obligated to the Spartans. (Athens had held both Nisaea and Pagae prior to the Thirty Years Peace.) Given the strain in Megarian-Spartan relations since the democratic coup, and the ease with which Sparta might comply with Athenian demands for Megarian territory, it may well have seemed that the Spartans were likelier to conclude peace at Megara's expense than that of any other ally. The situation was similar to that of the early 440's when Athens, anxious for peace, might have been tempted to trade Megara for a treaty with Sparta. Megara was once more in danger of becoming a pawn in the relations between the great powers—only this time it was Sparta who might sacrifice her. In the earlier instance, the Megarians, or rather the Megarian oligarchy, anticipated events by violently repudiating the Athenian alliance and voluntarily rejoining the Peloponnesian League. By 424, and perhaps earlier, the democratic leaders were ready to execute the same maneuver in reverse, but their problem was more complex for two reasons. First, the principle of prior consultation with the people, which lies at the root of democracy, could not be fulfilled because of the watchful presence of Peloponnesian troops at Nisaea and manning the long-walls. (The oligarchs had been under no similar obligation to seek popular consent for their move in 446.) Secondly, it is by no means clear that the democrats could have won popular support for their plan had they been able to present it to the Megarian assembly. The majority of Megarians

[30]Thuc. 4.22.2-3.

may have been anxious to see the war end on terms that were not devastating to Megara's vital interests, but years of suffering at Athens' hands had probably raised anti-Athenian sentiment to a high pitch, and there is no great likelihood that an appeal to the principles of *realpolitik* would have reconciled the majority to a new pact with Athens. In fact, the outcome of an open debate on this subject might well have been to undermine the democrats' support sufficiently to give their political opponents the opportunity for a countercoup. One is drawn to the conclusion that if the democrats were to be successful in bringing Megara into the Athenian camp, their move would have to be as secret and sudden as the oligarchs' had been in 446.

The democratic leaders were faced with no easy choice. If they remained firm in their allegiance to Sparta, it seemed likely that either their regime would be overthrown with Spartan acquiescence and possibly direct intervention, or that the Spartans would trade Megara's ports for a treaty with Athens, thus crippling the state and making it dependent on Athens. It also seemed unlikely that the Spartans could offer Megara even as much protection from Athens as in the past, should the war continue, since the Pylos situation had pinned down the Spartan army. If, on the other hand, Megara were willingly to join Athens, the democracy would be secure, supplies would once more come in by sea, and her new allies might be better able to protect Megara's land (as they had in the early 450's), should the war continue, than the Peloponnesians had been since 431. But popular hostility to Athens and the presence of Peloponnesian troops in the vicinity of Megara made this possible solution to Megara's problems extremely risky.

Thucydides' account of the crisis of 424 stresses the desire of the Megarian democrats to save their own necks, though it is possible to detect the broader issues, such as Megara's territorial interests and the survival of democracy itself in his detailed treatment. He begins by noting the material and psychological effects of the twice-annual Athenian invasion coupled with the raids carried out by the exiles at Pagae:

(The Megarians) began discussing the necessity of admitting the exiles, so that the city would not face ruin from two directions at once.

And the friends of the exiles, aware of the public outcry, began to urge more openly than before that the proposal be acted upon. But the leaders of the demos, realizing that the people would not be able to stand by them (if the exiles returned), because of all that they (the demos) had suffered, made overtures to the Athenian generals Hippocrates . . . and Demosthenes . . . out of fear, proposing to hand the city over to them. (The democratic leaders) thought there was less danger for themselves (in this course of action) than in allowing the return of those they had expelled.[31]

In this instance we ought to beware of allowing Thucydides' cynicism about human nature to carry us too far. There is neither more nor less reason to condemn the behavior of the democrats in this period than that of the oligarchs.[32] Both factions were powerfully influenced by considerations of self-interest—that is, their desires to prosper and rule, or at least survive—but both would also have claimed with some sincerity to have had the best interests of Megara at heart. Seldom do men see any clear distinction between their own welfare and the general good. Each faction would have believed that Megara's security was best served by the political ties that favored their personal interests as well. But it is certainly true that both sides were willing to compromise Megarian autonomy in pursuit of their objectives. The oligarchs had introduced Peloponnesian troops into their territory in 446 to support the revolt from Athens, and solidarity with the Peloponnesians had been the main theme of oligarchic policy thereafter. This course of action had drawn Megara deeply into the cold war con-

[31] 4.66.1-3.

[32] In fact, Thucydides was exiled from Athens in the very year these events took place, and he was away in the northern Aegean prior to that. This means that he is far likelier to have used Megarian oligarchic sources after 424 to reconstruct these events than to have consulted members of the democratic faction. Hence, his account may well be biased against the democrats. This state of affairs undermines the main objection to my analysis of the democrats' motives which has been raised by L. A. Losada, *The Fifth Column in the Peloponnesian War* (Leiden, 1972), pp. 51-56. Losada regards my hypothesis as "ingenious but speculative," and rejects it because Thucydides offers a different and less flattering explanation of the democrats' behavior. I continue to believe that Thucydides need not be followed so unquestioningly on matters of motivation (in distinction to matters of fact), and, as seems likely in this case, there is no reason to expect that he was always able to eliminate the prejudices of his informants from his narrative. If it were necessary, one might also question Thucydides' own objectivity in judging between oligarchs and democrats, given his preference for oligarchic rule.

flict of the 430's and made her a prime target of Athenian revenge during the early years of the Peloponnesian War. Ironically, this adherence to a hegemony which the oligarchs must have expected would preserve them from rising democratic sentiment led to a deterioration of Megara's position which was severe enough to bring about the downfall of the oligarchy. The rejection of the oligarchs in the coup of 427 may have been an accurate perception by their countrymen that their foreign policy was attuned to the needs of Megara's Peloponnesian allies rather than her own. Nor should we overlook the fact that the exiled oligarchs did not hesitate to attack Megara, despite her already dire condition. They apparently believed that a Megara without their presence was scarcely worth preserving. They continued to draw aid and comfort from Sparta, and, as we shall see, were helped back to power by the Spartans when the democrats' plot collapsed. In this context, it is unreasonable to reserve any special vituperation for the democrats and their plan to bring in the Athenians, as some have done. The more reasonable ground for criticizing the democrats is that their plot failed because they did not plan well enough. As for the rest, we need to recognize the prevailing standards of political conduct—both democratic and oligarchic—under the stresses of Greek hegemonal organization, and to avoid moral judgments based on significantly different political models.

The first stage of the democrats' scheme was to aid the Athenians in capturing the long-walls connecting Megara with Nisaea, thus isolating the Peloponnesian garrison from the main city.[33] When all had been arranged, several small Athenian contingents under the command of Hippocrates and Demosthenes crossed over to the mainland from Minoa under cover of darkness and waited in ambush outside the Megarian long-walls, while 4,000 Athenian hoplites and 600 cavalry made their way toward Megara long the road from Eleusis.[34] Just before dawn, the conspirators contrived to open a gate in the walls, which for some time they had been using to haul a small boat down to the sea and back at night.[35] This time, however, when the gate was opened to readmit the

[33]Thuc. 4.66.4.
[34]Thuc. 4.67.1-2, 68.5.
[35]Thuc. 4.67.3-5.

boat, the democrats prevented its being closed as the Athenians rushed forward from their ambush and poured through it. At first, the Peloponnesian garrison troops put up some resistance, but as more and more Athenians came through the gate, the Peloponnesians retreated to Nisaea.[36] Thucydides' description of the garrison's readiness to believe the Megarians had turned on them says much about the sorry state of relations between Megara and her nominal allies by 424:

> A few of the Peloponnesian garrison troops stood and fought at first, and some of these were killed, but most fled, frightened because the enemy had attacked them at night, and believing that all the Megarians had betrayed them, since the Megarian traitors were among the attackers. For it also happened that an Athenian herald, on his own authority, announced that any Megarian who wished could take up arms alongside the Athenians. When the garrison heard this announcement, it put up no further resistance, but, convinced that it was being subjected to a joint attack, fled to Nisaea.[37]

Thus far, everything had gone according to plan. By morning the Athenians, now reinforced by the troops from Eleusis, were in control of the long-walls, and the Peloponnesians were pinned down in Nisaea. Meanwhile, there was alarm and confusion in Megara, where the democrats were trying to implement the next phase of their plan, which would deliver Megara itself into Athenian hands:

> At dawn, the walls having been taken by then, and with the Megarians in the city in an uproar, those who had conspired with the Athenians and a great many others who were in on the plot declared that they ought to open the gates and attack (the Athenians). They had planned that when the gates were opened the Athenians would pour in, and they anointed themselves with oil so that they could be more easily recognized and no harm would befall them. . . . But one of the conspirators revealed the plot to the other faction, which gathered together, came (to the gates) in a body and argued that they should not sally forth—for they had never dared such a thing before, even when they were stronger—nor should they lead the city into such

[36]Thuc. 4.68.2.
[37]4.68.2-3.

obvious danger. And if any refused to listen, they threatened to attack them on the spot. However, they gave no indication that they were aware of the plot, but defended their proposals as being for the best. At the same time they remained by the gates standing guard, so that none of the conspirators could implement their plan.[38]

By this means, the oligarchs avoided either the opening of the gates or an outbreak of violence inside Megara which might have given the Athenians their opportunity. This unanticipated setback was to prove fatal to the democrats' plans.

When the Athenians sensed that something had gone wrong, they diverted their attention to Nisaea, which they quickly walled off from the mainland. The Peloponnesians surrendered to lenient terms on the second day of the siege of Nisaea. They were cut off both by land and by sea, without food, and, as we have seen, they assumed that Megara had already gone over to the Athenians. The Spartans present were taken prisoner, while the other Peloponnesians were permitted to ransom themselves.[39] One can imagine their chagrin when they discovered that relief was only a day away, and that Megara was still holding out. Athens took possession of Nisaea and, to secure the long-walls from a hostile Megara, demolished the section where they joined the city walls of Megara.

On the same day, the Spartan commander Brasidas, who had been gathering a large army near the Isthmus for a projected campaign in Chalcidice, reached Megara with a force substantially larger than that commanded by the Athenian generals.[40] He tried to get the Megarians to admit him into the city, promising to attempt the recapture of Nisaea, if possible. Not surprisingly, the democrats were as reluctant to admit Brasidas as the oligarchs were to open the gates to the Athenians, and a stalemate developed:

---

[38]Thuc. 4.68.4-6. The plot's betrayal by one of the democrats is a sobering reminder that shades of opinion existed among political factions in Megara and elsewhere, which we are seldom in a position to detect. Clearly, some of the democrats felt that their fellows were going too far.

[39]Thuc. 4.69. These troops turn up later in the same summer at Delium (Thuc. 4.100.1), having apparently gone directly from the Megarid to Boeotia. Perhaps they were wise not to return home immediately, in view of their failure of nerve at Nisaea.

[40]Thuc. 4.70.

The rival factions among the Megarians were frightened, the one that (Brasidas) might bring back the exiles and expel them, the other that in fear of this eventuality the demos might attack them and that the polis might be undone if civil war erupted with the Athenians lying in wait nearby. They therefore would not admit (Brasidas), both sides believing it was better to await events. For everyone expected that a battle would be fought between the Athenians and the relief force, and each side thought it would be safer to join their friends after the battle had been won.[41]

A skirmish between the cavalry of the opposing armies was fought under the walls of Megara, but the Athenians declined to do battle with the Peloponnesians.[42] This emboldened the oligarchic faction to throw open the gates to Brasidas and the allies: "the friends of the Megarian exiles opened the gates and received them (the Peloponnesians), and now that the pro-Athenian faction was frozen with fear, entered into negotiations (with Brasidas et al.)."[43]

The democrats had lost the initiative and stood in extreme personal danger. The stage was set for a countercoup. Thucydides says that both Brasidas' forces and the Athenians soon retired, but it seems certain that Peloponnesian troops remained in Megara for some time, given the unstable domestic situation and the proximity of an Athenian force at Nisaea. When the main armies had dispersed:

Those Megarians in the city . . . who were most deeply implicated in the conspiracy with the Athenians, realizing they had been detected, fled secretly, but the others of their faction, in consultation with the friends of the exiles, brought them (the exiles) back from Pagae after they had sworn sacred oaths not to bear grudges, but to counsel for the good of the polis.[44]

It was naive of the Megarians to put any trust in such a pledge; the active members of the democratic faction who fled Megara at this point were not so foolish. Thucydides narrates the sequel:

[41]Thuc. 4.71.
[42]Thuc. 4.72.1–73.4.
[43]Thuc. 4.73.4.
[44]Thuc. 4.74.2.

As soon as (the former exiles) gained office they held a review of the hoplites, separating them into companies and singling out their enemies and those they thought had been most heavily implicated in the conspiracy with the Athenians, about 100 men in all, and, forcing the demos to judge their guilt by an open vote, executed them once they had been convicted. Then they established an extreme oligarchy in the city.[45]

Thus ended Megara's brief encounter with democracy in the fifth century.

Thucydides closes his account of the Megarian *stasis* with a striking statement: "This (oligarchy) lasted longer than any regime established through revolution by such a small number of men."[46] The comment implies that Thucydides, who died about 399, lived to see at least some modification of the narrow regime that came to power in 424, but this relaxation was long in coming. One imagines that as long as Athens remained a serious threat to Megarian security, the oligarchs maintained tight control of the state. There is, however, no indication in Thucydides or elsewhere of the specific institutions or domestic policies of the extreme oligarchy. Purges of suspected democrats may have long continued, for there were 120 Megarian exiles fighting in the Athenian army in Sicily a decade later.[47]

In the winter following the oligarchic countercoup, "the Megarians, having taken the long-walls the Athenians had built for them, razed them to the ground."[48] Thucydides gives no hint that the Athenians put up any serious resistance to this move, and it seems reasonable that they were content to see it take place. Since they had lost hope of capturing Megara by force in the immediate future, the long-walls were as much a menace to their troops at Nisaea as they were to the Megarians, for they could provide cover for a surprise attack at either end. With the long-walls demolished, a no-man's-land was created between Nisaea and Megara, and this situation remained essentially unchanged for about fifteen years.

[45] 4.74.3.
[46] 4.74.4.
[47] Thuc. 6.43, 7.57.7.
[48] Thuc. 4.109.1.

During the same winter, the Megarians resumed their active support of the anti-Athenian coalition. Thucydides notes the presence of "some Megarians" among the Peloponnesian forces supporting the Boeotian attack on Delium at that time.[49] The number was apparently small, which is hardly surprising in light of the recent turmoil in Megara and the continued presence of Athenian troops in the vicinity. Thucydides mentions the destruction of the Megarian long-walls after his treatment of the Delium campaign, but no strict chronology is implied, and I suspect that the long-walls may actually have come down earlier; the Megarians might have felt marginally more secure at home, once the walls had been demolished, and therefore more willing to take part in military campaigns further afield.

Meanwhile, Brasidas had followed through with his original plan to operate in Chalcidice and Thrace, where he achieved considerable success.[50] This campaign threatened Athens' links with the Propontic and Black Sea states. Now the Spartans had a means of putting pressure on the Athenians, which they had lacked in 425. The Athenians were not yet reconciled to the need to settle for inconclusive peace terms, after their high hopes of the previous year, but they were at least persuaded of the desirability of a truce that would prevent Brasidas from further undermining Athens' position in the northeast. In 423 such a truce was worked out between the two sides.[51] Thucydides quotes the terms of the agreement, which, among other items, dealt specifically with the situation in the Megarid:

(The Athenians) in Nisaea and Minoa shall not cross the road which runs from the gates of the Temple of Nisus to the Poseidonion and from the Poseidonion straight on to the bridge to Minoa; neither shall the Megarians and their allies cross this road, and the Athenians shall keep the island which they captured [Minoa], and neither side shall communicate with the other.[52]

[49]4.100.1.
[50]Thuc. 4.78-88, 102-16.
[51]Thuc. 4.117 ff.
[52]Thuc. 4.118.4.

Thus the truce in no way permitted the Megarians to resume their naval activities on the Saronic Gulf. In fact, they were now pledged to make no attempt to reach the shore in the vicinity of Nisaea and Minoa. The truce was signed by two Megarian representatives, Nicasus, the son of Cecalus, and Menecrates, the son of Amphidorus (who were, doubtless, chief figures in the restored oligarchy).[53] At the same time, the Megarians might now begin the arduous task of reclaiming their land and rebuilding what had been destroyed over eight years of Athenian invasions, for the Athenians were similarly pledged to confine their movements to the coast.[54] But it is impossible to say with what zeal the Megarians undertook this project as long as the full scale resumption of the conflict remained distinctly possible.

The truce of 423 never really took hold in Chalcidice and Thrace, as the Athenians had hoped, and it was allowed to expire without having led to a permanent peace agreement. Had it not been for the deaths of Cleon and Brasidas in 422, the war would probably have resumed in earnest, but their demise enabled more conciliatory figures in Athens and Sparta to work out a peace treaty by the following year—the Peace of Nicias.[55] Sparta encountered considerable difficulty in persuading some of her allies to accept the terms of this agreement, which had apparently been negotiated without their prior consent. It is not difficult to understand why they objected, since the treaty neither resolved the original grievances of the allies, nor compensated them for any of their fresh injuries, which had resulted from the war itself. Megara was particularly aggrieved, for in addition to the treaty's complete silence regarding the Megarian Decree and Megarian shipping rights in the Aegean, the Athenians were not even required to surrender Nisaea or Minoa. Thucydides explains this last omission as a concession offered to the Athenians by the Spartans to compensate for Thebes' unwillingness to restore Plataea:

[53]Thuc. 4.119.2.

[54]They may also have begun to bring in some supplies through Pagae, if the Athenian blockade at Naupactus had been suspended or relaxed as a result of the truce. See Thuc. 4.118.5.

[55]See esp. Thuc. 5.16 ff. and Plut. *Nic.* 9.

for when the Athenians demanded Plataea back, the Thebans claimed that they had come into possession of it not by force but by consent (of its people) and that they did not win the territory by treachery, and the Athenians made the same claim for Nisaea.[56]

Neither claim had any real merit, since both Plataea and Nisaea had surrendered under duress, but these concessions were made by the major powers out of a recognition of strategic realities and a mutual desire to terminate hostilities, at least for the time being. What is important from our perspective is that Sparta had agreed to leave Athens in possession of the Megarians' principal port for a period of fifty years, the specified duration of the agreement. The sacrifice of Megarian naval interests was part of the price Sparta was willing to pay for peace, the return of Athens' Spartiate captives, and the restoration of Pylos. It is not surprising to learn that, in thrall as they were to the Spartan hegemony, the Megarian oligarchs could not bring themselves to endorse this pact, but joined a minority, including the Boeotians, Corinthians, and Eleans, in voting against acceptance of the Peace of Nicias.[57] Sparta convened a second meeting of her allies to put pressure on the holdouts, but to no avail.[58] After dismissing the recalcitrants, Sparta took the extraordinary step of concluding a separate agreement with Athens. This was a fifty-year alliance, which pledged both states to join in punishing any states who opposed the Peace of Nicias.[59] I doubt that Sparta seriously intended to go to war against her allies, but this second pact may have been intended to ensure Athens of the Spartans' sincere determination to make good on the terms of the Peace of Nicias and to apply further pressure on the allies who had not yet signed the earlier agreement. In all these moves, Sparta was far less concerned with the behavior of Megara than with that of Corinth or Boeotia, or even Elis. After all, the Megarians were hardly in a position to undermine the Peace of Nicias on their own, and the oligarchs were not even remotely likely to go over to the Athenians after the recent stasis in Megara.

[56]5.17.2.
[57]Ibid.
[58]Thuc. 5.22.1-2.
[59]Thuc. 5.22.2–24.2.

Thus Megara's unhappiness with the treaty could be safely disregarded for the moment.

Corinthian discontent was more dangerous to the peace. The Corinthians began to build an anti-Spartan coalition in the Peloponnese around the state of Argos, whose own treaty with Sparta had recently expired without being successfully renegotiated.[60] The Corinthians were playing a double game, whose main objective from the outset may have been to force Sparta to repudiate the Peace of Nicias. But Megara's attitude toward these machinations is instructive. As unhappy as she was with the terms of the peace, she held back from the new coalition: "The Boeotians and Megarians, following the same policy, remained quiet, awaiting events and considering that the Argive democracy was less congenial to them than the Spartan constitution, since they were oligarchies."[61] Here, if any further evidence is needed, we see clearly the connection between the Megarian oligarchs' self-interest and their foreign ties. Despite Sparta's adoption of a policy that spelled severe economic hardship for Megara, the oligarchs contented themselves with a half-hearted protest and shrank from any foreign connection that might have improved Megara's position while jeopardizing their own. Sparta could hardly have expected her oligarchic friends in Megara to do more if they were to retain any vestige of respect among their fellow Megarians.

Although Megara had rejected the Peace of Nicias, there is no evidence that hostilities resumed in her territory. If Thucydides' statement to the effect that she and Boeotia followed the same line during this period is literally true, she may have agreed to a series of renewable ten-day truces with the Athenians, as the Boeotians did.[62] Megara was reduced to a cipher, capable neither of applying

[60] Thuc. 5.25 ff.

[61] Thuc. 5.31.6.

[62] On the Athenian Boeotian truces, see Thuc. 5.26.2. At 5.38.1, Thucydides says the Megarians and Boeotians were acting "in concert." In fact, from as far back as 427, when exiled Megarian oligarchs were allowed to occupy Plataea temporarily, the Megarian oligarchs may have been closely tied to the Boeotians. (How much further back these ties reached is impossible to say, and there is no tangible evidence to suggest that these neighboring territories were normally close political allies, as is sometimes asserted. See, e.g., Meyer, "Megara," col. 181, who accepts the existence of close association between the two regions in historical times.)

leverage on her allies to defend her interests, nor of taking any effective action on her own behalf.

In the winter of 421/20, according to Thucydides:

> the Boeotarchs, the Corinthians [now allied to Argos and Elis], the Megarians, and the ambassadors from Thrace resolved first to swear oaths to one another that they would come to the assistance of any party in need of help and would make neither war nor peace except by mutual agreement. Then it was agreed that the Boeotians and Megarians, who were acting in concert, should conclude a treaty with the Argives.[63]

The defensive alliance noted here seems a direct response to the pact between Sparta and Athens, and thus far committed the Megarians and Boeotians only to their old allies. Had they gone ahead with the proposal that they ally themselves with Argos, something significant would have been added to the picture, but these alliances never materialized. Thucydides' language stops short of indicating that the Megarians and Boeotians even endorsed the suggestion that they align with Argos. He is more specific in the case of Boeotia, reporting that the Boeotian commanders failed to convince the government at home to ratify even the defensive alliance with Megara, Corinth, and the Thracian states, and thought it best not to bring up the more controversial proposal to join the Argives.[64] We do not hear what steps, if any, the Megarians took, but from the sequel it is apparent that the entire charade came to naught.

The Peace of Nicias was doomed to failure for many reasons which it would be inappropriate to dwell on here, but the unhappiness of many of Sparta's major allies (if not the Megarians' distress) was certainly a factor. When fighting resumed in 418, all the allies fell into line with Sparta, Megara among them.[65] They contributed to the Peloponnesian army which defeated the new Athenian-Argive axis at Mantineia as though nothing had happened to alienate them from the Peloponnesian League. Unfortunately, no in-

[63]5.38.1.
[64]5.38.2-4.
[65]Thuc. 5.57 ff., esp. 58.4, 59.2, and 60.3, on Megarian participation. On the Peace of Nicias and the reasons for its collapse, see my article "The Peace of Nicias," *Journal of Peace Research* (1969), 323-34.

dication is given of the size of Megara's contribution, which might have told us something about the degree to which she had recovered from the events of the 420's. Athenian land forces were active in the Peloponnese at various times between 419 and 417.[66] Though these forces might have been sent by ship, Thucydides gives no hint of this, and the likelier assumption is that they made their way through the Isthmus. But neither is there any indication that those expeditions caused damage to Megarian property. Following the collapse of Athens' ambitions in the Peloponnese, there is no evidence of further military activity in the region of the Isthmus for many years; nor is there reason to believe that the Athenians resumed their twice-yearly invasions of the Megarid. The struggle was being pursued in other arenas, and the Megarians were spared much additional suffering, although their economy can scarcely have revived.

In 409, according to Diodorus, the Megarians stormed Nisaea.[67] The date does not inspire great confidence, since Diodorus makes the event synchronous with Sparta's storming of Pylos, but there can be little doubt that Nisaea fell sometime after the summer of 411, when Thucydides' narrative comes to an end without having noted either occurrence. Diodorus gives no details of how the Megarians finally succeeded after so many years (and who knows how many abortive attempts?), though the sequel suggests that Megarian forces may have been augmented by Peloponnesian or Sicilian troops. It is also true that Athens was now harassed year round by the enemy force at Decelea, and was further preoccupied with efforts to rebuild her navy, hold the loyalty of her Delian League allies, and resolve her own political troubles. As a result, she may have taken the security of Nisaea too much for granted. In any case, the Athenians were not so burdened down by their other concerns as to ignore entirely the loss of Nisaea and the fate of its defenders. Diodorus describes an invasion of the Megarid, which the Athenians launched when they learned of Nisaea's fall:

> the Athenians attacked (Megara) with 400 cavalry under the command of Leotrophides and Timarchus. The Megarians came out to

[66]Thuc. 5.52.2, 55.4, 61.1, 75.6.
[67]13.65.1.

engage these troops with all their forces, augmented by some soldiers from Sicily, and positioned themselves near the hills called "The Cerata" [i.e., on the Megarian-Athenian border]. The Athenians fought splendidly and put to flight an enemy many times more numerous than themselves, but while many Megarians were killed, only twenty Spartans died. For the Athenians, angered by the seizure of Nisaea, did not pursue the Spartans, but concentrated their attack on the Megarians.[68]

There is some confusion here, as the Megarians are said at one point to have had the support of Sicilian troops and at another of Spartans. Only one is likely to be correct, but which of the two cannot be determined. One possibility is that the Sicilians might have been the refugees from the stone quarries at Piraeus who, Xenophon says, fled to Megara in 409.[69]

The scene of this Megarian defeat was along the coastal road that led from Eleusis into the Megarid, where the "horns" of Cerata divided Attica from the Megarid. The Megarians appear to have advanced to this point, anticipating an Athenian military response to the fall of Nisaea and hoping to bar the way. Diodorus does not say whether the Athenian victory and pursuit of the enemy were followed by further devastation of the Megarid, but this was the likely purpose of the expedition in the first place, and now there was nothing to prevent it. Since the Megarid had probably been spared for the greater part of a decade, there was quite a lot of damage to be inflicted. This may account for the Megarians' uncharacteristic and futile effort to resist the invasion. This failure was both an indication of Megarian weakness and a sharp setback to her hopes of recovery, since it led to the further depletion of her manpower and resources. Thus the taking of Nisaea proved a mixed blessing in the short run. The Megarians may nonetheless have decided to emphasize its positive aspects, dedicating a statue of Apollo, spear in hand, at Delphi to commemorate the event.[70]

[68]13.65.1-2. This passage derives from fr. A, col. 1.1-19 of the Florentine Papyrus of the Oxyrhynchus historian. See I. A. F. Bruce, *An Historical Commentary on the 'Hellenica Oxyrhynchia'* (Cambridge, 1967), pp. 28-30. The identification of Diodorus' source here is highly significant, since it points to his use of one of the best available authorities for this period, and lends added weight to his testimony.
[69]*Hell.* 1.2.14.
[70]See Paus. 10.15.1, which describes an image of Apollo at Delphi "dedicated by the Megarians for a victory which they won over the Athenians at Nisaea." The

The war's effect on Megarian naval power and economic strength may be seen in her meager contributions to the Peloponnesian fleet after 412, when the Athenian defeat in Sicily led to its reactivization in the Aegean. In 412 Thucydides says Sparta requisitioned a total of ten triremes from Megara, Troezen, Epidaurus, and Hermione.[71] At another point he notes the involvement of a single Megarian ship.[72] Megara's fleet had dwindled to the verge of extinction. In contrast, she retained a store of naval skill and good will among the Hellespontine and Propontic states which her allies were wise enough to employ. Thus despite the Megarian's minute contribution to the fleet of 412, a Megarian by the name of Helixus was named commander of one squadron of ten or fifteen ships.[73] He proved his worth by successfully maneuvering past the Athenian fleet at the Hellespont, making his way to Byzantium and raising it in revolt. It is hard to imagine anyone more suited to this mission than a Megarian captain. His success was the first step in threatening the Athenian grain supply.[74] We also hear of the employment of a Megarian metic by the name of Hermon who was pilot under several later Spartan admirals operating in the Aegean and Hellespont. He served under Callicratidas in 407 and under Lysander thereafter.[75] Hermon is credited with having opposed the ill-advised battle at Arginusae, which the Peloponnesians lost.[76] He was honored by Lysander with a statue at Delphi and an attempt to have him enfranchised in Megara.[77]

---

attempt by the Megarians to take Nisaea by force in 446 had failed, and therefore cannot have provided the occasion for this dedication. A passage in Plutarch (*Mor.* 402a) appears to refer to this same statue, but says it was erected "to commemorate a battle in which they (the Megarians) defeated and expelled the Athenians when they held the city after the Persian Wars." This set of circumstances clearly refers to 446, rather than post-412. It is impossible to reconcile these two plausible explanations of the Delphic dedication.

[71]8.3.2.

[72]8.33.1.

[73]Thuc. 8.80.3, which puts the squadron at ten ships; Xenophon (*Hell.* 1.1.36) says fifteen. The Athenians later captured eight of Helixus' ships at anchor (Thuc. 8.107.1), but Byzantium remained in revolt.

[74]See Xen. *Hell.* 1.3.15-21, for the subsequent exploits of Helixus and the Megarians at Byzantium. He was eventually captured when Byzantium was betrayed to the Athenians.

[75]Xen. *Hell.* 1.6.32 (under Callicratidas) and Paus. 10.9.4 (under Lysander).

[76]Xen. *Hell.* 1.6.32.

[77]Paus. 10.9.4. Cf. Dem. 23.212. Demosthenes says the Megarians refused to enfranchise Hermon. Pausanias, on the other hand, says he *was* granted

Pausanias notes a further Megarian sailor, Komon, one of the admirals whose statues were erected at Delphi for their role in the battle at Aegospotami in 405, where Athenian seapower was decisively crushed.[78] This is a remarkable record for a state which possessed very few ships and, until about 409, lacked an Aegean port.

In the year following their defeat at Aegospotami, the Athenians surrendered to Lysander, thus bringing to an end the Peloponnesian War. Athens was forced to hand over her fleet and disband her alliance, but—despite the objections of many of her allies, according to Xenophon—the Spartans refused to carry out the complete destruction of Athens.[79] Xenophon specifies the Thebans and Corinthians as being most prominent among those who demanded harsher punishment, but one can readily imagine the Megarians having taken the same line. Though it is not specifically noted by the sources, Minoa was doubtless restored to the Megarians at this time, if it had not already fallen, and of course the seas were open once again to unrestricted Megarian shipping. But the war had left Megara decimated and impoverished, and only time could restore her to health. There was, in addition, a legacy of bitterness and cynicism which must have affected postwar Megara. She was to prosper again, but she would never be quite the same. The short- and long-term effects of the Peloponnesian War and the changed direction of Megarian history in the fourth century are the subjects of the next chapter.

---

citizenship, but Demosthenes seems the preferable source here, because of his greater proximity to the event. Cf. Plut. *Lys.* 14, which may point to the alternate reward Lysander offered Hermon when Megarian citizenship was deined—i.e., participation in a new settlement at Sestos, where Lysander expelled the populace and distributed land to the pilots and boatswains of his fleet.

[78]Paus., *loc. cit.*
[79]*Hell.* 2.2.19-20.

CHAPTER 11

Megara's Middle Way

The Megarians feast as if they expect to die tomorrow, and build
their houses as if they were never going to die at all.
                    —Attributed to Diogenes the Cynic,
                        by Tertullian, *Apologeticum* 39.14[1]

THE PELOPONNESIAN WAR is frequently depicted as a watershed
in Greek history: The point at which the dynamic energy of the
polis lost its forward momentum and public spirit gave way to
selfish and self-destructive individualism. Internal political rival-
ries that had long existed in most poleis erupted violently in the
course of this protracted conflict, and they were rarely laid to rest
thereafter. The economic and material consequences of the war
could be overcome to a considerable degree, but its psychological
impact had a lasting effect. There is more than a bit of truth in this
picture, but it exaggerates the importance of the Peloponnesian
War, which was really only one phase of a pattern of conflict between the hegemonal states of the Greek world. This struggle had
begun by the 460's and continued past 350, when it was finally
overshadowed by the threat from Macedon. The alignment of
states shifted from time to time, as did the balance of power, but
the terms of the contest scarcely altered. The Peloponnesian War
was a symptom of deeper problems which its resolution did nothing to settle. The root of Greece's dilemma is to be found in the
nature of the polis itself, with its attitude of political exclusiveness

---

[1]Cf. Jerome (*Epist.* 123.14), who makes the same observation, but without attribution. The remark was also applied to other states, e.g. to Agrigentum in Sicily by
Plato, according to Ael. *VH* 12.29, also by Empedocles (D.L. 8.63), and to Rhodes by
Stratonicus (Plut. *Mor.* 525b). Aristotle is alleged to have applied this observation to
mankind in general (D.L. 5.20), but the sense of it suggests that it was applicable
only to notably prosperous states, i.e., the conspicuous consumers. As such, it
seems appropriate to fourth-century Megara, and, given Diogenes' clear association
with Megara (see below), Tertullian's attribution may well be authentic.

vis-à-vis even its closest neighbors and allies. The more powerful poleis continued to pursue the elusive goal of political domination over their rivals, rather than work toward greater stability through the sharing of power with one another. (Weaker states often behaved similarly among themselves.) The result was an unending series of wars in which the larger states combined and recombined their forces against one another, sweeping the middle-sized and smaller states along with them. The majority of the Greeks continued down this debilitating path, oblivious to the warnings of the few who saw the danger of internal exhaustion down the road. And attempts by a minority of states to break out of this self-destructive cycle of hegemonal rivalry were too feeble to make much difference. Fourth-century Megara may be studied as an example of a state which attempted, with mixed success, to escape the unending round of warfare and to find peace and prosperity amid the raging storm.

Megara had suffered more severely from the effects of the Peloponnesian War than most other participants, but her recovery was dramatic. It probably began even before the war had officially ended, since the Athenians were forced to adopt a more defensive posture in the last years of the struggle and gradually lost control of the seas. Under these conditions, the Megarians began to reclaim their land and to resume their commercial activities. One lingering effect of the war was a shortage of manpower. This was largely the result of Megara's decimation during the war, but, as elsewhere, there were probably a substantial number of her troops who could not readjust to civilian pursuits after so many years of warfare, and who turned instead to careers as mercenaries.[2] One of the mercenary captains who answered the call of Cyrus, the Persian pretender, in 401 was a Megarian by the name of Pasion.[3] He brought 300 men with him, and it is likely that many were also Megarian. He left Cyrus' service when his men were placed under the command of Clearchos.[4] Highbarger calls the decline of Me-

---

[2]See H. W. Parke, *Greek Mercenary Soldiers from the Earliest Times to the Battle of Ipsus* (Oxford, 1933), pp. 20 ff.

[3]Xen. *An.* 1.2.3.

[4]Xen. *An.* 1.4.7.

gara's free population "a real blessing," but the Megarians probably saw it as a serious problem.[5] As we shall see later in this chapter, they appear to have overcome the economic problems attendant upon insufficient free labor by turning to a greater reliance on slaves, but there was no evidence to suggest that they employed mercenaries to compensate for reduced military manpower. Thus fourth-century Megara recovered economically, but became militarily inconsequential, even in comparison with her limited military capacity in the previous century. This situation had a considerable impact on Megarian policy.

As noted in the previous chapter, the Megarians probably shared the unhappiness of other Peloponnesian allies over the peace terms imposed on Athens by the Spartans. After a war that had witnessed atrocities on both sides, it is hardly surprising that many would have demanded the complete annihilation of Athens as punishment for her crimes. Even lowly Megara might have profited materially from such an outcome, in terms of both commercial opportunities and border land in the region of Eleusis, though the main beneficiaries would most likely have been Thebes and Corinth. But Sparta was determined to prop up Athens under the control of a compliant oligarchic regime, the Thirty Tyrants. She defended her decision in high moral terms,[6] although the allies saw it as a means of denying them an opportunity to profit from the war and of securing the commercial, military, and other advantages of victory for Sparta alone.[7] This interpretation gained plausibility from Sparta's other willful acts in the postwar period, such as her refusal to share war booty with her allies[8] and the imposition of military governors (*harmosts*), garrisons, and committes of ten (*dekarchies*) in the former member states of the Delian League.[9] This last policy quickly established a new Spartan Empire, to which the Peloponnesian allies were only peripherally related, one which commanded wealth and resources equal to those of Athens at her height. It is small wonder that many of the allies felt cheated.

[5]*Megara*, p. 197.
[6]Xen. *Hell*. 2.2.20. Plut. *Lys*. 15.
[7]See Polyaenus *Strat*. 1.45.5.
[8]Xen. *Hell*. 3.5.5, 12; Plut. *Lys*. 27; Just. *Epit*. 6.10.
[9]Xen. *Hell*. 3.5.13; Plut. *Lys*. 13; Diod. 14.4.3. See Parke's treatment of this subject in "The Development of the Second Spartan Empire", pp. 50 ff.

Megara was too weak and vulnerable to challenge Spartan policy through major acts of defiance, as Thebes and Corinth might, but she showed her displeasure in several small ways. The Megarians joined other Spartan allies, most notably Thebes, in sheltering democrats and other refugees from Athens during the reign of the Thirty Tyrants.[10] The best known instance is the case of the wealthy Athenian metic, Lysias, who fled by ship to Megara in order to avoid proscription by the Athenian oligarchy.[11] But when the Spartans ordered all the states who were shielding Athenian opponents of the Thirty Tyrants to return them to Athens, Megara seems to have complied. Diodorus states that only Thebes and Argos defied this order, and Plutarch mentions only Thebes.[12] Megara's short-lived policy of providing sanctuary to enemies of the Spartan-backed oligarchy in Athens can hardly have been inspired by genuine sympathy with Athenian democracy. Rather, it was a gesture of dissatisfaction with Spartan policy in general and with her attempt to monopolize Athens in particular.

Megarian pique may also be detected behind several apparently related incidents involving the Spartan commander Lysander. The victor of Aegospotami was at the height of his power and prestige in 404, and many of the Spartan policies to which the allies objected appeared his own doing, in particular the establishment of the dekarchies. Even if Lysander was largely executing directives from the government at home, he was clearly personally ambitious, arrogant, and insensitive to the feelings of Sparta's longtime allies. These traits brought him into conflict with the Megarians. After the war Lysander attempted to reward his loyal lieutenants, including Hermon, the Megarian metic who had served as pilot to his predecessor Callicratidas, as well as himself, in a variety of ways. From the spoils of war he erected their statues (near his own) at Delphi, and Hermon's was given a prominent place.[13] Hermon was doubtless also one of the recipients of an allotment at Sestos, long an Athenian possession, when Lysander expelled the populace and divided the land "among his pilots and

---

[10]Xen. *Hell.* 2.4.1; Diod. 14.6 (which does not mention Megara explicitly); *Lys.* 7.4, 12.17; Plut. *Lys.* 27 (which names only Thebes).
[11]*Lys.* 12.17.
[12]Diod. 14.6; Plut. *Lys.* 27.
[13]Paus. 10.9.4.

boatswains."[14] The high-handed act was quickly undone when word of it reached Sparta. I suspect that at this point, though possibly earlier, Lysander, having failed to provide Hermon with a new domicile, asked the Megarians to enfranchise him for his services. According to Demosthenes, the Megarians responded that they would make Hermon a Megarian when the Spartans made him a Spartiate.[15] Perhaps this biting reply indicates nothing more than the Megarians' rigid attitude toward the extension of citizenship, comparable to the exclusive feelings of the Spartans. When they offered Megarian citizenship to Alexander the Great in the 330's, they claimed the step was unprecedented, and, apart from the case of Hermon, no evidence survives to contradict them.[16] But the sting of the remark suggests a certain degree of hostility (or bitterness) toward Lysander and the Spartans.

Lysander is widely reported to have issued a menacing rebuke to the Megarians in response to some unspecified remarks: "When some Megarian spoke boldly to him at a conference, Lysander replied, 'Stranger, your words lack a real city to back them up.' "[17] Perhaps these two fragmentary tales are connected, Lysander's rebuke being in response to the Megarians' harsh rejection of his request at some conference that Hermon be granted citizenship. If not, we must conclude that the Megarians expressed strong disagreement with Lysander on other issues as well. The wider implication of Lysander's remark is that Megara was too weak to brook his displeasure and might easily be brought to heel. Did the Megarians yield to this thinly veiled threat? Pausanias, without mentioning the dispute with Lysander, remarks simply that Hermon *was* granted citizenship by the Megarians,[18] and it is entirely possible that Megara backed down in this instance as she had on the matter of harboring Athenian refugees. But we must still contend with the Megarians' insistence that their gesture to Alexander

[14]Plut. *Lys.* 14.2.
[15]Dem. 23.212.
[16]Plut. *Mor.* 826.
[17]Plut. *Lys.* 22.1. Cf. Plut. *Mor.* 71e, 190e, and 229c; Them. *Or.* 27.344c. Plutarch once (*Mor.* 213a) attributes this remark to the Spartan king, Agesilaus, who is contemporary with Lysander, but this contradicts his other references to it.
[18]Paus. 10.9.4. Xenophon, who discusses Hermon's exploits during the Peloponnesian War, loosely refers to him as a Megarian (*Hell.* 1.6.32), but this reference is earlier than even the request for citizenship.

was without precedent. The answer to this question therefore remains in doubt.

The incidents we have examined suggest that Megara was unhappy but that her political response was controlled. It could even be argued that the Megarian regime tried to distinguish carefully between defiance of Lysander and opposition to Sparta itself, assiduously avoiding the latter. If that is a fair reading of the situation, Megara must have been pleased and somewhat reconciled to Sparta by the gradual eclipse of Lysander in 403 and 402 and the amelioration of his policies. The possibility exists, however, that she was severely punished by Lysander for her postwar behavior toward him by having a Spartan harmost and garrison imposed upon her while he still enjoyed a relatively free hand. The only direct statement to this effect comes in Demosthenes' description of the political situation in Greece during the interval between the Peloponnesian and Corinthian Wars: "when the Spartans ruled land and sea, and encircled Attica with harmosts and garrisons in Euboea, Tanagra, all the Boeotian towns, Megara, Aegina, [Ceos,] and the other islands."[19] Demosthenes' picture, three quarters of a century later, is far too sweeping, as applied to the entire decade between 404 and 395, and it is directly contradicted in the case of Boeotia by the statement in an anonymous Athenian oration (around 401) that Sparta had not interfered in the internal affairs of Boeotia, Phocis, Corinth, Achaea, Elis, Tegea, and the other Arcadian cities after the Peloponnesian War.[20] Megara, however, is conspicuously absent from this list, which adds some support to Demosthenes' view of her treatment during this period. If Lysander was, in fact, responsible for the imposition of Spartan military rule on Megara in 404, it probably was removed when his own influence declined, perhaps as early as the spring of 403, when King Pausanias of Sparta reversed Lysander's arrangements in Athens.

There is no direct evidence to suggest that Lysander might also have shaken the Megarian oligarchy or installed a dekarchy of his own local adherents, but something of this sort was the natural

[19]18.96.

[20]*Peri Politeias* 28.1. This speech is preserved among the works of Herodes Atticus. See H. T. Wade-Gery, "Kritias and Herodes," *CQ*, 39 (1945), 19-33 (rep. in his *Essays in Greek History*, Oxford, 1958), who argues that the tyrant Critias was the author.

concomitant of the establishment of a harmost and garrison elsewhere. When Thucydides described the extreme oligarchy that had come to power in 424, he observed that it lasted a very long time, considering the small number of men who created it.[21] The implication of this passage is that the narrow oligarchy had passed from the scene before Thucydides put down his pen, about 399. Perhaps Lysander's interference led to its collapse, and it was not able to reassert its prerogatives when the harmost was removed. This would allow sufficient time for Thucydides' observation about the narrow oligarchy's longevity to make sense. But whatever shifts may have taken place in the few years after the end of the war, there is no basis for concluding that oligarchy itself was in danger in Megara. The only reference we have to Megarian government in the early fourth century is Socrates' remark in the *Crito* that both Thebes and Megara were "well governed" (*eunomountai*).[22] This is a term which neither Plato nor his teacher would have applied to a democracy. The overriding impression of Megarian political behavior in the fourth century is of moderation, and it will be argued later in this chapter that Megara appears to have achieved this stability under a moderate oligarchical regime, which enjoyed broad support.

Although there is no evidence of Megarian disaffection from Sparta after the fall of Lysander, anti-Spartan feeling among the larger states continued to grow. By 395 a new anti-Spartan coalition had formed, including such unlikely bedfellows as Athens, Thebes, Corinth, and Argos.[23] Each harbored grievances against Sparta and ambitions that might be realized at her expense. Financial and military support from Persia was the catalyst that fused these traditional rivals into a formidable force. This new alliance posed a grave threat to Megarian security. A glance at the map will show that the anti-Spartan coalition dominated the Isthmus as well

[21] 4.74.4.

[22] 53b.

[23] For the formation of this coalition and the antecedents of the Corinthian War, see Xen. *Hell.* 3; Diod. 14.81 ff.; *Hell. Oxy.* 6-22. An excellent recent treatment of the war is C. D. Hamilton, *Sparta's Bitter Victories: Politics and Diplomacy in the Corinthian War* (Ithaca, 1979), though in common with older discussions, Megara is little noticed.

as the northeastern Peloponnese. Megara was completely encircled. Had she actively maintained her commitments to Sparta during the Corinthian War that followed, she would have been even more vulnerable than she had been during the early years of the Peloponnesian War. It would have been impossible for the Spartans to protect Megarian territory, and though they now possessed a strong fleet, supplies could not have been shipped to Megara if the coalition had decided to interfere, since Megara's long-walls had never been rebuilt. From a military standpoint, Megara's position was hopeless.

It would not have been surprising, under the circumstances, if Megara had bowed to reality and joined her neighbors in the war against Sparta. Some historians have presumed that this is precisely what she did.[24] In support of this view, one can cite the apparent ease with which the anti-Spartan coalition moved its forces through the Megarid, the lack of any evidence that the territory was plundered, and the complete silence of the sources regarding Megarian contributions to the Peloponnesian League forces in the course of the war.[25] Most proponents of this view would also argue that Megara was not troubled by the predominantly democratic caste of the new alliance, because she threw off her own oligarchy in the same period.[26] The case for democracy is based on a misreading of the implications of stasis in Megara a quarter of a century later, but even if Megara was democratic around 371, it is impossible to believe that a democratic regime could have survived the

[24]See, e.g., Beloch, *Gr. Gesch.* 3.1[2], p. 70n., and Meyer, "Megara," col. 192.

[25]The frequent passage of contingents of the anti-Spartan forces through the Megarid is implicit in Xenophon's narrative of the war. See, e.g., *Hell.* 4.2.14 ff. (Athenian and Boeotian forces at Nemea in 395), 4.3.15 ff. (Corinthian and Argive troops in Boeotia in 394), and 4.4.1 (all the allies make Corinth their base in 393 and thereafter). Cf. the opening of Plato's *Theatetus* (142c), which is set in Megara at the home of the Megarian philosopher Euclides during the Corinthian War. The wounded Athenian, Theatetus, has just been carried back to Athens from the allied army at Corinth, and Euclides laments that he did not choose to stop in Megara. The circumstances and the tone of this passage suggest that Megara and Athens were not openly at war with one another, and that individuals might pass freely from one state to the other.

[26]See, e.g., Meyer, "Megara," col. 192. Apart from the long-standing democratic institutions of Athens and Argos, Boeotia exhibited democratic tendencies during this period, and even staunchly oligarchic Corinth was converted to a democracy and joined to Argos at the height of the war.

resurgence of Spartan power after 386, when the Spartans put down democracies in other Peloponnesian states, Mantinea and Phlius, as punishment for their equivocal support in the Corinthian War.[27] In fact, the apparent lack of Spartan reprisals against Megara either during or after the war argues strongly that Megara had not joined Sparta's enemies. Nor is there any more evidence that Megara lent military support to the anti-Spartan coalition than to Sparta. Another solution to the puzzle of Megarian survival in the Corinthian War is possible and, I believe, more likely to be correct: Megara may simply have sat out the war—not formally severing her ties with Sparta, but incapable of honoring them either. Her policy, in other words, might have been *de facto* or even *de iure* neutrality.[28]

It is arguable that the pacific policy of the Megarians, which Isocrates praised in his speech *On the Peace* in 355, had its genesis at the time of the Corinthian War: "Why is it that (the Megarians), who live between the Peloponnesians, the Thebans, and our own city, remain always at peace?"[29] His answer is that they follow a sober and moderate policy (*sophrosynē*).[30]

One serious question, however, is why the major states tolerated Megarian neutrality during the Corinthian War. Possibly Megara was regarded as militarily too weak to bother about, so long as passage through her territory was unimpeded.[31] There is a close parallel to her situation, however, which may throw some light on her motives and those of the contending powers in the 390's. A generation later, after Sparta's disastrous defeat at Leuctra at the hands of the Thebans, Corinth remained loyal to Sparta and Athens in the face of mounting Theban pressure. But when

---

[27]This Megarian stasis after the Battle of Leuctra is discussed later in this chapter. On Sparta's punitive policy toward her recalcitrant allies after the conclusion of the King's Peace, see Xen. *Hell.* 5.2.1-7 (Mantinea) and 8-10 (Phlius). Cf. my article "Phliasian Politics and Policy in the Early Fourth Century B.C.," *Historia,* 16 (1967), 329-31.

[28]This interpretation is supported by, e.g., Hammond, *HG,* pp. 8, 522, and Meyer, "Megara," col. 194. Highbarger, *Megara,* p. 198, is more cautious, merely noting the "subordinate role played by Megara in public events in the fourth century."

[29]8.118.

[30]8.119.

[31]More is said on this issue below, in connection with the wars of the 370's and 360's.

Corinth became alienated from Athens in 366, her position became untenable.[32] The Corinthians therefore resolved to ask Sparta's permission to conclude peace, but not an alliance, with Thebes. According to Xenophon, the Corinthians went to Sparta to defend their proposal to become, in effect, neutrals in the conflict between Sparta and Thebes:

> Men of Sparta, we come here as your friends, and we ask that if you see any hope for us if we continue fighting, point it out to us. But if you judge our situation to be hopeless, that you join with us in making peace, if it suits your interests too, since there is no one in whose company we would rather seek safety. However, if you are determined to continue the war, please let us conclude peace. For if we survive, we may be of use to you at some time in the future, but if we are destroyed now, plainly we will never again be of service.[33]

Xenophon reports that the Spartans readily agreed to allow Corinth and any other allies who wished to make peace on these terms.[34] The case presented here by the Corinthians applies forcefully to Megara's situation in 395: If she were to be saved for Sparta in the future, she could not be expected to fight on in impossible circumstances at the present time. It is even possible that Corinth's arguments in 366 were affected by the earlier case of Megara. We cannot determine, however, whether Megara concluded a formal peace treaty with Sparta's Corinthian War enemies or worked out some informal understanding. Nor can we dismiss the possibility that this resolution of her predicament was proposed by Athens and the others, rather than the Megarians, possibly when the latter balked at joining the coalition outright. All that seems relatively certain is that Megara was an island of peace in the ocean of the Corinthian War. This circumstance must have greatly advanced the cause of Megarian economic prosperity in the early fourth century, and it undoubtedly had a lasting effect on Megara's attitude toward succeeding wars.[35]

[32]*Hell.* 7.4.4 ff.
[33]*Hell.* 7.4.8.
[34]*Hell.* 7.4.9.
[35]Another possible sign of Megarian neutrality in this period was her failure to rebuild her long-walls, despite the balance of naval power between the Peloponnesian League and its enemies in the fourth century—a circumstance that ought to have assured Megara's ability to resupply herself by sea. Apparently there was no need for such measures.

Before we leave the subject of the Corinthian War, a few words should be said about it as an illustration of the strategic importance of the mountain passes that led through Megarian territory. In the opening round of the war, before the anti-Spartan coalition took the offensive, the Road of the Towers in the northeastern Megarid apparently lay open to the Spartans. They launched a two-pronged attack on Thebes, one army marching through the Isthmus and over Mt. Karydi, descending into the Boeotian plain in the vicinity of Plataea, while the other seems to have been ferried across the Corinthian Gulf from Sicyon, reaching Boeotia via Phocis.[36] When the Spartans were defeated at Haliartus, Pausanias, the commander of the force that had advanced through the Isthmus, withdrew into Phocis under a truce.[37] His eventual return to the Peloponnese is nowhere explicitly described, but it is a reasonable assumption that he sailed back to avoid further contact with the aroused enemy. From this time forward, the only Spartan expeditions north of the Isthmus traveled by sea, as the anti-Spartan coalition concentrated its forces near Corinth, thus controlling the Gerania passes, and doubtless controlled the Road of the Towers as well.[38] Without the support of a militarily strong Megara, passage through the Isthmus was extremely hazardous for the Spartans, and they clearly preferred not to risk it as long as they had alternatives. This factor was to come into play once more in the wars of the 370's.

The Peace of Antalcidas in 386, otherwise known as the King's Peace because of the Persian king's role in dictating its terms, reestablished Spartan predominance throughout mainland Greece for the moment by requiring the dissolution of all alliances except the Peloponnesian League and the restoration of autonomy to all the poleis. Sparta blithely ignored the pledge of universal autonomy, and used the general peace as an opportunity to tighten control over her own alliance and to punish recalcitrant members.[39] As already noted, there is no evidence that Megara was punished for her passivity during the war. She appears to have resumed her participation in the Peloponnesian League quite smoothly.

[36]Xen. *Hell.* 3.5.6-7 and 17; Plut. *Lys.* 28; Diod. 14.81.
[37]Plut. *Lys.* 29.
[38]For instances of Spartan armies being ferried across the Corinthian Gulf, see Xen. *Hell.* 4.4.1 (Lysander's troops in 394) and 4.6.4, 14 (Agesilaus' army in 389).
[39]Xen. *Hell.* 5.2.1 ff.

Megara's moderate position in the previous period seems to have carried over into the era of the King's Peace, if we can credit a story told by Plutarch in his *Spartan Sayings*:

> When the Athenians selected the Megarian assembly to arbitrate some grievances they had against the Spartans, Agesipolis, the son of Pausanias remarked, "O Athenians, that the leaders of the Greeks should know less of justice than the Megarians!"[40]

The date of this episode must fall between 386 and 380, since Athens and Sparta were at war during the early part of Agesipolis' reign (though it is barely possible that it was the war itself which the Athenians offered to submit to Megarian arbitration—which would be dramatic proof of Megarian neutrality during the conflict). What the nature of the issues between Athens and Sparta might have been after 386 is a matter of speculation, but the choice of Megara as arbitrator *by the Athenians* is striking. A generation earlier that would have been unthinkable, and the offer must be judged as a significant testimony to the middle course Megara steered in the early fourth century. Agesipolis' rejection of the offer is more likely a sign that he expected Athens to yield to his demands—whatever they were—than an expression of distrust of Megara. We have no reason to believe that the proposed arbitration ever took place.[41]

One of the circumstances that may have induced the hegemonal states to accept Megarian neutrality at various times in the fourth century was her military weakness. She had become an extremely modest, if not negligible, asset in time of war. Megara's reduced military capacity has already been noted in general terms, and Isocrates refers to her possession of "only a small force" in the passage to which we earlier referred,[42] but better evidence can be extracted from references to the reorganization of the Peloponnesian League in the period of the King's Peace. In 383, the Spartans convened the league members to consider the Acanthian and Apollonian appeal for aid against Olynthus and the Chalcidic

---

[40]Plut. *Mor.* 215c.
[41]As Meyer, "Megara," col. 192, appears to assume.
[42]8.118.

League.[43] Here the Spartans proposed raising an army of ten thousand men by proportionate contributions of the allies. According to Xenophon, money payments could be substituted for troops:

> The policy was adopted that any state who wished might contribute money in place of men, at the rate of three Aeginetan obols a day per man, and that if anyone was responsible for cavalry, the value of four hoplites should be given for each horseman. If any state defaulted, the Spartans could impose a fine of a stater [two drachmas] per man.[44]

The ten thousand men assembled on this basis were then sent to Olynthus in 382, but the proportionate contributions of the member states of the Peloponnesian League to this expedition are not specified. Nor can we determine whether a state such as Megara chose to meet its obligation monetarily, rather than by mustering her troops. The main interest of this episode is that it served as a precedent for a thorough reorganization of the league in 378, when Megara's role was spelled out more clearly. This time Diodorus is our source. He describes it as a belated effort by the Spartans to treat their allies more fairly lest they secede.[45] The member states were grouped into ten divisions:

> The first division consisted of the Spartans, the second and third of the Arcadians, the fourth of the Eleians, the fifth of the Achaeans, the sixth was made up of the Corinthians and Megarians, the seventh of the Sicyonians, Phliasians, and the inhabitants of Akte [i.e., Epidaurus, Troezen, and Hermione], the eighth of the Acarnanians, the ninth of the Phocians and Locrians, and the remaining one of the Olynthians and the other allies in Thrace. One hoplite was considered equivalent to two light-armed troops, and one horseman the equivalent of four hoplites.[46]

These ten divisions are clearly geographic, hence the pairing of Megara with Corinth, but they also seem designed to be roughly equal in military strength.[47] Thus some divisions consist of a single state—for example, Elis—while others—for example the seventh—

[43]Xen. *Hell.* 5.2.11 ff.
[44]Xen. *Hell.* 5.2.21-22.
[45]15.31.1.
[46]15.31.2.
[47]Cf. *Hell.* 6.1.1, where Xenophon corroborates this proportionate principle.

consist of a large number of smaller states. The ratios for different types of armament are clearly related to the arrangements in 382, but it is not clear whether money was any longer an acceptable substitute for men.

The first campaign fought by the restructured Peloponnesian army permits us to attach some numbers to this organizational skeleton. Diodorus reports that Agesilaus marched against Thebes with more than 18,000 troops and 1,500 cavalry.[48] The force is said to have included five of the six Spartan brigades, totaling 2,500 men. This seems to confirm the approximate proportionality of the ten divisions of the new army, for if we weigh the horsemen at 1:4 and add the resulting 6,000 to the number of foot soldiers, we arrive at a total of more than 24,000, of which the 2,500 Spartiates constitute a bit more than 10 percent. This calculation presumes that the number of light armed peltasts was small, though we do hear of their activity during the campaign.[49] For our purposes it is sufficient to recognize that an underallowance for the peltasts leads to an overestimate of hoplite strength. Since the Spartans mustered five sixths of their forces for this campaign, it is reasonable to assume that the allies in the other nine divisions were expected to do likewise. This means that the entire levy of the league was theoretically 30,000 hoplites or their equivalent.

The purpose of this arithmetical exercise is to suggest the slender military capacity of fourth-century Megara. The point is somewhat obscured by the fact that she is coupled with Corinth, but only 3,000 troops were expected between the two, whereas they had mustered 8,000 at Plataea a century earlier. If the 5:3 ratio of Corinthian to Megarian strength which prevailed at the time of Xerxes' invasion had remained unchanged—and no one would suggest that Megara had gained population relative to Corinth in the intervening period—then the Megarians were now called upon to produce a mere 1,200 hoplites. If the Spartans' motive in making this reform was indeed to treat their allies better than in the past, it is possible that levies on this scale did not tax their manpower to the limit, but they can hardly have fallen far short either, in light of the formidable opposition the alliance faced. Thus it is safe to

[48]15.32.1.
[49]Diod. 15.32.6.

270

conclude that in 378 Megara would have been hard put to field an army of more than 1,200 to 1,500 men, which would have been less than half her strength in the early fifth century. It might be argued that the decline reflects the impoverishment of what had been the hoplite class in Megara, but the hypothesis flies in the face of ample evidence that this was a period of prosperity in Megara in which quite the opposite was likely to be the case.[50] The more reasonable explanation is a decline in the free population, reflected in the thinning of her hoplite ranks. The same decline probably took place among the poor, who might have served as peltasts and rowers. In fact, Megarian warships are entirely absent from our accounts of the fourth-century wars.

In 382, the Spartans strengthened their hand in Greece by aiding an olgarchic faction in Thebes to seize power and keeping a Spartan force on the Theban Cadmea thereafter.[51] This policy was to have dire consequences for Sparta, when in 379 the Thebans threw off the Spartan yoke and, supported by Athens, initiated the first of a series of clashes which were to shatter Sparta's military preeminence in Greece.[52] The reorganization of Peloponnesian League forces described above was prompted by the failure of Sparta's initial military response to the new Theban challenge.[53] As is clear from the terms of the league's new military structure, Megara participated in the early campaigns of this war on the side of her Peloponnesian allies, but there are no further references to her active involvement in the conflict, beyond what we have noted in Diodorus. The Megarid itself, however, was to play a key role in the course of this war. In the opening campaign in 378, King Cleombrotus of Sparta crossed the Cithaeron range—that is, the Road of the Towers—into Boeotia unopposed, but by the time he was ready to come home, the Athenians and Boeotians had occupied the pass over Mt. Karydi, and he was forced to take the treacherous route along the northern coast of the Isthmus from Creusis through Aegosthena, where high winds nearly destroyed

[50]The evidence for this prosperity is presented below.
[51]Xen. Hell. 5.2.25 ff., 5.4.1; Diod. 15.20.
[52]Xen. Hell. 5.4.1 ff.; Diod. 15.25 ff.
[53]Xen. Hell. 5.4.14 ff.; Diod. 15.27.1-3.

his army.[54] Having survived this ordeal, his army was disbanded in the Megarid. The lesson was not lost on Agesilaus, for in the following year, knowing that "unless one first gained possession of Mt. Cithaeron, it would not be easy to effect an entrance into the country of Thebes," he instructed his northern mercenaries to occupy the passes in advance of the campaign.[55] Thus when he led his newly organized army north, he was able to advance and later return over the Road of the Towers unmolested.[56] He followed the same procedure in the next campaign, succeeding in negotiating his passage in and out of Boeotia (though not in achieving the major objectives of the campaign).[57] Each time, the Peloponnesian forces were disbanded, once safely back in the Megarid. At the end of his second campaign in Boeotia, Agesilaus paid a visit to Megara before returning home.[58] He went first to the Temple of Aphrodite on the eastern acropolis, presumably to pray and sacrifice, and then set off for the Aesymnaton, the council house on the slopes of the western acropolis. But the trek up and down the steep hills of Megara proved too much for the aged warrior, and he burst a blood vessel in his leg on the ascent of Alcathoa. His condition was serious, and quite possibly he never held his parley with the Megarian leaders. We are left to wonder what he might have wished to discuss with them.

In 376 the Spartans planned a further invasion of Boeotia, with Cleombrotus in command, no doubt because of Agesilaus' continuing incapacity.[59] When Cleombrotus discovered that the Thebans and Athenians were already in possession of the Cithaeron passes, he gave up the campaign and disbanded his army in the Megarid. It is curious that neither side appears to have attempted to hold the passes along the Road of the Towers permanently, winter and summer, and that each year there was some doubt as to whether the passes would be open to the Peloponnesians. The towers in the Vathikhoria, described in Chapter 1, which seem to have been built in the mid-fourth century and later, may have been

---

[54]Xen. *Hell.* 5.4.14, 17-18. This passage is quoted above in Chapter 1.
[55]Xen. *Hell.* 5.4.36, 38.
[56]Xen. *Hell.* 5.4.41.
[57]Xen. *Hell.* 5.4.47-58.
[58]Xen. *Hell.* 5.4.58; Plut. *Ages.* 27.
[59]Xen. *Hell.* 5.4.59.

attempts by the powers of central Greece (Boeotia most likely) to hold the passes on a permanent basis. They were insufficient to hold the road against a large enemy army, though at one time[60] they may have been connected by defensive walls, but they might at least provide an early warning of a hostile force advancing over Gerania, giving time for larger forces to be rushed to defend the passes themselves. It is impossible, however, to fix the precise dates of the various towers or to associate them with any particular war—the general tactical problem arose time and again in the fourth and third centuries—and there is no indication in the historical sources that any towers existed during the wars of the 380's and 370's. Perhaps this was an idea whose time had not yet come. What is equally striking is that the Spartans do not appear to have entrusted Megara with the task of keeping the passes through her own territory open. Were the Megarians regarded as too weak, or perhaps as unreliable? The latter possibility raises the question of just how willing and enthusiastic allies of the Spartans the Megarians were after 386, and how far beneath the surface of Megarian politics lay the inclination to passivity and neutrality in the wars between Sparta and the other powers. Perhaps it is significant that Athens and Boeotia do not appear to have devastated the Megarid in the period after 379; it would have been perfectly possible for them to do so, as had been common practice in the fifth-century wars. Their restraint may reflect the lessened strategic value of the Megarid itself to an alliance which joined Athens with Boeotia and could control access to the regions north of the Isthmus with or without the cooperation of the Isthmian states. But it is also possible that Thebes and Athens did not seriously regard Megara as a hostile state.

Cleombrotus' decision not to attempt to force his way over the Cithaeron passes in 376 marked a turning point in the war. At a subsequent meeting of the Spartan alliance, it was proposed that the war against Thebes should be pursued by transporting the Peloponnesian army across the Corinthian Gulf by ship, rather than attempt to carry the mountain passes.[61] A fleet of sixty ships

---

[60]Professor Colin Edmonson believes there are traces of classical walls around the towers which Hammond, "Main Road," pp. 108-11, did not notice.

[61]Xen. *Hell.* 5.4.60 ff.

was readied for this purpose in 375, and Cleombrotus made the crossing with four of the Spartan brigades and "the corresponding contingents of the allies"—namely, two thirds of the league levy.[62] Megara may have continued her participation, or she may have resumed a neutral posture now that the Peloponnesians would no longer be regularly marching through her territory. One possible indication of Megarian passivity after 375 may be found in the composition of the fleets of sixty ships which were assembled to convoy the Peloponnesian army across the Gulf of Corinth and for an expedition to Corcyra the following year. Xenophon lists the following states as having contributed to the second armada: Sparta, Corinth, Leucas, Ambracia, Elis, Zacynthus, Achaea, Epidaurus, Troezen, Hermione, and Haliae.[63] Of the Peloponnesian members of the Spartan alliance, only Megara, Sicyon, and landlocked Arcadia are missing. As has been suggested, Megara may not have been a sizable naval power in the fourth century, but it is hard to believe that she could not have matched the likes of Troezen, Hermione, and Haliae had she wished to do so. Megara's absence from this armada is more likely the result of policy than resources, but whether her lack of involvement in this aspect of the Peloponnesian League's military effort points to her withholding all support cannot be proved.

Later in 374 Sparta and Athens concluded peace, and over the next few years the Thebans busied themselves in campaigning against dissidents in the Boeotian League.[64] In 371 the Persian king, Artaxerxes II, anxious to employ Greek mercenaries, exerted his influence to bring about another general peace in Greece, like that of 386.[65] Again, the autonomy of all was guaranteed, but this time Athens' second naval league, formed in 377, was recognized in addition to the Peloponnesian League. The peace did not, however, sanction Thebes' control of the Boeotian cities, and, not surprisingly, the Thebans refused to accept it. The high-sounding principles of the document scarcely cloaked the intention of Sparta and Athens to reduce the power of Thebes, which had grown alarming-

[62]Xen. *Hell.* 6.1.1.
[63]*Hell.* 6.2.3.
[64]Xen. *Hell.* 6.2.1.
[65]Xen. *Hell.* 6.3; Plut. *Ages.* 28; Diod. 15.50.4-6. Cf. Diodorus' treatment of events in 374 (15.38 ff.), which he seems to confuse with the aftermath of Leuctra.

ly over the past decade, while retaining their own might. Under these circumstances, the peace of 371 was stillborn and a resumption of war was inevitable.

The Spartans decided to press their advantage over the isolated Thebans by mounting a campaign immediately. King Cleombrotus invaded Boeotia through Phocis once more, which points to his continued reliance on naval transport rather than on the Megarian passes.[66] This campaign ended in disaster, when the Spartans were defeated at Leuctra.[67] When news of this catastrophe first reached the Peloponnese, the initial reaction of many of Sparta's allies was to rally around her. Xenophon singles out the Mantineans, Corinthians, Sicyonians, Phliasians, and Achaeans, but the list is far short of being a full roster of the Peloponnesian League, and Megara is among the missing names.[68] Archidamus, son of the still infirm King Agesilaus, rapidly marched north, sending word ahead for the allies to meet him in the northern Megarid at Aegosthena.[69] They arrived in time to meet the remnants of Cleombrotus' army, which had marched along the coast from Creusis. The routes of both forces clearly point to the fact that at this time Thebes controlled the main route over Cithaeron. Archidamus had hoped to press on into Boeotia and join Cleombrotus there, but when the full extent of the latter's defeat became clear, Archidamus decided to wait at Aegosthena for all the allied contingents to arrive and then led the whole army south as far as Corinth, where he dismissed the allies and continued toward Sparta with his own forces. The Spartans no longer felt safe enough in the Megarid to risk disbanding their armies there.

Sparta's losses at Leuctra were grave for a state with a relatively small population base, but the psychological impact of the defeat of her heretofore invincible phalanx was even more serious. The fear of Sparta, which had overshadowed Peloponnesian affairs for centuries, lessened dramatically, and long-held assumptions were cast in doubt. Within a few years the security cocoon that Sparta had patiently woven around herself and the captive helots began to

[66]Xen. *Hell*. 6.4.3.
[67]Xen. *Hell*. 6.4.4 ff. (which puts the Spartan dead at 1,000); Diod. 15.52.6 (which puts Spartan losses at 4,000!).
[68]*Hell*. 6.4.18.
[69]Xen. *Hell*. 6.4.25-26.

unravel. Now that Sparta was in trouble, even in the heart of the Peloponnese, there was little hope of her holding the active allegiance of Megara on the Boeotian border, an allegiance which, as we have seen, had been equivocal at best since the 390's.

Over the years after Leuctra, the Boeotians carried the war against Sparta into the Peloponnese, but there is only one reference to Megarian participation on either side of the conflict between 370 and the Battle of Mantinea in 362. Under the year 369, Diodorus describes an Athenian force which was sent into the Peloponnese in support of Sparta under the command of the professional general, Chabrias: "(Chabrias and his troops) reached Corinth and, recruiting more troops from Megara, Pellene, and Corinth, he raised his force to about 10,000 men."[70] From the manner of their recruitment, these Megarians, Pellenians, and Corinthians appear to have been mercenary soldiers recruited by Chabrias rather than citizen levies provided by Megara and the other states. We therefore have no evidence of official Megarian involvement in this war. In listing Theban abuses after Leuctra, Isocrates says that they "threatened the Megarians on their border";[71] but though the Corinthians complained in 370 of their country's devastation by the invading Thebans,[72] we have no reference that the Thebans actually took punitive action against Megara. When we put all of this together, the most likely state of affairs appears to be that Megara remained passive during the war between Thebes and Sparta, allowing the contending forces to traverse her territory unimpeded but lending direct support to neither. The Corinthian analogy from 366, cited earlier, is even more likely to reflect Megarian policy at this time, and Xenophon explicitly notes Sparta's invitation to her other allies to follow Corinth's path if they chose.[73] As suggested earlier, Megara, rather than Corinth, may have *led* the way. In any case, the Theban threat to Megara was either effective or superfluous if its purpose was to neutralize her.

It is possible, however, that Thebes' victory at Leuctra and, perhaps, her threats against Megara precipitated a domestic polit-

[70]15.68.1-2.
[71]5.53.
[72]Xen. *Hell.* 6.5.37.
[73]*Hell.* 7.5.9.

ical crisis. Diodorus reports a series of civil disturbances in Greece, mostly among the Peloponnesian states, including one in Megara, under the year 375/4.[74] He seems to have dated these outbreaks of stasis too early, since he portrays them as democratic movements encouraged by the collapse of Spartan hegemony and the ascendancy of Thebes. This situation did not exist until the period after Leuctra in 371. A further indication of chronological confusion in Diodorus' account of 375/4 is his report of Persian-dictated peace guaranteeing universal autonomy, which sounds suspiciously like the peace of 371 as recorded in other sources and even by Diodorus himself under the appropriate year.[75] We can confirm Diodorus' error in dating in the case of one of the civil disturbances, in Phlius, which Xenophon more plausibly puts in 369.[76] The confusion in Diodorus is probably due to two factors: a conflict in his sources, which caused him to record variants of the same events in more than one place and to misplace some events entirely, and a tendency to cluster events occurring over a period of years under a single year. I do not, however, regard the error in Diodorus' dating of the disturbance in Megara as sufficient grounds for doubting that the episode ever occurred.

Unfortunately, Diodorus says far too little about the stasis in Megara, and no other source mentions it at all. In a brief sentence he writes: "In the polis of the Megarians certain men attempted to overturn the constitution and were overpowered by the demos. Many were killed and not a few expelled."[77] Based on the involvement of the demos, the common people, this passage has sometimes been taken as proof that Megara had a democratic government that beat back an oligarchic challenge.[78] But one cannot assume that the demos of Megara would only have fought in defense of democracy. (Consider the equivocal role of the demos in 424, for example.) All one can legitimately infer from Diodorus' description is that the mass of the Megarian people supported the

---

[74]15.40.

[75]See above, note 65.

[76]Cf. Diod. 15.40.6 with Xen. *Hell.* 7.2.5 ff. See my article "Phliasian Politics," esp. pp. 335-36.

[77]15.40.4.

[78]E.g., by Meyer, "Megara," col. 192, and Highbarger, *Megara*, p. 192, who omits any mention of when this democracy might have come to power.

regime in power against another group. It should be kept in mind that Diodorus places this episode in the context of a wave of democratic movements against Spartan-supported oligarchies. If the Megarian disturbance was the opposite, we might as well discard Diodorus' evidence altogether. Again the case of Phlius is apt, since it is quite clear that the demos there supported an oligarchic regime against the exiled leaders of a democracy that had fallen a decade earlier.[79]

Without clearer evidence to the contrary, it seems reasonable to believe that the Megarian regime that successfully defended itself after Leuctra was the same one that Isocrates described as sophrosynē in the 350's, and that the challenge came from either a democratic or (though less likely) a more extreme oligarchic faction. The revolutionaries were no doubt inspired by the shifting political currents of the post-Leuctra era, but it is impossible to tell what principles or policies they stood for. The reaction of the Megarian people to this challenge demonstrates their support for the regime in power, and the outcome of this stasis enabled Megara to continue on the path of political stability and diplomatic moderation forged in the first third of the century.

Megarian neutrality seems to have continued in the period after the Battle of Mantinea in 362, when Thebes' brief hegemony collapsed. This was, in fact, the period in which Isocrates made the statement to which we have already referred regarding Megarian moderation and neutrality. *On the Peace* was delivered in 355 in the waning days of the Social War between Athens and her "allies" in the confederacy, and Isocrates was urging his fellow Athenians to abandon their aggressive and expansionist ways. In an extended contrast between the Thessalians and Megarians, Isocrates holds the latter up as an example of the benefits to be derived from political and diplomatic moderation, sophrosynē:

> What accounts for the fact that, on the one hand, the Thessalians, inheriting great wealth and possessing a large and excellent country, have fallen into poverty, while the Megarians, beginning with a small and worthless country, possessing neither farmland nor harbors nor silver mines, but forced to farm rocks, own the greatest houses in

[79]See "Phliasian Politics," pp. 335-37.

Greece? Why are the acropoleis of the former always in the hands of others, when they have more than 3,000 cavalry and peltasts beyond number, while the latter, with only a small force at their disposal, govern themselves as they wish? And why is it that the former are continually fighting among themselves, while the latter, who live between the Peloponnesians, the Thebans, and our own city, remain always at peace?[80]

However much one wishes to allow for rhetorical exaggeration in this passage, it becomes totally implausible unless one assumes that Megara had steered clear of political and military entanglements for a period of years leading up to 355.

This is appropriate point to consider the question of Megarian prosperity in the fourth century. Was this indeed the golden age implied by Isocrates' rosy portrait? To make his contrast more effective, the orator may have inflated the Megarians' success to the same degree he minimized their resources. Megara has some harbors and a modest amount of good arable land, and it is safe to assume that not all Megarians owned fine houses. But Isocrates' choice of Megara to make his point is still highly significant, and it must mean that Megarian success in the fourth century was familiar to his audience. I believe that the connection between political moderation at home and abroad, peace, freedom from interference in her internal affairs, and material prosperity, which Isocrates seeks to convey, was essentially valid for Megara. We have already found corroboration in other sources of all these elements, apart from the last, and substantiation of her economic success is also available. This is only what we ought to expect, if the rest of the picture is true. The material advantages to be gained by any polis which managed over a long period of time to avoid both foreign wars and internal disturbances should be self-evident. But let us turn to the evidence.

First, there are several further general observations that tend to support Isocrates' portrait. The Cynic philosopher Diogenes appears to have spent some time in Megara in the middle decades of the century, and two of his aphorisms deal directly with Megarian affluence and concern for material things, which he deplored.[81] The more famous of these appears at the head of this chapter: "The Megarians feast as if they expect to die tomorrow, and build their houses as if they were never going to die at all."[82] The allusion to substantial homes echoes Isocrates' remark about the great houses of Megara. We may conclude that Megara was graced with fine mansions in the fourth century, numerous and impressive enough to catch the eye of any visitor. But Diogenes' remark goes beyond this; gluttony and lavish homes are symbols of material excess and the neglect of other aspects of life. The philosopher apparently found Megara a handy symbol of great prosperity and its corrupting influence.

Diogenes' second comment has a related theme, but tells us something too about the basis of Megarian affluence: "In Megara, seeing the sheep wrapped with hides while the children went naked, he said, 'It is more advantageous to be a Megarian's ram than his child.'"[83] Again one notes the criticism of the acquisitive impulse run amuck, but the reference to sheep also confirms the prominence of the industry which probably constituted the material basis of Megara's good fortune in the fourth century—woolens.

A passage from Xenophon's *Memorabilia*, written about 381, though set in Socrates' lifetime several decades earlier, deals with another phase of the woolen industry. In a conversation with the businessman Aristarchus, Socrates remarks, "The Megarians support themselves by manufacturing woolen cloaks." Aristarchus replies, "True, for their practice is to buy barbarian slaves and force them to work diligently."[84] The cloaks in question were coarse garments intended for working men and slaves, which we have already encountered in Aristophanes' picture of Megarian commerce in the fifth century. I suspect that their manufacture goes back much further than this; but the scale of production implied by Xenophon and the employment of large numbers of slaves in the industry were likely to be post-Peloponnesian War developments

[81]For evidence of Diogenes' contacts with Megara, see D.L. 6.22, 24, 76. Cf. D.L. 6.21 for Diogenes' trip to Athens from Corinth, which probably took him through the Megarid, though he might have gone directly by ship.
[82]See above, note 1.
[83]D.L. 6.41.
[84]2.7.6.

brought about by the decline of Megara's free population and the ready availability of slaves in the early fourth century. Though it cannot be directly demonstrated, I believe that a large proportion of these slaves were women, since female slaves appear to have been the predominant labor force in the manufacture of Greek textiles in this period, if we may judge from contemporary Athenian manumission inscriptions.[85] Such slaves might be relatively easy to manage.

A further aspect of the woolen industry is verified by the Eleusis building inscriptions, where Megarian merchants are found supplying cloaks for the crews of public slaves.[86] Under the year 329/8, a Megarian cloak merchant by the name of Antigenes is listed, and two more sellers of cloaks, Callias and Midas, are listed in 327/6. Thus the Megarians appear also to have marketed their products abroad, though it would be desirable to have confirmation of overseas activities in addition to this evidence for their presence in neighboring Attica. Perhaps some indication that they remained active in naval commerce rather than working exclusively through the emporia of neighboring commercial states may be seen in the description of the Megarians by the early third-century poet Theocritus as "Megarians of Nisaea, champions of the oar."[87] As noted earlier, there is no evidence for a Megarian warfleet after the Peloponnesian War. It would seem, therefore, that if there was any justification for Theocritus' words, it lay in the sphere of naval commerce. Only one of the three Megarian merchants mentioned in the Eleusis inscriptions, Callias, can be positively identified as a citizen. The other two appear to have been resident aliens, very possibly manumitted slaves, who conceivably learned the business while enslaved.

One further episode substantiates the picture of a significant slave population in fourth-century Megara. In 307 the troops of Demetrius, son of the Macedonian general Antigonus, sacked Megara and carried off all her slaves.[88] No figures are given, but the impression created is that the number was fairly large. We have no

---

[85] IG 2². 1553-78. Cf. W. L. Westermann, *The Slave Systems of Greek and Roman Antiquity* (Philadelphia, 1953), p. 13.

[86] IG 2². 1672.103, 1673.45-46.

[87] 12.27.

[88] Plut. *Demetr.* 9. This episode is treated in the Epilogue.

sound basis for estimating the size of Megara's slave population in the fourth century, or for that matter at any time. Beloch reckoned it as equal to the free population—that is, about 20,000—even in the fifth century.[89] I suspect that this figure is far too high for any date in Megarian history, but it was most closely approached in the fourth century, as the citizen population diminished and the demands of industry grew.

Another indication of Megarian prosperity in the fourth century is the series of silver coins Megara minted down to 338—the first authenticated Megarian coinage.[90] The dates for this series are established by coin hoards, but we cannot determine how soon after the end of the Peloponnesian War coinage was initiated. There is reasonable certainty, however, that Megara ceased to mint at the time of the Macedonian conquest, and that her Hellenistic coinage commenced only in the last decade of the fourth century. The earlier fourth-century coinage exhibits the head of Apollo on the obverse and his lyre on the reverse. The three largest denominations are inscribed MEGARE on the didrachm, MEGA on the pentobol, and MEG on the triobol. The smaller denominations, diobol, obol, and hemiobol, follow the type but are not inscribed. The weights of these silver coins do not conform closely with the standard of any major currency of the period, nor are the weight ratios between the coins very precise. But the weights approximate the Athenian standard more closely than any other, including the widely used Aeginetan standard, suggesting what we have already concluded on other grounds—that Megara was on reasonably good economic and political terms with Athens, and operated within the Athenian trading sphere during the fourth century. Since larger denominations are not represented in the series, Gardner speculates that the Megarians may have relied on larger Athenian coins for major transactions, producing their own primarily for local use, where precise weights would have been less critical. It should be recalled that Megarian commerce appears to have managed without any local coinage up to this time. During this period, Athens and other states began minting smaller denomina-

---

[89]*Bevölkerung*, pp. 173-74.

[90]See B. V. Head, *Catalogue of Greek Coins in the British Museum; Attica, Megaris, Aegina*, ed. R. S. Poole (London, 1888), lxiii and pl. 21; and P. Gardner, *A History of Ancient Coinage, 700-300 B.C.* (Oxford, 1918), p. 368.

tions for the local market in copper, rather than silver.[91] Perhaps Megara ventured into the minting of small silver coins for the first time out of dissatisfaction with this shift on the part of states that had supplied her needs in the past.

A composite picture of the fourth-century Megarian economy would be as follows: The woolen industry flourished and Megarian commerce with it. Large herds of sheep were raised on the grazing lands of the northern Megarid, slaves concentrated in urban workshops were employed in processing the wool and turning out sturdy, low-priced garments for export, and Megarian merchants sold these goods abroad—in exchange, no doubt, for silver, grain, timber, and other commodities in short supply at home. A large proportion of this trade took place within the Athenian economic sphere. Probably there was a revival of Megara's other traditional exports: vegetables, fruits, and salt. Citizens, resident aliens, and slaves were involved in various aspects of this economic revival. There was still room, I suspect, for the small vegetable farmer and the shepherd who owned a small flock and supplemented his income with a certain amount of marginal farming. The general level of prosperity appears to have risen, and capital investment in slaves, large-scale production, and export shipping fostered a wealthy commercial class, whose mansions adorned the city. As a result of these trends, the city grew to its largest size.

We have a brief sketch of a wealthy Megarian citizen in Plutarch's account of the visit to Megara by Dion of Syracuse sometime in the late 360's:

> They say that Dion was once invited to visit Ptoeodorus, the Megarian, in his home. It appears that this Ptoeodorus was one of the wealthiest and most powerful men in the city. When Dion saw a crowd of people at the door and many preoccupations which made it difficult to speak to Ptoeodorus or even get near him, looking toward his friends, who were angry and irritated, he (Dion) said, "Why should we blame this man? For, we all behaved the same way when we were in Syracuse."[92]

The nature of Ptoeodorus' business, whether public or private, is not specified, but I suspect from the tenor of the anecdote that it

[91]I am grateful to Professor C. G. Starr for pointing out to me this change in the coining policies of surrounding states.
[92]*Dion* 17.4-5.

was a bit of both. We shall have another occasion to meet him in connection with civil strife in the 340's.

One result of Megarian affluence in this period was a burst of artistic patronage, resulting in the beautification of the city. This can be inferred from Pausanias' inventory of the city's monuments. Theocosmus, the native sculptor who had collaborated with Phidias on the chryselephantine statue of Zeus before the outbreak of the Peloponnesian War, remained active early in the fourth century. He is credited with the statue of Hermon at Delphi, and he probably produced new work in Megara too.[93] More significantly, most of the great sculptors of the century executed commissions in Megara. Praxiteles of Athens (370-329) was the most active, sculpting images of Tychē in her sanctuary near the Temple of Artemis, most if not all of a group of the twelve Olympian gods in Artemis' sanctuary, and still others in the Temple of Aphrodite and the sanctuary of Apollo Prostateros.[94] Other sculptors represented were Stronglion (late fifth and early fourth century), Bryaxis and Scopas (both mid-fourth century), and Lysippus (mid to late fourth century).[95] Some of the more notable statues were later copied on the coins of Hellenistic Megara and Pagae.[96] All this activity doubtless points to substantial new building and renovation of the temples and shrines that accommodated the statuary. Public expenditure on this scale is a sound indication of Megarian wealth and confidence. It may be added here that Megara also played a not insignificant role in the rebuilding of Apollo's temple at Delphi after its collapse around 369. Her contributions of more than 4,000 drachmae recorded in the fragmentary inscriptions concerning the project place her among the more generous patrons of Delphi, and the names of individual Megarians appear with some frequency among the official templebuilders (the *naopoioi*), though not consistently.[97] This was a significant level of involvement for a state which had never been a favorite of the Delphic Oracle.

[93]Paus. 10.9.4.
[94]Paus. 1.40.3, 43.6, 44.2.
[95]Paus. 1.40.3, 6, 43.6. For Lysippus, cf. *IG* 7.38.
[96]See F. Imhoof-Blumer and P. Gardner, "Numismatic Commentary on Pausanias, I," *JHS*, 6 (1885), 50-58.
[97]See *Fouilles de Delphes* 3 (5) A6 and C55, for Megara's financial contributions. Megarian *naopoioi* are listed at 3 (5) 19.34, 43, 77, 20.34. Cf. the comments on P. Cloché, *BCH*, 40 (1916), 78-142.

There are also indications that other aspects of the higher culture of Greece flourished in the confortable surroundings of fourth-century Megara. Early in the century, the philosophical school of Euclides, a Megarian disciple of Socrates, gained fame, particularly for its skill in dialectic.[98] Plato himself is said to have spent a period in Megara after the death of Socrates.[99] This so-called "Megarian School" sustained its momentum in the second half of the century under the leadership of Stilpo.[100] With the appearance of Praxion's *Megarika* by the mid-fourth century, local history also made its debut in Megara.[101] Praxion was followed by his son Dieuchidas, who also produced a local history, and several more appeared in the next century. These works seem to have shared many characteristics and a common outlook, concerning themselves with the legends and early history of the state and saying little if anything about events from the tyranny onward. These features of local history in Megara may be a further indication of a stable oligarchy, accommodating both commercial and agrarian interests, and a neutral course in foreign affairs; the Megarians may have preferred to read panegyrics to earlier days of glory than to debate the substance of foreign and domestic conflicts in more recent times, particularly those of the fifth century. But any judgments of the overall character of the Megareis' work and their attitudes toward the course of Megarian history after the loss of Salamis must be tentative in view of the limited fragments of their works which can be positively identified.

The Megarians' avoidance of conflict in the first half of the century proved difficult to sustain in the latter half. The first dispute which comes to light is a renewal of border controversy with Athens. This issue, of which we last heard prior to the outbreak of the Peloponnesian War, seems to have flared up again in the late 350's, casting a shadow over half a century of good relations between Megara and Athens. Our earliest reference to this trouble comes in Demosthenes' speech *On Military Affairs* (*Peri Syntaxeos*),

[98]D.L. 2.106-08. See K. Döring, *Die Megariker*, Amsterdam, 1972.
[99]D.L. 2.106, 3.6.
[100]D.L. 2.112.
[101]On the Megareis, see L. Piccirilli, *Megarika; Testimonianze e Frammenti*, Pisa, 1975.

delivered about 352. He refers to it in citing recent examples of Athenian public decrees which had not yet been fully implemented:

> Consider the decree you voted against the accursed Megarians when they appropriated the sacred land (*tēn orgada*), to march out, to prevent it, and not to allow it. . . . A fine resolution, O men of Athens . . . but action, there was none.[102]

Further details of the issue are purportedly related by Didymus in his commentary on this passage of Demosthenes. Didymus attempts to fix the date of the speech by tying this reference to the testimony of two fourth-century Athenian historians, Philochorus and Androtion, regarding a dispute between Athens and Megara over the unbounded lands in the vicinity of the hiera orgas in 350/49. His case for dating the speech this late has been convincingly demolished by G. L. Cawkwell,[103] but the events related by the two Atthidographers were undoubtedly connected with (though not identical to) the earlier eposide recorded by Demosthenes, just as the hiera orgas and the unbounded lands were linked in the dispute before the outbreak of the Peloponnesian War. Philochorus is said to have noted an Athenian invasion of the Megarid over the issue of the unbounded lands. He names the general Ephialtes

---

[102]13.32-33.

[103]See Cawkwell, "Anthemocritus," pp. 328-30. This issue is crucial to W. R. Connor's dating of the Decree of Charinus and the mission and subsequent murder of Anthemocritus to the mid-fourth century dispute over the hiera orgas, rather than to the quarrel that arose before the Peloponnesian War. See his articles, "Charinus' Megarian Decree," *AJP*, 83 (1962), 225-46, and "Charinus' Megarian Decree Again," *REG*, 83 (1970), 305-308. In the latter article Connor abandons his view that the decree belongs to 350/49 (which had been based on his earlier acceptance of Didymus' equating of Demosthenes' remarks in the *Peri Syntaxeos* with the issue described by the atthidographers), but he still insists on a date in the late 350's. The concession, however, has substantially weakened his case. The most compelling evidence he has left is the apparent reference to Anthemocritus' murder as a recent event in the *Letter to Philip* (Dem. 12.4) and several references to a statue raised to Anthemocritus' memory after 353 (Paus. 1.36.3 f.; Harp., *s.v. Anthemocritus*). Proponents of both views concede that the case for either falls short of being conclusive (Connor, "Again," p. 308; Cawkwell, p. 335), and in this I can only concur. But I believe that Charinus' Decree makes good sense in the context of fifth-century events, and I am inclined to place it in the final months before the outbreak of the Peloponnesian War. See above, Chapter 9. Perhaps the memory of Anthemocritus was revived in the fourth century, when the issue which allegedly led to his death came to the fore once again?

as the leader of the expedition, but either his account preserved no further details or Didymus did not see fit to report them. He does say that according to both Philochorus and Androtion the issue was resolved by the Delphic Oracle, which sanctioned the consecration of these lands and the placement of boundary stones. Since the two historians were contemporary with these events, and had an accurate list of archons to guide them, there can be little doubt that they described the later stages of this affair under the appropriate year.

One further piece of evidence related to this border dispute is an Athenian decree dated to the year 352/1—that is, the midpoint between our other references.[104] This enactment set up two commissions, one to replace the boundary markers of the violated hiera orgas, and the other to inquire of the Delphic Oracle if occupation of the sacred land ought to be permitted. The decree, furthermore, calls for the vigilance of the general charged with protecting the region in question, though no specific military action is authorized. Megara is not explicitly mentioned, nor is the precise region identified, but there can be no doubt that these measures were adopted with reference to the disputed land on the Eleusinian border.

Various reconstructions of the course of events outlined in these sources are possible, and the state of the evidence does not permit certainty, but the general trend is reasonably clear. The precise boundary between Attica and the Megarid had never been fixed to the mutual satisfaction of both states. Part of the problem was the extent of the sacred precinct dedicated to Demeter and Persephone on the Athenian side of the border and whether certain unmarked lands were really part of this precinct or in Megarian territory. We have no evidence to determine how the issue was resolved when Pericles raised it in the late 430's, and the land in dispute may have changed hands repeatedly in the course of the Peloponnesian War. It is conceivable that afterward, Megara was awarded the disputed territory. But we then lose sight of the issue for half a century, during which Athens regained much of her former strength and Megara assumed a relatively neutral stance, which deprived her of strong hegemonal support. Friction over the hiera orgas and the

[104]*IG* 2², 204.

unbounded lands may well have occurred sometime during this period. When the issue comes to light in the late 350's, it seems that Athens had been in possession of the disputed land and was now accusing the Megarians of having recently encroached upon it. The accusation may be true, but it is worth remembering that, as in the fifth-century flare-up, the *Megarian* view has not survived. It is certainly difficult to imagine that Megara, militarily weak and isolated, would have committed calculated acts of aggression against Athenian territory in the late 350's. (It is remotely possible, however, that the pro-Macedonian faction that was active in Megara in the mid-340's was already influential and provoked this crisis in order to divert Athenian attention from Philip's moves in northern Greece.)

In any case, the Athenians appear to have voted a military expedition that was never actually sent. Perhaps it was hoped that the threat alone would persuade Megara to back down. The decree of the following year may, indeed, imply a partial retreat by the Megarians, abandoning the previously marked area of the hiera orgas, thereby permitting an Athenian commission to replace the boundary markers without a resort to force. Perhaps the Megarians had also agreed to the consultation of Delphi regarding the status of the remaining disputed territory, as a form of mediation, though it is equally possible that this was a unilateral step by Athens to secure Delphic backing for her position in the conflict. The verdict of the oracle, sanctioning the incorporation of the unbounded lands into the sacred precinct and thereby resolving the issue in Athens' favor, may not have been accepted in good grace by the Megarians, leading to the military expedition recorded by Philochorus. Androtion's failure to mention it suggests that it did not amount to very much, and that Megara quickly relented, accepting the oracle's decision.

In his *Third Olynthiac* in 349, Demosthenes appears to make a reference to the military campaign against Megara which had recently been undertaken. He criticizes the Athenians for avoiding the grave menace posed by Philip of Macedon while seizing any excuse to "fly to arms against Corinth and Megara."[105] He is unlike-

[105]3.20.

ly to mean the military expedition which he says in his speech "On Military Affairs" was authorized in or before 352, since the point of the earlier reference was precisely that no such expedition had actually been sent—a poor example of Athens' readiness to "fly to arms." He evidently means something more recent and concrete. The scholia to this passage from the *Third Olynthiac* suggest two quite different explanations of what lay behind Demosthenes' comment. One version speaks of the Corinthians allying themselves with Megara in a war against Athens. The issues that led to such a war are not specified, and the border dispute between Athens and Megara provides the only obvious motive for Megara's involvement. Corinth might have had motives of her own, or, for reasons we cannot determine, she may have lent support to the Megarians. But no such war is attested elsewhere, and Demosthenes' comments alone need not lead to the inferences this scholiast appears to have made—namely, that the Athenians' expeditions against the Megarians and Corinthians were one and the same and that a full-scale war resulted. The alternate explanation of this passage in Demosthenes accounts for the reference to Corinth on the basis of a quite separate issue: her refusal to allow Athens to participate in the Isthmian games (in 350?), and Athens' subsequent military action to compel the Corinthians to allow her to take part. Again we lack any confirmation of this incident or any explanation as to why Corinth might have taken this unusual step. Cawkwell suspects that the scholiasts were engaged in "a good deal of guessing,"[106] and it would be futile to engage in further speculation on the subject. Yet we cannot rule out the possibility that Megara received some support from Corinth in regard to the hiera orgas dispute; there are no reasons to think that her relations with Corinth were less good than those with Athens during the greater part of the fourth century.

The Eleusinian border dispute appears to have left a legacy of bitterness in Megara which may be partly responsible for Megarian flirtation with Macedon in the 340's, when Athens had emerged as the main bastion of defense against the advancing juggernaut of Philip II. The Athenian politician Philocrates is alleged to have

[106]"Anthemocritus," p. 331n.

warned in 346: "many great dangers surround us. For we know that the Boeotians and Megarians are disposed to be hostile."[107] Another sign of Megarian hostility may be that the Athenian historian Androtion, exiled in the 340's, retired to Megara.[108] But rather than rely on these few hints, we ought to be guided by the logic of the situation. Many Megarians would have been angered by the outcome of the border dispute with Athens and would have been ripe for Philip's overtures. The Macedonian king was always ready to advance money and material support to factions (the Philipizers) within the poleis who were prepared to promote his interests. By the mid-340's, Philip had achieved considerable influence in central Greece, and the support or control of Megara would have carried his policy forward significantly, enabling him to outflank Athens and become more directly involved in Peloponnesian affairs. At just this time a pro-Macedonian faction in Megara attempted to seize power and deliver the state into Philip's hands. Demosthenes is responsible for most of what we know about the plot itself, referring to it in at least four speeches.[109] His most extensive description of the affair occurs in his prosecution of Aeschines in *The Treaty* in 343. He cites the recent crisis in Megara as an illustration of his claim that Philip has relied on prominent and respected political leaders (men like Aeschines) rather than on avaricious nonentities to betray their states to him. Demosthenes asks, rhetorically, the identity of those who attempted to betray Megara:

> Who are the men responsible for so many terrible crimes? Those who consider themselves worthy to be called friends of Philip, men who claim the right to military and political leadership, men who consider themselves better than the common herd. Wasn't Perillus put on trial in Megara just the other day in front of the 300, charged with going to Philip? And didn't Ptoeodorus, the leading Megarian by wealth, birth, and reputation, get him off and send him back to Philip? After that, didn't the one return with a foreign army, while the other connived at home? Something like that.[110]

[107]Theopompos *FGrH* 115 F 164.
[108]Plut. *Mor.* 605d.
[109]19.87, 204, 294-95, 9.17-18, 27, 10.9, 18.48, 71, 295-96.
[110]19.295.

Demosthenes' final phrase may be an attempt to avoid criticism for not getting the facts entirely straight, probably through gross over-simplification, but his remarks here are consistent with those he makes elsewhere. Ptoeodorus and Perillus are consistently identified as the key figures in the pro-Macedonian movement. A passage in *The Crown* adds a third name, Helixus.[111] These men were prominent members of the ruling class in Megara, who sought to enhance their personal power with the backing of Macedon. They aimed at establishing either a narrow oligarchy, or, on the analogy of Oreos in Euboea, where similar developments were taking place at the same time, a tyranny.[112]

Demosthenes describes Ptoeodorus as the most influential man in Megara, which is precisely how he is portrayed at an earlier stage of his career by Plutarch in his life of Dion.[113] Ptoeodorus' influence seems to overstep the bounds of legitimate political activity, and Demosthenes holds it up as a warning against the undue elevation of any individual:

> For there is nothing, absolutely nothing, which should be guarded against as much as permitting one man to become greater than the rest. Let no man be either saved or destroyed at the whim of a single individual. Rather, when the evidence dictates acquittal or the reverse, let the court vote the appropriate verdict. For that is the democratic way.[114]

It is impossible to say how early the pro-Macedonian faction within Megara took shape. One possibility already suggested is that it was in existence at the time of the Eleusinian border dispute in the late 350's, but it is more likely to have got under way some time later, even as late as Perillus' first visit to Philip around 344. Perillus made his trip apparently without authorization from the Megarian government, and was prosecuted for it when he returned. Under the influence of Ptoeodorus, the supreme tribunal in Megara—the three hundred (possibly the *aesymnatae* sitting as a court)—cleared Perillus of any charge of wrongdoing. Perhaps

---

[111]18.295. A descendant of the Peloponnesian War admiral?
[112]Dem. 9.33; Steph. Byz., s.v. Oreos.
[113]*Dion* 17.
[114]19.296.

many of those who voted were themselves part of the conspiracy. But whether Perillus' acquittal can be explained purely in terms of partisanship and influence peddling or was partly the result of Ptoeodorus' defense of his colleague's character and of the merit of opening contacts with Philip is unclear. Nor can we tell whether Perillus' second visit to Philip was officially sanctioned or not. Demosthenes says Ptoeodorus sent him back, but since he also credits Ptoeodorus with obtaining the acquittal, he may only mean that Ptoeodorus' prestige was sufficient for the three hundred to authorize Perillus' return to Pella. We can only speak confidently of a conspiracy from this point forward. Up to the time of the trial, the Philipizers may have contemplated merely bringing Megara into alliance with Macedon by peaceful means, leaving their own ambitions to be satisfied thereafter, although they may equally have contemplated a violent revolution from the start. But after their exposure in the trial, they acted to bring about the downfall of the Megarian regime as swiftly as possible.

Perillus obtained a mercenary force from Philip which he intended to lead back to Megara, while Ptoeodorus kept the pot boiling at home. Had Perillus managed to get through to Megara, his confederates inside the city might well have found the means to admit his troops and take control. In several later remarks, Demosthenes makes it clear that the plot came within an ace of succeeding,[115] but it is Plutarch rather than Demosthenes who tells us how it was ultimately frustrated. In his life of the Athenian general Phocion, he reports:

> When the Megarians secretly invited in the Athenians, Phocion was worried that the Boeotians would learn (of the appeal) and send help first, so he convened the assembly at dawn and reported the Megarian request to the Athenians. Then, as soon as they had voted, the trumpet signal was given and they left the assembly at once carrying their weapons. He was received enthusiastically by the Megarians, fortified Nisaea, and built two walls between the port and the metropolis, thus joining the city with the sea, so that she would have less to fear from her enemies on land and could be in close contact with the Athenians.[116]

[115] 10.8, 19.334.
[116] *Phoc.* 15.

292

The secrecy of the Megarians' appeal was probably due to the presence of conspirators in high places and the imminence of the threat. Secrecy was necessary to avoid precipitating the coup. As Plutarch tells it, Phocion was anxious to move quickly, not merely to avert Megara's loss to Philip, but to prevent the Thebans, who would also have been sympathetic to the Megarian appeal, from gaining an advantage. Phocion saw this as an opportunity to draw Megara closer to Athens after their recent rift. His rapid construction of new long-walls (perhaps using materials left from the fifth century) and harbor fortifications for Nisaea are reminiscent of Athens' policy after 460. In both periods, Athens was strongest at sea, and could use long-walls to bind Megara closer to herself. It is possible that Athenian intervention was opposed by Aeschines' faction in Athens at the dawn meeting of the assembly. Many years later in his speech on *The Crown*, Demosthenes alluded to Aeschines and his party having "turned all our nearest neighbors from friends into enemies, the Megarians, Thebans, and Euboeans."[117] Aeschines' rise to prominence was too late for him to have been an instigator of the border dispute from 352 to 349—one possible meaning of the reference here to Megara—and this leaves the events surrounding the pro-Macedonian coup as the only likely basis of this charge—that Aeschines took a line which nearly delivered Megara into Philip's hands. But the reference is too vague and the source too partisan in matters concerning Aeschines for us to place much weight on this interpretation.

No battle between Phocion's hastily assembled army and Perillus' mercenaries appears to have taken place. The mercenary force, which was probably large enough to effect a coup but unsuitable to engage the Athenian army in a full-scale battle, must have turned back when it became known that their opponents were alerted to the danger, Megara's defenses were being strengthened, and Athenian troops were present. Perillus appears to have remained in exile. Other conspirators may have been purged, but since the plot had never really been forced into the open, it is possible that many in the pro-Macedonian faction remained undetected and at large. We learn nothing of the fate even of such visible figures as

---

[117] 18.234.

Ptoeodorus and Helixus. Over the next few years, Megara seems firmly attached to Athens and the anti-Macedonian coalition. Demosthenes claims credit for having brought Megara into alliance with Athens, an occurrence that must have followed the collapse of the coup very quickly.[118] The Megarians joined in the expedition to Euboea around 342 to overthrow the tyrant Philistides, whom Philip had installed at Oreos.[119] Later, in 340, the Megarians made a substantial contribution to the coalition's war chest.[120] And though Macedonia is not specifically mentioned in our sources, it seems certain that Megara fought against the Macedonians at Chaeronea in 338. Yet even after the suppression of the coup in Megara, Demosthenes continued to warn of the danger of pro-Macedonian intrigue there.[121]

After Philip's decisive victory at Chaeronea, Megara followed most of the other defeated states by opening her gates to the conqueror.[122] If the pro-Macedonian faction was still in a position to capitalize on this turn of events, we hear nothing of it. With nearly all Greece at his feet, Philip chose not to garrison Megara, but made nearby Corinth the center of his Greek operations.[123] Megara must have participated in Philip's new Hellenic League, but her military weakness was such that she was not a significant factor in it. After Philip's assassination in 336, when a number of states, including Athens and Thebes, joined together to throw off the Macedonian yoke, Megara's role is equally obscure. Yet Megara may well have joined this ill-fated movement, if only because she no longer had the strength to resist the prevailing winds, however frequently they changed direction. Only when there was a relative equilibrium of forces in fourth-century Greece could the Megarians pursue an independent course.

After Alexander reasserted Macedonian hegemony in Greece in 335, Megara's acquiescence to this new state of affairs was swift and dramatic. According to Plutarch:

[118]18.237. Cf. Plut. *Mor.* 851b.
[119]Steph. Byz., *s.v. Oreos.*
[120]Aeschin. 3.95; Dem. 18.237.
[121]19.326; 8.18.
[122]Ael. *VH* 6.1.11.
[123]Diod. 16.89.1-3; Just. *Epit.* 11.5.1.

the Megarians voted Alexander citizenship, and when he made fun of their zeal, they told him that they had granted citizenship only once before, to Herakles, and now to him. Alexander was impressed and accepted an honor so rarely given.[124]

Our review of half a millennium of Megarian history gives us little reason to doubt their claim. The story of this interview with the leader of the coming age, with its paradoxical combination of Megarian pride and pragmatism, is an appropriate note on which to end the story of the classical polis.

---

[124]*Mor.* 826c-d.

Epilogue

Returning from Asia, when I was sailing from Aegina to Megara,
I had a panoramic view of the region. Behind me was Aegina,
before me Megara, to my right the Piraeus, and to my left
Corinth, all of which were once powerful and flourishing towns;
they now lay before my eyes overthrown and demolished.
—Servius Sulpicius Rufus to Cicero in 45 *Ad. Fam.* 4.5.4

WHAT lessons may be drawn from our survey of Megarian history? Several themes stand out. First, one cannot fail to be struck
by the tenacity of this small, relatively weak, and exposed state.
Despite the close proximity of three of the most powerful poleis, and
falling under the influence of one or another of them from time to
time, Megara survived as an independent state throughout the
classical era, and even achieved a high degree of prosperity in the
Indian summer of the free polis in the fourth century. Her successful struggle to endure and thrive in spite of the odds is, I believe, as
eloquent testimony to the durability of the polis and its institutions
as the more glamorous histories of her better endowed neighbors.

In the archaic period, Megara's position at the crossroads of
Greek civilization and her rapid maturation compensated for her
meager resources, and she was able to play a leading role. Thus
she was among the most adventurous colonizers, a pioneer in
commerce and engineering, and innovative in her political development. Her tyranny was one of the earliest, and the "unbridled democracy" was possibly the first experiment in popular rule
(however imperfect) in the whole of Greece. I suspect that the main
factors contributing to Megara's extraordinary early development,
apart from her strategic location, were the pressures exerted on her
by larger but not yet overwhelming neighbors. As a result of these
pressures she was forced to face the problems of land shortage and

296

overpopulation earlier than most Greek poleis, and her solutions broke fresh ground more than once.

With the passage of time the creative edge, which had enabled early Megara to play a role beyond her apparent means, disappeared, and she was consigned to a steadily diminishing role in Greek affairs. By the classical era Megarian history serves to illustrate the degree to which the survival of the smaller states depended on the active support of a larger patron. From the middle of the sixth century at least until the end of the Peloponnesian War, Megarian security hinged on the support of one or another hegemonal state, with Sparta playing the necessary role for most of that period. Lacking this support, Megara might have been swallowed up entirely by her neighbors. The hegemonal system, for all its faults, kept Megara afloat when she was no longer capable of defending her own interests. She became adept at shifting her allegiance from one hegemony to another to protect her vital interests (though with variable results at best). Megarian experience shows the hegemonal sword was double-edged. On the most obvious level, the leading state demanded loyalty and support in return for protection, and, as we have seen, the extreme sacrifices made by the all too vulnerable Megarians occasionally nullified any positive advantage they derived from the hegemonal connection; but we should not make the mistake of assuming that this was ordinarily the case. Long periods of peace and secure borders were at least partly the result of her hegemonal ties.

There were other offsetting advantages and liabilities which characterized Megara's experience with the hegemonal states. Close links to one of the more powerful poleis entailed not merely the surrender of an independent foreign policy, but the reduction of internal autonomy as well. Her long association with Sparta froze her into an oligarchic mold, which appears threatened only when the relationship between Megara and Sparta was shaky or had broken down completely. The crisis of the 420's provides a unique opportunity to see the connection between internal factionalism and hegemonal influence, with democrats and oligarchs each trying to harness the power of competing hegemonal states to achieve their own ends. Yet the situation exposed in this instance must have prevailed in other, less well documented periods too.

297

We can never hope to know what political forms Megara might have developed on her own after the adventurous early centuries if the constraints of hegemonal politics had not existed. On the other hand, Megara achieved a high degree of internal political stability from the sixth to the fourth century, through the oligarchs' willing dependence on the conservative Spartans, and we must balance the positive benefits of such stability against the sacrifice of the free political development it entailed.

In the fourth century Megara seems to have found a formula for avoiding direct involvement in the hegemonal wars while not entirely extricating herself from hegemonal ties. This policy appears to have been the work of a moderate oligarchic regime, which bent before the prevailing winds, adapting when these shifted, but maintained friendly relations with all the surrounding states and avoided military involvement whenever possible. Undoubtedly, Megara's modest military power made such a policy more acceptable to the larger states than it would otherwise have been, and the relative balance of power between the hegemonies may also have induced them to tolerate the Megarian position. It was a policy that worked to the immediate advantage of Megara but did nothing to help resolve the self-destructive tendencies of the community of poleis as a whole. Nor did it prepare Megara to participate effectively in the defense of Greece against a genuine external threat: Macedon.

A few further thoughts on the subject of peace may be in order. Though warfare was often profitable in antiquity, and a number of poleis made their fortunes through aggressive foreign policies, Megara's experience demonstrates the close connection between peace and prosperity in the smaller states. Megarian history shows that victory was less important to her well-being than peace—on almost any terms. Her periods of greatest prosperity followed wars in which she had suffered serious losses, either in territory or manpower—for example, in the seventh century after the loss of her western komai to Corinth; in the second half of the sixth century, after Athens had taken Salamis; and in the fourth century, after the devastation of the Peloponnesian War. In each case, the outcome of the conflict was less important than the bare fact that peace had returned. The point may seem too obvious and universal to need emphasis, but it is a healthy corrective to the tendency of historical narrative to stress warfare and measure the success or failure of states in terms of their military achievements.

The Macedonian conquest did not, of course, signal the end of Megara's existence or the extinction of the Greek city-state system. But the independent poleis were gradually subsumed into a world dominated by larger states and empires, in the process losing many of their unique political and social characteristics and increasingly partaking in a more ecumenical culture. There will be no attempt here to reconstruct in detail Megarian history after Chaeronea. The subject may have something further to teach us, but its problems differ fundamentally from the challenge of preserving an independent existence in the world of poleis which pre-Hellenistic Megara faced. The reader deserves, however, at least a brief picture of Megara's later experience.

The Hellenistic Age, no less than the preceding one, was a period of almost continual warfare, and the Megarid was frequently crossed by the contending armies. Megara was even less well equipped to resist these movements than in the past, and had to open her gates to foreign armies on a number of occasions. Several times the city was subjected to prolonged sieges in which the Megarians themselves were caught in the crossfire between contending powers. Not surprisingly, Megara changed her political allegiance at least ten times in the century and a half between Alexander's death and the Roman conquest—better than once a generation, on the average.[1]

The most serious crisis of the period occurred when Cassander garrisoned Megara in 307 and Demetrius, the son of the Macedonian general Antigonus, laid siege to it. According to Plutarch, the city fell while Demetrius himself was absent, and it would have been plundered had not the Athenians interceded on behalf of the Megarians.[2] Yet from the sequel as reported by Plutarch and others, it is apparent that the city was indeed looted before Demetrius returned and put a stop to it. This circumstance emerges from

[1]See Meyer, "Megara," cols. 194-97, for a summary of these political shifts.
[2]Plut. *Demetr.* 9. Cf. Diod. 20.46.3.

several anecdotes told of the encounter between Demetrius and the Megarian philosopher Stilpo, when the former had become master of Megara. Diogenes Laertius relates that:

> When Demetrius the son of Antigonus captured Megara, he spared (Stilpo's) house and saw to it that all that had been seized from him was returned. But when Demetrius asked him for a list of all that had been taken, he replied that nothing was missing which was genuinely his own.[3]

The philosophic point is, of course, that it is unwise to place value on material possessions, but the anecdote also implies that Demetrius' troops made off with all they could. Plutarch's story makes the same point, and he reports the confiscation of Megara's entire slave population:

> Megara was captured and the Athenians made strong entreaties on behalf of the Megarians, preventing the looting of the town by the soldiers. And Demetrius gave the city its freedom, expelling the garrison. While this was going on, he remembered the philosopher Stilpo. . . . Summoning him, Demetrius asked whether any of his property had been taken. "Nothing," Stilpo replied, "for I didn't notice anyone stealing knowledge." But nearly all the slaves *were* carried off. Demetrius was still solicitous and said as he left, "I leave your city in freedom, Stilpo." "You speak the truth," he replied, "for none of our slaves are left."[4]

One need not accept the literal truth of these stories to believe that Megara lost her slaves and much else in 307. When Demetrius' troops carried off the slaves of Megara, her economy was dealt a shattering blow, for, as we have seen, they played a vital role in the woolen industry, on which a substantial measure of Megarian prosperity was based. I suspect that Megara never fully recovered from this blow.

Megarian population seems to have continued its downward trend in the Hellenistic period. One indication is her meager contribution to the defense of Greece against an invading Gallic hoard in 280. Only 400 Megarian hoplites and a few horse took part in a

[3]D.L. 2.115.
[4]*Demetr.* 9.5-6. Cf. Seneca *Dial.* 2.5.6; *De Vir. Ill.* 63; Plut. *Mor.* 5e, 475c.

300

force in excess of 27,000 hoplites and 1,500 cavalry.[5] The occasion called for extreme military measures, and Megara's response is revealing. We possess (rather fortuitously, in view of the little evidence regarding Megarian population) three figures for her hoplite forces at nearly one-hundred-year intervals: 3,000 in 479 at Plataea; 1,200 (estimated) in 378; and 400 in 280. Even without making an attempt to extrapolate from these figures the total number of free citizens in Megara over this span, the magnitude of her decline in population is evident. It is possible, however, that Megara's effort against the Gauls was not representative. We can estimate her military strength more accurately from a series of *ephebe* lists from Megara and Aegosthena which were inscribed toward the end of the third century.[6] These lists (of the youths reaching the age of military service each year) suggest a yearly average of thirty-five or less for the Megarid as a whole. (The Megarian lists average twenty-two, those for Aegosthena—then an independent state—average seven, and some allowance must be made for Pagae, also independent, whose lists do not survive.) If, as Beloch argues, these twenty-year-olds represent about 4 percent of the armed forces, we arrived at a total of 900 hoplites. That may indicate a degree of recovery since 280, or it could mean that Megara did not exert herself to the fullest against the Gauls, but even if her total hoplite strength in the third century was 900 or 1,000, the downward trend is nevertheless apparent.

As implied above, the third century witnessed the further shrinkage of Megara's domain. As a condition of joining the Achaean League in the 240's, she had to grant independence to her northern ports, Pagae and Aegosthena.[7] Henceforth, down to Roman imperial days, these tiny communities remained separate states, to the undoubted distress of the Megarians. Megara was now reduced to her central agricultural plain, since Pagae and Aegosthena must have controlled to isolated valleys and grazing lands of the northern Megarid. Having now lost her slaves and her pasturage, the Megarians may have been reduced to subsistence

---

[5] Paus. 10.20.4.
[6] *IG* 7.27-31, 209-18, 220-22. Cf. K. J. Beloch, "Griechische Aufgebot II," *Klio,* 6 (1906), 55-56.
[7] Polyb. 2.43.5. Cf. 20.6.8; Plut. *Arat.* 24.3; Strab. 8.7.3; Trogus *Prol.* 26.

agriculture from this time forward. Entry into the Achaean League also forced a constitutional reform in Megara, bringing her into line with the other Achaean allies,[8] and that was probably only one of many such reforms which occurred as Megara shifted her political allegiance in the see-saw struggles of the age.

Even the Roman conquest did not bring about the revival of Megarian prosperity. Her fate during the Roman Civil Wars of the first century, though not as catastrophic as Corinth's, was miserable enough. After Pharsalus in 48, some of Pompey's supporters seem to have retained control of Megara, leading to an assault on the city by Caesar's legate Calenus:

> Athens and most of the other Greeks immediately came to terms with him (Calenus), but the Megarians held out despite this. They were captured some time later, partly by force and partly by treachery. As a result, many of them were put to death and the remainder were sold. Calenus did this so that men would see that they had gotten their just punishment, but fearing that the city might be completely destroyed, he sold them to their relations and at a very low price, so that they might regain their freedom.[9]

Several years later, in 45, when Cicero's correspondent, Servius Sulpicius Rufus, was making his way to Achaea to assume the proconsulship, he sailed to Megara from Aegina and sent back the bleak description of the prospect that appears at the head of this chapter. One can scarcely doubt the picture of desolation he related to Cicero, at least insofar as it deals with Megara; she was on the verge of extinction as a political entity, though at some level life went on.

The condition of Megara in this period is also the subject of an anecdote in Plutarch's life of Antonius. He is reported to have visited Megara after the Battle of Philippi in 42:

> When the Megarians wished to show him something beautiful, to rival the Athenians, they took him to see their senate-house [the *aesymnaton*?]. He climbed up and took a look, and they asked him what he thought of it. "It's small," he answered, "and decayed."[10]

[8]See Meyer, "Megara," col. 195.
[9]Dio Cass. 42.14.3-4.
[10]*Ant.* 23.3.

Perhaps this is only another joke at Megara's expense, but we can readily imagine that the Megarians had fallen so far that they were unable even to maintain the relics of their former prosperity. There is the flavor of Roman bluntness about Antonius' remark, but Plutarch does not describe him as entirely callous to the plight of Megara. He reports that during this same visit the Roman triumvir commissioned a survey of the temple of Pythian Apollo, promising to have it completed (restored?).[11] This was actually done more than a century later when the Emperor Hadrian faced the brick temple in marble,[12] and also widened the narrow path along the southern coast of the Megarid between Crommyon and Megara, the Scironian Way, so that chariots could pass one another.[13] The Megarians expressed their gratitude for Hadrian's benefactions by creating a fourth tribe, the Hadrianidae in his honor.[14] Yet despite these benefactions, comments Pausanias, the Megarians "were the only Hellenic people whose circumstances even the Emperor Hadrian was unable to improve."[15]

[11]Ibid.
[12]Paus. 1.42.5.
[13]Paus. 1.44.6-7.
[14]*IG* 7.72, 74, 101.
[15]1.36.3.

Selected Bibliography

Alexandris, O. "Reports from the Megarid." *AD,* 22B (1967), 118-22; *AD,* 23B (1968), 100-04; and *AD,* 24B (1969), 81-88. (In Greek.)
———. "The Ancient Wall of Megara." *AAA,* 3 (1970), 21-26. (In Greek.)
Allen, T. W. "Theognis." *CR,* 19 (1905), 386-95.
Amit, M. *Great and Small Poleis.* Brussels, 1973.
Andrewes, A. *The Greek Tyrants.* London, 1956.

Babelon, E. *Traité des monnaies grecques et romaines,* Pt. 2, Vol. 1. Paris, 1901.
Beattie, A. J. "Nisaia and Minoa." *RM,* 103 (1960), 20-43.
Beloch, K. J. *Die Bevölkerung der Griechischen-Römischen Welt.* Leipzig, 1886.
———. "Theognis Vaterstadt." *Jahrb. für Phil.,* 11 (1888), 729-33.
———. "Griechische Aufgebot II." *Klio,* 6 (1906), 55-56.
———. *Griechische Geschichte, von den Anfängen bis in die römische Kaiserzeit,* 2d ed., 4 vols. Strassburg, Berlin, and Leipzig, 1912-27.
Bengtson, Hermann. "Einzelpersönlichkeit und Athenische Staat zur Zeit des Peisistratos und des Miltiades." *Sitz. Bayr. Acad.* (1939), 67 pp.
Benson, E. F. "Aegosthena." *JHS,* 15 (1895), 314-24.
Bergk, T. *Griechische Literaturgeschichte,* Vol. 1. Berlin, 1872.
Berve, H. *Die Tyrannis bei den Griechen,* Vol. 1. Munich, 1967.
Biers, W. R. "Megara," in *The Princeton Encyclopedia of Classical Sites,* ed. R. Stillwell. Princeton, 1976.
Bliquez, L. J. "Anthemocritus and the *orgas* Disputes." *GRBS,* 10 (1969), 157-61.
Boardman, John. Review of Coldstream, *Greek Geometric Pottery.* In *Gnomon,* 52 (1970), 493-503.
———. *The Greeks Overseas,* 2d ed. Harmondsworth, England, 1977.
———, and F. Schweizer. "Clay Analysis of Archaic Greek Pottery." *BSA,* 68 (1973), 267-83 and plates 53-55.
den Boer, W. Review of de Ste Croix, *OPW,* in *Mnemosyne,* 27 (1974), 430-38.
Bol, P. C. "Die Giebelskulpturen des Schatzhauses von Megara." *AM,* 89 (1974), 64-75 and plates 31-35.

Bölte, F., and G. Weicker. "Nisaia und Minoa." *AM*, 29 (1904), 79-100.

Bowersock, W. "Pseudo-Xenophon." *HSCP*, 71 (1966), 33-55.

Bowra, C. M. *Early Greek Elegists*. Martin Classical Lectures, Vol. 7. Repr. New York, 1969.

Bruce, I. A. F. *An Historical Commentary on the Hellenica Oxyrhynchia*. London, 1967.

Brunt, P. A. "The Megarian Decree." *AJP*, 72 (1951), 269-82.

——. "The Hellenic League against Persia." *Historia*, 2 (1953), 135-53.

Burn, A. R. "Greek Sea Power, 776-540 B.C., and the Carian Entry in the Eusebian Thalassocracy List." *JHS*, 47 (1927), 165-77.

——. "The So-called 'Trade-Leagues' in Early Greek History and the Lelantine War." *JHS*, 49 (1929), 14-37.

——. *The Lyric Age of Greece*. London, 1960.

——. *Persia and the Greeks*. London, 1962.

Burnouf, E. "Nisée et Minoa." *CRAI*, 3 (1875), 209-21.

Bursian, C. *Geographie von Griechenland*, Vol. 1. Leipzig, 1862.

Bury, J. B., S. A. Cook, and F. E. Adcock, eds. *The Cambridge Ancient History*, Vols. 3-6. Cambridge, 1925-27.

Busolt, G. *Griechische Geschichte*, 3 vols. Gotha, 1893-1904.

——, and Swoboda, H. *Griechische Staatskunde*, in Müller's *Handbuch der Altertumswissenschaft*, 2 vols. Munich, 1920-26.

Cartledge, P. "Hoplites and Heroes: Sparta's Contribution to the Technique of Ancient Warfare." *JHS*, 97 (1977), 11-27.

Casson, L. *Ships and Seamanship in the Ancient World*. Princeton, 1971.

Casson, S. "The Topography of Megara." *BSA*, 19 (1912/13), 70-81.

Cauer, F. *Partien und Politiker in Megara und Athen*. Stuttgart, 1890.

Cawkwell, G. L. "Anthemocritus and the Megarians and the Decree of Charinus." *REG*, 82 (1969), 327-35.

——. Review of de Ste Croix, *OPW*, in *CR*, 25 (1975), 258-61.

Clarke, E. D. *Travels in Various Countries of Europe, Asia, and Africa*, Pt. 2, sect. 2. London, 1814.

Clinton, H. F. *Fasti Hellenici*, Vol. 1. Oxford, 1834.

Cloché, Paul. "Les Naopes de Delphes et la politique Hellénique de 356 à 327 av. J.-C." *BCH*, 40 (1916), 78-142.

Coldstream, J. N. *Greek Geometric Pottery*. London, 1968.

——. *Geometric Greece*. London, 1977.

Connor, W. R. "Charinus' Megarian Decree." *AJP*, 83 (1962), 225-46.

——. "Charinus' Megarian Decree Again." *REG*, 83 (1970), 305-08.

——. Review of de Ste Croix, *OPW*, in *Phoenix*, 28 (1973), 399-403.

Deane, Philip. *Thucydides' Dates, 465-431 B.C.* Ontario, 1972.

Delbrück, R. and K. G. Vollmöller. "Das Brunnenhaus des Theagenes." *AM*, 25 (1900), 23-33.

Desborough, V. R. d'A. *The Greek Dark Ages*. London, 1972.

Dickens, George. "The Growth of Spartan Policy." *JHS*, 32 (1912), 1-42.

Dodwell, E. *A Classical and Topographical Tour through Greece*, Vol. 2. London, 1819.

Döring, K. *Die Megariker*. Amsterdam, 1972.

Ducat, J. "Note sur la chronologie des Kypsélides." *BCH*, 85 (1961), 418-25.

Dunbabin, T. J. "The Early History of Corinth." *JHS*, 68 (1948), 59-69.

———. *The Western Greeks*. Oxford, 1948.

———. *Perachora*, Vol. 2. *Pottery, Ivories, Scarabs, and Other Objects*. Oxford, 1962.

Ehrenberg, Victor. Review of de Ste Croix. *OPW*, in *JHS*, 95 (1975), 242.

Fontana, M. J. *L'Athenaion Politeia del V secolo a. C.* Palermo, 1968.

Fornara, Charles. "Plutarch and the Megarian Decree." *YCS*, 24 (1975), 213-28.

———. *Archaic Times to the End of the Peloponnesian War*, Vol. 1 of *Translated Documents of Greece and Rome*, ed. E. Badian and R. K. Sherk. Baltimore, 1977.

Forrest, W. G. "Colonization and the Rise of Delphi." *Historia*, 6 (1957), 160-75.

———. "Two Chronographic Notes." *CQ*, n.s. 19 (1969), 95-110.

———. "The Date of the Pseudo-Xenophontic Athenaion Politeia." *Klio*, 52 (1970), 107-16.

———. Review of de Ste Croix, *OPW*, in *Times Literary Supplement*, 72 (1973), 541-42.

Frazer, J. G. *Pausanias' Description of Greece*, 6 vols. London, 1898.

French, A. "Solon and the Megarian Question." *JHS*, 77 (1957), 238-46.

———. "The Megarian Decree." *Historia*, 25 (1976), 245-49.

Frisch, Hartvig. *The Constitution of the Athenians*. Copenhagen, 1942.

Gardner, P. *A History of Ancient Coinage, 700-300 B.C.* Oxford, 1918.

Garnsey, P. D. A., and C. R. Whittaker. *Imperialism in the Ancient World*. Cambridge, 1978.

Gilbert, G. *Handbuch der Griechischen Staatsalterthümer*, 2d ed., Vol. 1. Leipzig, 1895.

Girard, J. *De Megarensium ingenio*. Paris, 1854.

Gomme, A. W. *The Population of Athens*. Oxford, 1933.

———. *A Historical Commentary on Thucydides*, Vols. 1-3. Oxford, 1945-56.

Graham, A. J. *Colony and Mother City*. Manchester, 1964.

Greenhalgh, P. A. L. *Early Greek Warfare*. Cambridge, 1973.

Van Groningen, B. A. *Theognis. Le premier livre édité avec un commentaire*. Amsterdam, 1966.

Gruben, G. "Das Quellhaus von Megara." *AD*, 19A (1964), 37-41.

Halliday, W. R. *The Greek Questions of Plutarch with a New Translation and a Commentary.* Oxford, 1928.

Hamilton, H. C., and W. Falconer. *The Geography of Strabo,* 3 vols. London, 1892.

Hammond, N. G. L. "The Heraeum at Perachora, and Corinthian Encroachment." *BSA,* 49 (1954), 93-102.

——. "The Main Road from Boeotia to the Peloponnese through the Northern Megarid." *BSA,* 49 (1954), 103-22.

——. "The Family of Orthagoras." *CQ,* 50 (1956), 45-53.

——. *A History of Greece to 322 B.C.,* 2d ed. Oxford, 1967.

——. Review of de Ste Croix, *OPW,* in *EHR,* 88 (1973), 870.

Hanell, Krister. *Megarische Studien.* Lund, 1934.

Harrison, E. *Studies in Theognis.* Cambridge, 1902.

Head, B. V. *Catalogue of Greek Coins in the British Museum: Attica, Megaris, Aegina.* Ed. R. S. Poole. London, 1888.

——. *Historia Numorum: A Manual of Greek Numismatics.* Oxford, 1911.

Heath, R. M. "Proxeny Decrees from Megara." *BSA,* 19 (1912/13), 82-88.

Hermann, K. "Die Giebelrekonstruktion des Schatzhauses von Megara." *AM,* 89 (1974), 75-83 and plates 36-39.

Highbarger, E. L. *The History and Civilization of Ancient Megara.* Baltimore, 1927.

Hignett, C. *Xerxes' Invasion of Greece.* Oxford, 1963.

Hudson-Williams, T. "Theognis and his Poems." *JHS,* 23 (1903), 1-23.

Illinois Greek Club. *Aeneas Tacticus, Asclepiodotus, Onasander.* Cambridge, Mass., 1948.

Imhoof-Blumer, F., and P. Gardner. "A Numismatic Commentary on Pausanias, I." *JHS,* 6 (1885), 50-59.

Inscriptiones Graecae, Vol. 7: *Inscriptiones Megaridis et Boeotiae,* ed. G. Dittenberger. Berlin, 1892.

Jacoby, Felix. *Die Fragmente der griechischen Historiker.* Berlin and Leiden, 1923–.

Jeffery, L. H. "Comments on Some Archaic Inscriptions." *JHS,* 69 (1949), pp. 31-32.

——. *The Local Scripts of Archaic Greece.* Oxford, 1961.

——. *Archaic Greece: the City-States c. 700-500 B.C.* New York, 1976.

Johnson, A. C. "Ancient Forests and Navies." *TAPA,* 58 (1927), 199-209.

Kagan, D. *The Outbreak of the Peloponnesian War.* Ithaca, 1969.

——. *The Archidamian War.* Ithaca, 1974.

——. Review of de Ste Croix, *OPW,* in *AJP,* 96 (1975), 90-93.

Kahrstedt, U. *Griechisches Staatsrecht, 1. Sparta und seine Symmachie.* Göttingen, 1922.

Kirsten, E., and A. Philippson. *Die Griechischen Landschaften,* Vol. 1, Pt. 3. Frankfurt, 1952.

Knight, D. W. *Some Studies in Athenian Politics in the Fifth Century B.C.*, Historia Einzelschriften 13. Wiesbaden, 1970.

Lang, Mabel. "The Kylonian Conspiracy." *CP*, 62 (1967), 243-49.
Larsen, J. A. O. "Sparta and the Ionian Revolt: a Study of Spartan Foreign Policy and the Genesis of the Peloponnesian League." *CP*, 27 (1932), 136-50.
_____. "The Constitution of the Peloponnesian League." *CP*, 28 (1933), 257-76, and *CP*, 29 (1934), 1-19.
Leahy, D. M. "Chilon and Aeschines Again." *Phoenix*, 13 (1959), 31-37.
Leake, W. M. *Travels in Northern Greece*, Vol. 2. London, 1835.
Lebègue, J. A. *De oppidis et portibus Megaridis ac Boeotiae*. Paris, 1875.
Legon, R. P. "Phliasian Politics and Policy in the Early Fourth Century B.C." *Historia*, 16 (1967), 324-37.
_____. "Megara and Mytilene." *Phoenix*, 22 (1968), 200-25.
_____. "The Peace of Nicias." *Journal of Peace Research* (1969), pp. 323-34.
_____. "The Megarian Decree and the Balance of Greek Naval Power." *CP*, 68 (1973), 161-71.
Lenschau, T. "Forschungen zur griechischen Geschichte in VII. und VI. Jahrh. v. Chr., Die Tyrannis in den Isthmosstaaten." *Philologus*, 91 (1936), 278-307.
Lepper, F. A. "Some Rubrics in the Athenian Quota-Lists." *JHS*, 82 (1962), 25-55.
Linforth, I. M. *Solon the Athenian*. Berkeley, 1919.
Lolling, H. G. "Nisaia und Minoa." *AM*, 5 (1880), 1-19.
Losada, Luis A. *The Fifth Column in the Peloponnesian War*. Leiden, 1972.

McKay, K. J. "Studies in Aethon II: Theognis 1209-1216." *Mnemosyne*, 14 (1961), 16-22.
Markianos, S. S. "The Chronology of the Herodotean Solon." *Historia*, 23 (1974), 1-20.
Marshall, F. H. *The Second Athenian Confederacy*. Cambridge, 1905.
Meiggs, Russell. *The Athenian Empire*. Oxford, 1972.
_____, and D. M. Lewis. *A Selection of Greek Historical Inscriptions to the End of the Fifth Century B.C.* Oxford, 1969.
Merle, H. *Die Geschichte der Städte Byzantion u. Kalchedon*. Kael, 1916.
Meyer, Ed. *Forschungen zur alten Geschichte*, 2 vols. Halle, 1892-99.
_____. *Geschichte des Altertums*, Vol. 2. Berlin, 1893.
Meyer, Ernst. "Megara." *RE*, Vol. 15, Pt. 1 (Stuttgart, 1931), cols. 152-205.
_____. "Tripodiskos." *RE*, Ser. 2, Vol. 7, Pt. A2 (Stuttgart, 1939), cols. 201-202.
_____. "Pagai." *RE*, Vol. 18, Pt. 1 (Stuttgart, 1942), cols. 2283-93.
Michell, H. *The Economics of Ancient Greece*. Cambridge, 1957.
Miller, J. "Ist Byzanz eine megarische Colonie?" *Philologus*, 56 (1897), 326-33.
Moggi, M. *I sinecismi Interstati Greci*, Vol. 1. Pisa, 1976.
Moretti, L. *Olympionikai*. Rome, 1957.

Munro, H. "Some Observations on the Persian Wars. 3. The Campaign of Plataea." *JHS*, 24 (1904), 144-65.

Murray, Oswyn. Review of de Ste Croix, *OPW*, in *G&R*, n.s. 20 (1973), 204-5.

Naval Intelligence Division, British Royal Navy, *Regional Geography*, Vol. 2: *Greece*. London, 1945.

Nicopoulou, Y. "Reports from the Megarid." *AAA*, 2 (1969), 339-43, and *AD*, 25B (1970), 99-120. (In Greek.)

Noonan, T. S. "The Grain Trade of the Northern Black Sea in Antiquity." *AJP*, 94 (1973), 231-42.

Novikova, J. F. "Greek Tyranny in the Archaic Period in the Isthmus of Corinth." *VDI*, 94 (1965), 112-26. (In Russian.)

Oliva, P. Review of de Ste Croix, *OPW*, in *Eirene*, 12 (1974), 143-45.

Oost, Stewart I. "The Megara of Theagenes and Theognis." *CP*, 68 (1973), 186-96.

Orsi, P. "Thapsos." *Monumenti Antichi*, 6 (1895), cols. 90-150.

Parke, H. W. "The Development of the Second Spartan Empire." *JHS*, 50 (1930), 37-79.

——. *Greek Mercenary Soldiers from the Earliest Times to the Battle of Ipsus*. Oxford, 1933.

——. *The Delphic Oracle*, 2d ed., 2 vols. Oxford, 1956.

Payne, Humphrey G. G. "A Bronze Herakles in the Benaki Museum at Athens." *JHS*, 54 (1934), 163-74.

——. *Perachora*, Vol. 1. *Architecture, Bronzes, Terracottas*. Oxford, 1940.

Piccirilli, L. "Su alcune Alleanze fra Poleis: Atene, Argo e I Tessali – Atene e Megara – Sparta e Megara." *Scuola Normale Superiore Annali*, 3 (1973), 717-30.

——. *Megarika. Testimonianze e Frammenti*. Pisa, 1975.

Pritchett, W. Kendrick. *The Greeks at War*, 2 vols. Berkeley, 1971.

Reinganum, H. *Das alte Megaris*. Berlin, 1825.

Richter, G. M. A., and I. A. Richter. *Kouroi. Archaic Greek Youths*, 3d ed. New York, 1970.

Roebuck Carl. "The Economic Development of Ionia." *CP*, 48 (1953), 9-16.

——. *Ionian Trade and Colonization*. New York, 1959.

——. "Some Aspects of Urbanization in Corinth." *Hesperia*, 41 (1972), 96-127.

de Ste Croix, G. E. M. *The Origins of the Peloponnesian War*. Ithaca, 1972.

Sakellariou, M., and N. Faraklas. *Ancient Greek Cities*, Vol. 14: *Megaris, Aegosthena, Ereneia*. Athens Center for Ekistics, Athens, 1972. (In Greek.)

Salmon, J. "The Heraeum at Perachora and the Early History of Corinth and Megara." *BSA*, 67 (1972), 159-204.

_____. "Political Hoplites?" *JHS*, 97 (1977), 84-101.

Schachermeyr, F. "Theagenes." *RE*, Ser. 2, Vol. 5A (Stuttgart, 1934), cols. 1341-45.

Sealy, R. "The Causes of the Peloponnesian War." *CP*, 70 (1975), 89-109.

_____. "Zum Datum der Solonischen Gesetzgebung." *Historia*, 28 (1979), 238-41.

Seltman, C. "Aegean Mints." *NC⁵*, 6 (1926), 138-43.

Semple, E. C. *The Geography of the Ancient Mediterranean*. New York, 1931.

Simpson, R. H., and O. T. P. K. Dickinson. *A Gazetteer of Aegean Civilization in the Bronze Age*, Vol. 1: *The Mainland and Islands*. Studies in Mediterranean Archaeology, Vol. 52. Göteborg, 1979.

Smart, J. D. Review of de Ste Croix, *OPW*, in *CW*, 68 (1974), 179-80.

Snodgrass, A. M. *Arms and Armour of the Greeks*. London, 1967.

Starr, Chester G. *The Origins of Greek Civilization, 1100-650 B.C.* New York, 1961.

_____. Review of de Ste Croix, *OPW*, in *AHR*, 78 (1973), 662-63.

_____. *The Economic and Social Growth of Early Greece, 800-500 B.C.* New York, 1977.

Sutherland, C. H. V. "Corn and Coin: A Note on Greek Commercial Monopolies." *AJP*, 64 (1943), 129-47.

Thamm, M. *De re publica ac magistratibus Megarensium*. Halle, 1885.

Threpsiades, J. C. "Megarika." *AE* (1933), pp. 119-30. (In Greek.)

_____. and J. Travlos. "Archaeological Discoveries in Megara." *PAAH* (1934), pp. 39-57. (In Greek.)

_____. "Excavations in Megara." *PAAH* (1936), pp. 43-56. (In Greek.)

Tillyard, H. J. W. "Two Watch-towers in the Megarid." *BSA*, 12 (1905/6), 101-108.

Tod, M. N. *A Selection of Greek Historical Inscriptions to the End of the Fifth Century*, 2d ed. Oxford, 1946.

Tomlinson, R. A. *Argos and the Argolid*. London, 1972.

Travlos, John. "Megara." *Encyclopedia Domē*, no. 274/5 (1978), 202-208.

Trever, A. A. "The Intimate Relation between Economic and Political Conditions in History, as Illustrated in Ancient Megara." *CP*, 20 (1925), 115-32.

Unger, G. F. "Die Heimat von Theognis." *Philologus*, 45 (1890/1), 18-33.

Ure, P. N. *The Origin of Tyranny*. Cambridge, 1922.

Vallet, G., and F. Villard. "Les dates de fondation de Mégara Hyblaea et de Syracuse." *BCH*, 76 (1952), 289-347.

_____. "La date de fondation de Sélinunte: Les données archéologiques." *BCH*, 82 (1958), 16-26.

_____. "Céramique grecque et histoire économique." In *Etudes archéologiques*, ed. P. Courbin (Paris, 1963), pp. 205-17.

Vallet, G., F. Villard, and P. Auberson. *Mégara Hyblaea,* Vol. 1: *Le quartier de l'Agora Archaïque.* Paris, 1976.

Verdelis, N. M. "Der Diolkos am Isthmus von Korinth." *AM,* 71 (1956), 51-59.

Vogt, G. *De rebus Megarensi um ad bella Persica.* Marburg, 1857.

Völkl, K. "Das megarische Psephisma." *RM,* 94 (1951), 330-36.

Wade-Gery, H. T. "Classical Epigrams and Epitaphs, III, The War Monument in the Megarian Agora." *JHS,* 53 (1933), 95-97.

———. *Essays in Greek History.* Oxford, 1958.

Welcker, F. T. *Theognidis Reliquae.* Frankfurt, 1826.

Whibley, L. *Greek Oligarchies.* London, 1896.

White, Mary. "The Date of the Orthagorids." *Phoenix,* 12 (1958), 2-14.

Wick, T. "Megara, Athens, and the West in the Archidamian War: A Study in Thucydides." *Historia,* 28 (1979), 1-14.

Wickert, K. *Der peloponnisische Bund von seiner Entstehung bis zum Ende des archidamischen Krieges.* Erlangen, 1961.

Wilamowitz-Möllendorf, U. von. "Die megarische Komodie." *Hermes,* 9 (1875), 319-41.

Will, Edouard. *Korinthiaka.* Paris, 1955.

Wiseman, James. *The Land of the Ancient Corinthians.* Studies in Mediterranean Archaeology, Vol. 50 (Göteborg, 1978).

Woodhouse, W. J. "The Greeks at Plataiai." *JHS,* 18 (1898), 33-59.

Wright, J. H. "The Date of Cylon." *HSCP,* 3 (1892), 1-74.

General Index

Index of Ancient Authors and Inscriptions

Pages on which translations appear are listed in italics.

MEGARA

Designed by R. E. Rosenbaum.
Composed by Eastern Graphics,
in 10 point Palatino, 3 points leaded,
with display lines in Palatino.
Printed offset by Thomson/Shore, Inc. on
Warren's No. 66 text, 50 pound basis.
Bound by John H. Dekker & Sons, Inc.
in Holliston book cloth
and stamped in Kurz-Hastings foil.

Library of Congress Cataloging in Publication Data

Legon, Ronald P   1941-
    Megara, the political history of a Greek city-state to 336 B.C.

    Bibliography: p.
    Includes indexes.
    1. Megara, Greece—Politics and government. I. Title.
DF261.M43L43   938'.4   80-25668
ISBN 0-8014-1370-2